MARKETING
AN INTRODUCTION

MARKETING
AN INTRODUCTION

Rosalind Masterson and
David Pickton

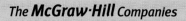
The **McGraw·Hill** Companies

London · Boston · Burr Ridge, IL · Dubuque, IA · Madison, WI · New York · San Francisco
St. Louis · Bangkok · Bogotá · Caracas · Kuala Lumpur · Lisbon · Madrid · Mexico City · Milan
Montreal · New Delhi · Santiago · Seoul · Singapore · Sydney · Taipei · Toronto

Marketing: An Introduction
Rosalind Masterson and David Pickton
ISBN 0077098765

Published by McGraw-Hill Education
Shoppenhangers Road
Maidenhead
Berkshire
SL6 2QL
Telephone: 44 (0) 1628 502 500
Fax: 44 (0) 1628 770 224
Website: www.mcgraw-hill.co.uk

British Library Cataloging in Publication Data
A catalogue record for this book is available from the British Library

Library of Congress Cataloging in Publication Data
The Library of Congress data for this book has been applied for from the Library of Congress

Senior Development Editor: Caroline Howell
Marketing Director: Petra Skytte
Senior Production Editor: Eleanor Hayes

Text design by Claire Brodmann, Lichfield, Staffs
Fakenham Photosetting Limited, Fakenham, Norfolk
Cover design by Fielding Design Ltd
Printed and bound in Spain by Mateu Cromo Artes Graficas, Madrid

BRIEF TABLE OF CONTENTS

DETAILED TABLE OF CONTENTS

PREFACE

About the book

This is an introductory text and it is squarely aimed at students who are just starting out on their studies. It is the product of years of experience in teaching first year undergraduates and other new students. It has been produced by the Marketing Department at the Leicester Business School, host to one of the largest (if not **the** largest) introductory marketing courses in the UK. Explanations are simply phrased and technical terms defined in everyday language – no prior knowledge is assumed.

That's not to say it may not prove useful to students in the later stages of their careers. Nor is it to say that this is a cut down version of other, weightier texts. With this book the authors set out to do two things:

▶ to get students engaged in the study of marketing

▶ to provide a solid foundation for further study – and that means filling some important gaps that we believe are fundamental to good marketing but which many longer books still don't tackle.

As well as the essentials of each topic, the book includes a number of learning aids; lists of key concepts, illustrations and deeper explanations set apart from the text, definitions of key terms, activities, questions, further reading and mini case studies. We have also covered many of the key concerns of modern marketing. In particular, there are five key themes running through this text that we considered significant enough to warrant special attention (see focus boxes below).

Key Features

Focus boxes

Each chapter contains a number of coloured boxes, which show how these key concepts affect, and are affected by, the chapter's topic:

▶ global focus

▶ crm focus

▶ e-focus

▶ b2b focus

▶ ethical focus

These are all issues that challenge today's marketers. The focus boxes explain and illustrate their impact on modern marketing.

There are three other types of boxes in the book: insight boxes, activity boxes and glossary boxes.

Insight boxes

These are asides designed to shed further light on a topic. They may contain more detail, explain a specialist angle or provide an example.

Activity boxes

The activities are designed to help readers understand the subject in more depth. They are not traditional academic exercises but practical things that students can do to see how marketing actually works.

Glossary boxes

Some terms are highlighted as they appear in the text. These are terms that appear in the glossary. If they are terms that are important at that point, then they may be explained in a small box by the side as well.

Key concepts

Each chapter starts with a list of the most important things that the chapter will cover, as well as related issues covered in other chapters.

Marketing is a vast subject and it does not break down into neat little boxes. However you try to split it up, there are overlaps in topics. Students find it helpful to have subjects broken down into manageable chunks as this facilitates learning – even though it is not always realistic. Also books are traditionally written in chapters.

So some of the items in the key concepts list will not be covered in depth (or at all) in that particular chapter. In those cases, a chapter reference is given so that readers can look the terms up in their respective chapters. Alternatively, they can ignore them in the first instance, then look back at all the key concepts later in the course (or at the end, approaching exam time) and see how things fit together.

Marketing Challenges

At the beginning of each chapter there are some 'marketing challenges'. These are designed to show why the topic in question is significant and give an indication of some of the things the reader should be able to do by the end of the chapter (learning outcomes). It is assumed that novice students will not be able to answer them at first and it is not intended that they should. These challenges are food for thought – designed to provide some real-world settings to show why the chapter's contents are important and how they can be applied.

It is hoped that students will go back and look at the challenges again when they have read the chapter. They should look much easier than they did at the start.

Alternatively, these challenges can be the basis for class discussion – either before or after the topic is studied – or both.

Self-review questions

At the end of each chapter there are self-review questions. These relate directly to topics covered in the chapter. They are designed to make sure that students have understood the chapter, and can also be used as revision aids.

It is better to write down the answers before looking back in the chapter. Students who look the answers up before really trying to answer the questions themselves may get a false impression of how much they know. It is very easy for a person to think they knew an answer already when they've just been told what it is. It is not always so easy to know the answer without a prompt.

Case studies

There are mini case studies at the end of each chapter. Most of these are based upon real-life situations and all are written with their associated chapter in mind.

These case studies are designed to help students to apply their knowledge and to improve analysis skills.

The postscript: careers in marketing

Many people study marketing as part of another degree, often business. Others are specialist marketing students (as are many at the Leicester Business School). Whether the reader is planning a career in marketing or not, it is helpful to know what careers are available and what marketers actually do. After all, marketing may be an academic discipline but it is primarily a business function. At the end of this book there is a postscript that provides further insight into the practicalities of marketing and possible future careers.

All these features have been designed with a view to blending the academic and the practical. We want students to understand their subject well, to be able to analyse situations and select appropriate marketing tools, to evaluate proposed courses of action and justify their choices. We also hope that many of them will go on to great marketing careers.

Rosalind Masterson and David Pickton
October 2003

ACKNOWLEDGEMENTS

The publishers would like to thank the following reviewers for their comments at various stages in the text's development:

John Crosbie Glasgow Caledonian University
Aidan Daly, National University of Ireland, Galway, Ireland
Charles Dennis, Brunel University
Chris Dodd, Heriot-Watt University
David Evans, University of Lincoln
Mel Godfrey, South Bank University
Ian Grieg, Lancaster University
Anthony Henry, University of Central England
Steve Hogan, University of Brighton
William Mott, Wolverhampton University
Lindsey Muir, Liverpool John Moores University
Sue O'Neil, University of Westminster
Brendan Richardson, University College Cork, Ireland
Jill Ross, Teesside University
Peter Simcock, Liverpool John Moores University
Nick Wilde, University of Greenwich
Frank Withey, Unversity of Huddersfield

We would also like to thank the organizations that granted permission to reproduce material in this textbook.

Thanks also go to members of the Marketing Department at Leicester Business School, De Montfort University for their contributions and support, and particularly to Leuela Rickard for her work on the early stages of the manuscript.

GUIDED TOUR

Part opening page – each part opens with a schematic that highlights the area of marketing under study, and with an outline of the chapters that make up the part.

Chapter opening page – each chapter opens with a set of 'marketing challenges'. These are real-life challenges that you could face as a marketing professional. As you read the chapter, think about how you would tackle each challenge.

Margin notes – to help you to spot the important terms you will need for revision purposes, each new concept is defined in the margin where it first appears in the text.

Glossary terms – technical terms highlighted in the text are defined in the glossary at the end of the book.

Insight boxes – insight boxes encourage you to pause from your reading and take time to think about the topic in more detail.

Activity boxes – each chapter contains a number of marketing-related activities, which you can try out on your own or in class.

Summary – recaps the key topics for review at the end of each chapter.

Reading around – suggested titles for further reading to enhance your background knowledge.

Self-review questions – test your understanding of the key marketing ideas in the chapter.

Case study with questions – apply your marketing knowledge by reading a case example and working through the case questions.

FOCUS BOXES

There are five important themes in the book, which are highlighted in these application boxes. These themes are relevant to contemporary marketing and provide examples of how each topic is applicable to marketing practice. The five themes to look out for are:

 **ethical focus –** a closer look at marketing and social responsibility

 **global focus –** cases of international marketing in a global economy

 **crm focus –** illustrations that demonstrate customer relationship management in practice

 **b2b focus –** business-to-business marketing examples

 **e-focus –** examples of how technology impacts marketing

TECHNOLOGY TO ENHANCE TEACHING AND LEARNING

VISIT *www.mcgraw-hill.co.uk/textbooks/mastersonandpickton* **TODAY**

Online Learning Centre (OLC)

After completing each chapter, log on to the supporting Online Learning Centre (OLC) website. Take advantage of the study tools offered to reinforce the material you have read in the text, and to develop your knowledge of marketing in a fun and effective way.

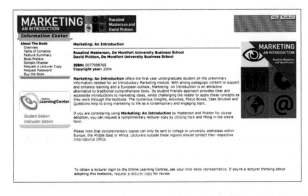

Resources for students include:

▶ self-testing multiple-choice questions for each chapter provide quick online tests for revision

▶ chapter overviews highlight the key topics within each chapter

▶ glossary of all key concepts used within the book, for revision and reference

▶ additional case studies with questions to help students to apply their new marketing knowledge in practical situations

▶ useful web links for marketing studies, and links to new articles/updates on all of the cases or companies referred to in the text.

Also available for lecturers:

▶ lecturer's manual with chapter synopsis and guides, and suggestions for using the textbook's features such as insights, activities and questions

▶ PowerPoint slides for use in lecture presentations and on course handouts

▶ multiple-choice test bank questions for tests and assessments

▶ teaching notes and solutions for the case studies featured in the book

▶ artwork from the book for use in class or lecture presentations.

For lecturers: Primis Content Centre

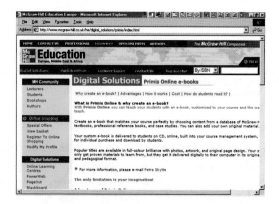

If you need to supplement your course with additional cases or content, create a personalized e-book for your students. Visit www.primiscontentcenter.com or e-mail primis_euro@mcgraw-hill.com for more information.

Study skills

Open University Press publishes guides to study, research and exam skills, to help undergraduate and postgraduate students through their university studies.
Visit www.openup.co.uk/ss/ to see the full selection.

Computing skills

If you'd like to brush up on your computing information technology skills, we have a range of titles covering MS Office applications such as Word, Excel, PowerPoint, Access and more. Get a £2 discount off these titles by entering the promotional code **cit** when ordering online at www.mcgraw-hill.co.uk/cit.

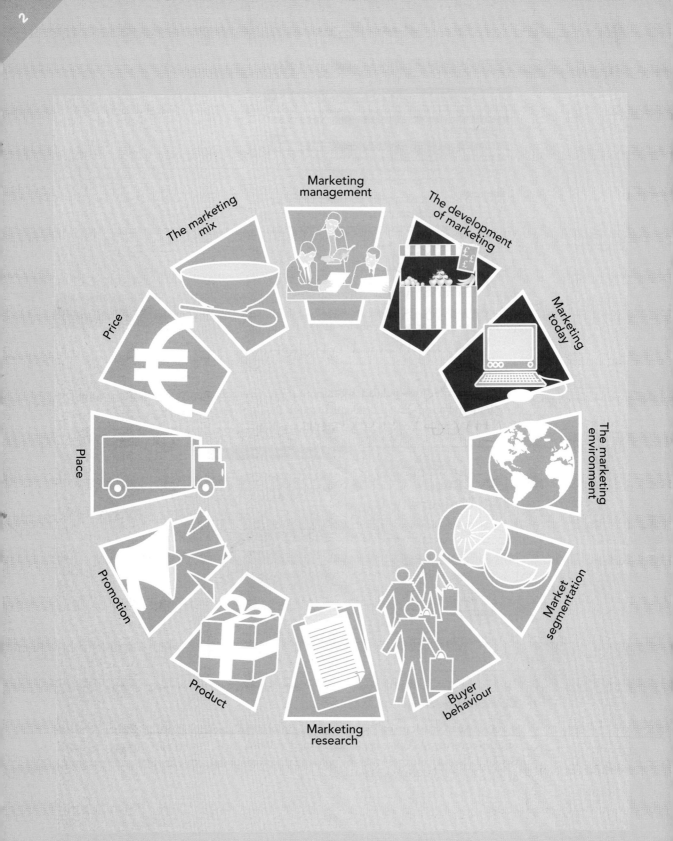

Marketing management

The development of marketing

Marketing today

The marketing environment

Market segmentation

Buyer behaviour

Marketing research

Product

Promotion

Place

Price

The marketing mix

THIS IS MARKETING

THIS PART CONTAINS:

Chapter 1: The development of marketing

Chapter 2: Marketing today

WHAT THIS PART IS ABOUT:

The term 'marketing' comes literally from 'market': a place where traders go to sell and customers come to buy. Sellers have always tried to show their products to advantage, and buyers have always looked for good value. This has not changed. However, marketing has come a long way since the days when traders travelled around the market towns with their goods packed in a wagon.

The first part of this book looks at marketing history. It explains why marketing is more important today than it was in earlier times. It looks at how it has evolved into such a sophisticated business function and also briefly considers the key aspects of modern marketing.

THE DEVELOPMENT OF MARKETING

MARKETING CHALLENGES

At the start of each chapter in this book, you will find several challenges. They are there to help you see the significance of the chapter you are about to read. *You aren't expected to know how to deal with the challenges now*; just bear them in mind as you read the chapter and see what you can find that helps.

▶ You tell friends who are studying sciences that you are doing a marketing course. One says, 'You're studying advertising, what fun.' Is he right – is marketing just another name for advertising?

▶ Another of your scientist friends says, 'But how can that be an academic subject – what's it about?' What will you say to her?

▶ Most of the products in your local shop are much more expensive than those in the supermarket five miles away, yet the shop survives. How would you account for this?

▶ You are the marketing manager for a large university. Funds are always short. A local bar owner has offered the Registry a substantial amount of money for its list of student names and addresses so that he can text them with a very tempting offer to visit the bar. The Registry wants your advice.

KEY CONCEPTS

Throughout this book, key concepts for each chapter will be listed. Most of these will be covered within the chapter itself, but some may be cross-referenced to other chapters in the book. Marketing is an integrated subject. The cross-referenced concepts should help you to build up the whole picture.

markets
marketing
exchange relationships
value
demand and supply
branding (see Chapter 7)
relationship marketing
business to business (b2b)
ethics in marketing
crm (customer relationship management)
international marketing
e-marketing

INTRODUCTION

A traditional market

A market is a place where things are bought and sold. It is often defined as: 'a place where buyers and sellers meet'.

Marketers are the sellers. They set out their stalls, displaying goods to their best advantage, and then try to attract buyers. Of course, modern marketing is rather more complex than a town square or street market, but it is still about attracting customers, selling them things, competing with others and making a profit (usually).

This chapter will introduce modern marketing through a brief look at how it evolved to become what it is today. We will consider current marketing issues and where marketing might be tomorrow. This chapter, and this book, will consider both marketing theory and marketing practice: concepts and definitions of marketing, the marketing industry, its key players and their roles. Towards the end of this chapter, you will find introductions to five 'focus' themes that will run throughout the book: e-focus, ethical focus, global focus, b2b (business to business) and crm (customer relationship management) focus. These are key areas in modern marketing. Each one has been singled out for extensive commentary so that its role within marketing can be appreciated fully.

DEFINITIONS OF MARKETING

Definition 1

❝The management process which identifies, anticipates and satisfies customer requirements efficiently and profitably.❞ **(The Chartered Institute of Marketing)**

This definition relates marketing to management. That should not be too much of a surprise as there are lots of marketing managers about. They manage all the things that need to be done in order to market products and services. These managers must understand what their customers really want from them. This means more than just what sort of product customers want. It must suit their needs physically (e.g. it should work), psychologically (e.g. they should feel good about owning it), financially (e.g. they should be able to afford it) and timewise (e.g. it should not take too long to actually get it). For the company, this may involve considerable **market research** and analysis. (Remember, the words in colour can be found in the Glossary at the back of the book.)

Take a new pair of shoes as an example. There are certain fundamentals such as they need to fit and they need to be within your price range. They may also need to be comfortable, though there are, of course, degrees of this depending on whether they are high-fashion shoes or walking boots. It is unlikely that customers will be prepared to travel too far to buy a pair of shoes, so they need to be easily purchased. The importance of the shop becomes apparent here. It does not matter how much you want those Nike trainers, if you just cannot get them anywhere in your size then you will have to buy something else or go without. Finally, the customer will walk up and down in the shop, look in the mirror, see if the shoes suit them. Do they feel right? Do they look good? Do they make the wearer feel good? With our plethora of choice, this is often the most important consideration.

Definition 2

❝Marketing is the process of planning and executing the conception, pricing, promotion and distribution, of ideas, goods and services to create exchanges that satisfy individual and organizational objectives.❞   (The American Marketing Association)

The American Marketing Association's definition looks for balance between the needs of the firm and the needs of the customer. The objectives of both must be satisfied. This definition uses the traditional **marketing mix** as the means through which these needs will be satisfied. The marketing mix is the subject of Part 3 of this book. Briefly, it is a set of marketing tools, commonly referred to as the 4Ps: product, price, place and promotion. (The latter is also called marketing communications – although unfortunately that does not start with 'P' and would therefore spoil the acronym!)

WHAT MARKETING IS NOT

The world, even the business world, has some erroneous ideas about what marketing is. It is worth being aware of these (it may save you some confusion) but it is important to be clear that marketing is not just selling, advertising, promotion or marketing communications. Let's take selling first. Selling is a part of marketing, an important part. The underlying aim of most marketing activity is to make sales. However, this could be said to be the underlying aim of most businesses. After all, where is the profit without sales?

Selling is about persuading customers to buy. It may be a hard sell or a soft sell. Hard selling is pushy, an aggressive stance that is usually resented by customers and is therefore not a good tactic if you want them to come back again. It is often used in selling items that people are reluctant to buy, such as replacement windows. A soft sell, just as it sounds, is a gentler approach – more persuasive.

globalfocus

The hard sell

It may seem obvious that the soft sell is the better sales technique, but it depends. In many countries, and some situations, a hard sell is needed. It may even be part of the local culture. If you have ever been a tourist anywhere, but particularly in a less-developed country, then you will almost certainly have been subjected to a hard sell. Trinkets, local crafts, postcards, boat tickets even accommodation are thrust at tourists as soon as they arrive anywhere. Many sales are made (and many are later regretted by the new owner of a stuffed donkey or undrinkable local liqueur).

A typical one-off transaction

Peter Drucker famously said, 'The aim of marketing is to make selling superfluous.' If the product is something that the customer actively wants to buy, then a hard sell is unnecessary.

crmfocus

The right relationship

Think back to the earlier example of hard selling to tourists. Tourists are, by their very nature, not in a place for very long. They are often actively seeking mementoes and gifts on which to spend their money.

Is it better for vendors to build a relationship with the tourists or to make a quick sale?

Many of those souvenirs are made in factories and workshops in other parts of the country (or even in other countries altogether). Think about the craftsperson hundreds of miles away; should he or she be selling hard to the street vendor or would it be better to develop a relationship so that he or she can rely on selling more products next month?

So selling is a part of marketing, but not all of it. In fact, it would be more accurate to say that selling is a part of marketing communications or **promotion** (these are alternative terms for the same thing), and that marketing communications is part of marketing. Marketing communications (promotion) will be covered in more depth in Chapter 8, it is a collective term for all the activities that an organization undertakes to promote its products to its customers. Such activities may include holding press conferences, designing appealing packaging, making promotional offers such as prize draws and **bogofs**, supporting websites, sponsoring sports teams and **advertising**, which means that advertising is only part of marketing communications, which in turn is part of marketing. Clearly there must be more to marketing too than just advertising. So what is included in marketing besides promotional activities?

activity

What do you think 'bogof' stands for?

If you don't know, look it up in the glossary at the back of the book (all terms in coloured text can be found in the glossary and some particularly important terms are defined in the margins).

One of the biggest areas of marketing is market research (see Chapter 6). Research is vital in understanding customer needs, buyer behaviour (see Chapter 5) and how to design products and services to meet those needs. Without new product development (see Chapter 7) a company will die. Marketing is also concerned with getting the right products to the right place at the right time, and so distribution (**place**) is key (see Chapter 9). Those products also need to be at the right price (Chapter 10) or they will not sell.

Marketing is also about understanding your competitors (**competitive intelligence**) and devising strategies to beat them. Strong **branding** is a competitive strategy that is often used today. Think of the sportswear market; it has some of the strongest, most valuable brands: Nike, Adidas, Reebok, Sergio Tachini, Umbro, Head. There are many of them but some are stronger than others and therefore have a **competitive advantage** over their rivals. Yet how much is there to choose in terms of quality, value for money, even style, between Nike shorts and those made by Adidas?

Marketing, then, encompasses a large number of business activities. An examination of Exhibit 1.1 will give you more detail on its scope.

competitive advantage

something about an organization or its products/services that is better than rival offerings

BEFORE MARKETING

In a subsistence economy, such as the poorest in the world today, there is very little trade. Only when people have a surplus of goods do they trade them. So if farmers have an abundance of apples, say, they may go to market and try to trade them for something else. If they have only enough to feed their own families, there will be no apples left over for others to buy. So markets, and marketing, are only found where the economy has developed beyond these very early stages.

In Europe, before industrialization, the emphasis was on making enough goods to supply people's needs, not on persuading them to buy them. There is no need to do that when there are not enough shoes, soap or sugar to go round anyway. There was a time when farmers and craftspeople could sell everything they could make. Goods were produced in small quantities and sold locally. There were enough local buyers and so no need for the expense, and risk, of travelling to find more custom.

So marketing is a relatively new discipline. Businesses have always needed managing and they have always needed financing. Someone had to make goods to be sold. There had to be a place to sell them in and people to take the money and hand over the goods. However, there was a time when people had no need to do anything beyond set up the stall in the market square with their goods displayed, and buyers would come.

supply led

shortages of goods mean that suppliers can dictate terms of business

demand driven

a surplus, or potential surplus, of goods to be sold gives buyers more power

Those markets were **supply led**, not **demand driven**. That is, the problem lay in producing enough to meet customers' needs. In such circumstances, there is no need for marketing. However, as factories opened and towns developed, so people became more reliant on buying goods and services from others to meet their needs. Town dwellers did not have land on which to grow their own vegetables or keep animals. They needed to buy food with the wages they earned. Farms became larger and so produced surpluses that could be sold at market. Smaller farmers sold their surplus food to **intermediaries**, who would take them to market for them, where they would be sold alongside other products from other parts of the country, or even abroad.

This represented a major change in the way that goods were sold. Sellers no longer had direct contact with their buyers. There were agents and shopkeepers in between. This had two effects: first, it meant that they were not as aware of customers' requirements, relying as they did upon these intermediaries, and, second, it meant that customers no longer knew their suppliers – they only knew the shopkeepers or stallholders.

So the smarter producers made conscious efforts to find out what customers wanted – that is, they began to conduct rudimentary market research (largely through those same intermediaries). Some also badged their products so that customers could recognize them. These makers' marks were an early form of **branding**.

The new factories brought with them an even more significant change. Their new mass-production techniques meant that there was a greater supply of products and that they were cheaper. Initially, the focus was still on finding more efficient ways to produce larger quantities as people queued up to buy all these new cheap products. There was more than enough **demand** to keep the early factories going.

demand
quantity of goods that customers buy at a certain price

Manufacturing in the old days before modern mass production techniques

However, technology continued to improve and the volume of products available grew until there was no longer a shortage but a surfeit of almost everything. These days suppliers cannot rely on people to buy everything they produce. They have to compete for customers. In such a situation, they need good marketing skills.

MODERN MARKETING

Before mass production, there was very little need for marketing. Value for money, pleasant service, a shop sign, a maker's mark and a reputation built by word of mouth were enough. Modern marketing is clearly more complex than that, although those early good-business principles are still valid today. Initially, more sophisticated marketing techniques were limited to the everyday, high-volume items that the new mass-production techniques had made readily, and cheaply, available to the masses: washing powder, toothpaste, shoe polish, soap, foodstuffs, etc. They were easier to make and so there were more companies making them. At the same time, transport improved. There were roads, railways and canals available to ship goods to other parts of the country. Competition became an issue.

These mass-produced products acquired brand names, had posters and press advertisements, were sold on special offer, and were adjusted to suit customer tastes and to be better than rival products. Manufacturers clearly could not sell such large volumes to so many customers directly and so the intermediaries, the shopkeepers and **wholesalers** became more significant. They were wooed, persuaded to stock products (and perhaps not to stock rivals' products), to display them more prominently than others, to recommend them to customers.

So a number of factors led to the birth of modern marketing, the main ones being:

▶ breakthroughs in production technology
▶ advances in the technology for transporting goods (particularly railways)
▶ social changes such as the move away from the countryside and into towns
▶ increased competition.

These forces still drive marketing today. Modern technological breakthroughs (such as the Internet) still have the power to change the way we sell goods and services. Air freight has made it possible to have fresh foods from around the world. It means we can have tropical fruits in northern Europe all year round. The changing age profile of our population means more products are developed for, and aimed at, older age groups. In many parts of the world, people are leaving rural areas and heading for the towns to find work. Competition now is global, no longer limited to rivals based in the same town, or even the same country. European Union (EU) companies compete fiercely with each other across the region – and across the world. The wealth of Europe attracts American, Canadian, Japanese, Chinese, African and Asian competitors. Almost all countries across the world are home to at least some internationally competitive companies.

You will learn more about how these forces shape marketing – and indeed our world – in later chapters, particularly Chapter 3 which looks at the marketing environment. 'Global focus' boxes throughout the text will provide further insights into the nature of global competition.

THE MARKETING FUNCTION

First, let's distinguish between the marketing function and the marketing department. Function is a wider concept. It embraces all marketing activity within the organization – whether or not it is carried out by members of the marketing department. The department is a defined part of the organization in which specialist marketers work. They report to marketing managers and directors who lead the department.

The distinction is important because, in a truly marketing-orientated organization (see Chapter 2 for a detailed explanation of **marketing orientation**), everyone will think marketing and, at least some of the time, carry out marketing-related activities. For example,

exhibit 1.1

Marketing activities

marketing research and analysis
where and who we are now

market research – who are our customers and what do they want?

competitive research – who are our competitors and what do they do?

what is our position in the market? (**market share**, customer views)

organizational research – what are we good at? (organizational strengths)

what are we bad at? (organizational weaknesses)

what have we done that worked well in the past? (e.g. promotions)

how much money can we spend? (budget)

are we risk takers?

objective setting
where and who we want to be

targets – e.g. **market share**, profits, sales, **brand image**, brand awareness, numbers of sales outlets, locations where products are available (at home and abroad), new product launches, product updates, customer satisfaction levels . . .

marketing tasks
how we are going to make it happen

planning – selecting and scheduling marketing tasks

staff – suitably selecting and training

budgets – allocating to activities

promotional activites – **advertising**, **PR**, **sales promotions**, sales force support, **direct marketing**, packaging, website, etc.

sales – finding new customers, getting repeat business

pricing – setting prices, discounts, credit terms, etc.

distribution – stock holding, packaging, shipping, order handling, etc.

product management – development, dropping old products, standardization, adaptation to suit different customers, etc.

branding – **branding strategy**, maintaining brand image, logos, colours, etc.

market entry – selling in new markets (directly or through a third party)

customer service – loyalty schemes, complaints handling, after-sales service, warranties and guarantees

customer management – customer database, events/actions designed to build relationships

collecting feedback and controlling activities
how we will keep track of things

objectives – have they been achieved? are they likely to be achieved?

customer feedback – complaints, compliments, recommendations, repeat buys, satisfaction surveys

checklists and deadlines – have things happened on time?

market position – are we doing better/worse than our competitors?

the finance people will make sure that bills and receipts are customer friendly and queries dealt with promptly and pleasantly, human resources will make sure that job advertisements project a positive image of the company, delivery staff will be friendly and helpful, and perhaps even advise customers on products and services, etc. As one of the founders of Hewlett Packard once said, 'Marketing is too important to leave to the marketing department.'

So what activities fall under the heading 'marketing'? The answer is a large number, the most typical of which are shown in Exhibit 1.1.

DEMAND AND SUPPLY

supply
quantity of goods that sellers are prepared to put on the market at a certain price

The concepts of **demand** and **supply** are fundamental in business – and in marketing. The word 'demand' causes some confusion. It is being used here in its economic sense, i.e. it means what people *will* buy, not just what they would like, if only they could afford it, find it, etc.

Today, most markets are **demand driven**. This means that the amount of goods made available for sale is dependent upon the customers and how much they will buy. In a supply-led market, the amount of goods available would depend on how much could be produced.

In a **supply-led** market, the most successful companies will be those that are the most efficient producers. Everything they can make will be bought. However, in a demand-driven market, companies have to compete for custom, hence the modern-day importance of marketing. It is the job of marketers to stimulate demand, to provide the goods and services that people want, and to persuade them to buy.

Ideally, the firm wants demand to equal supply exactly. At this point it maximizes sales without having anything left over.

The point where the supply curve and the demand curve cross (see Exhibit 1.2) is called the equilibrium point. At this price, customers will want to buy just exactly the amount that suppliers want to sell. Let's take the example of a book publisher. The easiest way to make

insight

Modern markets

Although most modern markets are demand driven, there are still some that are supply led. Some products are in short supply just by their nature (e.g. precious stones or antiques), others by design (e.g. limited-edition prints or collectibles).

Have you ever struggled to buy a concert or football match ticket? Perhaps you have even paid more than the marked price? These are modern-day, supply-led markets.

sure that all its books are sold would be to produce fewer books than demanded. However, this would mean that some customers will be unable to get copies. The publishing firm will miss out on potential sales and so make less profit. It would be in its interest to print more books.

If the publisher wants be sure that it makes all the sales it possibly can, satisfying all potential customers, then it will print more books than could ever be required. The problem with this is that it will have books left over. It will probably end up selling these at a reduced price, maybe even at a loss. (For more on how demand and supply affect prices, see Chapter 10.)

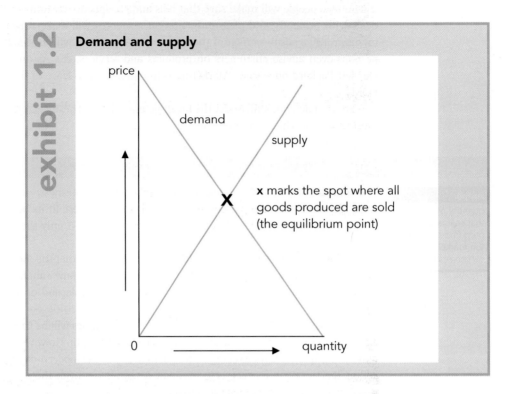

exhibit 1.2

Demand and supply

x marks the spot where all goods produced are sold (the equilibrium point)

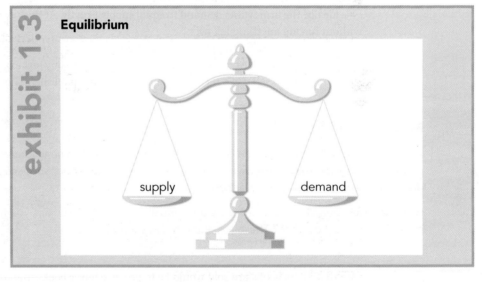

exhibit 1.3

Equilibrium

EXCHANGES

exchange

when two parties swap items perceived to be of approximately equal value

It is often said that marketing is about managing the **exchange** process. If you exchange something, you part with something of value (e.g. products, services, ideas) in return for something else of value. The 'something else of value' is, of course, usually money, though it could be other goods or services.

Clearly there must be two parties to an exchange: the seller and the buyer. Each wants to exchange something for something else that they value more. So the car that the customer is buying must be a car that he or she wants more than the money he or she will part with in order to obtain it, and the car dealer would rather have the money than the car standing on the forecourt. This may sound obvious, but it is a concept worth hanging on to as you move into more complex marketing ideas. This valued exchange is at the heart of marketing. If we cannot offer customers goods and services that are worth more to them than whatever they have to give up to obtain them, then we will not sell much.

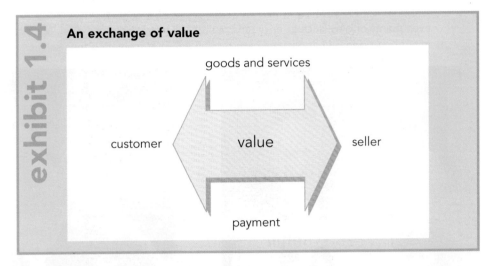

exhibit 1.4

An exchange of value

goods and services

customer

value

seller

payment

Customers give up more than just money. They give up time: the time taken to check out the other options, to test drive other cars, for example. They put in effort that could have been expended doing something else. They have to weigh up the pros and cons of each possible car in order to make their decision. Sometimes customers will pay more for something just because it is less hassle, or quicker, or safer, or for any number of other good reasons. For example, train tickets are cheaper if booked in advance, but it is often just not convenient to book ahead. Many products can be bought more cheaply on the Internet, but many people do not yet trust Internet sales. Vegetables are usually much cheaper when bought from a market stall than from supermarkets, but still you see lots of people with supermarket carrier bags full of them.

People will only exchange something for something that is of higher value *to them*. The exchange must be satisfying to both parties. Good marketing will create and maintain satisfying exchange relationships. This may be a very short-term relationship, if the sale is a one-off, or it may be ongoing, if a company is looking for repeat business. To be sure of repeat business, a company needs to make its customers loyal. Loyalty should, of course, be a two-way street. The company needs to be consistent in its good treatment of its customers if it wants the same in return. (See Chapter 2 for more on customer loyalty.) This idea of ongoing relationships with customers will be revisited many times throughout this book, particularly in the crm (customer relationship management) focus boxes and below, under the subheading 'Relationship marketing'.

MARKETING'S CHANGING EMPHASIS

In its short history, marketing has moved its focus from the immediate sale to the preservation of future sales. Good marketing practice today involves thinking beyond the one-off sale. It means longer-term planning and that makes it a more complex process to manage.

Promoting fame

In modern marketing the original idea of an exchange has been pushed to its limits. Marketing stretches far beyond the selling of goods and services into almost all aspects of life. Politicians, places (see the case study at the end of the chapter), events, sports, entire companies, ideas – even points of view (such as environmentalism) all have to be marketed. Many modern celebrities might be said to be people who have proved adept at marketing themselves.

A few of today's
well-marketed
celebrities

A strong **brand image** was probably the most highly prized and sought-after marketing weapon of the late twentieth century. While branding is still vital in many markets now, its own image is getting a little tarnished as **consumers** see through brands without substance. Some of the famous brands of the 1980s and 1990s are losing ground. Supermarket own-labels are beginning to dominate the UK food market. Even McDonald's, possibly the most famous brand of all, faces a consumer revolt against over-processed foods.

consumer
the individual end user of a product or service

It is not yet clear what will replace branding as the weapon of choice for today's companies. There is a trend towards more socially responsible marketing (though for many organizations this is currently no more than a token gesture – a chance to be seen as doing the right thing), and cynics would say that this is merely another positive image projection for competitive effect. It may be that firms seek to build even stronger relationships with their customers – though, again, there is evidence that customers do not always want to have relationships with their suppliers (O'Connor and Galvin, 2001). Many firms seek technological edge and cost savings through increased use of the Internet and call centres. Then again, others are returning to a more old-fashioned idea of service. The HSBC subsidiary bank First Direct boasts that customers always get through to a real person – no automated call-handling systems there. For First Direct this is a key competitive difference.

Transactional marketing

transactional marketing
focuses on the immediate sale

There is still a place for the one-off transaction that is sometimes referred to as **transactional marketing**. Here there is no intention to continue with the relationship. Both parties are satisfied by that one sale and they go their separate ways. A transactional exchange is likely to be appropriate where the product is a basic commodity, such as salt, or an occasional purchase, such as a house. Alternatively, the circumstances of the exchange may dictate that it be transactional. For example, the buyer may just be passing through, a visitor to the area. The seller may only have one thing to sell, perhaps a private sale of a car or furniture that is no longer wanted, or they may be winding a business down.

Relationship marketing

66 Relationship marketing is a long term, continuous series of transactions between parties. **99**
(Doyle, 2002)

relationship marketing
a long-term approach that nurtures customers, employees and business partners

Relationship marketing was a revolutionary idea that turned sales and marketing on their heads. No longer were the end-of-year sales figures the prime measure of success. Companies wanted to look ahead to next year, and the year after that. Could they count on repeat business from this year's customers?

But which parties? The other new and exciting thing about relationship marketing was that these long-term relationships were to be built not just with customers, but with all members of the **supply chain**, both up and down. The key to maximizing long-term profitability was seen to lie not just with loyal customers, but also in ongoing relationships with suppliers. Keeping the same suppliers saves the time and risk involved in finding new ones. It can also have more direct benefits, as a supplier who is secure and has a good working relationship with the buyers is more likely to be flexible, to try harder.

Although the term relationship marketing can be traced back to Berry (1983), the importance of building long-term customer relationships really became apparent from some groundbreaking studies in the 1990s. Researchers found that retaining customers for just a little longer increased a company's profitability significantly, while other studies discovered that it was much cheaper to hold on to existing customers than to find new ones. Loyal customers may prove a company's best form of promotion: they tell their friends about their good experiences with the company and so word of mouth spreads. Who would you be more likely to believe when they recommend a product, a friend or the company's salesperson?

THE RISE OF CONSUMERISM

consumerism
the belief that
increasing
consumption is
economically
desirable

In the Western world, we have more material wealth, more stuff, than any society has ever had before. The amassing of goods is seen as a sign of success. Expensive, desirable possessions confer status. **Consumerists** believe that it is economically desirable to consume (i.e. eat, drink, use) more and more. Modern production techniques mean that we have more than enough of everything. Every day, Western businesses and households throw away millions of excess goods. In the meantime, there are parts of the world that are so poor that they are short of basic necessities: food, water, clothing, shelter. This disparity provokes envy and conflict yet still, even where governments have the will to do so, it is difficult to even things out.

With this surplus of goods, the power has shifted to consumers. Today, most producers of goods and services are more reliant on their customers than the other way around. A customer can usually go to another supplier but, for the supplier, a replacement customer is harder to find. This would suggest that customers have the upper hand but this is not always true. Large customers, which are usually big companies, can indeed dictate terms to their suppliers. UK supermarkets have such dominance in the food market that they can demand low prices, specially packed products and frequent (often several times a day) deliveries. However, it is harder for an individual consumer to make demands on a large corporation. Even with the current levels of competition for customers, just one customer among thousands is not so significant a loss.

As a consequence, just as workers formed trades unions in the early twentieth century, consumers in the latter half of that century got together and formed pressure groups. The power of numbers can make large corporations listen. Organizations such as the Consumers' Association have significant influence. The media can make an impression too – even the largest of multinationals wants to protect its reputation. Most newspapers have consumer advice columns and are prepared to take on any size of organization, as are television programmes such as the BBC's *Watchdog*.

activity

Think of something you may purchase in the near future (e.g. a CD, foodstuff, clothing, shoes, book). Make a list of the different types/brands you could purchase and the different places you could buy them. (Hint: look down the high street, surf the web, check out newspaper/magazine ads and the *Yellow Pages*.) What would make you switch from your first choice of supplier to your second?

Consumer protection

In the West, consumers have rights. In 1962, US President John Kennedy proclaimed four basic consumer rights. These were the right to:

▶ be safe

▶ have information

▶ choose

▶ be heard.

There are laws to protect consumers. In the UK, for example:

▶ all loans and other credit agreements have to display their true costs in a way that consumers can compare with other offerings (APR)

▶ there must be no hidden product costs (e.g. it must be clear whether or not VAT is included)

▶ many purchases (e.g. insurance policies, timeshare holidays) have a cooling-off period during which customers can change their minds and cancel with no penalty

▶ direct debits (automatic bank payments) have a guarantee of immediate refund if a customer complains

▶ adverts must be truthful

▶ consumer information should not be used for any purpose other than that agreed to by the consumer (Data Protection Act)

▶ descriptions in mail-order catalogues and other direct mail items must be accurate (Sale of Goods Act).

Other countries have similar laws although there are, or course, some differences in detail. For example, data protection laws across the EU are much stricter than they are in the USA.

The fall of consumerism?

Despite all these protective measures, there are consumers who still feel exploited and who believe that **consumerism** is wrong. Their concern is that we are using up the Earth's resources, in effect destroying our world. They feel that there is an overemphasis on materialism and that its main point is to make a few fat cats richer. The anti-globalization protesters who make the news every time the World Trade Organization (WTO) or some other such body meets are part of this anti-consumerism movement. They champion the rights of the underdog: the less-developed countries (LDCs), the poorer workers and consumers. Unfortunately, a small but significant number of more aggressive protesters often turn their demonstrations into vandalism and clashes with the police. Bricks may be aimed at symbols of Western (most commonly US) domination such as McDonald's. This is a clash of views that will continue for some time. You can follow its progress through TV news and documentaries, newspapers and magazines. Look out for new consumer protection laws, changing government attitudes on green issues and trading with LDCs. Many of the protesters hold marketers as much to blame as governments. This is an interesting time to be studying marketing – and thinking of a marketing career.

THE FOCUS THEMES

Throughout this book there are 'focus' boxes that relate the chapter's subject matter to certain key marketing themes. The boxes are:

▶ e-focus

▶ global focus

▶ b2b (business-to-business) focus

▶ ethical focus

▶ crm (customer relationship management) focus.

The themes have been chosen to reflect marketing's current major preoccupations. Marketing is a broad subject that overlaps with many other business functions: corporate strategy, human resource management, operations management, research and development, design and corporate communications. It also draws on many other academic disciplines, for example: psychology, economics, management strategy, inter-cultural relationships, media studies and sociology.

e-marketing

The Internet has changed the way many businesses operate. It has far-reaching effects throughout the business world, affecting the ways that businesses communicate with their customers, their suppliers, their own staff. The Internet has shortened **supply chains** by cutting out trade **intermediaries** such as **wholesalers** and **retailers**, and allowing manufacturers to deal directly with their end customers. It has broadened the geographic reach of companies by providing a fast, cheap way to communicate with customers in other countries. It has increased the levels of competition in many industries, and the ways in which firms compete, by making it easier for companies to get into new markets and for smaller companies to compete with larger ones for business. For example, Amazon did not exist pre-Internet but it is now a serious global competitor in bookselling. It has taken enormous amounts of trade away from the more established bookshops, and is rapidly branching out into other areas too.

Web pages provide a shop front to the world. Many companies now do very well without a high-street presence. Online, everyone looks the same size so there is no immediately obvious disadvantage for a smaller firm like there is for a smaller shop. It still has to deliver the goods of course, as only a few businesses manage to do that online (e.g. software and music downloads, and some services such as banking).

The influence of the Internet has been so great that many have declared it a new economy or a new market. Few marketers now take that position, referring to it instead as **new media** or a new **marketing channel** (i.e. way to sell to customers). The confusion arises because of the differing definitions of 'market'. Traditionally, a market is a place where buyers and sellers meet – in which case the Internet is a new place. However, increasingly, the term market is used to refer to customers en masse. In this case, the Internet is not a new market; Internet buyers just buy online rather than offline, they are not necessarily new customers. If a firm finds new customers in another country via the Internet, then that is a new market – but the old way of describing them as a new geographic territory is still valid, indeed necessary, if their needs and wants are to be met effectively.

E-marketing does not stop at the Internet. Further new communications technologies are being developed all the time. Mobile phones are becoming a marketing tool – particularly useful for reaching the young. Digital television is in its infancy but interactive TV (**iTV**) may radically change the way we watch TV – and do TV advertising.

Throughout this book we will take the opportunity to reflect on the impact of new technologies and how they can be used to market goods and services.

International/global marketing

There seems to be a general consensus that all marketing today is international. If this is not quite universally true now, it is certainly the way the trend is going. Almost all large firms have to deal with foreign competitors either in their home markets or abroad or both. Foreign rivals may not be much in evidence in the local shop, but foreign products are, and it may be foreign-owned supermarkets that are taking away its customers.

However, there are a large number of small to medium-sized businesses that have little or no dealings outside their own country. Many **services** businesses (e.g. cleaning, consultancy, law, accountancy, hairdressing and plumbing) have no significant international dimension. Will they all be crushed by the march of the **multinationals**? It seems unlikely that everyone will desert their regular hairdresser (especially those that make home visits and therefore have very low costs and, consequently, low prices), or that individuals and small businesspeople will prefer to hand over their tax returns to an anonymous corporation or Internet service rather than the accountant round the corner.

All businesses, however small, need to be aware of the forces of globalization though. They need to look out for new competition, new products and services and new opportunities. (See Chapter 3 for more about monitoring changes in the organization's environment.)

The patterns of trade are changing. The twentieth century was the era of free trade with richer countries pushing for the lowering, or abolition, of barriers to trade between nations, such as import duties, quotas (specified maximum amounts of imported goods), embargoes (bans on certain imported products) and subsidies (grants to producers that make home-produced goods cheaper). The twenty-first century may well prove, at least in its early part, to be a time of re-consolidation, but along new lines. Countries are clamouring to join trading blocs such as the EU, the North American Free Trade Association (NAFTA), the Association of South East Asian Nations (ASEAN) and Mercosur (an alliance of South American nations). Between them, the EU and NAFTA account for the bulk of world trade. Within their borders, member countries conduct trade on preferential terms. For example, within the EU, there are no import taxes and EU citizens can move to any country to work without obtaining work permits.

Business-to-business (b2b) marketing

FMCG (fast moving consumer goods)

low-cost products that are bought regularly (their shelves empty quickly)

Marketing grew from a start in **consumer** goods – in particular, FMCG (**fast moving consumer goods**); the term FMCG describes products that move off the shelves fast, i.e. they are bought frequently and so shops need to restock them regularly. These are everyday products such as soap, washing-up liquid, toothpaste, shampoo, breakfast cereal and bread – low-cost, kept in the cupboard all the time, items. Because of this heritage, modern marketing techniques favour the selling of these kinds of items to individuals for their own use. It is also the type of shopping that most people are more familiar with, so they usually relate to it better than **b2b**.

However, just consider how much more money businesses have to spend than individuals. Large companies spend millions every year. When they do buy the everyday items that we do (pens, paper, sticky tape, etc.) they buy them by the crate. This is a good **market** to be in.

The purchasing habits of businesses are rather different to those of individuals. Typically they:

▶ buy in larger quantities

▶ negotiate harder on delivery terms

▶ expect reduced prices for bulk buying

▶ may require tailored products

▶ are harder to please

▶ have more people involved in making the decision to buy

▶ have longer, more complex decision-making processes.

Businesses buy in larger quantities just because they are buying goods and services for more people. You may buy one or two biros; a company would need several boxes just so that each employee could have one. If the goods they are buying are actually for use in their production process (e.g. Birds Eye buying rice as an ingredient for its ready meals) or for selling on (as shops do), then they will have to buy enough for all their customers.

activity

Look around your room. What items can you see that a business would also buy? How might their use of the items differ from yours?

If you order something, such as a new CD or a new computer add-on, then usually you want it to arrive quickly, just because you cannot wait to play it or plug it in. Businesses have a more pressing need to know that their orders will arrive on time. A company's whole production process may well depend on having sufficient rice to make its paella, or there may be just one time slot, say a national holiday, when it can install its new computer hardware without too much disruption. So businesses tend to insist on particular delivery times and, if their orders are large enough, suppliers will comply.

Organizations are well aware that they are more valuable customers than individual purchasers. Often they expect something in return. They may settle for superior customer service, or they may insist on a **discount** as an incentive to place a large order.

Some business customers will ask for their own version of a supplier's products. For example, Zanussi has made special washing machine models for UK high-street stores such as Dixons. There are a number of reasons why businesses may want this. In the case of Dixons, it would almost certainly be to confer a **competitive advantage** by offering a model that other stores do not have. Businesses may want cars in the company colours or pens with their name on. They may want the rice they buy to be of uniform quality so that they can be sure it will all cook through when they cook it in a large batch. It would not usually be worth the supplier's while to customize its products for an individual customer, but for a large organization? Well, that's a different matter.

Organizations often employ experts, specialist buyers. These are people whose job it is to thoroughly understand what is available in terms of products or services in their field, and to get the best possible deal for the company. So, if they are a computer buyer, they will be technically expert in IT and will require more detail and demonstration than the average individual customer. The organization may have a large and complex network, and any new equipment will have to fit in with what is already installed – this may mean it has to be tailored to suit or specially installed.

When you want to buy something, the decision is usually yours although you may consult other people, particularly if you are not paying the whole cost yourself. Within organizations, it is rarely just one person that makes the decision on any significant purchase. There is a group of people who are referred to as the **decision-making unit** (DMU).

Take the example of a new car. There may be the fleet manager (who will specify which cars may be bought), the buyer (who will choose a supplier and negotiate terms), the finance department (which will set the budget and pay the invoice) and, of course, the person who is actually going to drive the car: the user. A potential supplier may have to deal with all these people and more. (See Chapter 5 for more on decision-making units.)

With all these people involved, it takes longer to decide to buy something. There are often forms that must be filled in, committee meetings called, procedures that must be followed. The organization is likely to have rules about how many suppliers must be invited to bid for a contract. All of them must get a fair chance, and so there are more rules and procedures to ensure that this happens. It is a lot more complicated than when you decide to buy a new printer for your PC.

Marketing ethics

Different businesses operate according to different ethical codes. There was a time when it was considered perfectly acceptable for an employer to own his workers and their children, yet now such a practice would cause outrage. Ethics change with the times. There are a number of different ethical models under which an organization can operate.

There are different views on who should be the main beneficiaries of business activities. Many companies are ostensibly run for the sole benefit of their owners or shareholders, whose primary requirement is likely to be profit. In practice, though, a business cannot run without workers, and so they must benefit too, usually through wages or salaries. Then again, if the firm's products and/or services do not benefit anyone, why would customers buy them? So perhaps a firm is run primarily for the benefit of customers?

The **stakeholder** view of business ethics takes all of these interests, and more, into account. The argument is that the benefits to all of an organization's stakeholders should be considered by the management team. (For more on stakeholders, see Chapter 2.)

A firm's overall ethical stance will, of course, influence its marketing approach. However, there are some, more specific, ethical questions that marketers have to address. At one extreme is the view that all marketing (and in particular marketing communications) is unethical. If an organization is supplying good products/services, then marketing is superfluous; it can only be designed to con people into buying things they do not need – or even that are bad for them (which would make them unethical products).

When an ethical position is generally accepted within a country, it is likely to be formalized by the passing of a law. Regulations and codes of practice are watered-down laws. They still reflect what is generally accepted as right or wrong. There are many laws governing marketing, e.g. product liability, consumer protection, trades descriptions, pricing, anti-competitive practices. There are regulations and codes of conduct covering **advertising**, **sponsorship**, **sales promotion**, Internet trading, **telesales**, data protection and many other marketing activities. For example, the UK Sale of Goods Act requires goods that are delivered to be the same as the ones that were shown to the customer. This is particularly important for mail order where the pictures and descriptions must be accurate. In many European countries, a code of practice prevents overt **product placement** on television (although the practice is considered acceptable in the USA).

ethicalfocus

Does his face ring a bell?

Continued deregulation in the UK telecommunications market meant that, in 2003, directory enquiry services were opened up to competition. A new operator, The Number, quickly gained an impressive 50 per cent **market share** thanks to its unusual advertising campaign featuring two athletes who appeared to have run straight out of the 1970s.

However, former world record holder David Bedford felt that they looked all too familiar and consulted lawyers. The Number denied basing their characters on him, saying that the look was typical of 1970s sportsmen.

He wasn't the only famous runner to appear in adverts around that time. Prince Charles (or rather, what appeared to be Prince Charles) made it on to Belgian billboards, in lycra shorts and looking surprisingly fit, to advertise tours to Britain. The Queen also appeared in that campaign – skirt flying just like Marilyn Monroe's.

Clearly the royal appearances were the construct of modern imaging technology. Advertisers can also place dead stars with products they could never have seen (e.g.

Steve McQueen driving a modern Ford). They can change a photo's background and a subject's appearance. In 2002, racing driver Eddie Irvine successfully sued a radio station that had used a digitally altered picture of him in promotional material without his permission.

We are used to seeing famous faces in adverts and assume that these people are paid for the use of their image. If people are in the public eye, even actively seek out publicity, should it be OK to use their image without their permission? If not, then how close must the resemblance be for us to say that it really is that famous face?

Products can be unethical. There are a number of products that are banned in most countries (e.g. recreational drugs). Many would argue that cigarettes should not be on sale either. Sales of some products are severely restricted (e.g. guns, alcohol – which is banned in some countries – and strong medicines).

Unethical pricing practices include fixing prices so that consumers are forced to pay too much. This usually involves collusion between competitors (e.g. as a **cartel**), or the existence of a **monopoly**, or a severe shortage of goods. In wartime, there are people who exploit other people's misery by charging dearly for essential goods, and so they become rich.

dumping

when a company exports its products at a very low price and so undercuts competitors in the target country

Too low a price may be considered unethical too. The outlawing of **dumping** is called for at meetings of the WTO (World Trade Organization) and there are now severe restrictions on its legality. Dumping is an anti-competitive practice whereby a company exports its products at a very low price and so undercuts competitors in the target country. These competitors are then unable to compete and eventually go out of business, and so jobs and wealth are lost in that country. The low price is, of course, unsustainable. The company that has dumped the products will either raise its prices or will stop exporting; so the residents of the dumped-on country end up with either no products of that type or more expensive ones.

Professional marketers, and marketing associations such as the Chartered Institute of Marketing, strive to behave ethically towards all their organization's stakeholders. There are still those who doubt their motives, however, and consider their caring stance to be enlightened self-interest or just good PR.

Customer relationship management (crm)

One of the trickiest things about crm is getting people to agree on what it is. In this textbook, we have taken the acronym to stand for customer relationship management, but you will see it billed in many other places as customer relationship marketing. The two terms are used interchangeably by some (e.g. Kotler, 2003) and to add further to the confusion, crm (or CRM) is often used to refer to **cause-related marketing**, which is a form of **sponsorship** and therefore a different thing altogether.

The term management is preferred here because it has more scope. If you are managing a relationship, then you are nurturing it, progressing it – perhaps in the end terminating it. If you are using a relationship for marketing purposes only, then you are using your knowledge of someone to further marketing aims: to woo them into loyalty, persuade them that the brand's image is right for them, sell them more products and over a longer time period. Both sets of activities are valid and both go on. However, the management of customer relationships is more likely to contribute to the long-term health of the company. Some even claim that it is more important to manage the life cycles of these customer relationships than it is to manage the life cycles of products, claiming that this is the route to strategic advantage (Wilson, 1996).

So there is some confusion over what crm stands for, and further differences of opinion surface over what it actually means in practice. There is a school of thought that takes crm as a set of technological tools that capture customer information and enable an organization to use it to market its products more effectively: 'the application of technology to learning more about each customer and being able to respond to them one-to-one' (Kotler, 2003).

This is really a sophisticated form of **database marketing**. It enables a company to **cross-sell** (i.e. sell existing customers additional, different products) and **up-sell** (i.e. sell customers a more expensive version of the product).

Again, that is not the way the term crm will be used here. Customer relationship management is more than just technologically enhanced customer service. It is the use of procedures and management techniques that enhance the customer's experience of the organization, build loyalty and contribute to long-term profitability.

It is as important to be skilled in ending relationships as it is to be able to maintain them. A customer will end a relationship when the exchanges no longer have value (see 'Exchanges' above). The organization must be prepared to be similarly ruthless. Some customers, particularly long-standing ones, can in fact cost the firm money. (See Chapter 2 for more on managing customers.)

> **database marketing**
> use of computerized customer data to communicate with customers and promote further sales

SUMMARY

This chapter has been an introduction to the marketing concept and to the themes that run throughout this textbook. We have looked at what marketing is, and what it is not. Marketing has been defined and the modern marketing concept explained. The origins of marketing should help you to understand how the discipline has developed and where it might go next.

Some basic economics have been considered. Economic theory is highly relevant to marketing and informs much of what marketing managers do. In particular, an overview of demand and supply analysis has been presented. There are many other disciplines that are relevant to marketing (for example, psychology). Marketers are always keen to understand their customers in depth, and psychological theories form a platform for theories of customer behaviour (see Chapter 5). Finance and accounting are among the other relevant disciplines – after all, marketers seek to make exchanges that are profitable.

This book has been carefully designed to help inexperienced students and/or those new to marketing as a subject. As well as the questions and case studies that you would expect to find in a textbook of this type, we have included challenges, activities and focus boxes. The focus themes are key, current marketing issues and they, along with the 'insight' boxes you will see throughout the text, should help build a bridge from your academic studies to the marketing practitioner's world – and your future marketing career.

Challenges reviewed

Now that you have finished reading the chapter, look back at the challenges you were set at the beginning. Do you have a clearer idea of what's involved?
Hints:

▶ see 'definitions' and 'what marketing is not'

▶ think about the concept of value and also relationship marketing

▶ always act ethically; also, check the Data Protection Act.

READING AROUND

books
Naomi Klein (2000) *No Logo*, Flamingo HarperCollins.
book chapters
John O'Connor and Eamonn Galvin (2001) Marketing's challenge, Chapter 1 in *Marketing in the Digital Age*, FT Prentice Hall.
magazines
Marketing Week
Marketing
(Most libraries will have these magazines – possibly online – ask your librarian.)

SELF-REVIEW QUESTIONS

1. Define a market. (see pages 6 and 20)

2. Is marketing an alternative term for advertising? (see page 8)

3. What is another term for marketing communications? (see page 8)

4. Why is marketing less important when there is a shortage of goods? (see page 9)

5. Give 5 examples of fmcg items. (see pages 11 and 21)

6. Why is it desirable for a product's demand and supply to be in equilibrium? (see page 13)

7. Why is value such an important part of an exchange? (see page 14)

8. In what circumstances might transactional marketing be appropriate? (see page 17)

9. What is relationship marketing? (see page 17)

10. Who has more power today: consumers, big companies or small businesses? (see page 18)

MINI CASE STUDY

Read the questions, then the case material, then answer the questions.

Questions

1. What are the problems that Liverpool faces in attracting tourists? (Use the information in the case study, but you may also want to look up Liverpool, and rival cities, on the Internet.)

2. How could it overcome these problems?

3. Write an insert (approx. 200 words) on Liverpool for a tourist guide. You should identify different aspects of the city that will appeal to different types of visitor.

4. How could relationship marketing help Liverpool?

Relaunching Liverpool

In its heyday as England's busiest port, Liverpool saw the launching of many fine ships. Those glory days are long gone and now the city finds itself in need of a relaunch itself.

For years Liverpool has suffered from jokes and abuse – for being more famous for its sense of humour than its work ethic. The media, through such programmes as *Bread*, *Brookside* and *The Fast Show*, have built a picture of Liverpool as a city of lazy, dole-beating chancers. Tourists, shoppers and business travellers avoid it, fearing for their wallets and their safety. Yet locals claim that the city's poor image was invented by the media and that the truth is very different.

Liverpool has recently received a major boost, however; it has been chosen as the European Capital of Culture for 2008. Over £2 billion will be invested in the city over the next five years.

Plans include one of Europe's biggest regeneration projects to turn the Paradise Street area into a suitable venue for a variety of entertainments, including street theatre and music. As a city of culture, it hopes for an additional income from visitors of over £50 million a year.

As well as writers such as Beryl Bainbridge, Willy Russell, Alan Bleasdale, Catherine Cookson and Roger McGough, Liverpool has produced many pop-cultural icons. The city has produced more artists with number-one hits than any other. Its most famous sons are, of course, The Beatles. These symbols of the 1960s were born and bred in the city and first played at the Cavern club – now redeveloped as a Beatles museum. The National Trust recently acquired John Lennon's childhood home (a gift from his widow, Yoko Ono-Lennon) and opened it to public view. Liverpool Football Club has been one of the country's premier clubs for decades. Comedians as diverse as Ken Dodd, Jimmy Tarbuck and Lily Savage all hail from the city. Cilla Black started her days (as Priscilla White) singing in Liverpool, and more recent pop exports include Atomic Kitten, Space, the Lightning Seeds, the Coral and Cast.

Even so, if the city is to market itself as a cultural capital that should be on every tourist's list, it has a lot of image rebuilding to do.

A spokesperson for the City Council said, 'People just haven't been listening. Unemployment is reducing and it is one of the safest cities in the country. Liverpool has art galleries, shopping centres and trendy bars. We are also close to becoming the film capital of Britain with the number of films shot here. I don't see why it should be a problem marketing ourselves to the UK and abroad.'

Unusually for a city, Liverpool has been abroad itself. The wealth of architectural styles and impressive buildings within the city have made it an ideal film double for a number of European cities, including Moscow, Dublin, Paris and, most surprisingly, Venice. The most dramatic aspect of Liverpool is, of course, its waterfront. The Albert Dock is already home to thriving bars, restaurants and shops, as well as upmarket apartments and the Tate art gallery. By 2008, it will be reborn as a twenty-first-century vista with a grandeur that will rival the original docks.

Sources: BBCi, 2003; Liverpool City Council, 2003; Singh, 2003

REFERENCES

BBCi (2003) *Capital of Culture* (web page) accessed 10/8/2003. Available at www.bbc.co.uk/capitalofculture.

Berry, L.L. Relationship marketing (1983) in Berry, L.L., Shostack, G. and Upah, G., *Emerging Perspectives on Services Marketing*, American Marketing Association.

Doyle, P. (2002) *Marketing Management and Strategy*, FT Prentice Hall.

Kotler, P. (2003) *Marketing Insights from A to Z*, John Wiley & Sons, Inc.

Liverpool City Council (2003) *Liverpool, European Capital of Culture* (web page) accessed 10/8/2003. Available at www.liverpool.gov.uk.

O'Connor, J. and Galvin, E. (2001) *Marketing in the Digital Age*, FT Prentice Hall.

Singh, S. (2003) Can Liverpool set the record straight? *Marketing Week*, 12 June. Available at www.mad.co.uk.

Wilson, Kevin (1996). 'Managing the industrial sales force of the 1990s' In Hartley, Bob and Starkey, MIchael W., Editors, *The Management of Sales and Customer Relations*, International Thomson Business Press London.

MARKETING TODAY

MARKETING CHALLENGES

The following are illustrations of the types of decisions that marketers have to take or issues they face. *You aren't expected to know how to deal with the challenges now*; just bear them in mind as you read the chapter and see what you can find that helps.

▶ Your cousin has an idea for an apparently foolproof way to stop mobile phones being used by anyone but their owners. He has enough cash to produce the system but no more and he doesn't want to borrow to fund further activities such as marketing. He thinks his idea is so good that everyone will want it anyway. What are the dangers here? Could any marketing techniques help?

▶ A friend's bookshop is not doing as well as it used to. It's in a great location but Internet bookshops are just so much cheaper. How can she make better use of the shop to attract more customers in and make the ones who are there spend more?

▶ Winston Smith installs CCTV systems for a living. He is self-employed and all his jobs are one-offs. Today he's very annoyed because he's just seen someone else adding to one of his systems. The customer was pleased with the work Winston did but couldn't remember his name, so he got someone else in when the system needed enlarging. How could Winston have got that job himself?

KEY CONCEPTS

crm (customer relationship management)
strategic orientation (particularly sales, marketing, customer and societal orientations)
customer focus
markets
customers
consumers
market leaders
marketing objectives (see also Chapters 11 and 12)
marketing strategies (see also Chapter 12)
customer retention

INTRODUCTION

Marketing can be viewed in many different ways. It is:

▶ a concept

▶ a philosophy

▶ an orientation

▶ a function

▶ a discipline.

This chapter will try to sort through the different aspects of marketing, and introduce the differing views, and so arrive at an understanding of marketing's place in the world today.

The role of marketing has changed as our economic systems have developed, and it is viewed differently in different countries. Some organizations emphasize their marketing activities, seeing themselves as marketing companies, while others see themselves as primarily manufacturers, or as financially excellent, or perhaps as innovators. This is one of the important things to understand: different organizations focus on different business activities and, much as marketers might like to think that organizations will never be successful unless they view marketing as the most important thing, some firms do seem to get by without putting very much effort into marketing activities. Of course, it is always possible that they would do much better if they were more marketing focused.

MIXED TERMINOLOGY AND MIXED CLAIMS

The following are all activities that come under the heading of marketing:

▶ selling

▶ advertising

▶ pricing

▶ product distribution

▶ new product development

▶ brand management

▶ public relations (PR)

▶ customer service

▶ promotion

▶ market research

▶ dealer support

▶ in-store displays

▶ exhibitions and demonstrations.

There are more too, of course; however, not all of these activities are the exclusive province of marketing. For example: accountants and economists lay claim to pricing; operations managers often take charge of distribution; research and development staff may take the lead in new product development; PR may be seen as a separate, corporate function.

The *discipline* of marketing is of primary interest to students and their tutors. Discipline means 'field of study' (Allen, 2000). Organizations are more likely to consider marketing as a *function* or a *department*. Function is a broader concept; it encompasses all an organization's marketing activities, whether or not they are carried out within the marketing department. For example, reception staff could be said to play a key role in the maintenance of a company's image and the building of relationships with customers; they do not report to the marketing manager, are not part of marketing staff, but they do perform a marketing function as part of their job. Marketing roles and the marketing department will be covered in more depth at the end of the book (see Postscript).

Academic researchers are more concerned with the marketing concept, marketing philosophy and marketing orientation. The distinction between these terms is sometimes unclear. They are used differently within different texts and journal articles. Sometimes they are even used interchangeably. For example, Dibb *et al.* (2001) make no real distinction between the terms. They define the marketing concept as, 'the philosophy that an organisation should try to provide products that satisfy customers' needs through a co-ordinated set of activities that also allows the organisation to achieve its goals.' So they see concept and philosophy as the same, and they are in good company. Kotler *et al.* (2001) also make no distinction between these terms. However, Hooley *et al.* (1990) suggest that the marketing concept is a process, rather than a philosophy (or way of thinking). Jobber (2001) also sees the marketing concept as a process, i.e. something that organizations do. He defines it as, 'the achievement of corporate goals through meeting and exceeding customer needs better than the competition.'

These differences in definition are less important than the principles behind marketing – and are not something to be too concerned about at this stage. An awareness that such terms are often substituted for each other, without there being any great significance to the way they are used, is all that is required.

Marketing orientation is another term that gets thrown into this mix. Again, Dibb *et al.* (2001) do not make any significant distinction between terms. Kotler *et al.* (2001) do not use this term at all. So what does it mean?

An organization's orientation provides 'the guiding principles that influence a firm's marketing and strategy making activities' (Noble *et al.*, 2002) and so determines how it will interact with its marketplace. Orientation literally means the way a person, or organization, faces. Marketing-orientated firms, then, look to marketing. Jobber (2001) also refers to this as **customer orientation** but, strictly speaking, a market is made up of buyers and sellers, so a truly marketing-orientated organization ought to be both customer *and* competition facing.

For the purposes of this textbook, the terms marketing concept and marketing philosophy will be used in a similar way. Marketing orientation will be used to mean the implementation of the marketing philosophy (or concept), i.e. to describe those firms that have embraced the marketing philosophy (or concept) and use it to inform their activities and strategies. So a marketing orientation requires marketing actions, not just thoughts or intentions.

marketing orientation

the provision of customer value determines an organization's direction

MARKETS

A market is a place where buyers and sellers meet. The term is often made more complex, but it is worth hanging on to that simple definition.

There are lots of different markets (e.g. consumer markets, industrial markets, b2b markets, overseas markets). These are broad groups of buyers and sellers, and they can be narrowed down into smaller groupings such as product type (e.g. **white goods** market) or customer type (e.g. youth market) or a combination (e.g. children's clothing market). Often, when people refer to 'markets' they are using the term interchangeably with 'customers'; however, a market needs sellers too and so any true study of a market should also include the seller – and its competitors.

white goods

large electrical household appliances such as fridges and washing machines (traditionally coloured white)

exhibit 2.1

Market classifications

consumer markets	personal purchases	e.g. household weekly shop
industrial markets	things that will be used in the making of other things	e.g. glass to go into headlights for cars, cooling fluids for machinery
b2b markets	things for use in the course of another business	e.g. delivery vans
not for profit markets	purchases and marketing activities by charities, government organizations, trades unions, clubs and associations, etc.	e.g. computer equipment and supplies, marketing services
government markets	purchases by central government, local government, health services, schools, public libraries, armed forces, police, etc.	e.g. office supplies
reseller markets	goods to be sold on, e.g. by retailers, wholesalers, distributors, dealers, etc.	e.g. anything found for sale in a shop
overseas markets	all above categories – but in other countries or outside of the home country's trading bloc (e.g EU)	could be anything at all
internal markets	other divisions, subsidiaries or employees of the organization itself	e.g. own product sales (usually at discounted prices), services provided by one division for another in the same organization

MARKET DYNAMICS

market leader

the company with
the highest sales
within a market

Some companies are said to be **market led**, others to be **market leaders**. Strictly, the market leader is the company that sells the most. It is important to be clear which market you are referring to when talking of a market leader. Cadbury's may well be the market leader in chocolate in the UK but not in the USA, where it is more likely to be Hershey's, or in any other European country each of which has its own favourites.

The term market leader is often used more loosely, however, to refer to a firm that leads the way in a market. This may be in terms of setting prices, releasing **innovative products**, devising new forms of promotion, moving into different **market segments**, or any number of other ways of starting an industry trend. Such leaders are not necessarily large organizations. Often the recognized market leader is a smaller firm that is more innovative (e.g. Dyson and its vacuum cleaners), or that has more expertise (e.g. some specialized consultancy and accountancy firms), or has unique talent (e.g. fashion designers such as Stella McCartney and Alexander McQueen).

If a company is said to be market led, then it follows other firms within that market. Such firms are often termed **market followers**. Market followers take their lead from competitors and copy their successful ideas and strategies. This does not mean that they produce only me-too designs or campaigns, only that they wait for more radical ideas to be tested by others first and cash in on their research. Throughout the 1990s, many fast-food chains waited for McDonald's to set up a new store and then set up their own stores nearby. They assumed that McDonald's had done the research and found an area with good potential.

The disadvantage of this is that the followers are, by definition, second (or third, fourth, etc.) into the market and therefore do not usually get the benefit of **first mover advantage**. Often, the first significant company to move into a market becomes the leader. It can be hard to dislodge as it is the brand people know, the one they tried first and presumably liked or there would be no market.

Coca-Cola was the first company to make a cola drink and it still outsells all others in most countries. The Body Shop was the first to build a retailing chain around the idea of more ethically produced toiletries. Amazon was the first company to sell books online with a view to making a large business of it and the resources and skills to make that dream a reality. All these firms had first mover advantage.

However, being first into the market does not guarantee success, as many IT and Internet companies have found. Sometimes the first is a very small company, unable to exploit the market to the full or it may make mistakes, thus letting another, larger or more able company steal the high ground. The first company bears the brunt of the risks and so may fail where later companies succeed. If it is successful, it is likely to attract the attention of larger competitors. A highly praised Internet browser called Netscape pre-dates Microsoft Explorer. Which one do you use?

asset-led marketing

basing marketing
strategy on the
organization's
strengths rather than
on customer needs
and wants

Not all organizations are marketing focused, so they cannot be said to be either led by the market or driven by it. For example, some companies are **asset led**. These companies concentrate on doing what they already have the resources and skills to do, rather than looking for market opportunities and adapting to fit them. The asset in question might be equipment, people, contacts, a distribution network, shops – almost anything. In the UK, many shoe repairers also cut keys, and frequently now take in dry cleaning. They have suitable shop premises to do this. Their shops are major assets to be exploited. Many universities rent out rooms in their halls of residence to tourists in the summer months, using an asset that would otherwise stand empty. Theatres, museums and art galleries rent out their foyers for upmarket parties. Did any of these organizations conduct research to discover people's needs and then design their offerings to fit? No, they realized they had spare space and came up with something profitable to do with it.

It is not just spare space that can be exploited profitably. Mars started making ice cream versions of its products, trading on the considerable asset that is its brand name. IBM realized it had hundreds of highly trained management and computing personnel whose skills could be offered to clients as consultants. Many years ago, when textile production was dying in the UK, the factory owners realized that the same machines could be used to knit tea bags.

So, is it best to build your strategy around what your customers want, or around the assets you already have? This is an occasion where companies look for the best of both worlds. The ideal is to meet your customers' needs while making the best possible use of all your assets.

Sometimes circumstances allow you to be more proactive about this – for example, when moving, or building new premises. When Leicester City football club had its new stadium built, for instance, it incorporated private rooms of various sizes into the design so that it could develop its business of hiring out space for meetings, lunches and other functions.

Leicester City's new stadium is not just for football fans

An example of asset-led marketing – partying in the art gallery

Minarik

Andrew Minarik runs a hairdressing salon. It is a family business, passed down from mother to son. The business thrives, thanks to its well-established (and well-heeled) clientele and a prime position on a busy road. There was no absolute need to diversify, but the salon had spare rooms and bored clients sitting around. As anyone who has had their hair coloured knows, it's a long and tedious business. So, if you've got the premises and a regular, captive audience, why not find more things for those customers to buy?

So now there's a beauty salon upstairs. You can have your nails painted at the same time as your hair changes colour. Regular hair clients become regulars at the beauty salon too – making separate appointments for facials and massages – and walking past the handmade jewellery display on the way to each. Sometimes, there are gifts and knick-knacks for sale too. In another room, you can get an all-over tan in 10 minutes or so. The machine is looked after by another company which maintains and services it and takes a cut of the proceeds.

Some people do still go there just to get a good haircut.

MARKETING STRATEGIES

A strategy is a long-term plan designed to achieve the organization's objectives. Strategies are perhaps the most important influence on a company's success or failure. Consequently, larger organizations spend a lot of time devising their strategies and designing plans to implement them. Academics and consultants also spend a lot of time thinking about strategies, analysing what makes them successful and designing standard approaches to commonly faced situations. You will learn more about marketing strategies and planning later in the book (in particular, in Chapter 12). What it is important to grasp now is that most successful organizations are not managed on an ad hoc basis, but work to an overall plan with a particular end in mind.

OBJECTIVES

Different organizations are trying to achieve different things. However, there are some things that most hope to achieve, for example:

▶ survival

▶ **profits** (however, not for profit organizations, such as charities or hospitals, usually just aim to **break even**)

▶ a good reputation

▶ **competitive edge**

▶ increased **market share**.

At different times, organizations may have other objectives, for example:

▶ the takeover of another company

▶ a move into a new market (perhaps another country)

▶ the launch of a new product

▶ the recruitment of more skilled staff

▶ increased **sales volume** (i.e. quantity of goods sold)

▶ cost cutting

▶ the acquisition of another **brand**.

Compare the second list to the first. The second list could be said to be secondary objectives, i.e. they contribute to the first. For example, the purpose of moving into a new market is almost certainly to make more sales. More skilled staff are likely to contribute to a better reputation for the organization. Cost cutting should help profits. Acquiring a competitive brand is a fast track to increased market share.

Organizations have a number of different objectives and must make plans in order to achieve them. It is important that these objectives support each other, rather than conflicting, otherwise how can an organization possibly achieve all of them? For example, it is hard to cut costs and increase market share at the same time. An increase in market share often requires considerable upfront spending, e.g. on new advertising or product variations.

STRATEGIC ORIENTATIONS

Different organizations take different approaches when it comes to achieving their objectives. Almost all (the successful ones anyway) will have a strategy but there are many ways to achieve success. The strategies themselves, and the thinking behind them, varies. If an organization has embraced the marketing philosophy, then the needs and wants of its customers, coupled with a recognition of what competitors offer them, will be the driving force behind its thinking. That organization will be **marketing orientated**.

However, marketing is not the only strategic orientation an organization could adopt. Exhibit 2.2 shows some of the other options.

exhibit 2.2

Strategic orientations

orientation	focuses on	typical objectives
production	production efficiency	higher profits through reduced costs
product	product quality and features	increased sales through product improvements
sales	sales techniques and advertising	sales volume – often short term
customer	customers' needs	increased long-term sales through customer loyalty, positive image
marketing	customers' needs and competitors' strategies	long-term profits through good customer relations and a sustainable **competitive advantage**
cooperative	workers' needs	long-term job security, good working conditions
financial	financial ratios and other measures	return on investment (ROI), higher share prices and dividend payments
societal	society's well-being	environmental regeneration, community welfare

Many textbooks ascribe these orientation strategies to specific eras, usually making production the earliest and marketing the most recent. However, there are still organizations that are product or production orientated, even though marketing orientation is widely accepted as better in terms of business performance.

Cooperative and financial orientations are beyond the scope of this book. The next section goes into detail on the other, more marketing-related orientations. Production is included as it often appears in marketing texts, though it is definitely out of favour with modern-day management thinkers. Societal orientation is included because of its links with positive corporate image.

Production orientation

Putting the factory first

Firms that have a production orientation focus on production efficiency. They try to make their products and services as quickly as possible and at the lowest possible cost. A production-orientated firm will take great pride in its production facilities which may well be state of the art.

Such firms place great emphasis on **economies of scale** and so are likely to be large-scale producers. It is usually most cost effective to produce a large amount of a product because it makes it worthwhile to have the largest, fastest machinery or specialist tools, gains bulk discounts on component parts, and enables workers to concentrate on certain tasks and so become expert in them. This efficiency often comes at the cost of product range. If a firm is making a huge quantity of one product, then it cannot also make others. In fact, it is in the interest of such a firm to offer its customers limited product choice. The most famous example of a production orientation is the original Ford car, the model T, of which Henry Ford is alleged to have said, 'They can have any colour they like, so long as it's black.' This lack of consideration for customer requirements means that a production orientation is not in keeping with the marketing philosophy. However, today, technological developments are making it possible to achieve production efficiency and lower production costs without the need to go into large mass-production quantities.

Product orientation

Putting the product first

Firms with a **product orientation** are concerned with making the best possible product. They put great effort into product development and improvements, adding new features, expanding ranges, improving quality, etc. Their view is nicely summed up by the nineteenth-century American philosopher and poet Ralph Waldo Emerson, who said, 'If you build a better mousetrap, the world will beat a path to your door.'

This is often used as an indictment of marketing communications; showing it to be unnecessary. However, there are a number of flaws in this product-orientated view – not least that the world can only beat that path to your door if it knows about the mousetrap and where to get one. So communication in some form is required. If you build a better mousetrap, chances are that someone will steal your idea – or build an even better one, or make a cheaper one. Technology moves on and it is hard to keep ahead of the competition even with groundbreaking new ideas. Also, sometimes the mice just get smarter.

In his famous article 'Marketing myopia', Levitt stated that product-orientated industries died. The example he used was that of the North American railways, which believed themselves to be in the railroad business and were therefore surprised when they lost all their customers to airlines. They had not appreciated that they were all in the transport market.

Product-orientated firms believe that, if they provide a good quality product, at a reasonable price, then people will buy it without much further effort on the firm's part. This concentration on product improvement has its advantages. For example, it may well produce groundbreaking new products. Many technology companies are product orientated; they produce new computers, machinery, gadgets and gizmos believing that other people will be as caught up in the invention and its cleverness as its designers are.

Sometimes this works. Vacuum cleaner manufacturer Dyson is a modern example of a successful product-orientated firm. After all, people find it hard to imagine products or services that do not currently exist. Someone, often someone with technical expertise, has to come up with the ideas before they can run them past potential customers to check their likely popularity. Imagine a world without DVDs. Would you have come up with such an idea? How about recorded music generally? That is only a twentieth-century invention. Before that, if you wanted to hear music, you had to learn to play an instrument, or befriend others who could. If you had only ever known communication over distance by letter, would you have asked for a mobile phone? (See Chapter 7 for more on product innovation.)

Of course there are some basic needs that we know we want fulfilled, even without imagining new technology. For example, we want cures for a number of diseases, from cancer and HIV through to the common cold. We want to be able to get to places faster and more reliably. Many of us want to be slimmer. Often, it is more useful to ask people what they want to be able to do, what desires they have, rather than what new products they would like.

activity

Get a small group of friends together and suggest ideas for new products that you would like to own. Alternatively, just make a list yourself.

How many of your ideas require a technological breakthrough before they can be made reality?

Technological breakthrough products, then, usually require a leap of imagination, and faith, on the part of their providers. Most such products fail. The ones that do succeed tap into a real customer need, either a pre-existing one that was being met less well (or not at all) previously, or a need not previously recognized (for example, to be able to talk on the phone, hands-free of course, while driving a car).

Other situations where product orientation may be effective are when there is little effective competition or a shortage of that type of product. For example, where a company has a **patent**, as Dyson had on its vacuum cleaner technology, or a **monopoly**, as many train operators have in their designated areas or under the terms of their franchises. Product-orientated companies that do not have these advantages may need to do some very hard selling.

Sales orientation

Saying that the customer comes first

Firms that are sales orientated spend a lot on sales training, sales aids and support materials (brochures, presentations, etc.). They do a lot of **sales promotion** (short-term special offers such as 'buy one get one free', coupons, competitions) and often use hard-sell advertising ('amazing special offer', 'this week only', 'never before available to the public', etc.). They are likely to have a large salesforce that may be quite pushy. Such firms seem to believe that customers will not want to buy their products unless they are pushed into doing so. They are trying to overcome customers' reluctance to buy. Double-glazing firms and timeshare sellers are often sales orientated.

The emphasis here is on the seller's need to shift stock or to make the targets, rather than on customers' needs. However, as part of the heavy sales drive, the salespeople may pay lip-service to marketing – perhaps by calling sales managers 'marketing managers' (as IBM used to do) and by taking an interest in the customer's requirements (so they can sell them other products). This may really just be part of their sales technique, a way of generating rapport with a prospect. Sales-orientated firms are far more interested in their own needs than those of their customers and their salespeople often have high quotas of products to sell with the prospect of large commissions if they succeed. So the success of a sales-orientated firm depends largely upon the skill of its salesforce.

Sales-orientated companies are stuck in the old **transaction exchange** way of thinking (see Chapter 1). Pushing a customer to buy something that they may not really want or need, and may later regret, is no way to build a relationship.

According to Peter Drucker, 'The aim of marketing is to make selling superfluous.' A firm that has developed products to meet its customers' needs, and that presents them well, will not need the hard sell. A sales orientation is, at best, a short-term route to success.

ethicalfocus

The timeshare scam

The bubble truly seems to have burst on timeshare deals now. **Classified ads** sections are full of owners wanting to sell – but nobody's buying.

Not so long ago, timesharing was a popular way to own a holiday home. You could buy a share in your very own villa or apartment for a fraction of the cost of owning it outright. Your share effectively made you the owner of the property for a specified two weeks or so every year. Holidays sorted!

Timeshare-sales companies employed attractive young people in holiday resorts, dressed them in beachwear and trained them to persuade relaxed holidaymakers to sign up for another holiday next year, or to attend a party (at which they would hear all the benefits of timeshare). They offered inducements like cheaper rates for those who signed up before they went home (and got their feet back on the ground). They told people that there were only a couple of apartments left; the others had all been snapped up.

Back home, they lured prospects with amazing deals and promises: 'Just attend our presentation,' they said, 'with absolutely no obligation to buy, and we'll give you a fine lunch, unlimited champagne and a free gift.' They sent out invitations telling the lucky recipients that they had definitely won a prize. Soon people wised up to the way that the prize always turned out to be the cheapest thing on the list (a pen, a scarf – often with the company's name emblazoned on it), so the companies upped the offer. The prize would be nothing less than a television or a stereo. After two hours or so of hard selling, during which people found it almost impossible to leave (and if they did they didn't get a prize at all), many caved in and signed up.

One of the main objections that potential purchasers raised was that it tied them to the same time and the same place every year. While some people liked this, others thought it might become dull and would prefer a change. 'No problem,' said the timeshare sellers (who were well versed in objection handling), 'you can swap with someone else and go during their timeslot. You can even sell your two weeks if you want to and, if you get tired of the place altogether, there's a waiting list of people who want to buy. This is an investment. Sell in five or ten years at a nice fat profit.'

For many it hasn't worked out like that, though. There are now thousands of timeshare holiday homes across Europe standing empty and unwanted.

Customer orientation

Actually putting the customer first

Many writers do not distinguish between customer orientation and marketing orientation – but there is a key difference. A market is made up of buyers *and* sellers so, within this text anyway, a marketing orientation will be taken to include serious consideration of the competition.

However, a customer orientation is held by most to be essential to long-term success. How strange then, that so few organizations are customer orientated. Many pay lip-service to the idea but fail to gear their systems to satisfying customers, focusing too much on the needs of the organization itself instead.

An organization has a number of types of customer. A company that focuses on end customers, without considering trade customers, may find that its products are not actually available for sale (trade customers include retailers, wholesalers, distributors, and import and export agents).

The move to a true customer orientation is not easy and takes a long time. Organizations typically experience considerable resistance from individual departments and employees. Any organizational change has to be managed carefully to ensure that it is accepted and works, but turning an organization around, so that all its processes are geared

b2bfocus

Dave the decorator

Dave the decorator has a thriving business. He is booked up at least six months in advance. He doesn't need to advertise as word of mouth brings in all the business he needs. Many of his customers are regulars, so impressed by his work that they wouldn't dream of employing anyone else, and most certainly wouldn't do the decorating themselves.

Because he has a lot of experience in interior decorating, Dave has become quite an expert on which paints and papers look best in which situations and which last longest. People ask Dave for his opinion on their proposed colour schemes and for his recommendation on types of paint.

Currently, Dave favours an eggshell finish rather than gloss for woodwork. He thinks it looks smarter and says it doesn't fade as quickly. He dislikes ceiling paper and thinks some of the supposedly better wallpapers are overpriced.

People say you can tell Dave's work, not just by the quality of the finish, but by the trademark eggshell woodwork, the plain ceilings and the brand of paper.

So, from Dulux, Crown or any wallpaper manufacturer's point of view, who is the key customer here – consumer or trade?

towards the customer, can be particularly gruelling and may cause major conflict. An organization's orientation is a feature of its culture. Organizational culture can loosely be described as 'the way we do things around here'. The procedures an organization follows are evidence of its culture. The culture may be formal (as in many banks) or informal (as in many software companies). It may be traditional (like Harrods) or wacky (like, say, Virgin radio). The tone of it is often set by the chief executive or founder and their lead influences the behaviour of all members of the organization – all successful members that is.

An organization's culture is possibly the hardest thing about it to change. It can be a source of great strength but, if it is too rigid, it can hold an organization back and prevent it from moving with the times (as happened with IBM in the late 1980s). Changing an organization's culture is rather like asking you to become another nationality – and to behave appropriately, forgetting all of your original beliefs and behavioural patterns. You would have to learn to like different food, support a different football team (possibly a whole new sport), maybe wear different clothes, talk another language, etc. Very few firms have yet managed to adopt a true customer orientation that permeates their whole organization. Do not underestimate the obstacles in their way.

Marketing orientation

Putting the customer first, while watching the competition

A true marketing orientation requires a focus on both customers and competitors. Marketing is about providing products and services that meet customers' needs, but it is also important to do that better than your competitors. Many marketers believe that there is a third, vital, component of a true marketing orientation, and this is coordination between the different functions of the business. Kohli *et al.* (1993) defined marketing orientation as:

> the organization-wide generation of market intelligence pertaining to current and future needs of customers, dissemination of intelligence horizontally and vertically within the organization, and organization-wide action or responsiveness to market intelligence.

Much recent evidence suggests that organizations that are marketing orientated enjoy better overall performance than those with other orientations and marketing practitioners see clear-cut benefits from the adoption of this orientation. This is in no small part due to these organizations' emphasis on marketing research. They use their superior market information to find new marketing opportunities in advance of the competition.

Marketing-orientated organizations take marketing research seriously. Research is essential to an understanding of customers and their needs. It may not be formal marketing research; many smaller companies are able to maintain personal contact with their customers which is by far the best way to get to know them. Larger companies have to find more cost-effective ways to understand their much larger customer base. These may include customer satisfaction surveys, websites, loyalty schemes, owners' clubs, helplines and customer service desks.

Marketing-orientated firms take a long-term view of their markets and the products and brands they develop to serve them. Not for them the quick fix that will make this year's sales targets at the expense of next year's – that's a tactic more likely to be employed by a **sales-orientated** company. For example, if you were an industrial machinery salesperson with a quota of sales to make before the year end, achievement of which would gain you a large bonus, then you would want a customer to order sooner rather than later. However, suppose the customer said they could only afford the smaller machine this year, but if you wait until their next financial year they would buy the larger, newer model. Might you offer them discounts and other incentives to order early so that you get your bonus and your company makes its targets (and makes you a hero)? Then, next year, when the new, improved model comes out, how welcome is that customer going to make you? Will they buy any more from you? Probably not.

However, the other orientations should not all be dismissed out of hand – they may work for specific organizations in particular circumstances (Noble *et al.*, 2002).

The advantages of a marketing orientation are:

▶ better understanding of customer needs and wants
▶ better customer relations
▶ a better reputation in the marketplace
▶ more new customers

- more repeat purchases
- improved **customer loyalty**
- more motivated staff
- **competitive edge**.

Societal marketing orientation

Putting consumers and their society first

Societal marketing involves meeting customers' needs and wants in a way that enhances the long-term well-being of consumers and the society in which they live. Some of the products and services on sale today (e.g. cigarettes) are known to be bad for consumers. Some are damaging to our environment, either in use or in production (e.g. cars). Organizations that adopt a societal marketing orientation recognize the wider implications and responsibilities of marketing and take them into account when formulating strategies. For example, they may design packaging that is minimal, made from recycled materials and biodegradable. Their product design may take into account how the product can be disposed of at the end of its life. Their advertising will encourage responsible product use. For example, they would not encourage children to overindulge in high-sugar treats. Perhaps the most famous example of a successful societally orientated company is the Body Shop.

---

insight

Know when to stop

In 2003, Diageo (the company that makes Guinness and Smirnoff vodka) introduced an unusual ad campaign. Titled 'Know when to stop', the TV campaign encouraged people to drink less. Diageo claimed it was part of its corporate **social responsibility** programme.

The drinks industry has been heavily criticized in recent years for not doing enough to tackle problems caused by drink, particularly drunk-driving and under-age, excessive drinking. Anti-drinking charities welcomed the campaign as a step in the right direction but pointed out that it didn't amount to much when set against the £200 million (€280 million) or so that is spent each year on alcohol advertising in the UK.

Whose responsibility do you think it is to promote sensible drinking – if anyone's?

---

activity

Visit the Body Shop's website at www.thebodyshop.com. In what ways is the company trying to improve our well-being? Why do you think it does that?

Cynics would say that this is just another marketing ploy: responding to a current trend. Societally orientated companies may be motivated by enlightened self-interest or they may have a genuine desire to do good. Consumers are beginning to choose organic foods and other green products, and these are proving lucrative niche markets as customers seem prepared to pay a little more for them (not too much more though).

FOCUSING ON CUSTOMERS

" The customer is king! **"**

A somewhat sexist and hackneyed phrase, but with a serious point. Companies cannot exist without customers. Their main function is to provide customers with something of value in exchange for money. It would therefore seem to make sense to design the company around the customer, gearing everything to serve the customer better. This focus on the customer is at the heart of good marketing and is one of the hallmarks of a marketing or **customer orientation** (see above).

> **stakeholders**
>
> individuals or groups that are involved in, or affected by, the organization's actions and/or performance

All organizations have a number of **stakeholders**, of which customers are just one group – but perhaps the most important one. The other two key groups are employees and investors. Any organization needs these three stakeholder types just to exist, and all three must be kept satisfied. A successful organization will focus the attention of all its stakeholder groups on the customer. Happy, loyal employees will work better, provide better customer service and be the most ardent recommenders of the firm's products. If investors trust the firm's directors and managers, and are happy with their returns, then they will continue to provide funds. It is important that employees recognize that they are there to meet customers' needs and wants, not their own. It is no good a delivery person standing on the doorstep and saying 'but this is the best time for me to deliver' if it is not a good time for the customer. It is important that investors also recognize that without the customer there is no company. A few years ago, Gerald Ratner of Ratner's, a large UK chain of jewellery shops, was widely reported as saying that the firm's products were of poor quality – not what he would buy. The firm's share price, and Mr Ratner's standing, plummeted.

Customers or consumers?

There is a distinction between customers and consumers, both of whom are vital to business success. A customer is someone who buys the firm's products or services; however, they may not actually use the product themselves. The eventual user of the product is called the **consumer**. The difference is perhaps easiest to understand in the context of food as that is something that really is consumed.

There are lots of customers for flour in the world. Big food companies buy it to include in ready meals, which are bought by shops to sell on. Bakers buy it to make bread and cakes. Chefs buy it to use in their sauces. People buy it to make pastry at home. None of the first

exhibit 2.3

The heart of the organization

three are buying for their own consumption; they are customers but not consumers. The consumers are the people who eat the ready meals, the bread, the cakes, the sauces, the homemade pies. Their opinion of the flour is also important. If the sauce is lumpy or the cakes too solid then they will not consume them and so the customers will not buy them again. The customers have no direct dealings with the flour mill, they are not mill customers, but they are important in terms of marketing strategy.

Consumers may, or may not, also be customers. Take the example of the person buying flour for use at home. This person is a customer and, assuming that he or she eats the pastry, is also a consumer. However, he or she will probably not eat alone. It is likely that family or friends will join in the meal. They did not buy the flour but they are consumers of it. So you can be a customer but not a consumer, or you can be a consumer but not a customer, or you can be both.

Consumers are important influencers on purchase decisions (see Chapter 5 for more on this). They may well make the actual decision on what to buy. Children's toys, particularly those designed for young children, are usually bought by other members of their family or friends. They are the customers but the child is the actual consumer. Most perfume is bought as a gift, usually from a man to a woman. So while perfume consumers are clearly predominantly female, the perfumiers' customers are mainly men.

Obviously, it is essential that a company has buyers and consumers. However, not all are of equal value. In fact it is possible for some customers to actually cost the company money. This is the reason behind the closure of uneconomic shops, bus services and post offices in some rural areas. There are customers but they do not use these services frequently enough, or pay enough for them, to cover the company's costs. The customers cost more than they bring in; they are therefore uneconomic and the business closes. Unfortunately, there are a surprising number of businesses that do not realize that some customers are just not worth having. They continue to support loss-making customers to the point where the firm itself makes a loss. A business cannot continue in this way.

There are, of course, a number of reasons for continuing to support loss-making customers, either temporarily or as part of a customer group that includes more profitable customers that can support the losses made. Perhaps:

▶ this is a new customer and the company wants to nurture them, hoping that they will become a good customer in the future

▶ the company is trying to break into a new market, perhaps in a different country, and can afford to sustain losses for a while (see the section on **penetration pricing** in Chapter 10)

▶ there are considerable social benefits (often in the case of rural services) that outweigh the financial considerations – for some, altruistic, organizations (or those with a government-controlled charter or franchise that lays down rules of operation, e.g. UK bus and train companies) the social benefit will be enough justification; others may see this as a way to enhance their corporate image.

Retaining valuable customers

Long-standing, regular customers can be valuable assets. They buy more products, tell their friends good things about the company (**word of mouth advertising**), are less time consuming (because they already know how to handle orders with the company and they trust its products) and less likely to be put off by a price increase. It costs approximately five times more to attract a new customer than it does to keep an existing one happy. Customer relationship management (crm) has evolved in response to this need to retain customers and increase their value to the company (see Chapter 1).

exhibit 2.4

Customer end user descriptors

customer type	description	value to seller	suggested strategy
consumer	uses/eats (i.e. consumes) product(s)	variable, depends on degree of influence on purchase decision	persuade consumers to ask for products regularly
buyer	makes the decision to buy	variable, depends how often purchase is made and at what price	persuade to buy regularly, at fair price
reseller	a company or an individual who sells product on to another customer, e.g. a shop	variable, depends on how many products are sold and at what price	help them to sell more
industrial	a company that buys products/services for use in the making of something else	variable, depends how often purchase is made, at what price and how products are used	persuade to buy regularly, at fair price and make best use of products so that they are seen as reliable and are well liked
brand loyal	a customer who (almost) always buys the same brand	usually very high	build relationship in order to retain
brand switcher	the opposite of brand loyal	usually very low	aim for greater loyalty
regular	makes repeat buys often	high	build relationship in order to retain
occasional	rarely buys company's product(s)	limited	try to turn into a regular
first-time buyer	often needs a lot of care	has potential	nurture them, after-sales service is particularly important

It is often said that 20 per cent of a firm's customers generate 80 per cent of its profits (the Pareto principle). The other 80 per cent of customers only account for 20 per cent of profits and so may not justify the time and money spent on servicing their needs. This is not a hard-and-fast rule, of course – for example, new customers take up a lot more time than older ones who know the ropes – but a firm must have new customers if it wants to grow and thrive. They may well turn into profitable customers in time.

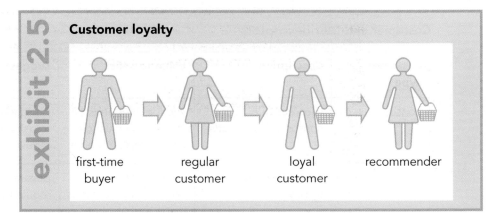

exhibit 2.5

Customer loyalty

first-time buyer → regular customer → loyal customer → recommender

crmfocus

Punishing loyalty

There is a war going on in the UK. Credit cards are employing some highly destructive weapons in their fight for new customers.

The bait they offer is 0 per cent interest on balances transferred from other cards. This free offer has a time limit of course, often six months. After that, the customer has to pay a standard interest rate. The offer is not usually available to existing customers, only to new ones when they first take out a card.

Many customers play a lucrative game with this, taking out a new card with a new company at the end of the honeymoon six-month period, transferring their outstanding balance on again and so still getting their 0 per cent finance. Some forget and so have to pay some interest at least some of the time. Are the credit card companies actively encouraging disloyalty? It seems hard to believe this was their intention.

How would you feel as a long-standing customer who isn't getting such a good deal?

Those new customers may become regular customers. If the relationship is good enough, then they may become loyal – and then they are likely to recommend the company's products to their friends.

So firms try to build customer loyalty. To do this, they try to build a relationship based on trust. Trust is a vital ingredient of any long-standing relationship. Think of friends. They know each other well and each has expectations of how the other will behave. If a friend behaves in an unexpected, bad way, we are disappointed and feel our faith in them is misplaced. Now think of a firm you deal with, or a product that you buy regularly – perhaps a drink or a snack. Imagine that one day, it lets you down. It tastes bad or fails to perform to expected standards in some other way. You revise your expectations downwards: you rethink your loyalty.

Loyalty is based on familiarity and is a kind of emotional attachment. Not all regular customers are loyal, and a strong brand is not enough to create loyalty on its own (although it helps). For example, customers may buy products regularly just because they are cheap or convenient, and when something else becomes available, either more cheaply or more conveniently, then they may switch. Someone who usually buys milk from their local petrol station is unlikely to be a loyal customer, just a rather disorganized person who runs out of milk a lot. They could be lured away quite easily by milk delivery or another, more convenient, retail outlet.

Customer satisfaction is a key contributor to loyalty, but not all satisfied customers will be loyal. For example, you may have really enjoyed the last holiday you took, the flight, hotel, resort and value were all great, but you will probably want to go somewhere else next time, just for a change. Satisfied customers will have a positive attitude towards the company and will probably intend to buy from it again. This, however, may not be enough to clinch the actual sale. A positive attitude is only a predisposition to behaviour; often other things get in the way and cause a person to do something else. They may even go out with the intention of buying one thing but come home with another. (For more on attitudes and their relationship to behaviour, see Chapter 5.)

activity

Pick a favourite product – one that you are loyal to (a chocolate bar, drink, restaurant, brand of sports equipment, TV programme). Make a list of what might cause you to buy/watch (consume) something else instead.

Customers remain loyal because they value what they get from a firm (Reichfeld, 1994). This value mainly comes from product quality, functionality and style, service and support. These things are not all within the control of the marketing department, so if a company wants to build loyalty, it needs all departments to work together to achieve this. There needs to be an integration of customer-related activities across the whole organization. This is easier for companies with a customer focus (see above).

Loyalty schemes

This is really a misnomer. You cannot buy true loyalty, it has to be earned through excellence in product/services and customer care. The cards available from so many large retailers today are, more accurately, **reward cards**, and they are a sophisticated form of **sales promotion** and a source of customer data. Customers earn points on their bill, which they can exchange for money off the next bill or other treats such as days out or tickets for the cinema or other entertainment venues. The Boots Advantage Card is one of the largest, and most generous, reward schemes in the UK, with about 15 million cards in circulation. Advantage Card holders earn four points for every pound spent. Each point is worth a penny off future purchases. In-store machines give out points balances, vouchers and details of special offers.

Most of the people who have a supermarket reward card have at least two. One of the biggest supermarket chains, ASDA, has never had a card scheme, claiming that research shows that its customers prefer lower prices. ASDA's sales figures suggest that this strategy works well. Safeway dropped its ABC card scheme for similar reasons. Traditional retail thinking is that shoppers are largely motivated by convenience, i.e. they go to the nearest store or the one where they can park. Nowadays they may even choose the one with the best website.

These reward card schemes cost millions. Tesco issues vouchers worth £200 million (€280 million) each year. On top of that, there is the cost of mailshots, the administration of the scheme, the customer support. Why are these companies prepared to spend all this money? Mainly, they do it for **market research** and improved **target marketing**. Every time a customer uses their card at the checkout, a computer records all their purchases. This information, combined with the personal information the cardholder gave when they filled out the application form, helps the companies build up a detailed **customer profile** of shoppers. They then use this information to improve their marketing by stocking the products such customers are most likely to buy and by tailoring offers to suit them.

Customer data can highlight a marketing opportunity that sales data would not. For example, according to sales data, the market for birdseed and feeders was very small. However, by analysing its customer data, Tesco found that people who bought bird feeders were also likely to buy organic foods. So it stocked a wider range of bird feeders, told its organic food customers about them – and watched the sales rocket (Shabi, 2003).

@

e-focus

Reaping the rewards

The Nectar scheme, used by a consortium of large UK companies including Sainsbury's, Debenhams and Barclaycard, reportedly cost over £50 million (€70 million) to launch. About half the households in the UK have a Nectar card, using the points collected to claim money off purchases or special treats like a day at a theme park.

The information gained from Nectar application forms and computer records of individual purchases builds to a detailed profile of each Nectar card holder. The data is stored in a huge central database so that a variety of queries can be made and reports run off. For example, the information held will reveal whether you have pets and what kind they are – even whether your dog is large or small. From the amount of toilet roll bought, the computer can calculate how many people there are in a household. Purchases reveal whether there are any children and approximately how old they are. A suitably written database query can even work out when you are going on holiday.

Knowing their customers profiles enables the stores to stock the kinds of products that will appeal to those customers. For example, if a lot of large families shop there, it makes sense to stock family and economy sizes. If there are a lot of young professionals, then upmarket ready meals may sell well. This profile information also allows the companies involved to target their communications better – for example, by not sending special offers on meat to someone who appears to be vegetarian.

There are some consumer concerns though. Just how comfortable are you with a firm knowing so much? Just think how this data could be misused if it was in the hands of less reputable organizations.

activity

When you get home after your next shopping trip, take a look at what you've bought. What could a company work out about you from your purchases?

The information that stores gain from their reward card schemes is worth a lot to them. Market research can be expensive, yet here the stores have customers volunteering their information, electronically, every time they present their card at the till. The set-up costs are high but the research information pours in.

Database marketing

The reward card schemes would not be possible without sophisticated information technology to manage the data collected. The data is held in a database, which is really an electronic filing system with extensive cross-referencing and processing capabilities.

database marketing
the use of computerized customer data to communicate with customers and promote further sales

Database marketing pre-dates loyalty schemes, of course, and is used by most companies today – with varying degrees of sophistication and success. Customer data is stored electronically and used to identify **prospects**. These people are then targeted for marketing and sales activities, usually by being placed on specific **mailing lists**. Take the example of a department store. It may have lists for men, women, parents, customers of specific cosmetics companies, people who buy designer clothes, people who have its store card, people who do not have its store card, people who purchased electrical goods such as televisions or household appliances. This information is gathered from purchases made in store, data provided by customers when they fill in forms (such as applications for store cards, credit agreements, competition entries) and bought in from other sources (there are companies that specialize in buying in data and selling it on).

exhibit 2.6

Examples of customer database information

type of information	possible source(s) include
customer contact details	order forms, sales team
customer sales history	past orders, loyalty cards
customer demographics	order forms, credit applications, market research reports
customer psychographics	customer surveys, sales team
customer preferences	customer correspondence, enquiries, sales team
customer business details	annual report and other publicly available documents, company website, sales team

The targeted customers may be sent mailings, telephoned, e-mailed or just added to a list to receive regular newsletters, updates, etc.

Databases have been used for years to analyse customer buying patterns and identify prospects for other products and services. The technology has, of course, got more sophisticated and powerful and so have the uses to which it can be put. Today, many companies have **data warehouses** and use **data-mining** software to sift through the enormous amounts of data stored in them and make the connections between the data. For example, a company can match up customer profiles in different parts of the country with past sales at specific times of year and use this link to identify new ranges that might sell well. There is almost no limit to the connections data mining might make – as long as the data exists in the database, of course.

It is likely to be through data mining that Tesco learnt that people who buy bird feeders and seed also tend to buy organic food. This demonstrates a particularly clever form of a traditional marketing technique: **cross-selling**. Usually, cross-selling means selling a related product to a customer, e.g. if you have a customer buying suede shoes, you recommend suede cleaner as well. The wealth of data that the reward card schemes provide also helps companies to **up-sell**, i.e. persuade customers to buy a more expensive version of a product. For example, they might send an average beer customer a money-off coupon for a premium beer, or someone who usually buys pre-packaged fish might get a voucher for the fresh fish counter.

data mining
using specialist software to analyse large amounts of data (held in a database) to predict trends and likely customer behaviour

cross-selling
persuading a customer to buy extra products

up-selling
persuading a customer to trade up to a more expensive product

activity

Gather together all the promotional items that you receive in a week (through the post and by e-mail). Then sort them according to their relevance to you.

▶ How many did you receive?
▶ Whose mailing lists are you on?
▶ How did you get there?

These sophisticated computer systems are at the heart of crm. Organizations have more information on customers than they ever had before, and the technology and techniques to use it to understand and serve their customers better. There really is very little excuse for poor customer service today, and yet it still exists in some places. Have you ever received a standard response to a query that really just did not answer it? It can be a mistake to become over-reliant on automation.

The changing role of salespeople

Earlier in the chapter we suggested that a sales orientation is not a good route to long-term success. This does not mean, however, that salespeople are not required. They have a valuable role to play in most organizations (and being a salesperson can prove a highly lucrative career for those with the right talents). Salespeople are often the face of the organization, the one that customers see most often. It may well be the salesperson that customers build a relationship with, rather than the organization itself. This can be a problem for the company if the salesperson moves on, so the salesperson's role needs careful management.

There are a number of different types of salespeople including:

▶ account managers – often quite senior, in charge of the relationship with one or more customers, maybe head of a team

▶ b2b/industrial salespeople – selling products/services to other organizations to assist them to make their business targets, e.g. office supplies, ingredients, raw materials

▶ sales representatives (reps) and field marketers – make sales into retail environments (shops, petrol stations, etc.) and provide retailers with sales support (e.g. how best to display products)

▶ demonstrators – show potential customers how a product works, they may then make the sale themselves or they may pass the prospect on to a salesperson

▶ sales assistants – work in a shop or other retail environment

▶ door-to-door salespeople – literally knock on doors, with a bagful of products or a catalogue to show; this is declining in popularity as it is expensive, time consuming and such people get a lot of doors closed in their faces

▶ telesales – a modern form of door-to-door, but using the telephone instead of personally visiting – again they get a lot of refusals – and a lot of abuse; good telesales is carefully targeted so that the recipients of sales calls are likely to be interested

▶ dealers/agents – resellers of products, often b2b, may sell one brand exclusively or a range.

(For information about careers in sales, see Postscript at the end of the book.)

There have been some major changes in the role of salespeople over the last decade. Traditionally, they work on commission and to a quota. They are set a target of how many sales they have to make and are rewarded for succeeding in making that quota. Then they are paid over-performance bonuses for any further sales. This is how good salespeople make a lot of money. The drawback with this is that the emphasis is on the meeting of short-term targets, sometimes to the detriment of the longer-term health of the company. Hence the change in sales roles. Today, salespeople are expected to build relationships with their customers. They nurture them and encourage repeat purchases and brand loyalty. Good salespeople have, of course, always built relationships. They are usually selected for their friendliness and ability to get on with people. After all, we would all rather buy something from someone we like and we resent giving our money to someone we dislike.

This emphasis on relationship building represents a major change in the way we do business. It is a change of emphasis from maximizing short-term sales and profits (and therefore returns to shareholders) to looking after the long-term health of the company. Loyal customers are the key to this (see above).

SUMMARY

Marketing strategy is a means to an end – that end being the achievement of the aims and objectives of the organization. In this chapter, we have started to consider how marketing can help organizations to achieve their objectives.

An organization will have a strategic orientation, mostly by design but sometimes by accident. This is how it looks at itself and the world around it. Marketers would usually recommend a marketing orientation that involves being customer focused while also keeping an eye on competitors. A customer focus is generally held to be the best route to long-term profit, but not all organizations manage this. There are still a number that have a product or financial orientation.

A more modern (or possibly much older) approach is a societal orientation, such as that adopted by the Body Shop.

One of the advantages of a customer focus is that it makes it easier to develop customer loyalty. Loyal customers stick with a company, making repeat purchases and even recommending it to friends. Salespeople have always had a valuable role to play in the development of loyalty. More recently, a number of firms have introduced customer loyalty schemes, although these are sometimes more like sale promotions.

These loyalty schemes have generated vast amounts of customer data which is held in databases (or data warehouses) and used by companies to improve the targeting of their marketing activities. (For more on targeting, see Chapter 4.)

Challenges reviewed

Now that you have finished reading the chapter, look back at the challenges you were set at the beginning. Do you have a clearer idea of what's involved?
Hints:

▶ 'If you build a better mousetrap, the world will beat a path to your door'; is this true?

▶ asset-led marketing

▶ customer retention and crm.

READING AROUND

website
www.theidm.co.uk This is the website for the Institute of Direct Marketing. Go to its knowledge centre, use the jargon buster, try the quiz, see what else is there.

book chapters
Michael J. Baker (1999) One more time – what is marketing? Chapter 1 in *The Marketing Book*, CIM Butterworth Heinemann.

David Pickton and Amanda Broderick (2001) Customer contact management, Chapter 3 in *Integrated Marketing Communications*, FT Prentice Hall.

John O'Connor and Eamonn Galvin (2001) Relationship marketing, Chapter 8 in *Marketing in the Digital Age*, FT Prentice Hall.

SELF-REVIEW QUESTIONS

1.   List five activities that are part of marketing. (see pages 30/31)

2.   Define the word 'market'. (see page 32)

3. What is a b2b market? (see page 32)

4. If an organization is asset led, what kind of assets may it be led by? (see page 33)

5. Name a typical objective of a product-orientated company. (see page 36)

6. What kind of strategic orientation do most timeshare companies have? (see pages 38–9)

7. List five advantages of a marketing orientation. (see pages 41–2)

8. Why is customer retention important? (see pages 44–47)

9. Can you buy loyalty? (see page 47)

10. What is the data gained from loyalty schemes used for? (see pages 47–8)

11. What is data mining? (see page 49)

12. Name five types of salesperson. (see page 50)

MINI CASE STUDY

Read the questions, then the case material, then answer the questions.

Questions

1. Why did Virgin introduce a loyalty scheme?

2. Why do you think Virgin tested it in Australia?

3. How could Virgin use it to cross-sell?

4. Check the Internet (e.g. do a Google search, visit the Virgin website, check out any marketing publications databases you, or your university, subscribe to) or visit a Virgin store. Is the loyalty scheme still going? How has it changed?

Virgin loyalty

For many years, the Virgin brand name has been the envy of its rivals for its ability to inspire customer loyalty. The brand encompasses a diverse collection of products and services, from an airline to cosmetics. Aside from the brand name, these companies and their marketing have been kept largely separate.

That changed in 2003 when Virgin Mobile launched a customer loyalty initiative together with its Megastore and Megastore Xpress chains. The surrounding launch campaign was named 'Flash It' and both campaign and concept had been tested in Australia, and then in 10 UK stores, before being launched across the UK. The initiative was promoted through in-store marketing (including eye-catching point-of-sale material), Virgin Mobile's printed catalogue and all Virgin websites. The initial 10 stores reported a 50 per cent rise in the sale of mobile phones during the test. It is hoped that CD sales will benefit similarly as global sales of recorded music are falling fast, mainly because of downloads and piracy.

The loyalty scheme offered Virgin Megastore customers who flashed their Virgin Mobile phones £1 of free airtime for every £10 they spent in the store. The reward was handed over at the till immediately in the form of scratch-off, top-up cards. Virgin customers were also entitled to further discounts at third-party retailers, bars, clubs and restaurants.

Target audiences for Virgin Mobile and the Megastore chain are similar in profile: young music lovers who frequently use their mobile phones. It was hoped that the scheme would encourage Virgin Mobile customers to shop at Megastores, and Megastore customers to join the mobile network. 'We know Virgin Mobile customers love music and entertainment, which is why, working with Virgin Megastores, we have introduced this benefit for our customers,' said brand owner Sir Richard Branson.

Previously, Virgin Mobile's store presence had been limited to shelf space at Megastores and the facility for customers to top up their phone credit. The loyalty scheme coincided with the mobile

▶

operator's plan to expand its retail presence on Britain's high streets in order to boost its position in the market. The plan was to open Virgin mobile phones stores within Virgin Megastores – a store-within-a-store concept. These new mini-stores promoted the range of services available through the network and helped customers to set-up their phones in-store.

The first stage of the loyalty scheme roll-out was just for the mobiles and the Megastores, but Virgin would not rule out the idea of extending it across the whole of its empire. The company is hoping to find loyal Virgin customers everywhere.

Sources: Goodway, 2003; Porter, 2003

REFERENCES

Allen, R. (ed.) (2000) *New Penguin English Dictionary*, Penguin Books.

Dibb, S., Simkin, L., Pride, W.M. and Ferrell, O. (2001) *Marketing Concepts and Strategies* (fourth European edition), Houghton Mifflin Company.

Goodway, N. (2003) Branson in mobiles loyalty ploy, *Evening Standard* (1 August).

Hooley, G.J., Lynch, J.E. and Shepherd J. (1990) The marketing concept: putting theory into practice, *European Journal of Marketing* 24, 7–24.

Jobber, D. (2001) *Principles and Practice of Marketing* (third edition), McGraw-Hill.

Kohli, A.K., Jaworski, B.J. and Kumar, A. (1993) MARKOR: a measure of market orientation, *Journal of Marketing Research*.

Kotler, P., Armstrong, G., Saunders, J. and Wong, V. (2001) *Principles of Marketing* (third European edition), Pearson Education Ltd.

Kotler, P. (1977) From sales obsession to marketing effectiveness, *Harvard Business Review* 55 (Nov–Dec), 67–75.

Noble, C.H., Sinha, R.K. and Kumar, A. (2002) Market orientation and alternative strategic orientations: a longitudinal assessment of performance implications, *Journal of Marketing* 66, 25–39.

Porter, N. (2003) Virgin unveils customer loyalty scheme, www.mad.co.uk (accessed 11 August 2003).

Reichfeld, F.F. (1994) Loyalty and the renaissance of marketing. *Marketing Management* 2, 10ff.

Shabi, R. (2003) The card up their sleeve. *Guardian Weekend* (19 July), 15–23.

Wilson, K. (1996) Managing the industrial sales force of the 1990s, in Hartley, B. and Starkey, M. W., (eds) *The Management of Sales and Customer Relations*, International Thomson Business Press.

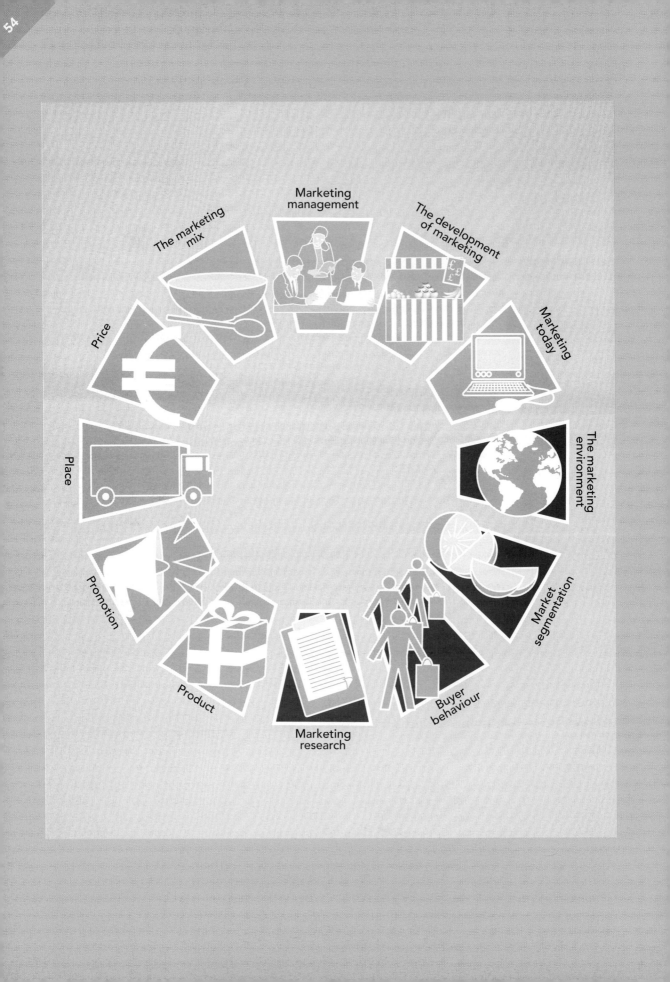

PART 2

MARKETING ANALYSIS

THIS PART CONTAINS:

Chapter 3: The marketing environment

Chapter 4: Market segmentation

Chapter 5: Buyer behaviour

Chapter 6: Marketing research

WHAT THIS PART IS ABOUT:

Part 2 goes behind the scenes and looks at the forces that shape an organization's marketing activities.

No organization exists in isolation. It has to interact with other organizations and with individuals. Successful marketing depends upon a thorough understanding of the surrounding environment and particularly of customers, their worlds and their needs. Consequently, marketers spend much time, effort and money on research and analysis. They draw on other social science disciplines to shed further light on their customers' behaviour: economics, psychology and sociology in particular. Such in-depth market understanding confers a valuable competitive advantage.

THE MARKETING ENVIRONMENT

ENVIRONMENTAL CHALLENGES

The following are illustrations of the types of decision that marketers have to take or issues they face. *You aren't expected to know how to deal with the challenges now*; just bear them in mind as you read the chapter and see what you can find that helps.

▶ You work in the marketing department of a multinational which has a large investment in the Middle East. Your company often considers pulling out. Can you devise a system for monitoring the often volatile situation there?

▶ You are the manager of a small chain of cafés. Business has been a bit slower this year than it was last, but you are better off than many of your competitors, some of whom have gone out of business. Do you know why that happened to them? Are you in danger too?

▶ You run a mail-order business and have been piloting selling over the Internet. You've heard rumours that the EU may introduce laws that will make e-commerce more difficult. You do not know whether this will affect your business and nothing is definite yet. Is there anything you could be doing to prepare?

▶ You work for an oil company and Greenpeace protesters are currently camped outside the refinery. They are protesting over a proposed new pipeline and no one at the oil company seems surprised that they are there. In fact, the counter-arguments were prepared in advance and the press release has gone to all the newspapers. Greenpeace kept its intentions a secret, so how was this possible?

▶ You work in banking and a colleague has just come up with a new service idea that has got the whole bank talking and will probably get him a promotion. It takes advantage of a new IT product that IBM has just announced. Why didn't you come up with that idea?

KEY CONCEPTS

PRESTCOM
PEST
SWOT
competitive environment
external environment
internal environment
environmental scanning
situation analysis
stakeholders
market segmentation (see Chapter 4)
profiling (see Chapter 4)
data collection and analysis (see Chapter 6)
marketing research (see Chapter 6)
marketing planning (see Chapter 12)

CHAPTER OVERVIEW

INTRODUCTION

The word 'environment' has come to be associated with conservation, with the green movement. However, that is not the sense in which the word is used in this chapter. The *New Penguin English Dictionary* (Allen, 2000) defines environment as 'the circumstances, objects, or conditions by which somebody or something is surrounded', and this is closer to the way the term is used in marketing.

Organizations do not operate in isolation. They have to take account of other organizations and individuals in their plans and in their day-to-day dealings. They operate within a specific marketing environment.

Organizations build up information on what is happening in the world around them so that they are better able to deal with any threats to their business or to take advantage of any new opportunities before their competitors do. For example, companies that do business in the Middle East should have been monitoring the political situation carefully in 2002. Those that did were ready to pull their people out before the invasion of Iraq.

A firm's environment is commonly split into two parts: its **external environment** and its **internal environment**. Things that happen in the external environment are largely outside of the firm's control and so are referred to as **uncontrollables** (or 'uncontrollable variables'), for example: wars, crop failures, a change of government, new technology. The internal environment ought to be more easily controlled and so occurrences within it are often referred to as **controllables** (or 'controllable variables'), for example: skill levels of employees, finance available, product range.

uncontrollables

events, issues, trends, etc. within the external environment

This chapter will consider these variables, the threats and opportunities they present and how to deal with them.

USES OF ENVIRONMENTAL INFORMATION

Environmental information is used in two main ways:

1. as input to the planning process

2. as part of ongoing analysis of marketing opportunities and threats (**environmental scanning**).

Input to the planning process

Particularly during the planning process, it is useful for a firm to have a framework in which to place its environmental data. It can then assess the data's impact and what to do about it. For example, a firm would wish to identify its key competitors and investigate their strategies; it is then in a position to develop counter-strategies if necessary. It would want to know about the lives of its customers, then it can develop products and services to meet their needs.

Planners do not stop at identifying relevant trends or competitors. They take the environmental data, feed it into a SWOT analysis (see page 84) and so arrive at a fuller understanding of the organization's current situation on which they can build their plans.

Environmental scanning

Wise organizations continuously scan their environments so that they can keep up with changes and are ready to deal with market developments, be they good or bad. This is an ongoing research exercise. The collected data helps build a better picture of their world. Perhaps they will find that a new law or regulation is being proposed and that it will affect their interests adversely. Take, for example, the proposed EU ban on tobacco sponsorship. This cuts off a significant marketing communications avenue for the tobacco companies; consequently they have been lobbying to weaken the legislation and so reduce the ban's impact on their businesses.

Some firms have research departments, or employ outside research consultants, to scan their environment. However, most do this on a more ad hoc basis.

Most managers rely on personal contacts for their environmental knowledge, possibly because it can be difficult to get hard facts on external environmental trends (economics, for example, has never been an exact science). These personal sources are supplemented by, or cross-checked in, newspapers, magazines, trade journals and other secondary sources (for sources of secondary data, see Chapter 6). The approach that academic commentators recommend, however, is to analyse the external environment as a team, i.e. to consult a range of employees from senior managers to the most junior staff. This way the firm benefits from a wide range of viewpoints (Mercer, 1995).

How do managers decide what is, and what is not, relevant?

Taken to its extreme, the whole world and everything in it could be considered as having an impact upon the organization – particularly if it is a very large organization such as IBM or ICI. Clearly it is not practical to study absolutely everything and so the management team must initially decide what to include. There are a number of models to help them do this, but again academia and management practice do not always agree in this. Most firms rely upon judgement. The insight box provides an example process.

Environmental scanning process

The environmental scanning process involves the following stages.

Monitor – broad trends, issues and events. In addition, develop a list of relevant publications, which should be checked regularly.

Identify – trends, issues, events that are significant to the organization. It is helpful if the management team sets, and regularly reviews, criteria to determine what is likely to be significant and what is not.

Evaluate – the impact of the trends etc. upon the organization's operation in its current markets.

Forecast – where the trends are heading, and examine the threats or opportunities they are likely to bring in the future.

Evaluate – the impact of those threats and opportunities on the firm's long-term strategies.

Source: adapted from Brownlie, 2000

Unfortunately, this sometimes means that pressing matters take precedence over long-term thinking. Many organizations have come unstuck by not looking beyond the requirements of current decision-making. The firm's most immediate operating environment (customers, suppliers, distributors, etc.) is likely to change rapidly and to receive more management attention than its wider environment (Brownlie, 2000).

For example, sales of red meat have been falling for some time. There have, of course, been a number of health scares associated with the eating of meat (high cholesterol, BSE, foot and mouth disease, excess growth hormones, etc.). It would be easy for farmers to blame their troubles on these scare stories. At the same time, however, many people are eating more chicken or fish, rather than red meat, for more general health reasons and, in many countries, significant numbers of people are becoming vegetarian. These people are unlikely to return to their meat-eating habits when the latest scare dies down.

SITUATION ANALYSIS

It is very hard (and often spectacularly unsuccessful) to plan a route ahead without an understanding of the starting point. Take the example of a journey to London. The travel agent is going to need to know the journey's starting point before he or she can possibly recommend a method of travel. It makes a big difference whether the traveller is currently in Paris, New York or Leicester.

Similarly, a company needs to know where it stands at the moment before it can make plans to improve its position. Acquisition of another chain might well be a suitable way for a large chain of stores with a dominant market position to grow, but a smaller chain, with fewer resources, is unlikely to be able to do this.

An analysis of the current situation is the starting point for most plans. It tells a firm where it is now.

The basic planning process looks like this:

Where are we now?
(situation analysis)
↓
Where do we want to be?
(objectives)
↓
How will we get there?
(the plan)
↓
How will we know when we've arrived?
(evaluation and control)

There are a number of techniques and models that the organization can use to analyse its situation. The most widely recognized technique is a **SWOT analysis** (see page 84). This analysis is based on organizing environmental data.

MARKETING ENVIRONMENT MODELS

The data that an organization collects through its environmental research must then be analysed. This process involves sorting the data, categorizing it and then looking for trends, changes in trends, patterns, dangers and opportunities. There are a number of models of the marketing environment that an organization can use to help it to analyse environmental data.

Probably the best-known environmental model is **PEST**:

Political

Economic

Social

Technological.

Common variants are STEP, SLEPT and PESTEL. The L in the last two acronyms stands for legal. The extra E in PESTEL can be environmental or ecological. All of these models are a way of looking at a firm's external environment. The **macroenvironment** is the term favoured by economists and refers to the broadest, external environment in which a firm operates.

Baker (1998) uses PEST but adds in QUEST (QUick Environmental Scanning Technique) as well, and ETOM (Environmental Threats and Opportunities Matrix). Adcock *et al.* (2001) use STEP but as part of a four-level system. Dibb *et al.* (2001) eschew acronyms, as does Jobber (2001). This would seem to suggest that PEST and its variants have had their day; however, they are a useful aide-memoire. Perhaps their current lack of favour can be attributed to a tendency to follow them too slavishly rather than use them as a prompt. If there is nothing of significance happening in one of the categories, then it should be passed over. The important thing is to have thought it through.

What is commonly referred to outside of business theory as 'environmentalism' causes commentators some problems of classification. First, there is the issue of what to call it; Jobber (2001) has 'physical forces', Kotler *et al.* (2001) have 'the natural environment', while Dibb *et al.* (2001) use the term 'green forces'. In this text the term 'natural environment' will be favoured (with due acknowledgement to Professor Kotler). 'Green' is used in a less than complimentary way in some quarters, and 'physical forces' seems too close to 'physical force' with its connotations of violence.

Second, there is the question of whether the natural environment requires its own heading in an environmental analysis, or fits under some, or all, of the others. Certainly there are political aspects to environmentalism, especially when lobbyists such as Greenpeace, Friends of the Earth or (perhaps at the other end of the political spectrum) the Countryside Alliance are involved (the Countryside Alliance is an organization that campaigns to preserve certain traditional aspects of British country life, such as hunting). Regulation is relevant in terms of laws and codes governing issues such as pollution or recycling. The using, or spoiling, of irreplaceable natural resources has economic implications. Social attitudes towards green issues are changing. Technology has the power to harm or heal the natural world. Being seen to be more green than rival firms can give a company a valuable competitive edge – there is a significant minority of customers who choose environmentally friendly products.

The natural environment affects an organization in numerous ways. Whether this means it should be treated separately or within the context of other forces is a choice the analyst must make. It will probably depend upon the nature of the organization, its products and the rest of its operating environment. In the cause of flexibility, this book will follow both courses; considering the natural environment where it is relevant within other categories, but then pulling its key elements together separately as well.

PEST, and its variants, only cover *part* of the organization's **external environment**. Marketers must consider all of the external environment and the **internal environment** as well. This more immediate environment is what economists refer to as the **microenvironment**. It comprises competitors, distributors, suppliers and the organization's own internal resources.

The macroenvironment refers to broad influences that affect all organizations in a market, whereas the microenvironment contains influences specific to the nature of the business, its suppliers, marketing intermediaries, customers and competitors.

So PEST does not give the whole picture: it only covers the macroenvironment. In order to complete the picture, Pickton and Broderick (2001) proposed a more comprehensive, environmental model: **PRESTCOM**. PRESTCOM provides a framework for the analysis of both the internal and the external environments.

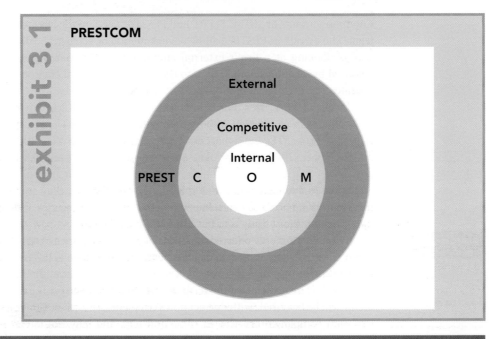

exhibit 3.1

PRESTCOM

External

Competitive

Internal

PREST   C   O   M

PRESTCOM

PRESTCOM is an acronym that stands for:

Political

Regulatory

Economic

Social

Technological

Competitive

Organizational

Market.

This chapter will now cover each of these categories in turn, commencing with the one so often ignored: the organization itself.

THE ORGANIZATIONAL ENVIRONMENT (THE INTERNAL ENVIRONMENT)

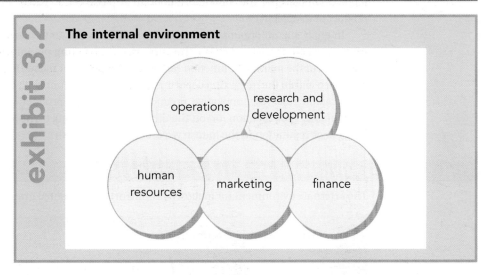

exhibit 3.2

The internal environment

operations

research and development

human resources

marketing

finance

There are five basic functions within a business (see Exhibit 3.2), of which marketing is one. It is important that these functions work well together and support each other. This requires good communication between staff and a culture that encourages interaction and mutual support. If all functions display a **customer orientation** (see Chapter 2), then this harmony will be easier to achieve. One of the key things that the company wishes to achieve from this cooperation is a consistent image.

customer orientation

the whole organization is focused on the satisfaction of its customers' needs

The following are examples of how these functions interact.

The human resources department (HR), which used to be known as personnel, is primarily responsible for ensuring that there are suitable staff, both in terms of quantity and quality, in place in order to carry out all the activities of the business. Their duties include various administrative functions such as hiring, firing and paying, as well as more strategic activities such as training, career management and succession planning. HR and marketing may liaise over the writing and production of communications such as staff newsletters and recruitment advertising. HR should also be kept appraised of product development and future growth plans to ensure that staff with appropriate skills are hired or trained.

The finance function includes accounting and also strategic financial planning. These departments will be heavily involved in the setting of marketing budgets and will also require regular reports on sales and forecasts of future incomes. Finance is often involved in aspects of costing, pricing and the collection of overdue customer accounts, all of which require close liaison with marketing/sales.

Operations is often called 'production' in manufacturing industries. Operations personnel actually make the products or deliver the service. For example, in a cleaning company, the cleaners are operations personnel. Clearly it is important for marketing and operations to work together closely to ensure sufficient supply of goods and services – but not oversupply, which would be wasteful and cost the firm money. Getting the balance right requires accurate demand forecasting This is particularly difficult with new products but, if stocks run out, this could scupper the product's launch. Marketing also needs to make sure operations are consulted in advance before any sizeable promotional campaign is undertaken. Sales will (hopefully) rise and production will need to increase to match.

Research and development (R&D) is where new ideas are uncovered and tested. This is a crucial function for any firm that operates in an innovative market, where new products are key to competitive advantage. The marketing function has a part to play in the introduction of new ideas as well as in the dissemination of them. Marketers, particularly salespeople, are more in tune with customers and their needs. There should be a process in place for this vital information to be passed on to R&D (See Chapter 7 for new product development).

In analysing an organization's internal resources, the analyst is looking for sources of advantage and disadvantage. For the purposes of marketing planning, these should be of relevance to the marketing function (although that does not mean that they will always be contained within the marketing department). Examples include skilled product researchers, large capital reserves, innovative products, leading-edge production technology, strong brand name, good location, or, on the other hand, high staff turnover (people do not stay long), poor reputation in the industry, a dreary shop, no cash.

THE EXTERNAL ENVIRONMENT

The external environment (or macroenvironment) is represented graphically in Exhibit 3.3.

exhibit 3.3

The macroenvironment

economy   politics

technology   regulations   society

The political environment

Players in the political environment include:

▶ government – i.e. domestic government bodies (central, regional and local, and government-appointed committees); supranational government bodies (e.g. the EU) and foreign governments

▶ special interest and pressure groups – i.e. political organizations that exist to further a cause (e.g. Friends of the Earth) or the interests of a particular group of people (e.g. trades unions)

▶ political parties.

These groups affect an organization and its operations in a number of ways.

The philosophy of the government in power sets the business climate. Government policy has a direct effect on the way in which businesses are allowed to operate. For example, some governments are characterized as interventionist, and others as non-interventionist. The interventionists are far more likely to interfere in the running of businesses; by introducing laws, setting up watchdog committees, levying new taxes, imposing new bureaucratic rules, even by nationalizing an industry. On the other hand, a non-interventionist government may scale down all of these things, and even privatize previously nationalized industries. Right-wing governments tend to be less interventionist than more left-wing, or socialist, governments. Generally speaking, communist governments exert the most control of all.

This demonstration against the Iraq war was organized by a number of pressure groups

A country's tax regime is important to businesses. Taxes are the government's primary means of raising income, which it can then spend on public works such as road building, or on health and education services, defence, etc. However, taxes can also be used to encourage, or deter, businesses and consumers from certain actions. For example, the British government reduced tax on diesel and unleaded petrol while increasing it on traditional, leaded fuel in order to encourage motorists to switch and so reduce pollutants. In a government attempt to deter smoking, and to help pay smokers' medical bills, cigarettes in Britain are taxed at a rate that would horrify the French. This has been a somewhat less than successful strategy. Cigarettes are, of course, addictive and therefore not

price inelastic demand

product sales are not very sensitive to price changes

very price sensitive (they have **price inelastic demand**, see Chapter 10). Also, France is easily reached from England, and therefore French cigarettes, with their lower taxes, are easily come by.

The government of a country may also exert influence through its commercial dealings. Most governments have enormous spending power and can therefore be lucrative, if demanding, customers. Many national governments have at some point followed a policy of giving their own country's suppliers preference when placing orders. Many more have imposed taxes, or quotas, on foreign imports.

The relationship between two governments may act as a help or a hindrance to trade. In the late 1990s, British firms lost deals in Malaysia because of a diplomatic incident.

A country's political stability has a huge bearing on its attractiveness to investors, especially to foreign investors. For example, foreign-owned multinationals were reluctant to invest in Britain during the late 1970s and early 1980s because of the large number of strikes that were called at that time. Today, many firms are unprepared to risk investments in parts of the Middle East; Iraq and Afghanistan are only for the extreme risk takers. On the other hand, foreign investment in China is now booming – a situation that would have looked very unlikely back when the tanks rolled into Tiananmen Square. That incident not only deterred investment in China, but also in the neighbouring countries of Hong Kong and Taiwan which were well within the range of China's military might.

Western Europe is currently a relatively stable political environment. However, a change of government can cause firms some problems. Policies change to match the political persuasion of the new government. Just the holding of an election affects sales. The feel-good factor kicks in as election promises of tax cuts are fulfilled. Often disposable income rises, as does employment. This does not always last the full term of the government, of course.

The most extreme political risk a firm will encounter is the outbreak of war, and there are usually clear signs that this is a possibility. More common risks include being subjected to pressure group activity. This is a frequent occurrence for a number of large, high-profile firms such as McDonald's and Shell. Nike has suffered too as protestors voiced their objections to its manufacturing methods, particularly the use of child labour in developing countries.

The assessment of political risk is especially important when considering whether to start trading in another country. Many countries have unstable governments that may be able to exercise powers that Western governments would not. Take the situation in Zimbabwe as an example: there, the government has encouraged the seizing of white-owned farms – not a good time for foreigners to move in. This contrasts with South Africa, which suffered from trade **embargoes** for many years while it was an apartheid state. Now that the regime is more stable, the economy is enjoying an influx of foreign investment.

globalfocus

Watch me!

In the summer of 2003, Mexican security forces drew up a list of 80 anti-globalization activists who were thought to be intending to disrupt the WTO meeting due to be held in their country. Their intention was to make it easier to keep those people under surveillance. They wanted to avoid a repeat of the riots at the Seattle summit in 1999. It was to be expected that this would provoke an angry response from the human rights-conscious activists. And it did – from those who were missed off the list!

Hundreds of activists wrote, and signed, a letter addressed to 'government agents bent on restricting civil liberties'. It read:

> 66 I recently found out about the 'watch list' prepared by Mexican authorities, purportedly to quell the voice of civil society at the upcoming WTO Ministerial in Cancun. Despite heavy expenditures of tax money on intelligence gathering ... we are concerned that you were only able to find 60 internationals and 30 Mexicans who are opposed to the World Trade Organization. Haven't you noticed that the tide of public opinion is turning decidedly against the WTO? ... Please add my name to your 'watch list' immediately! 99

The authorities feared that hundreds, possibly thousands, of demonstrators would turn up to make their points. While most restrict themselves to carrying placards and shouting, there are those who prefer to make their protests more forcefully. In Seattle, hundreds of thousands of pounds worth of damage was done.

Source: adapted from Campbell, 2003

The regulatory environment

The actions that an organization can take are constrained by the rules imposed upon it and by the duties it owes to other organizations or individuals. These rules and duties may be formalized as laws (e.g. the Human Rights Act) or as codes of practice (e.g. those governing what is, and what is not, acceptable in adverts) or they may be merely accepted behaviour (e.g. an advertising agency not handling competing clients).

Laws and regulations vary from country to country; there are very few laws that span borders; those that do come from bodies such as the EU. This variety of laws in countries is one of the things that makes international marketing additionally complicated. Take sales promotion laws as an example: in some countries, such as Britain, it is perfectly acceptable to entice customers to buy your product by giving them a money-off voucher. In other countries, such as Germany, this is not allowed.

A law is the formalization of a moral code that is generally accepted by the community. Laws cover the most serious business transgressions (fraud, theft, sale by deception, etc.) and must not be broken. Less serious rules are articulated in a less formal way – often as a code of practice. The UK Advertising Standards Authority (ASA) administers a code of practice for non-broadcast advertising. It is based on four principles. Advertising must be:

▶ legal – it must not break any law

▶ decent – it must not cause widespread, or serious, offence

▶ honest – no exploitation of the audience's credulity or ignorance

▶ truthful – no misleading by inaccuracy, omission, ambiguity, or exaggeration.

Advertisers who fail to live up to these standards are censured and asked to withdraw the offending advertisement. They have not broken a law, no one is going to prison (as they might for fraud), but they have broken the code. Just as the punishment for not complying with a code of practice is less severe than the punishment for breaking the law, so the consequence of simply failing to behave in an acceptable manner is relatively mild. A firm that fails to deliver when promised will find itself with a bad reputation and, eventually, less custom.

Laws are developed by governments, or the judiciary, and usually take a long time to come into force. This gives organizations (or at least those that have identified the proposed laws through their environmental scanning) an opportunity to try to influence the content of laws during their development. This activity is called **lobbying**.

Lobbying is a means of influencing the politicians. It is often employed by pressure or interest groups (e.g. trade associations) rather than by individual firms. The tobacco industry and farmers both have strong lobbies in many EU countries. Trained lobbyists will identify the key members of committees that are debating the proposed changes in law, and put their arguments to them. They hope to persuade the committees to make favourable changes or to drop any harmful proposals altogether. In Britain the tobacco lobby has been particularly effective: even when it had been agreed that cigarette companies should no longer be allowed to sponsor sports, it managed to get motor racing and snooker exempted.

ethicalfocus

Friends of the Earth

Friends of the Earth is an environmental pressure group that lobbies governments to get them to introduce laws that will protect the environment. One recent effort was the 'Real Food' campaign, which aimed to raise the public's awareness of the levels of pesticides in food, as well as the danger posed by modern farming practices such as the introduction of GM (genetically modified) crops.

As part of the campaign, FoE sent pre-printed postcards to its supporters asking them to sign them and send them on to politicians.

It also put pressure on supermarkets by publishing a league table ranking them in order of which ones were the best at trying to eliminate pesticides from their products. Website visitors could take advantage of a direct link to e-mail the stores and tell them what they thought of their performance on green issues. There were also e-mail links to relevant central government and EU ministers, as well as the opportunity to vote on whether farmers should be given subsidies to protect the environment.

Farmers have their own lobby and in the EU they are very strong. They try to persuade governments to protect their industry – often by providing subsidies.

The activities of these two powerful, but often opposing, groups are a key part of the environment of food manufacturers and retailers.

Visit the Friends of the Earth website (www.foe.co.uk) and see what campaigns the group is running now.

The economic environment

All firms are affected by changes in their macroeconomic environment. The macroeconomic environment is what is commonly referred to in newspapers as 'the economy'. It is made up of all the buying and selling that goes on in a country (the national economy), or in the world (the global economy). Economic trends today are increasingly global rather than affecting a country in isolation. This makes it harder for countries to manage their own economies. Most Western governments publish data on economic trends, as do professional organizations such as the Chartered Institute of Marketing (CIM) and international bodies such as the Organization for Economic Co-operation and Development (OECD).

The level of economic activity varies. Most governments set targets for economic growth, sometimes very high targets. In theory, this would mean that everyone within that country would be better off. However, there are many today who argue that high growth rates are not sustainable in the longer term. They come at too high a price – and that price is the health of the planet.

A more immediate problem with rapid economic growth stems from the old adage 'what goes up, must come down'. Many Western economies are characterized by recurring cycles of **boom** and **slump**. Booms are the good times, characterized by high consumer spending and business profits, and low unemployment. Unfortunately, this increase in demand for goods and services may lead to shortages and so to raised prices (**inflation**) and the need to import more while exporting less (balance of payments deficit). A slump is likely to follow. Consumers cannot afford the high prices and so demand falls. Businesses find they have surplus capacity and cut back, and so unemployment rises.

exhibit 3.4

The trade cycle

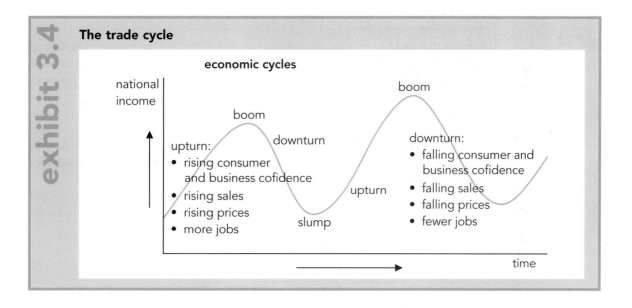

So what is the impact of all this on marketing? Clearly booms and upturns (as an economy moves from slump to boom) are good times to sell more products. With high consumer demand for products, this might be the time to introduce new, higher-specification models more often – as customers are likely to replace products sooner. With more money to spend, companies are likely to have higher marketing communications budgets. Those that do not, risk being left behind. It is a good time to break into new areas, perhaps by setting up new sales outlets. Prices are likely to rise but pushing prices up without good reason is a dangerous strategy. That is the path to inflation which is likely to spell the end of the boom. It is also likely to be very unpopular with customers, of course, and they may desert the firm at the earliest opportunity.

A slump, or downturn in the economy, brings with it a lot of marketing headaches for most businesses. There are a few businesses that are said to be **recession** proof (recession is another term for a downturn). These are companies involved in making and selling essentials such as food, power, health products and services. However, most companies will see falling sales and reducing profits. They may need to reorganize because of cutbacks in the workforce or the loss of distributors. It is likely that budgets will be cut. Often, promotional activity is one of the first things to go.

Stopping promotion is a mistake for at least three good reasons. First, other firms may be cutting back on advertising and so this is a good time to make a real impression – there will be fewer other ads to distract your audience. Second, if brand recognition is lost, then it costs much more to build it up again once the good times return. Third, competition will be cutthroat and advertising is needed to protect market share. Price cutting and special offers are popular tactics during the hard times, but these are not image enhancing and should be treated with care by those who have invested heavily in brand building. Many businesses will fail during a slump.

Most firms will hold off new product launches during a slump and it is almost certainly not the time to launch the latest luxury model. It may, however, prove a good time to launch cut-down, budget versions of products, e.g. the no-frills version of a mass-market car. Prices are likely to need careful monitoring and may need to be changed more often than in better economic times. It is important to remember the negative implications of reducing prices though; for example, a low price may be associated with lower quality (see Chapter 10).

Just as some companies are said to be recession proof, so are some individuals (i.e. the very rich). Businesses that target wealthy consumers, for example top designers such as Christian Dior and luxury goods makers such as Rolex, are less likely to suffer significant drops in sales because of changes in the world economy. Income distribution is as important as average income. In some counties (e.g. Saudi Arabia) a small proportion of the population controls the bulk of the country's considerable wealth.

Firms that trade internationally will have to take account of the economies of all the countries in which they trade. They will also need to take account of import duties (taxes) and other import barriers when devising their marketing plans. This is not an issue for EU countries trading with each other as a large part of the point of the EU is to remove such barriers. Exports to many other countries are more complicated though.

A firm that understands the economic environment in which it operates is far better placed to take advantage of changes in income and spending. Even a slump can be turned to competitive advantage by well-informed and talented marketers.

The social environment

Population changes, demographic trends (including age profiles and gender balance), the switch to urban living, lifestyle changes, cultural considerations – all of these come under the heading of the social environment.

Next to the technological environment, this is the area that has perhaps seen the most changes over the last century. Populations have exploded in some parts of the world (notably China and India), while declining in others (notably the Western nations). This has led to a significant shift in the world's population and put a massive strain on the resources of some countries, while the richer nations try to close their doors to a potential flood of immigrants.

In many Western countries, the average age of the population is rising. This has major implications for product developers. We are seeing an increasing number of products, services, even whole companies that are aimed at this 'seniors' market: e.g. Saga holidays, *The Oldie* magazine.

This is partly a result of the increased birth rate in the years after the Second World War. Baby boomers, as they are called, were the teenagers of the early 1960s, the parents of the 1970s and 1980s and are looking forward to their retirement within the next 10 years or so. These people have had a major impact on demand for goods and services throughout their lives. Take housing as an example: when they were young adults they would have wanted flats; as young parents in the 1970s, they would have bought small family houses and then moved up to larger, more expensive ones when their incomes, and families, grew. Now their children are leaving home and many are looking for smaller houses again – perhaps (for the higher income brackets) with a second home in Spain or France. Soon, there should be a boom in retirement homes. At every stage of their lives, these baby boomers have created high demand for the products relevant to them.

The baby boomers influence does not stop with them. Their children form a baby boom in themselves. Born in the late 1960s through to the 1970s, this is Generation X. A privileged group, born in a time of wealth and peace, Generation Xers have high expectations, especially of brands that they have given their allegiance to. They have grown up during the rise of consumerism. They are cynical and advertising literate. They will not accept shoddy products and they see through insubstantial campaigns. Because they know the advertisers and their tricks so well, they like clever campaigns with insider jokes.

This cycle of population booms continues of course, as each baby boomer becomes a parent, until enough time has passed for the effects to even out. The children of Generation X form a smaller population peak themselves.

It is not just a population's age mix that changes; the very way we live our lives is changing all the time. It is not so long ago that most women were housewives. Now nearly 70 per cent of UK women are in employment (UK government Labour Force Survey, spring 2002). In the past, marketers could just target all women's products and household items at housewives. It is not so easy now. They have to address a variety of different types of women, with different lifestyles, and different requirements. Take a look at 1950s adverts for cleaning products or foodstuffs; they are comically patronizing to today's eyes.

Adverts have changed, along with social attitudes

According to David Nichols, managing director of brand consultancy Added Value:

"even the women who stay at home and don't work have very different lives from 50 years ago and a variety of things to focus on. Now people want quick solutions from products so that they can either spend time with their families or get on with the things that they like doing. Everything that used to be the housewife's life has been shrunk to as small a job as possible."

(Mortimer, 2002)

The result of this has been a boom in **convenience** goods, such as cleaning wipes and ready meals. It has also led a retail revolution as shoppers seek convenience through home delivery services, mail order, Internet shopping and personal shoppers.

insight

Gender trends

Men's and women's roles are changing. Women's earnings are increasing and this seems to have left some brands distinctly confused about how to sell to the new female market. Some have found a new approach that works: the motor industry has succeeded in marketing car brands, for example, the Fiat Punto, the Renault Clio, and the Ford Fiesta and Focus, to women; pubs have catered for the female market with more female-friendly bars, and drinks manufacturers have spent much of the past decade dreaming up new alcoholic drinks that appeal to women.

Women do not seem to mind taking up brands that were previously aimed at men. Examples of this are numerous. Apart from the car brands, such as Audi, Saab and MG, there are beers such as Stella Artois and Hoegaarden that appeal to today's women. Even shaving products, such as Gillette, which now has the Venus shaving system for women, are getting in on the sister act.

Men, on the other hand, are sensitive about adopting brands that may appear feminine. They are wary, for instance, of many personal care and alcopops brands, which they perceive as having a female bias.

Knowledge of such trends and attitude changes enables marketers to develop brands that suit today's, and tomorrow's, consumers and to position them accordingly.

Nestlé, which makes Yorkie bars, has aimed its recent advertising at men, even turning the 'o' in Yorkie on the packaging into a street-sign image of a woman with a red line across. Its posters and print ads have included lines like 'not available in pink' and 'king size, not queen size'.

Clearly Nestlé wants men to buy the bars but, if it has judged the trends well, its advertising shouldn't put women off either.

Source: adapted from Benady and Charles, 2002

It is not just women's lives that have changed; men's have too. The 1990s saw the birth of the new man – just as able as a woman to change a nappy or cook a meal. New man is a caring, sharing sort of bloke, much beloved by women in adverts, but less apparent in real life where surveys consistently show that women still take responsibility for, and do the lion's share of, domestic chores.

insight

Tipping your hat

Attitudes and what constitutes acceptable behaviour change all the time. A hospital consultant was interviewed on BBC Radio 4 in 2002, where he complained about the rudeness of a number of patients who never removed their baseball caps when in hospital. The wearing of baseball caps off the baseball field, and the attitudes of non-wearers to the fashion, would make an interesting sociological study in itself. A number of people expressed views in support of the consultant, and

▶

of the patient. It was clear that many people just would never have considered the patient's behaviour to be rude, and really did not understand why the consultant was offended. Revealingly, the consultant explained that part of the offence came from not being able to see the baseball cap wearer's eyes. Not being able to look the patient in the eye made it harder to communicate with him/her and to establish whether there was a need to probe further into their symptoms. Yet looking directly into someone's eyes is considered offensive in some cultures. So rules of courtesy are by no means universal. They differ between social classes, ages, nationalities – it is so easy to offend, and so difficult to retrieve the situation – far better for marketers to ensure that they understand their market well in the first place.

The natural environment

There is increasing concern about the way we have exploited the planet on which we live. Any responsible analysis must take into account the impact that a firm's marketing will have on the world around us – the Earth is rich in resources but these are not limitless. There is a growing trend towards only harvesting things that can be replaced or regrown. Wooden and paper goods proudly declare it if they are made from sustainable sources. Organic food has become big business in the UK, where consumers are worried about pesticides and genetically modified (GM) products. However, the natural environment is not just about green issues. It is not just a way to make manufacturers feel guilty. Nature provides a wealth of opportunities for marketers too.

Economists have long since recognized that a firm's costs are not limited to the things that it buys and pays for. A manufacturer's activities may cause pollution, and someone has to pay to clean it up. It may appear cheaper to run extra large lorries rather than use rail transport, but the lorries will put a heavy load on the roads, and are noisy and potentially polluting, and eventually someone else will have to pay for these things. These **social costs** often end up the responsibility of the government, or, to be more precise, the tax payer.

The end of the line for packaging is often a dump such as this one

The natural environment is something that marketers particularly need to take account of when designing products and packaging, and organizing distribution.

Product design

How will products be disposed of when they are obsolete? Britain has a mountain of old fridges awaiting safe disposal. Products such as washing machines used to be designed with built-in obsolescence – they would not last more than about 10 years. This was a marketing idea, not a technological limitation. Is this a responsible use of resources?

The late twentieth century was a throwaway society: convenience was all, things were not mended, it was cheaper to buy new ones. However, is it really cheaper? It may cost an individual less in the short term to buy a new vacuum cleaner rather than to get the old one fixed, but the new one is using valuable resources in its manufacture, while the old one is adding to a rubbish tip somewhere. In the very long term, it could cost us the ability to make such things at all.

Packaging design

It is increasingly common to see a symbol on packaging that indicates that it can be recycled, although the facilities are not always available to do this. Much twentieth-century packaging was not biodegradable so it can hang around in landfill sites, potentially forever.

Distribution

As companies have got larger, and marketing has become global, so warehouses and distribution networks have grown. It may appear to be cheaper (thanks to **economies of scale**) to put one huge warehouse in the Netherlands and use it to send goods all over Europe, but this will use more petrol (a scarce resource) and cause more pollution. Bigger is not always better.

Some governments have introduced laws to make firms responsible for these costs; for example, Germany has laws governing the recycling of packaging. The producer is responsible for disposing of packaging. If companies do not take action soon (and some now do perform 'green' audits), then it is likely that more such laws will follow.

The technological environment

In the last two centuries, technology has changed at an unprecedented rate. In the life spans of just three generations, people in the UK have moved en masse from a way of life based on agriculture, to industry with its mass production, and on to jobs in a microprocessor-based service economy. The more developed countries are now becoming postindustrial information and communication-based societies.

Recent significant technological advances include:

▶ more sophisticated information technology

▶ the convergence of computer and telecommunications technologies (as in WAP phones)

▶ the large numbers of people with access to PCs and other new technologies

▶ the development of high-speed, unifying communications networks (e.g. broadband)

▶ high credit card ownership and use,

Technology has made parts of the world much richer but, from the nineteenth-century factory wreckers to the twentieth-century print workers (who went on strike against the introduction of computerized printing equipment in the 1980s), technological change has always been resisted.

It is not just our working lives that change with technology, our whole lives would be radically different if technology had not progressed at the pace it has. Houses would be colder and a lot less convenient. The kitchen would be a very different place in which to cook. Hygiene standards would be lower as hot water would be a more complicated treat. There would be fewer home offices if the recent advances in communications and personal computing had not happened.

Technological change has far-reaching effects. Its impact can be felt right across the **external environment**. Technological innovation is a key driver of economic growth and a major determinant of a company's competitiveness (Baker, 1998).

The technological environment has to be watched very carefully. Most environmental changes happen quite slowly, over a considerable period of time, but a technological breakthrough can change an organization's prospects overnight. Long-established businesses often lose their market leadership to younger rivals with better technology.

Swiss watches used to be reckoned the best in the world, until the Japanese put microprocessors in their. IBM, once the undisputed leader in almost all forms of computing, lost out to Microsoft's more user-friendly Windows operating system. Cars and planes harmed the railway industry and vinyl has become a **niche market** thanks to the invention of CDs. How long will video hold out against DVDs and devices like TiVo?

Some industries (e.g. telecommunications, computing, video gaming and aerospace) exist solely to provide technology to others, but all industries, no matter how low-tech, will be affected by technological change in some way.

Some of the ways in which technology affects marketing are:

▶ the invention of new products and services (see '*Innovation*', below)

▶ marketing research is easier thanks to database systems, CD-ROMs, the Internet

▶ CAD (computer-aided design) has radically changed the way products are designed; designers can try out alternatives and run simulations without building prototypes

lead time
the time it takes for an order to reach the customer

▶ more responsive manufacturing operations mean shorter customer **lead times**

▶ automated warehousing gets goods to the customer faster

▶ computerized order taking and online order tracking speed up the ordering process and provide better customer service

▶ point-of-sale systems (computerized tills) automatically reorder items, avoiding stock-outs and so increasing sales

▶ e-mail and other communications technologies cut down travel times and help firms keep in touch with their customers

▶ laptops and mobile phones mean salespeople can spend more time with customers, and less time in the office.

Innovation

Some industries compete largely on the strength of their new ideas (e.g. computer games, mobile phones, convenience foods) and for firms in these industries it is particularly important to invest in research and development. They need original, well-researched product ideas in order to stay competitive.

Just how innovative an organization and its products are depends on a number of things, including:

▶ how old the product, or the technology the product is based on, is – the older the technology, the more likely it is to be replaced; younger technologies may be able to be refined

▶ the size of the organization – small firms are often more inventive, it is easier for new ideas to get heard; unfortunately they often lack the resources to develop an idea fully and so may lose out to a larger firm

▶ how competitive the market is – lots of competitors may drive a firm to innovate; however, **monopolies** are more likely to have the money, if they see the need

▶ how quickly consumer tastes change – anything that could be considered a fashion item will change frequently; anything that customers will tire of (films?) will be replaced regularly.

activity

What are some of the (probably) unforeseen consequences of the invention of:

▶ cars

▶ PCs

▶ credit cards

▶ mobile phones

▶ e-mail

▶ laser printers

▶ the World Wide Web?

Technology is a catalyst for change. Once a breakthrough has been made, there's no going back, only further development. Technology spreads, leaping across boundaries to areas where it was never intended to go. The Internet was originally designed as a means for academics and scientists to share their research – look at it now.

(For further discussion of innovative products, see Chapter 8.)

The competitive environment

The competitive environment is part of the external environment.

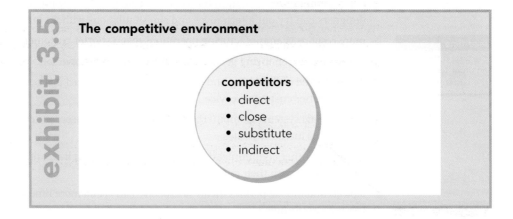

exhibit 3.5

The competitive environment

competitors
• direct
• close
• substitute
• indirect

Many companies devote considerable time and effort to competition watching. Some industries are more competitive than others – for example, the rivalry between UK supermarkets is high, with frequent price undercutting and heavy promotional activity; one supermarket even offers to accept the loyalty points that customers have built up at a rival store. Some firms are arch-rivals. Often these companies are vying for each other's market share – perhaps to take over as the **market leader**. PepsiCo and Coca-Cola, for instance, compete fiercely.

Firms analyse the competitive environment to see how they compare with rivals, and to try to understand their competitors' strategies – what they are doing now and what they intend to do in the future. This is essential if the firm is to develop counter-strategies and maintain, or improve, its market position.

The first thing to work out is: who are the competition? Competitive products can be categorized as:

▶ direct
▶ close
▶ substitutes
▶ indirect.

Direct competition

A direct competitor offers a product or service that is similar to the company's own. For example, Heineken is a direct competitor to Carlsberg, just as Coca-Cola is to Pepsi.

Close competition

A close competitor offers a similar product – one that satisfies the same need. Other soft drinks such as Tango could be said to be close competitors to Coca-Cola and Pepsi. Close competition might be said to extend to any drink, in fact.

Substitutes

These are products that are different to the company's own, but might be bought instead. Again they satisfy the same, or similar, needs. An ice cream is a substitute product for a chocolate bar – either could be eaten as a sweet snack.

Indirect competition

This is competition in its widest sense. People have limited amounts of money to spend and so all products compete for that spending ability. A woman might go out to buy a jacket but then see an irresistible pair of shoes. If she does not have the money for both, the jacket and shoes are in competition.

Competitive analysis: Porter's five forces

Porter's five forces analysis (Porter, 1980) helps firms to analyse the strength of competitive threats and is particularly useful to a firm considering entering a new market.

Threat of new entrants

barriers to entry
things that prevent new firms from entering a market easily (or at all)

An organization needs to monitor the activities of potential competitors as well as existing competitors. The lower the market's **barriers to entry**, the more likely it is that these potential rivals will become actual rivals.

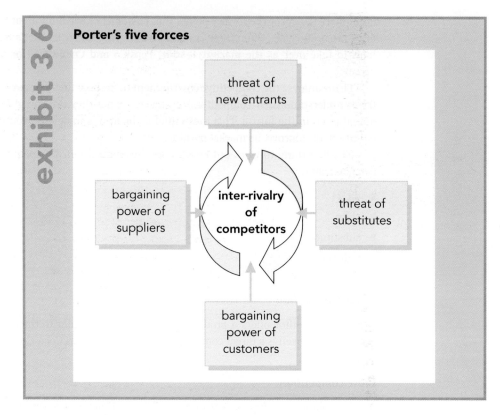

exhibit 3.6

Porter's five forces

Barriers to entry include:

▶ high capital outlay – perhaps to buy expensive production machinery, e.g. the nuclear power industry

▶ existing powerful brand names within the market – e.g. new entrants into the chocolate market would have to compete with Nestlé, Cadbury's, Mars, Suchard, etc.

▶ the size of the market – it may be too small to support any more competitors, e.g. a local high street may already have two good bakeries

▶ legal/regulatory barriers – e.g. a licence may be required to trade (selling alcohol, running a casino); foreign firms are often banned from owning businesses in key sectors such as defence or the media; **patents** are another means by which firms keep out potential rivals

▶ existing companies that control key resources – such as distribution chains or raw materials supplies

▶ existing companies that are large enough to benefit from **economies of scale** and therefore have lower cost bases than any new entrant would; this would mean that a new rival would be unable to match their prices without making a loss.

Threat of substitutes

The more alternative products and services there are, the harder it will be to maintain a competitive advantage and to make a good profit.

Crossing the channel: ferries and planes are substitutes for the Eurostar and Le Shuttle

Bargaining power of customers

Customers will be powerful if they, as individuals or buying groups, are more important to the suppliers than the suppliers are to them. Recently, major grocery retailers such as Tesco and Aldi have been able to dictate terms to most of their suppliers because the bulk of groceries are sold through their stores. Manufacturers such as Kellogg's and Nestlé have to be seen on these supermarket giants' shelves. Smaller manufacturers actively compete for the supermarkets' shelf space. This has led to pressure on prices and, in some cases, insistence upon manufacturer-funded special offers such as bogofs (buy one get one free).

Bargaining power of suppliers

If raw materials or ingredients are scarce, then their suppliers can dictate terms. For example, after the recent bad coffee bean harvest, the price of coffee rose sharply in the shops (though little of this money went to the smaller coffee growers). Suppliers can redress the balance of power with retailers by developing strong brands. It would be a brave supermarket that refused to put Heinz baked beans on its UK shelves. Market leaders have a distinct advantage.

Inter-rivalry of competitors

Just as some people are more competitive than others, so are some companies. Markets such as grocery retailing and fashion are highly competitive. In the first case, this is shown in the **price wars** and intense **below-the-line** activity. In the second, it is apparent in the high advertising spend. Just how intensely firms compete with each other depends on a number of factors, one of which is the **market growth rate**. In a growing market, there is more business available for everyone and so firms do not need to steal each other's **market share** in order to make more sales.

If a company is to develop a **competitive edge**, then it must understand its competitors' strengths and weaknesses. An in-depth, up-to-date analysis of the competitive environment is the basis of any sound competitive strategy. (This model is explained further in Chapter 12.)

The market environment

The market environment is part of the external environment.

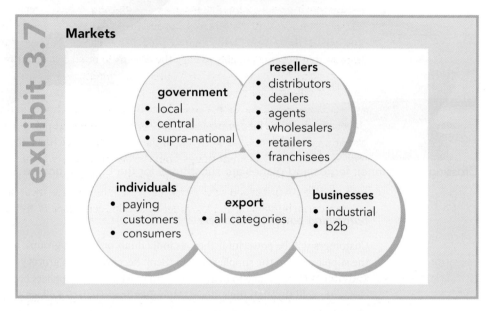

exhibit 3.7

Markets

government
- local
- central
- supra-national

resellers
- distributors
- dealers
- agents
- wholesalers
- retailers
- franchisees

individuals
- paying customers
- consumers

export
- all categories

businesses
- industrial
- b2b

Where would an organization be without customers? Increasingly, the recipients of products or services are referred to as customers even when they are not paying, as in the case of charities and other **not for profit** organizations. This is an attempt to improve the effectiveness of organizations by focusing their attention on the people they exist to serve (see the section on customer orientation in Chapter 2).

Markets can be classified according to the customers within them; the major groups are described below:

▶ Individuals, i.e. consumer markets: where private individuals buy goods for their own use, or perhaps to give to someone else. For some purchases, a distinction can be made between customers (who pay for products) and consumers (who use the products). For example, children's clothes are bought by adults (customers) but worn by children (consumers) – both groups are important.

▶ Business markets – which may be either industrial or b2b (business to business).

▶ Industrial buyers use the products they buy as an ingredient, or component, in the making of something else (e.g. Peugeot buying tyres to fit on to new cars) or to contribute directly to the manufacturing process (e.g. oil for machinery). Those tyres could, of course, have been bought by an individual to replace the worn-out tyres on their own car – and that would be a consumer purchase, and from a different source (and almost certainly more expensive).

▶ Organizations also need general supplies, office stationery, etc., which they use rather than make something with it; the sale of such goods is a b2b market.

▶ Government markets (see list in Exhibit 3.7) – governments are extremely large customers, spending millions on goods and services annually.

▶ Reseller markets – resellers sell on the products they buy to someone else, e.g. wholesalers, distributors, dealers, franchisees (see Chapter 9).

▶ Export markets – i.e. all the above, but in other countries.

Market fragmentation

The invention of mass-production techniques brought in the era of **mass marketing**. Now we are moving into an era of **customized marketing**, which is really at the opposite end of the spectrum. Mass marketing sold one design of product to a wide range of people. This was fine when there were only limited products available but, as production techniques improved, it became possible to vary the designs to build a range of products. Rather than all cars being black (as decreed by Henry Ford's famous edict), cars could be many colours and have different features.

Customers became more demanding, They had more choices and they exercised them. It became desirable for companies to make products that were different to the rest. Marketers recognized that customers were not all the same; that they had different needs and preferences, and wanted different things from the products they bought. Some people like plain burgers, some want cheese, some blue cheese. Some like mayonnaise, some do not. The same applies to pickle and salad. Today there are almost endless variations on a hamburger – even curry burgers (in the UK at least) and burgers made of fish, beans, even lamb (in India).

---

insight

Consumer choice

Toothpaste was once considered a basic product – not any more. At one time, people used soda to clean their teeth, now that's just a nostalgic option. Here are just some of the varieties of toothpaste that can be found in the shops today:

▶ anti-plaque

▶ whitening

▶ breath freshening

▶ tartar control

▶ 'total', i.e. all (or most) of the above

▶ with fluoride

▶ without fluoride

▶ for sensitive teeth (in various flavours, whitening)

▶ smokers'

▶ bicarbonate of soda

▶ peppermint

▶ spearmint

▶ chocolate

▶ strawberry

▶ striped.

On top of that, there are various packaging and size options – and you could probably add many more varieties.

So **end user** markets could no longer be treated as one **undifferentiated** mass; they had to be split up. People with similar tastes could be sold to as groups. This is called **market segmentation** (see Chapter 4). Companies can select (target) certain segments with specific products from their range. The trend today is towards **mass customization**; an attempt to treat all customers as individuals, and tailor the company's products, and their marketing efforts, specifically to each one. It is, again, a technological advance that has made this possible – though this time it has more to do with computing than it does with manufacturing. The power of microprocessing, the sophistication of database programs and the communications abilities of the Internet are making personalization so much easier.

activity

1. Get together with a couple of friends and see how many variants on the following basic products you can think of:
   - milk
   - household cleaning products
   - margarine.
2. Visit Sainsbury's or Tesco's online shopping site, search on 'milk' and see if there are any you missed.
3. Why do you think all these different products exist?

As consumer markets are fragmenting, many industries are reconsolidating. A **fragmented industry** is one in which there are a lot of players, few of whom have any sizeable market power. At its extreme, this is similar to what economists would refer to as **perfect competition**. Design agencies formed a fragmented industry in the 1980s and 1990s, and there are still a large number of small agencies in that field.

There has been a recent trend (notably in retailing and among advertising agencies) towards consolidation, i.e. companies are becoming larger and smaller ones are being pushed out. The advertising agencies have been achieving this mainly through mergers and takeovers of other agencies. Retailers employ a number of growth strategies. Franchising has been a particularly successful one for many (e.g. the Body Shop, McDonald's).

So this is a turbulent part of the organization's external environment and one that needs careful monitoring.

e-focus

A computer with a personal touch

Probably the most significant influence on marketing in the last decade of the twentieth century came from the technological environment. The Internet has had a huge effect on the way we market goods and services. A debate has raged over whether the Internet is a whole new marketplace or just another channel to market or new medium. That debate seems to have settled down now in favour of new channel/new medium, but still the impact of this technology has been greater than that of previous innovations such as telemarketing.

The power of the computing technology behind the Internet has allowed companies to collect enormous amounts of information on visitors to their sites. What's more, they can use this information to address customers on an individual basis. This personalized, **one-to-one marketing** is far more subtle and effective than the old direct mail techniques ever were. Where *Reader's Digest*'s mailers would address you by name throughout the text, Amazon's website knows who your favourite authors are and what kind of music you like. You get personal recommendations, your own page showing which items you've looked at – even an invitation to sell your past purchases online, with an estimate of their worth.

Cross-selling is so much easier with all that computer power behind you. Before a visitor checks out of Amazon's site, a list pops up: 'Other customers who bought books in your basket, also bought . . .'

THE INTERNATIONAL ENVIRONMENT

Many would argue that all marketing is now international. Even firms that do not sell their products and services abroad have to deal with foreign competition at home. The Internet has intensified that competition by giving companies easier access to customers across the world.

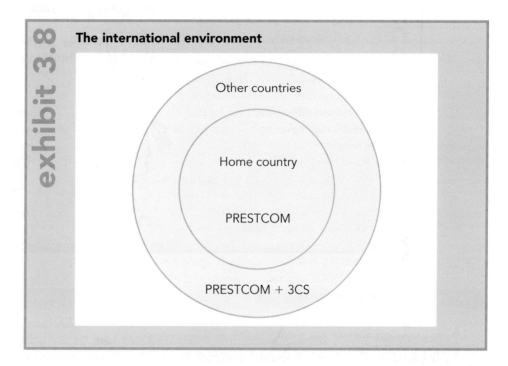

exhibit 3.8

The international environment

Other countries

Home country

PRESTCOM

PRESTCOM + 3CS

It is even more important to conduct a formal analysis of the environment when trading abroad. Firms are usually quite familiar with their home territories, but much less so with foreign markets which can provide some nasty surprises. Managers have to learn that different countries do things in different ways and it is dangerous to rely upon the familiar, to assume that attitudes, values, humour, interests, etc. will be the same the world over. It is not safe to assume that distribution channels operate in the same way, nor that the same advertising media will be available, nor the same laws apply.

Environmental analysis becomes more complex when overseas markets are included because you have to do a PRESTCOM analysis *for each country*. There are also some further variables to take into account; the 3Cs:

▶ country
▶ currency
▶ culture.

Country refers to geographical features, access issues (e.g. the need to cross mountains), climate, etc. Currency could be included in the economic environment, but is worth stressing as currency fluctuations have a huge effect upon the profits of international marketers – if the exchange rate worsens, profits are suddenly worth less when transferred back home. Culture is the key difference between behaviour and attitudes in different countries, and the cause of the greatest problems. An appreciation of the target market's cultural norms, their way of life, their beliefs, their tastes, superstitions, etc., is essential to overseas success.

Cultural differences

Christmas is not a traditional festival in Korea. The card's message reads:

"I wish his merry Christmas and I clean his room so I'm very happy now."

The perception of Christmas in Korea is clearly very different to that in Western cultures. What questions do such cultural differences raise for international marketing?

SWOT ANALYSIS

activity

Pick a company that is in the news. What has been going on in its environment that has helped put it there?

A SWOT analysis is a general management tool rather than being peculiar to marketing. However, it is widely used as a basis for marketing planning. Selected **environmental variables** from the PRESTCOM analysis (see page 62) are placed under one of the four SWOT headings:

Strengths

internal

Weaknesses

Opportunities

external

Threats

Strengths and weaknesses are internal factors, while opportunities and threats are external. So, only organizational factors go into strengths or weaknesses. The rest of the PRESTCOM analysis is external and so feeds into opportunities or threats.

A strength is something that the firm has, or something that it does, that is better than its competitors. For example, a stronger brand name would be a strength.

A weakness is the opposite of a strength: something that the firm has (or does not have), or does, that is worse than the competition. For example, an outdated product range would be a weakness.

Threats and opportunities are part of the external environment and therefore an organization will have far less (if any) control over them.

A threat is something that is going on in the firm's external environment that is likely to cause it problems. The tobacco industry is threatened by proposed new regulations that will make it much more difficult to promote cigarettes.

An opportunity is the opposite of a threat: it is something that is going on in the external environment that is likely to be good for the organization. For example, an upturn in the economy is an opportunity for many firms.

Opportunities have deliberately been left until last as they seem to be the cause of much student confusion. It is important to realize that the word opportunity is being used in a very particular way here: *an opportunity is not an action*. It is not something that the firm could *do*. It is just something good that is happening outside, that the firm might be able to take advantage of – somehow.

Further examples of possible opportunities are:

▶ the election of a government that is pro-foreign trade in one of the firm's export markets

▶ the relaxation of rules governing what can, and what cannot, be sponsored

▶ a drop in interest rates

▶ a baby boom

▶ digital iTV

▶ a competitor goes out of business

▶ a new store opens locally.

Not all of these opportunities will apply to all organizations. For example, the last one (the new local store) may only be of relevance to local suppliers – but, to them, it is clearly a great opportunity. They may be able to sell more. How they go about persuading the store to stock their products (if indeed they decide that they want to do that) comes further along in the planning process. The SWOT analysis just identifies that an opportunity exists.

activity

Pick one of the following companies and make a list of relevant PRESTCOM trends, issues, events (i.e. **environmental variables**). Then categorize them under the SWOT headings.

Companies to choose from:

▶ Microsoft

▶ Virgin

▶ Gap

▶ Vodafone

▶ or choose your own company.

When you've completed the exercise, check the following points.

▶ Do all your strengths/weaknesses come from the 'organization' heading? Are they all particular to the firm and (mainly) its responsibility?

▶ Do all your opportunities/threats come from the external environment (the other PRESTCOM headings)? Do they all affect other companies too?

▶ Are any of your opportunities actions or things the company could do? If so, then they are strategies or tactics, *not* opportunities!

Matching

SWOT analysis does not stop at listing the relevant variables under their correct headings – that is just the start. Many firms rank the variables in order of their importance to the company, but the really interesting bit of the analysis comes during a process called matching.

The firm looks for opportunities that play to its strengths (that match them). If there is an opportunity that matches a strength, then these will be key to the company and objectives and strategies will be built upon them.

For example, AOL merged with Time Warner and so gained access to its cable pipes. This coincided with increased interest from customers in broadband services (such cable pipes are needed to deliver broadband). The pipes were an AOL strength, while broadband presented the company with an opportunity. The two 'matched'. The exploitation of this opportunity became a key part of its marketing strategy (although at the time of writing, it still had not fully capitalized upon it).

It is also important to watch out for threats that prey upon weaknesses. These are significant threats, and action needs to be taken to reduce their effect. Let's take the example of AOL again. AOL grew into one of the biggest Internet service providers (ISPs) by offering a standard suits-everyone-style of service. As the Internet market matured, people wanted different types of product – for example, home users wanted something simpler and with more support; AOL did not have this. The standardized service was a weakness that was matched by the market's new demand for different types of service.

For further reading on SWOT, the following texts are recommended: Johnson and Scholes (1993); Wilson and Gilligan (1997). A critical commentary of SWOT analysis can be found in Pickton and Wright (1998).

STAKEHOLDERS

There are a large number of individuals and groups that exist within a company's environments, and that have an interest in the company and its activities. These are its stakeholders. Freeman (1984) defined stakeholders as 'any group or individual who can affect or is affected by the achievement of an organization's activities'. All organizations have a large number of stakeholder groups and they will be different for each one.

Typically stakeholder groups include:

▶ customers (who buy goods and services)
▶ consumers (who use the goods and services – for further discussion of this distinction see Chapter 2)
▶ employees, including directors
▶ pensioners, i.e. ex-employees who receive their pension income from the firm
▶ suppliers of goods and services, e.g. advertising agencies, raw materials providers
▶ distributors, e.g. wholesalers, retailers, agents
▶ government (local and central)
▶ local community, from whom customers, employees and pressure group members (e.g. local residents' organizations) may be drawn
▶ shareholders, who own the company
▶ pressure groups, e.g. trades unions, consumer groups
▶ bankers, who may have lent the company money
▶ other investors, e.g. venture capitalists
▶ professional bodies, e.g. the Chartered Institute of Marketing.

These groupings are very like the audiences that PR people refer to as **publics**.

Stakeholder groups will want different things from the firm, and often their objectives for the firm conflict. For example, customers usually want the best quality but at the lowest possible price. Shareholders, on the other hand, will want the company to make high profits so that their dividends are higher and their shares worth more. Pressure groups such as Greenpeace will want the company to spend money on protecting the environment and will consider any resulting increase in prices, or decrease in profits, as perfectly acceptable. Trades unions may want higher wages and better working conditions. This will, again, push up the company's costs and so it may have to raise its prices (which the customers will not like) or cut its profits (which the shareholders will not like). Top management must aim to set objectives that will resolve the conflicts between these differing groups (see Cyert and March, 1963).

The idea of a firm having a responsibility towards its stakeholders is relatively new in management thinking. Previously, a company's prime duty was thought to be to its shareholders, or owners, alone. This led to many organizations' main objective being short-term profit maximization, which was often not in its best interests in the longer term. Current managerial thinking takes account of other stakeholder groups when setting the organization's direction. Just how far to take this has become a moral question that has prompted significant debate. (See Hummel (1998) for the arguments.)

SUMMARY

No organization exists in isolation. What is happening in and around it largely determines its ability to succeed in achieving its goals. Monitoring changes in the environment helps a company to spot key opportunities and threats, and forms the basis for sound marketing planning. Some firms do have formal processes for the collection of environmental data but many gather their information in a more ad hoc manner, relying on the judgement and contacts of managers.

There are a number of acronyms that can be used as frameworks for the analysis of the external environment. The one proposed here is PRESTCOM, which encompasses not just the **macroenvironment**, but the competitive and internal environments as well.

The key environments to be monitored are: political, regulatory (or legal), economic, social, natural, technological, competitive, the organization itself (internal), distribution and customers (market). When an organization is trading internationally, it will have to assess these environments in its home country and in all the others in which it trades.

For many firms, the technological environment is a key determinant of competitive edge. Technological change may speed economic growth, provide a means for innovation, change the way people work, spend their leisure time, even how they think. It can also make an organization more efficient. Often, technologies, such as production and transport, have an impact upon the natural environment that may need to be watched out for.

Environmental data can be input into a situation analysis using a framework such as SWOT. This categorizes and prioritizes the information, and so identifies the key opportunities and threats that the organization should address. That situation analysis then becomes the base upon which the organization's marketing plans are built.

Challenges reviewed

Now that you have finished reading the chapter, look back at the challenges you were set at the beginning. Do you have a clearer idea of what's involved?

Hint:

▶ think about PRESTCOM and environmental scanning – what signs might you have spotted?

READING AROUND

websites
Visit the World Trade Organization's website at www.wto.org and find out what it does.
Go to www.statistics.gov.uk and check out the latest UK social trends.
books
Stephen Croall (2000) *Introducing Environmental Politics*, Icon Books.
book chapters
Philip Cateora and Pervez Ghauri (2000) The international business environment and Geography
    and history: the foundations of cultural understanding, Chapters 2 and 5 respectively in
    International Marketing (European edition) published by McGraw-Hill.

SELF-REVIEW QUESTIONS

1. Define 'marketing environment'. (see page 58)

2. What are 'uncontrollables'? (see page 58)

3. What are the two ways in which environmental information is used? (see page 58)

4. How is environmental data gathered? (see page 59)

5. What does PRESTCOM stand for? (see page 62)

6. Name three ways in which the political environment can impact upon a firm's marketing operations. (see page 64)

7. List four characteristics of a downturn that would adversely affect a firm's ability to sell its goods. Why is that? (see page 69)

8. What are social costs? Why do some people think that companies should account for them? (see page 73)

9. Why is innovation important? (see page 76)

10. List, and describe, four types of competition. (see page 76)

11. What are the five main internal functions of a business? (see page 63)

12. Define an opportunity. What is the key difference between opportunities and threats, and strengths and weaknesses in a SWOT analysis? (see page 84)

MINI CASE STUDY

Read the questions, then the case material, then answer the questions.

Questions

1. Do a PRESTCOM analysis of the travel industry, drawing on the information given below.

2. Now do a SWOT analysis.

3. If you were a marketing consultant, what would you advise a travel operator, such as Thomson Holidays, to do? You should *explain and justify* your suggestions.

The trouble with travel

At the start of the twenty-first century, the whole of the UK package holiday industry was struggling to survive recession and shifting consumer demands. Demand for package tour holidays had slowed and the UK's biggest tour operator, MyTravel, was fighting for its life.

MyTravel's troubles stemmed from a combination of general economic slowdown and anxieties about travelling after the terrorist attacks in New York and Bali. However, even before those horrors, trouble was already brewing for an industry that had apparently ignored the changes in its environment.

People were still going on holiday. In fact, they took more holidays than ever before. However, they were booking different types of holiday. High-end operators with tailor-made offerings, such as Kuoni or Mark Warner Holidays, were doing much better then their **mass market** counterparts. It was the mass-market product, which relies on small **profit margins** and **economies of scale** to produce a profit, that was under threat from changing consumer trends and demographics. Today's travellers want exotic destinations or short city breaks. They aren't all families with two children wanting to take a one or two-week all-inclusive holiday.

Package tour companies' prices were being forced down by heavy price competition. At the same time, the industry's bottom line was being squeezed by the need to invest in multidistribution channels, from retail outlets to websites to call centres. The situation was made worse by the large number of people who like to wait for a last-minute bargain before they book.

Further pressure on the travel sector's cost base came from rising hotel rates in Spain, a country that has seen vast improvements in its economy. Spain is still the favourite destination of UK holidaymakers and took 42 per cent of the package holiday market in 2000. Operators were faced with the dilemma of cutting already slim margins or passing on the price rise to customers.

One of the reasons they did not want to raise prices was the new competition from budget airlines such as easyJet. Their no-frills, low-cost flights encourage bolder holidaymakers to put together their own holiday packages. However, the European Commission's new passenger compensation rules, if introduced, will lead to higher costs for all airlines and therefore ticket price rises. As they will be less able to absorb these extra costs, the budget airlines may have to become less competitive in price.

Travelling habits have changed in lots of ways and for lots of reasons, but the biggest upheaval came from two social trends: the growth in the number of singles and of older people; and the fact that holidaymakers are becoming more adventurous and demanding more choice. Society has evolved. People's expectations of holidays have changed – but the package tour operators have not. **Source: based on Johnson, 2002**

REFERENCES

Adcock, D., Halborg, A. and Ross, C. (2001) *Marketing Principles and Practice*, FT Prentice Hall.

Allen, R. (ed.) (2000) *New Penguin English Dictionary*, Penguin Books.

Baker, M.J. (1998) *The Marketing Manual*, Butterworth Heinemann.

Benady, D. and Charles, G. (2002) The battle for the sexes, *Marketing Week* (4 April), Centaur Communications Ltd.

Brownlie, D. (2000) Environmental scanning, Chapter 4 in Baker, M.J. (ed.) *The Marketing Book* (fourth edn), Butterworth Heinemann, 81–107.

Campbell, D. (2003) Indignant activists demand names go on police list, *Guardian* (1 September).

Cyert, R. and March J.G. (1963) *A Behavioural Theory of the Firm*, Prentice Hall.

Dibb, S., Simkin, L., Pride, W.M. and Ferrell, O. (2001) *Marketing Concepts and Strategies* (fourth European edn), Houghton Mifflin Company.

Freeman, R. (1984) *Strategic Management: A Stakeholder Approach*, Pitman.

Hummels, H. (1998) Organizing ethics: a stakeholder debate, *Journal of Business Ethics* 17, 1403–9.

Jobber, D. (2001) *Principles and Practice of Marketing* (third edn), McGraw-Hill.

Johnson, B. (2002) Storm clouds gather over tour operators, *Marketing Week* (31 October), Centaur Communications Ltd.

Johnson, G. and Scholes, K. (1993) *Exploring Corporate Strategy* (third edn), Prentice Hall.

Kotler, P., Armstrong, G., Saunders, J. and Wong, V. (2001) *Principles of Marketing* (third European edn), Pearson Education Ltd.

Mercer, D. (1995) Simpler scenarios, *Management Decision* 33.

Mortimer, R. (2002) Consumer life made easy, *Brand Strategy* (12 June).

Pickton, D. and Broderick, A. (2001) *Integrated Marketing Communications*, FT Prentice Hall.

Pickton, D. and Wright, S. (1998) What's SWOT in strategic analysis? *Strategic Change* 7(2).

Porter, M. (1980) *Competitive Strategy: Techniques for Analyzing Industries and Competitors*, Free Press.

Wilson, R.M.S. and Gilligan, C. (1997) *Strategic Marketing Management* (second edn), Butterworth Heinemann.

MARKET SEGMENTATION

MARKET SEGMENTATION CHALLENGES

The following are illustrations of the types of decisions that marketers have to take about market segmentation. *You aren't expected to know how to deal with the challenges now*; just bear them in mind as you read the chapter and see what you can find that helps.

▶ You are the marketing director of a loss-making brewery. You need to develop new products to revitalize the business but you do not have the resources to launch a full range. How will you choose what type of beer to sell and to whom?

▶ You have just joined the marketing department of a car company. Your managing director has asked your advice about the launch of a new product. The investment to date on product development has been large and high sales targets have been set. Should you try to appeal to as wide a market as possible aiming to attract as broad a cross-section of customers as possible?

▶ You are a marketing manager for a firm of solicitors. Research has indicated that you are operating in a marketplace where people see little difference between rival solicitors' services. How could a deeper understanding of the customers help you to find profitable opportunities?

▶ You work in a travel agency. Recently published market research has revealed the existence of a variety of different types of customer who book package holidays. What criteria will you use to select one or more to concentrate your marketing efforts on?

KEY CONCEPTS

market attractiveness
market segmentation
perceptual mapping
positioning
target market
target marketing (targeting)
targeting strategies

INTRODUCTION

Marketers are interested in satisfying the wants and needs of customers and consumers but not everybody wants the same things. This poses a problem for marketers. If they try to market the same goods or services to everybody, they are unlikely to be successful except under some special circumstances. If they try to provide something unique for each individual, it would not be cost effective unless, again, there are some special circumstances. There has to be a compromise, and fortunately, there is. Marketers can take advantage of the fact that some people share similar wants and needs. They can be grouped according to these similarities; **market segmentation** is about breaking up a market into sections or segments so that marketing effort can be focused better towards particular segments. This is efficient and effective marketing.

In practice, there are different ways of segmenting a market and the particular approach taken will depend on the nature of the market and the way in which a company wishes to deal with it. The way a company segments a **b2b** market will be different from the way a company segments a consumer market.

This is not where the process ends, though. It is the starting point. Having identified the different segments in a market, decisions have to be made about which ones and how many to target. This is referred to as **target marketing**. These decisions lie at the very heart of marketing decision-making as they will affect the range of marketing activities undertaken. In choosing targets, marketers will need to consider competing brands and position their brands accordingly in order to reduce unnecessary direct competition. This is called brand, or competitive, **positioning**.

This chapter emphasizes the need to determine which markets are attractive, and explores different approaches to the important process of segmentation, targeting and positioning.

MARKET ATTRACTIVENESS

Choosing which markets to focus on, based on their **market attractiveness** to the organization, is one of the most fundamental aspects of marketing. It involves a matching process based on an assessment of:

▶ market opportunity – to identify what is possible
▶ competitive advantage – to determine the degree of challenge
▶ the objectives of the organization – to confirm what the organization wishes to achieve.

These aspects will allow organizations to decide on their marketing strategies and tactics. How many opportunities are selected will depend on the thinking of top management and the objectives of the firm. Some will want to be innovators and will be keen to search out new opportunities; some will be followers and quickly imitate the leaders. Others will consider themselves to be low risk takers and will be slow to adopt change even if this, ironically, may create risk because they are failing to move with the times.

To stand the best chance of achieving marketing success, a thorough understanding of the market is absolutely necessary. It is the purpose of this chapter to emphasize this fact and highlight the main concepts that form an integral part of this understanding. It is unusual for an organization to attempt to capture an entire market. What is more likely is that one or more sections, or 'segments', of the market will be deemed to be attractive. For profit-making organizations, whose objectives will be based around financial gain, this will typically revolve around such issues as sales volume, sales value, profits and projected growth rates, and these will usually vary from segment to segment. For both profit-making and for not for profit organizations, segmenting and targeting their efforts will result in the more effective use of resources and will increase their chances of achieving successful outcomes.

What are markets?

segments

distinct parts of a larger market; customers and consumers in each segment share similar characteristics

Markets are people. Or, more accurately, markets are a composite of individuals or organizations that have a willingness and ability to purchase products. A market can consist of a single segment or multiple **segments**.

Even though markets may be described in terms of products, such as the 'drinks market', 'car market' or 'market for nuclear power stations', it is important that marketers never forget that markets are composed of people.

In basic marketing terms, markets are composed of **customers** (buyers) and **consumers** (users) but will also include other groupings as well, such as sellers and competitors (see Chapter 1). From the point of view of segmentation, targeting and positioning (all of which will be explained in this chapter) we are particularly concerned with understanding customers (actual and potential) and consumers (actual and potential). Many texts tend to

These typical shoppers are part of a consumer market

refer to the importance of customers but this, in many ways, is an oversimplification. Markets are, without doubt, very complex environments, as was highlighted in Chapter 3, but identifying markets only in terms of customers can overlook one other important dimension: that of the role of consumers. While customers are strictly the purchasers of products, consumers are the users. Recognition of the respective roles of both in the marketplace is important to marketers.

WHY SEGMENT AND TARGET MARKETS?

66One of the most profound realizations to strike any marketer is that there is a great diversity among customers.99

(Louden and Della Bitta, 1993: 30)

mass marketing
delivering the same marketing programme to everybody without making any distinction between them

Until fairly recently, marketers would speak in terms of **mass marketing**; this was generally founded on the belief that if large numbers of customers/consumers shared sufficiently common needs and wants, the same marketing programme could be delivered to everybody. It is easy to presume that this has always been the way marketing is carried out but this is certainly no longer the case in the vast majority of circumstances in today's markets and probably was not the approach adopted in the past. As pointed out by Lindgren and Shimp (1996), mass marketing is a very recent phenomenon. Up until the early 1900s most goods were produced to meet the needs of specific customers, but as populations and demand grew, this became an inefficient process. Henry Ford, founder of the Ford Motor Company, is frequently attributed with developing and popularizing the concept of mass production, in which he standardized his production techniques to achieve **economies of scale**. The consequence was that he could produce more cars at lower prices and thereby satisfy the demands of the market for cheaper and easily available vehicles. This mass-marketing strategy, however, meant that Ford offered just one product (the Model T), in one colour (black), at one price ($360) to the entire market.

In times of scarce supply of products, customers will make do with whatever is available. In many countries, we now live in times of oversupply of most products. We are demand driven, rather than supply driven (see Chapter 1). As a consequence, markets are fragmenting and we are moving away from mass marketing to more targeted approaches. Under such circumstances, trying to apply mass-marketing techniques, offering a single product and marketing programme across the total market, while achieving economies of scale, runs the risk that few customers will be adequately satisfied (Dibb and Simkin, 1996).

mass customization
tailoring product offerings almost to meet individual needs

In contrast to mass marketing, some now talk of **mass customization** to refer to the way, even in very large markets, organizations are being challenged to tailor their product offerings almost to meet individual needs. Once again, technology is being harnessed to provide solutions.

Marketers need to recognize that potential customers and consumers want different things, and that this creates opportunities to develop different markets and sub-markets *and* to develop different marketing programmes for each. So numerous and diverse are people's requirements that it would be impossible for any single organization to satisfy everybody. This creates competitive opportunity and the potential for competitive advantage.

crmfocus

Technology provides the means to market one-to-one

Fortunately, at a time when there is greater need for marketers to be able to cope with an increasingly complex marketplace, technology comes to the rescue.

66Today it is a thousand times cheaper to hold a customer's details on a computer than it was 20 years ago. Media and markets are fragmenting. Marketing budgets are being squeezed. The ability for marketers to identify key customers and prospects is no longer a 'nice to have' but a necessity. This is achieved through the use of databases for segmentation and targeting.

Over the last ten years, companies have embraced database marketing and now know who are the best customers. Over the next ten years, leading companies will move to one-to-one marketing by developing customer relationship management (CRM) capabilities so that they can give the right offer, to the right person, at the right time and through the right channel.

One-to-one marketing requires changing the business focus from share of market to share of customer. CRM and a good segmentation strategy, particularly if it is based on share of customer, can make one-to-one marketing technically and administratively more practical and achievable.99

Mark Patron, Executive Vice President, Claritas (Europe) BV (quoted in Pickton and

Broderick, 2001: 383)

Although everybody is different, we have the advantage that people do at least share similarities and it is this feature that allows companies to direct their efforts with greatest effectiveness, efficiency and economy.

What is market segmentation?

Market segmentation is the splitting of a market into smaller groups (segments) so that marketers can better direct or focus their efforts. Segmentation can be defined as:

the process of dividing a total market into subgroups (segments) such that each segment consists of buyers and users who share similar characteristics but are different from those in the other segments.

Ideally, from the marketing point of view, a segment would be those people who share the same buying behaviour and practices in every respect, but this is not possible. Instead, marketers make use of a variety of measures or techniques that approximate this. It is possible, therefore, to segment according to such things as age, where people live, their interests and lifestyles, and so on. In the case of business to business (b2b) marketing, organizations can be segmented according to their location, industry grouping, etc. These segmentation approaches or variables give an indication of likely similarities and behaviour between members of the segment. They could be described as surrogate or substitute measures for the real thing, which would be to measure and model actual buyer and usage behaviour. A fuller description of the variables used as bases for segmentation follows the next section.

Criteria for determining good market segments

Today there is a veritable wealth of information available to marketers to help them segment markets. But good segmentation should meet particular criteria. Segments should have the features outlined below.

▶ *Measurable* – without being measurable, a segment cannot be assessed for its size and profit potential. Marketers need to know the characteristics of who is in each segment, how many potential customers are in each segment, and what their buying and usage behaviour is like (as well as other environmental and competitor factors).

▶ *Homogeneous* (similar) within – the customers/consumers in a market segment should be as similar as possible with respect to their likely responses to marketing mix variables (i.e. they should display similar behavioural responses).

▶ *Heterogeneous* (different) between – the customers/consumers in different segments should be as different as possible with respect to their likely responses to marketing mix variables (i.e. they should display different behavioural responses). Ideally, the less segments overlap each other, the better.

▶ *Substantial* – the segment should be big enough to be profitable (or otherwise be capable of meeting the objectives of the organization).

▶ *Accessible* – segments need to be reached and served effectively, not only in terms of delivery of product but also in terms of being able to communicate with the members of the segment. It is in this area that some of the most intractable implementation difficulties can apply. It may not be possible, for instance, to arrange new, or rearrange existing, distribution systems cost efficiently to reach a chosen segment (Dibb and Simkin, 1996).

▶ *Operational* – the segmentation approach adopted should be useful for identifying and distinguishing between customers/consumers and deciding on marketing mix variables. In this context, the stability of the segment in the short, medium or long term may also be important.

While the above factors may be applied to evaluate whether or not a segment is likely to be suitable for targeting marketing effort, Dibb and Wensley (2002) make the point that other important considerations also have to be borne in mind if market segmentation is to be effective. Quoting the research of other authors, they identify the need for the commitment and involvement of senior managers within the organization, the readiness of the company to respond to market change, the role of inter-functional coordination and the need for well-designed planning. Such factors are about turning segmentation analysis into effective marketing action.

Even the biggest companies can't do it all

Although described as appealing to wide and mass markets, major world brands such as KFC and McDonald's have their limitations. Strong branding helps to focus products into particular market segments and for this reason they can become very successful. But their brand associations mean they cannot take advantage of other segment opportunities. It would be virtually impossible for such fast-food chains to expand into upmarket, high-quality, gourmet restaurant businesses using the same names and identities. Similarly, they would not appeal to health-conscious, healthy eating and vegetarian market segments.

SEGMENTATION APPROACHES

There are many ways to approach the segmentation of a market and a summary of these is given in Exhibit 4.1. Although the approaches can be used singly, it is common to use them in combination. Exhibit 4.2 gives an indication of how this works to produce a much more

exhibit 4.1

The main variables used as bases to segment markets

Consumer (b2c) markets	Examples of variables
• demographic segmentation socio-economics	age, gender, family size, life stage, e.g. family life cycle (FLC), religion, race, nationality, education, ethnic group
• geographic segmentation	income, occupation – social grade (A, B, C1, C2, D, E) – country, region, city, urban–rural
• geo-demographic segmentation	house type and house location (e.g. ACORN, MOSAIC)
• psychographic segmentation	lifestyles, values, motives, personalities, e.g. VALS
• mediagraphic segmentation	media habits (i.e. TV viewing, papers read, etc.)
• behavioural segmentation	
purchase occasion	day-to-day purchase, special occasion
benefits sought	value-for-money, service, status, quality, brand image
usage rate	heavy, medium, light user
user status	none, ex, potential, first time, regular user
readiness stage	unaware, aware, informed, interested, desirous, intending to buy, bought, used
attitude to product	enthusiastic, uninterested, positive, negative
involvement	low involvement, high involvement (see Ch 5 for more details)
adopter type	innovator, early adopter, early majority, late majority, laggard
loyalty status	total, strong, medium, light, none

Business to business (b2b) markets *macrosegmentation variables*	Examples of variables
• geographic location	country, region, city, urban–rural, industrial estate
• type of organization	manufacturer, service, government, local authority, private, local, international
• industry grouping/business sector	standard industrial classification (SIC), e.g. textiles, computing, telecommunications, etc. subgroupings can be determined so that finance can be grouped as insurance, banking and investment, for instance
• customer size	large, medium, small, key customer

microsegmentation variables	
• user status	none, ex, potential, first time, regular user
• trade category	agent, wholesaler, retailer, producer
• benefits sought	economy, quality, service
• loyalty status	total, strong, medium, light, none
• readiness stage	unaware, aware, informed, interested, desirous, intending to buy, bought, used
• adopter type	innovator, early adopter, early majority, late majority, laggard
• purchasing practices	centralized, decentralized, tendering
• buy class	straight rebuy, modified rebuy, new task

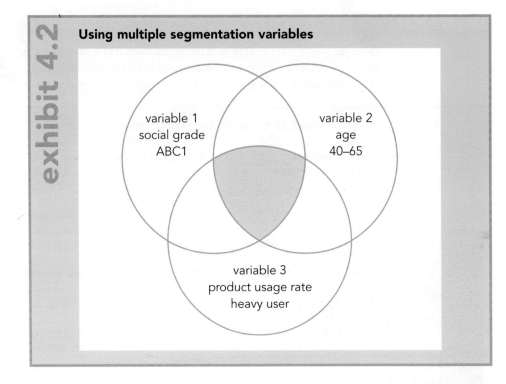

exhibit 4.2

Using multiple segmentation variables

variable 1
social grade
ABC1

variable 2
age
40–65

variable 3
product usage rate
heavy user

focused segment for targeting. Variables used singly would still represent a fairly indiscriminate market, while, used collectively, a more clearly defined segment emerges.

Segmentation in consumer markets

Geographic and demographic segmentation are probably the most popular forms of segmentation. Where customers are physically located (**geographic segmentation**) is of obvious concern to marketers, and determines the length and breadth of their marketing activities from the very local to global, international marketing. Markets can be segmented by areas, regions and by country. In many markets, the Internet and World Wide Web have opened up national and international opportunities to even the smallest of companies. Operating in many countries or areas, however, can have significant resource implications and should only be entered into after careful consideration. McDonald's, for example, operates around 22,000 restaurants in 109 different countries.

globalfocus

The world is getting smaller

The world is getting smaller, or so it seems, with improvements in transportation and telecommunications technologies. Writer and thinker Marshall McLuhan has coined the term 'global village'. International trade is increasing all around the world and trade barriers are being lifted. With an Internet website, e-mail and text messaging, even the smallest company can attract and satisfy international customers. But you do not need to market overseas to face international competition. International competitors are on your own doorstep. Moving into international markets is not without its problems, though. Even greater attention to segmentation may be needed to avert failure. Around 230 nations each have their own unique cultures, subcultures, languages, customs, ethics, beliefs, religions and demographic patterns. All these differences complicate the segmentation process, especially as the quantity and quality of relevant information will vary significantly from country to country.

Demographic segmentation (demographics) has to do with the study of population characteristics and provides a range of useful variables. These variables have the particular advantages that they are relatively easy to measure and that a wealth of information on them is readily available from both government and commercial sources. As can be seen in Exhibit 4.1, demographic segmentation variables include age, gender, ethnic group and many more. If you are a manufacturer or retailer of shoes, even size of feet would be relevant; or size of chest/bust if you make clothing. By focusing on large sizes only, retailers Long Tall Sally and High and Mighty have made use of size to segment and target the women's and men's market respectively for clothes. Life stage is another useful variable and an example of this is the **family life cycle** (FLC), which is described in the accompanying insight box. In this segmentation, the stages in the family life cycle create different needs. Young families have very different purchasing behaviour and leisure activities than solitary survivors.

People at different stages in
the family life cycle

insight

Stages in the family life cycle

Family life cycle segmentation is based on the recognition that we pass through a series of quite distinct phases in our lives, each typified by a different set of circumstances, and within each we display some very different behaviour. Each stage gives rise to, or is associated with, different needs, social behaviour and purchasing patterns. The buying and consumption needs of a family with a young child or children (Full Nest I) are very different from those of an older couple with no children (Empty Nest II).

Since its first inception, there has been far greater emphasis placed on the buying and influencing behaviour of children and, given the increasing longevity of life, the Empty Nest and Solitary Survivor stages.

Stage	Characteristics
Bachelor	young, single, not living at parental home, few financial burdens, recreation orientated – holiday, entertainment
Newlyweds	young couples, no children, better off financially, two incomes – purchase home, some household consumer durables
Full Nest I	youngest child under six, home purchase is significant emphasis, increasing financial pressures, may have only one income, purchase of household necessities
Full Nest II	youngest child over six, financial position improving, some working spouses
Full Nest III	older married couples with dependent children, financial position better still, replace household furnishings and products
Empty Nest I	older married couples, no children at home, home ownership is peak, renewed interest in travel and leisure pursuits
Empty Nest II	older couples, no children at home, retired, drastic cut in income, medical services emphasized
Solitary Survivor I	still working, income good but likely to sell home
Solitary Survivor II	retired, low income, special needs for medical care, affection and security

Social grading is when *occupations* (of heads of households) are classified to provide groupings, which in the UK are best known as A, B, C1, C2, D and E. These are often inaccurately referred to as social classes, which is a related and overlapping concept but has wider connotations than just the occupational measure that is used in social grading. By implication, measures of occupation are closely linked to income and so social grading is classified as a socio-economic segmentation variable. Social grading has proved to be a particularly useful measure as it is used so widely in market research and the collection of government statistics. For this reason, there is a wealth of data available to the marketer that relates social grades to buying behaviour, disposable and discretionary income, media habits, hobbies and interests – all the sorts of things that marketers need to know. Unfortunately, social grading is not very good at determining discrete segments (homogeneous within, heterogeneous between), which is an important aspect of analysing market segments. The information may be fairly easy to collect and it may be widely available, but it is limited in its usefulness. Despite this, it remains popular. Of course, as pointed out above, segmentation variables do not have to be used singly, they can be combined to improve their usefulness.

To clarify, the implication behind demographic segmentation is that age or life stage or occupation, etc. will be factors that will tend to affect your buying and usage behaviour. Thus, for example, an older person is likely to want different things to a younger person. A 20-year-old male will exhibit different purchase and use behaviour to a 50-year-old female.

exhibit 4.3

Social grading

Social grade	Occupational categories
A	higher managerial
B	intermediate management
C1	supervisory, clerical, junior management, administrative
C2	skilled manual
D	semi-skilled and unskilled manual
E	pensioners, casual and lowest-grade workers

Geo-demographic segmentation has become an increasingly popular method for segmenting consumer markets. It combines aspects of both geographic and demographic data (hence its name). Developed first in the early 1980s by the CACI organization, ACORN (A Classification Of Residential Neighbourhoods) makes use of household census data (data collected by the government on the total population) and specifically focuses on where people live and what types of houses they live in. Using sophisticated statistical techniques it has been possible to 'cluster' the population into defined groups according to two variables: house location and house type. The implication is that the area and the sort of house we live in say something about the sort of people we are and, importantly for the marketer, the sort of things we do, buy and use. We can contrast this with social grading that attempts to relate the sort of people we are and the things we do with our occupations (and income). Geo-demographic systems that have already analysed and grouped the population for every area in the country (in all large economies) are commercially available to the marketer to analyse a huge range of markets (for example, ACORN, MOSAIC, EuroMOSAIC, GlobalMOSAIC, PIN and SuperProfile; details of ACORN are provided in Exhibit 4.4). Significantly, geo-demographic groupings have been extensively cross-referenced with other shopping and behaviour databases, such as Target Group Index (TGI) and BARB (see also Chapter 6) so that the actual buying habits of these groups are widely known and analysed.

activity

Walk around an area of housing you are familiar with. Using the brief ACORN descriptions given in Exhibit 4.4, try to guess what categories the types of houses fit into. How much do the houses vary? How many different categories can you identify?

Psychographic segmentation attempts to measure and understand people's lifestyles, values and personalities. As an approach, it more directly addresses the issue of understanding buyer and usage behaviour through an understanding of the buyers and users themselves. It is a particularly useful approach for creating a more detailed understanding of particular segments within an overall market and can be used in conjunction with other approaches such as demographic segmentation. For example, classifying shoppers into different types, as follows, is an interesting and useful lifestyle approach:

▶ the convenience shopper

▶ the recreational shopper

▶ the 'shop-til-I-drop' shopper

exhibit 4.4

ACORN geo-demographics

Categories	Group name	Approximate % UK population
A Thriving	A1 wealthy achievers, suburban areas	15

> Example: there are further subdivisions of each group, these are the ones for A1:
> 1.1.   wealthy suburbs, large detached houses
> 1.2.   villages with wealthy commuters
> 1.3.   mature, affluent home-owning areas
> 1.4.   affluent suburbs, older families
> 1.5.   mature, well-off suburbs

Categories	Group name	Approximate % UK population
	A2 affluent greys, rural communities	2
	A3 prosperous pensioners, retirement areas	2
B Expanding	B4 affluent executives, family areas	3
	B5 well-off workers, family areas	8
C Rising	C6 affluent urbanites, town and city areas	2
	C7 Prosperous professionals, metropolitan areas	2
	C8 Better-off executives, inner-city areas	3
D Settling	D9 comfortable middle-agers, mature home-owning areas	13
	D10 skilled workers, home-owning areas	11
E Aspiring	E11 new home owners, mature communities	10
	E12 white-collar workers, better-off multi-ethnic areas	4
F Striving	F13 older people, less prosperous areas	4
	F14 council estate residents, better-off homes	12
	F15 council estate residents, high unemployment	3
	F16 council estate residents, greatest hardship	3
	F17 people in multi-ethnic, low-income areas	2
Unclassified		0.5

Note: ACORN is a registered trademark of CACI Ltd

- the price-bargain shopper
- the store-loyal shopper
- the traditionalist shopper
- the outgoing/individualistic shopper
- the quality service shopper
- the socially conscious shopper
- other directed shopper (concerned about asking others for opinions).

A popular psychographic classification model is VALS (Values and Lifestyles) developed by SRI International. The most recent version is VALS 2, which consists of eight categories based on a combination of demographic and lifestyle factors such as age, income, education, level of self-confidence, social considerations and interest in consumer issues. Exhibit 4.5 shows the eight types grouped into three broad categories of people: those who are *principle orientated* (guided by their views of how the world should be); those who are *status orientated* (guided by the actions and opinions of others); and those who are *action orientated* (guided by a desire for social or physical activity, variety and risk taking). The right-hand column represents available resources in the forms of income, education, intelligence and health, which range from abundant at the top to minimal at the bottom. Limited resources naturally reduce the opportunity for fulfilment. More details of the VALS 2 model can be found at www.future.sri.com/vals.

exhibit 4.5

VALS 2 segmentation (Values and Lifestyles)

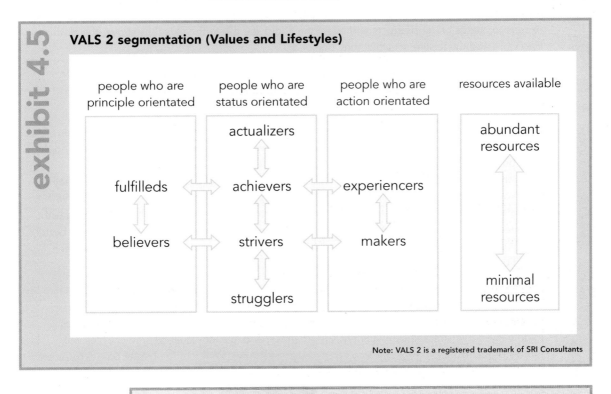

Note: VALS 2 is a registered trademark of SRI Consultants

activity

Visit the SRI website (www.future.sri.com/vals) and make notes on each of the eight types identified in the VALS 2 model. Click on 'survey' and match your own lifestyle or that of a relative or acquaintance with the VALS typology.

Mediagraphic segmentation is based on the reading and viewing habits of the population. This might at first appear a strange approach to segmentation as it measures media behaviour rather than attempting to measure buying or product usage behaviour. However, the original developer of this approach, Carat International, maintains that the approach is more discriminatory than demographics or geo-demographics. The company has cross-referenced data collected through readership and television viewing surveys (e.g. NRS and BARB, see Chapter 6) with purchase surveys (e.g. TGI, see Chapter 6) and has developed a range of mediagraphic categories, each relating media behaviour to purchase behaviour. The implication being that the sort of media 'consumed' says something about the sort of products purchased and used. At an obvious level, this can clearly be related to the reading of specialist magazines and particular purchases. For example, somebody interested in reading hi-fi magazines is likely to be interested in hi-fi products too.

Behavioural segmentation is described by Dibb (2000) as grouping customers and consumers according to how they buy, use and feel about products, and, as such, can be

Lifestyle groups

There are many strange terms used to describe specific lifestyle groups. 'Yuppies' – young urban professionals – aspired to a good life. This grouping was popular in the 1980s and early 1990s. They were young, upwardly mobile and were high achievers. Their disposable income was the envy of many and their spending followed suit. They were 'conspicuous consumers'. They bought expensive, status-brand products and everyone could see this in the cars they drove, the clothing they wore and the leisure activities they pursued.

Although not so popularly referred to today, Yuppies (as status-conscious parents) have given birth to 'Yuppy Puppies', children who they dress in kiddie designer clothing by Versace, Moschino, Hermes and Kenso.

'Baby boomers' is a term used to describe people born after the Second World War between 1946 and 1964. 'Generation X', a term coined by the writer Douglas Copeland, describes people born between 1965 and 1979. They grew up with television and computers. They are independent minded and cynical due to the economic and social problems present when they were young (economic recession, AIDS epidemic, etc.). 'Generation Y', people born since 1980 have also been called the 'Digital Generation' ('Generation D') because they have grown up with the Internet, and computer and communication technologies. They are more opportunistic, better informed, more empowered and entrepreneurial. Older members of the population have been called the 'grey market' and 'Woopies' – well-off older persons.

Other intriguing titles include: 'Dinkies', double income (young couples) with no kids yet; 'Biddies', baby boomers in debt; 'Skippies', school kids with income and purchasing power; 'Guppies', grey upwardly mobile professionals; 'Maffies', middle-aged affluent folks; 'Mossies', middle-aged overstressed semi-affluent suburbanites; and 'Dimps', dual-income couples with money problems.

Source: based on Duncan, 2002

very effective in identifying segments. She quotes the example of tea consumption to illustrate the point:

> Research into tea consumption has revealed that most consumers no longer prepare the beverage in a teapot. Instead, they place a single teabag directly into their cup and add hot water. Unfortunately, these consumers often find that the teabags drip when taken out of the cup. Now manufacturer Tetley has devised a new teabag design to appeal directly to these consumers. The bag features two drawstrings that are meant to ensure that when it is removed the liquid all drains into the cup.
>
> Dibb, 2000: 391

Similarly, a change in behaviour has accompanied the growth of out-of-town and edge-of-town supermarkets and shopping malls. As most shoppers arrive in cars, it has been possible to increase the size of bulk packaging of such items as soap powders as they now only have to be transported to the car park. In contrast, social changes and growth in what the Henley Centre for Forecasting has described as the 'secular household', in which individuals 'do their own thing', has resulted in increased sales of pre-packaged meals-for-one that can be prepared quickly in the microwave.

Behavioural segmentation can involve many different variables, as indicated in Exhibit 4.1, and these can include product or brand loyalty, frequency of purchase or rate of consumption, attitudes towards the product, whether the product is perceived as a high-involvement product in which great care will be taken over the purchase, or a low-involvement product that may be bought more out of habit (see Chapter 5), what the product is bought for – general use or a special occasion such as a party – and so on.

Some have described behavioural segmentation as the 'best' segmentation approach. Others disagree with this contention, not least based on the argument that relevant information is not so readily available or can be expensive to collect. In fact, it would be difficult to state that any one segmentation approach or variable is the 'best' – it would typically depend on the particular application. What *is* true is that behaviourally based variables can provide very 'powerful' descriptors for distinguishing between segments.

Of increasing interest is 'loyalty status'. As the value of maintaining loyal customers has become more widely recognized, degrees of loyalty have become more relevant to marketers. In today's market environment, it is difficult to believe in totally loyal customers. Even those that hold loyalty cards frequently hold such cards from a variety of competitors. One way of classifying customer loyalty is as follows.

▶ Hard core loyals: have absolute loyalty to a single brand or company (e.g. brands AAAAAA).

▶ Soft core loyals: divide their loyalty between two, or sometimes more, brands or companies (e.g. brands AABABBA).

▶ Shifting loyals: brand-switch, spending some time on one brand, or favouring one company, and then moving to another (e.g. brands AAABBB).

▶ Switchers: show no brand loyalty, often purchasing products that are the lowest price or have a special offer (e.g. brands BCBAACD).

User status (non-user to regular user) and usage rate (light usage to heavy usage) may seem similar to loyalty status as they share related aspects. Like loyalty, they are both important concepts to marketers. Even though in all other respects potential customers/consumers may be within a specified segment of interest to the marketer, their user status or usage rate may either heighten their worth or reduce it to zero. Understanding user/usage behaviour is something to which marketers should pay particular attention. Increasingly, the concept of **customer lifetime value** has been a focus of attention for marketers, as the importance of longer-term customer relationships has become more widely recognized. The use of customer databases allows organizations to maintain vast amounts of data on their customer purchasing habits and segment different customer groups accordingly.

customer lifetime value
a calculation of the long-term worth of a customer using estimates of expected purchases

The actual benefits sought by customers/consumers is another interesting way of distinguishing between them. The key benefit for some might simply be low price, for others ease of use. In the toothpaste market, we can see how different brands are aimed at different benefit groups. Brands for sensitive teeth such as Sensodyne, brands for tooth whitening such as Pearl Drops, brands for fresh breath such as Aquafresh, brands for tartar and plaque control such as Crest, brands that tackle tough smokers' stains such as Topol, brands that fight against cavities such as Oracle, and those that claim 'total' care such as Colgate. Each relevant benefit can provide a substantial market segment and help to create opportunities for brand positioning.

activity
Visit a supermarket and choose a category of heavily branded products such as soap, detergents or toiletries. Take a close look at the different brands and their packaging, and identify what benefits each is trying to emphasize. Think about the different ways the competing products are trying to be positioned in terms of the similarities and differences in the benefits they claim to offer.

Finally, in this section, adopter categories is another way of conceptualizing purchasing behaviour that many marketers have found helpful. Researchers have found that people tend to be more or less adventurous in their purchase and use behaviours, and these findings have been linked to particular **personality** and behavioural tendencies. Exhibit 4.6 briefly summarizes the different adopter groups (Chapter 5 discusses them more fully).

exhibit 4.6

Categories of adopter

Category	Characteristics	Percentage of the population
Innovators	Risk-takers, often affluent and well educated	2.5
Early adopters	Adopt early, are opinion leaders in their communities and a source of information about new things	13.5
Early majority	Follow the lead set by the early adopters, delay while making sure of new ideas and things	34
Late majority	Older than average and often less well educated, tend to be more sceptical, more traditional and more comfortable with older values	34
Laggards	Suspicious of innovation, often associated with lower education and low income, often social outsiders	16

Segmentation in business markets

Although attention has been given so far to consumer markets, segmentation principles apply in just the same way to business markets: markets that we may refer to as b2b (business to business) or industrial markets or commercial markets – those situations where one business does business directly with another, rather than with an individual for personal use. Although marketing is most readily associated with consumer markets (or b2c markets as they are also known) and even more particularly with fast moving consumer goods (**FMCG**) markets (for example, the sorts of products we associate with supermarkets), a great deal of marketing takes place b2b. The importance of this is frequently underestimated. Not only would such marketing take place in industrial and commercial contexts, it is also a fundamental part of marketing in consumer market environments. If we consider for a moment the very well-recognized large consumer goods companies, such as Unilever and Procter & Gamble, Coca-Cola and PepsiCo, Ford and General Motors, Sony and Philips, and very many more, most, though not all, of their marketing efforts are directed towards doing business with businesses. They rarely, if ever, sell directly to us, the final customers, even though they do advertise and promote themselves and their brands to us (what we call **pull** marketing activities, see Chapter 8). They put significant marketing effort into working through the trade – **wholesalers, retailers, agents,** franchisees, etc. (what we call **push** marketing activities, see Chapter 8). However, in describing their markets, it is the final customers and end consumers that are significant.

For true b2b organizations, their customers and consumers are other organizations and so it is these that need to be segmented. As shown in Exhibit 4.1, similar variables can be used in b2b markets to those used in consumer markets. For example, what may be of specific interest to the marketer might be where their potential customers are located, what type of business or industry they are in, size of business, and so on. In b2b markets, the segmentation variables can be grouped into macrosegmentation variables and microsegmentation variables, as shown in Exhibit 4.1. As with segmentation in consumer markets, the advent of cheaper databases has drastically reduced the cost of collecting, and vastly increased the opportunity of maintaining, mountains of customer information on a continual basis, making the segmentation process much easier.

Shapiro and Bonoma (1984) have proposed a detailed, nested approach in which they identify five general segmentation bases arranged in a nested hierarchy. The process of segmentation should work from the more general outer area (macrosegmentation) towards the more specific inner area (microsegmentation), probing deeper as it goes (see Exhibit 4.7). The five general segmentation bases are as follows.

1. *Demographic variables.* These are used to give a broad description of the business segments based on such variables as location (which Shapiro and Bonoma included as a demographic, rather than geographic, variable), size of business, type of business and business sector (e.g. SIC code, for details see below).

2. *Operating variables* enable a more precise identification of existing and potential customers within demographic categories. Here might be included user status and technologies applied.

3. *Purchasing approach* looks at customers' purchasing practices (e.g. centralized or decentralized purchasing); it also includes purchasing policies and buying criteria, and the nature of the buyer/seller relationship.

4. *Situational factors* consider the tactical role of the purchasing situation requiring a more detailed knowledge of the individual buyer, others involved and the specific buying situation. This might include potential order size, urgency of order and any particular requirements.

5. *Personal characteristics* relate to the people who make the purchasing decisions. Different customers may display different attitudes to risk and different levels of loyalty to suppliers.

exhibit 4.7

The nested approach to b2b segmentation

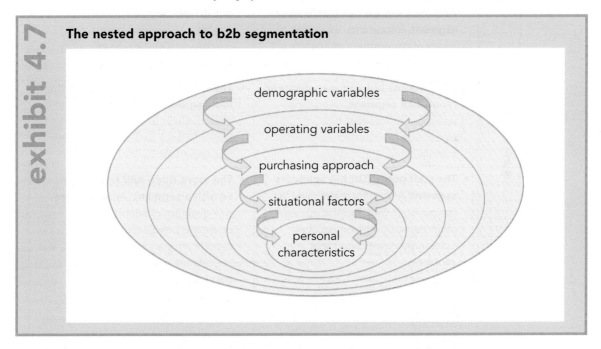

b2bfocus

Selling buses to America

Approximately 5000 transit buses are sold per annum in North America (1998 figures) to some 350 transport authorities. Segmentation in this b2b bus market has historically involved the macrosegmentation approach to segmentation analysis, namely focusing on customer size and geographical variables. Essentially, the most important consideration has been the size of the bus fleet. Transport authorities with over 750 buses are considered 'large', authorities between 200 and 750 are 'medium', and authorities with fewer than 200 buses are 'small'. In addition, the North American market is divided into 11 geographical regions.

b2bfocus

Research into microsegmentation characteristics in this market has revealed two new approaches to segmentation. The first highlights the importance of the purchase decision process and the second highlights the importance of the product evaluation process (which emphasizes the significance placed by buyers on particular product features). Six distinctly different decision process segments, and a further six product feature segments have been identified. These new ways of segmenting b2b markets are providing far greater insight into marketing issues, and overcoming the criticisms voiced and difficulties faced over not being able to adequately operationalize segmentation approaches into marketing strategy (Dibb and Wensley, 2002).

The researchers (Crittenden *et al.*, 2002) have termed these two different groups of segments as shown in the table below.

Decision process segments	Product feature segments
• **The rider-conscious and low-cost bid segment**. Importance was given to standardization of products with current fleet, low-cost bid and rider opinion.	• **The drive train and not drivers segment**. Importance was given to drive train and low maintenance cost but not to efficiency of use for divers.
• **The government regulation-prone advanced design bus (ADB) lovers segment**. Importance was given to issues of government intervention and compliance.	• **The cool climate drive train and not drivers segment**. Similar to segment above, but both air conditioning and driver efficiency were less important.
• **The low-cost bid and manufacturer reputation segment**. Importance was given to low-cost bid, perception of manufacturers and manufacturers' nationalities.	• **The rider-sensitive and forget the fuel segment**. Concern was given to attractiveness and air conditioning. Fuel efficiency and bus power were less important.
• **The staff-poor ADB big spenders segment**. Importance was given to comparisons with and the opinions of other transport authorities. Staff opinion was considered less important.	• **The more rider- and less driver-sensitive segment**. More concern was given to location-specific operating conditions, air conditioning and exterior styling, less importance given to maintenance cost and driver efficiency.
• **The large, new-look buyers segment**. Importance was given to standardization with current fleet, perception of manufacturers and local manufacture.	• **The power-hungry segment**. The unique characteristic of this segment was the importance given to bus power and location-specific operating conditions.
• **The 'others' opinions and not dollars count' segment**. Importance was given to board of directors' opinions and opinions of other transport authorities. Of low importance was low-cost bid.	• **The style conscious and cool segment**. This segment was primarily characterized by high ratings for exterior styling and low ratings for bus power and air conditioning.

SIC (Standard Industrial Classification)

system of classifying products by allocating numbers (codes) to every product category, industry or business sector

As with consumer markets, a great deal of information may already be available in published form. For example, type of business/industry will be defined by industrial classifications, such as the **SIC (Standard Industrial Classification)**, which governments use to categorize the companies within their countries. Government publications summarize this data and company details can readily be found in a wide range of business directories. The SIC system simply allocates numbers (codes) to every industry or business sector. Exhibit 4.8 gives some indication of the codes used. The first digit, or couple of digits, indicate the broad industry area. The succeeding digits provide greater detail and are more specific about individual products or product groupings. The exhibit shows example details of UK SICs by providing just the first digit of the code showing the major industry and service areas. The North American SICs (North American Industry Classification System – NAICS) code examples show how the code number is 'built up' from the general to the specific. European SICs and other countries' SIC approaches adopt similar principles.

exhibit 4.8

Standard Industrial Classifications (SICs)

UK SIC code	Description
0	Agriculture, forestry, fishing
1	Energy and water-supply industries
2	Extraction of minerals and ores (excluding fuels), manufacture of metals, mineral products and chemicals
3	Manufacture of metal goods, engineering, vehicles
4	Other manufacturing industries
5	Construction
6	Distribution, hotels/catering, repairs
7	Transport and communication
8	Banking, finance, insurance, business services, leasing
9	Other services

NAICS code	Description
	The first two digits of the NAICS code show the Major Group Category, for example:
20–39	digits in this range are for the Manufacturing Industry Division, for example:
34	these first two digits give the industry group code for 'Fabricated Metals'
342	the addition of the third digit, 2, gives the industry group code for 'Cutlery and hand tools'
3423	the addition of the fourth digit, 3, gives the specific industry code for 'Hand and edge tools'
34231	the addition of the fifth digit, 1, gives the product class code for 'Mechanics hand service tools'
342311	the addition of the sixth digit, 1, gives the specific product code for 'Pliers'
	So, allocating Code 342311 to a company (among any other codes it might also be allocated) would indicate that it was a manufacturer of pliers

TARGET MARKETING

Target marketing involves making decisions about which part of the market an organization wishes to focus on. It follows from market segmentation in which the total potential market is subdivided according to its characteristics. Targeting is then the choice of which single segment or group of segments the organization wishes to select. A **target market**, therefore, would actually be better described as a target submarket or target segment.

target market

a group of buyers and consumers who share common needs/wants or characteristics, and whom the organization focuses upon

Evaluating a segment for targeting

There are five principal characteristics that will make a market segment particularly attractive for targeting but, before selecting, the organization must undertake a full PRESTCOM analysis (see Chapter 3), which will include consideration of their own company resources and capabilities, their strengths and weaknesses, the competition and the company's objectives. The characteristics of an attractive segment are that it:

▶ has sufficient current and potential sales and profits

▶ has the potential for sufficient future growth

▶ is not over-competitive

▶ does not have excessive barriers or costs to entry or exit

▶ has some relatively unsatisfied needs that the company can serve particularly well.

It should be noted that the distinction here is really about the way in which a company *focuses* its marketing efforts towards those customers (targets) that it really believes will give it greatest success. Customers from outside the target can, of course, be accepted, but these, simply, will not be the focus of attention. The result could be that companies may lose some potential customers but, within their limited resources, they will have directed their efforts in ways that they have decided are likely to be most effective and cost-efficient. Certainly, marketers recognize that trying to appeal to *everyone* may well have the effect of not appealing successfully to *anyone*.

Reasons for targeting and positioning

The underlying rationale behind the total process from market segmentation to targeting and positioning is well accepted in marketing and is a logical development of the marketing concept that was introduced in Chapter 2. As all marketing authors emphasize, these concepts are key decision areas in marketing and strategic planning, and have formed a basis of marketing management since its early inception as a business discipline.

Applying the principles outlined in this chapter allows organizations to handle market diversity by focusing resources on particular customer/consumer groups. Having a better understanding of the media habits, buying behaviour and product use of subgroups of the market creates the opportunity for organizations to fine-tune their offerings, allocate scarce resources more effectively, and provide the basis for strategic marketing decisions. Analysis of the market allows organizations to improve their competitiveness, exploit market gaps, avoid or reduce direct competition, and develop their competitive advantage. In short, they are fundamental parts of good marketing, facilitating marketing effectiveness, efficiency and economy. How well an organization then puts these to use is an implementational issue that will be affected by managerial willingness and ability.

ethicalfocus

Targeting children

A number of companies are now quite directly targeting children. This is clearly evident during Saturday-morning TV and in marketing activities focused directly at schools. Companies are providing books, other teaching and learning materials, and free gifts.

While it can clearly be argued that children benefit from the donations and support given to their schools, what do you consider the motives behind this support to be? What ethical issues are raised by these companies' actions?

Targeting strategies

targeting strategies

used to select a single target market, or a group of target markets

Having analysed the chosen market and determined the attractiveness of the various segments in that market, a decision then has to be made concerning which segments to target. There are some basic options available. Exhibit 4.9 lists these and Exhibit 4.10 illustrates the different **target marketing strategies** visually.

exhibit 4.9

Target marketing strategies

undifferentiated marketing

differentiated marketing

concentrated marketing

niche marketing

customized marketing

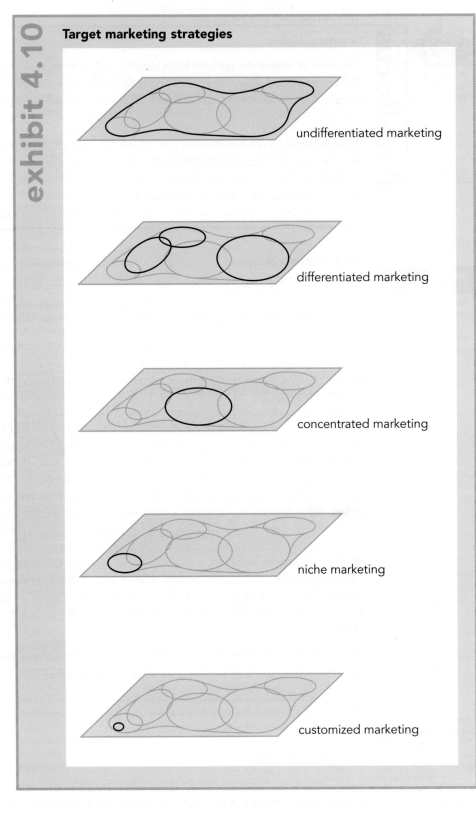

exhibit 4.10

Target marketing strategies

undifferentiated marketing

differentiated marketing

concentrated marketing

niche marketing

customized marketing

Undifferentiated marketing

undifferentiated marketing

where the market is believed to be composed of customers/ consumers whose needs and wants from the product are fundamentally the same

Undifferentiated marketing is where the market is believed to be composed of customers/consumers whose needs and wants in the context of the product being offered are fundamentally the same, i.e. there is no basic difference between them, they are undifferentiated. This is the area of **mass marketing**. In undifferentiated or mass marketing, a single marketing programme is used for all. Although this may result in lower costs and prices (and/or higher profit margins), it is very difficult to satisfy all customers/consumers with one marketing mix. An organization using undifferentiated marketing may also be providing an excellent opportunity for its competition to capture a portion of its sales by appealing to the desires of specific segments. Few, if any, products are marketed totally in this way. Usually, some form of differentiation takes place, even if only on a small scale. Products such as Coca-Cola and Pepsi are reasonable examples of undifferentiated marketing, although it should be recognized that some modifications are made to the marketing effort in different countries even if this is only to recognize language differences. Both companies have also recognized particular benefit segments within the general market and so, in this way, really practise a differentiated marketing strategy to some extent. For example, Coca-Cola has Diet Coke and Pepsi has Pepsi Max as a sugar-free alternative.

Undifferentiated marketing may be a strategy employed by marketers even when some differences between customer/consumer groups are recognized. The segments are aggregated in the belief that the differences are not significant or can otherwise be ignored. However, too much aggregation of segments can be risky. Combining segments to enlarge the target, and adopting mass-marketing approaches, inevitably means that the target becomes less and less homogeneous – the differences between each segment begin to outweigh their similarities. Thus, the mass marketer (when adopting an undifferentiated targeting strategy) needs to be convinced that the nature of its product offering can, indeed, meet the requirements of a large market, as primarily appears to be the case in the cola market. Other organizations, such as McDonald's, Burger King, Wendy's and KFC, take a similar stance, although it is not widely recognized that each of these businesses does, indeed, modify its product offering in different countries (geographical segmentation) to reflect different cultural preferences (demographic segmentation). It is each company's intention, though, to maintain its general image and promotional effort throughout.

Lindgren and Shimp (1996) point out that by pursuing an undifferentiated marketing strategy an organization can build and maintain a specific image with customers/consumers, minimize its production costs, achieve greater efficiencies and be able to offer its products at competitive prices (or otherwise achieve higher profit margins). They cite three instances, in general, when a mass, or undifferentiated, marketing strategy is most appropriate:

1. when the market is so small that it is unprofitable to market to just a portion of it

2. when heavy users are the only relevant target because they make up a large proportion of the market

3. when the brand dominates the market and draws its appeal from all segments of the market, thus making segmentation unnecessary.

Differentiated marketing

differentiated marketing

differences between market segments are recognized and two or more target markets are selected, each receiving a different marketing programme

Differentiated marketing occurs when differences between market segments are recognized and two or more target markets are selected, each receiving a different marketing programme. The Ford Motor Company is a very good example of an organization that uses a differentiated target marketing strategy effectively. By developing a range of models, it is able to meet the needs of a wide range of targeted segments. Most large organizations have adopted the principles of differentiated marketing, even if the specific approaches they have adopted vary (see Chapter 7, on **branding** strategies). Even the Coca-Cola Company, as an organization, has adopted a differentiated approach to its total business. Although Coke may be relatively undifferentiated, as an organization it owns and markets a range of drinks brands to cater for different segments.

The Ford Galaxy and Ford Ka were designed to meet the needs of different market segments

Concentrated marketing

Concentrated marketing: the term 'concentrated' is used to describe this strategy because only one, single, market segment is chosen for targeting – hence, there is a concentration of marketing effort. If the market is relatively small, well defined and very focused, the term **niche marketing** is used. In the car market, this might apply to Aston Martin and Morgan cars. At an even greater level of focusing, where individual customer preferences are important to the organization, marketing effort may be defined entirely by the need to satisfy a single customer. Here, the term **customized marketing** may be used. In consumer markets, this can occur for one-off products such as items hand built to a customer's specification. Tailors will custom-make suits; architects will design and build new houses for clients. More frequently, we tend to associate this degree of targeting with b2b markets and especially large-value orders; this might apply, say, to a custom made factory, engineering project or the organizing of a special event on behalf of a company.

Targeting strategies can, therefore, be seen as a continuum of strategies ranging from the very broad to the very narrow (see Exhibit 4.11).

customized marketing

producing one-off products/services to match a specific customer's requirements, e.g. a made-to-measure suit or the organization of a product launch party

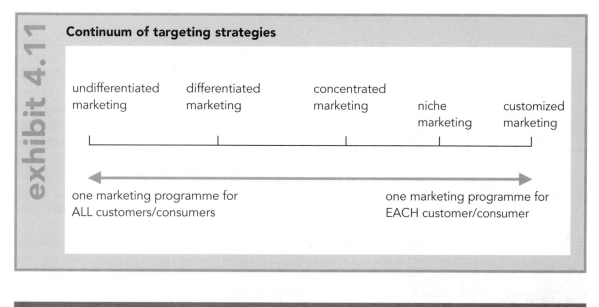

exhibit 4.11

Continuum of targeting strategies

undifferentiated marketing

differentiated marketing

concentrated marketing

niche marketing

customized marketing

one marketing programme for ALL customers/consumers

one marketing programme for EACH customer/consumer

POSITIONING

Positioning follows naturally from the targeting decision, and forms a direct link between the target marketing strategy and marketing programmes. But, having selected one or more target markets, and before developing marketing plans and programmes, an understanding of customer/consumer perceptions of the competing brands in that (those) target(s) is necessary. By carrying out a detailed analysis of the target market(s), an appreciation of competing offerings and where one's own brand might fit into the market can be developed, especially in the context of how customers/consumers think and feel about the **brands**. It is to do with their perceptions and preferences. This will typically be a consequence of their previous knowledge and experience of the brands themselves and the companies associated with those brands – thus a brand is frequently a function of perceptions held about both the company *and* its products. Sony, for example, creates close links between itself as a company and its brands (e.g. Walkman). Likewise, Cadbury's chocolate brands adopt a similar strategy. In contrast, some companies prefer to allow their brands to stand alone. Kiwi shoe polish is actually a brand of the Sara Lee company but very few people would realize this. Whiskas is a cat food, but few may recognize that it is made by Pedigree Petfoods, and fewer still may realize that this is a part of the Mars group, manufacturer of Mars bars (see Chapter 7 for more details about branding).

Positioning, then, is the place a brand is perceived to occupy in the minds of the target market relative to other competing brands. It has been referred to as a battle for the hearts and minds of customers/consumers.

Perceptual maps

perceptual mapping

the process of visually representing target market perceptions of competing brands in relation to each other

Rothschild (1987) highlights two particularly important techniques in ascertaining customer/consumer perceptions relative to competing bands. These are both represented visually as **perceptual maps**, which are also called brand maps, position maps or space maps. The first technique is **Multi-attribute Attitude Mapping (MAM)** and the second is **Multidimensional Scaling (MDS)**, both of which sound significantly more frightening than they really are. Both forms of analysis can be presented pictorially, which makes the comparison between brand perceptions very straightforward.

Multi-attribute Attitude Mapping (MAM)

MAM is achieved by, first, determining the key features or attributes of products in the group – for cars these might include fuel consumption, style, comfort, etc. People are asked to assess competing brands against these attributes by indicating how important each attribute is (from high to low) and how each brand is rated for each attribute (from high to low). Scoring can be used in both cases. For example, a mark out of 10 might be given. In all cases, it is important to confine the analysis to the perceptions of the members of the target market(s). Obtaining the views of the general market or general population would only serve to confuse the findings. The findings might then be presented as shown in Exhibit 4.12. The horizontal lines indicate how important each of the five identified attributes are perceived to be, and the relative position of brands A, B, C, D and E are shown against each of these attributes. Also shown is what is deemed to be the ideal position according to the respondents, this is identified as brand 'I'.

From this, comparisons can be made between competitor brands and also against the ideal position. Brand D, for example, is in the ideal position regarding price, brand E is close to the ideal position regarding low fuel consumption. None of the brands appears to be close to the ideal regarding style and comfort, although it may be argued that brand C frequently exceeds the expected ideal.

exhibit 4.12

Possible Multi-attribute Attitude Map for a compact car

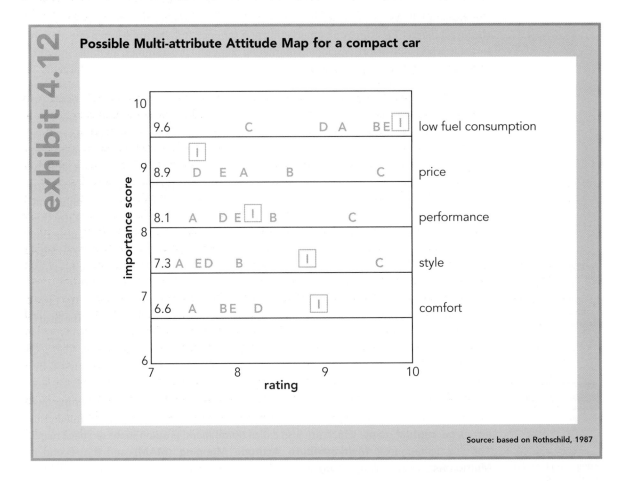

Source: based on Rothschild, 1987

Rothschild emphasizes a further feature of the MAM approach. If it is recognized that, for any one purchase, a range of people may be involved (see Chapter 5 for more on the **decision-making unit (DMU)**), then different constituent members of the target market may hold different views about the importance of specific attributes because of their particular interests or perspectives. Under these circumstances, the views of the different DMU members can be isolated, rather than being aggregated into the total data, and a multi-attribute attitude map produced for each. He quotes an industrial market example to illustrate this:

> 66 The most important attributes for the engineer are related to the technical specifications of the product, while the purchasing agent is most concerned with price issues. In such a case the firm can develop a technical ad for engineers and deliver it in Engineering Digest, while developing a price/value ad for purchasing agents that can be delivered in Purchasing Agents Weekly. 99
>
> **Rothschild, 1987: 89**

MAM is a useful tool in analysing and determining positioning in that it is easy to implement, it identifies which attributes are important to customers/consumers, it identifies how competitors are perceived in relation to each other and to an ideal, and provides further insight into positioning strategies for different constituent customers/consumers within the target market. In the context of this latter point, understanding perceptions of product attributes can assist in highlighting benefit segments, which may then be specifically catered for by launching new products, changing marketing programmes and repositioning.

Multidimensional Scaling (MDS)

Multidimensional scaling is a popular approach to visualizing brand positions. It is easiest to illustrate this approach by considering an example. Eight competing brands of soap are compared by asking members of the target market to consider the brands in groups of three. This is known as **triadic comparisons** and is a technique that is used because it is easier for respondents to compare such groups rather than try to consider all the brands together in one go. The respondents simply have to say which two of the three are most similar or, in other words, which they feel is the odd one out. The respondents do not have to work out why they feel this, it is enough that they can choose. All combinations of three brands are assessed in this way and a picture is developed of how similar or dissimilar the brands are to each other. These relative positions are analysed by a computer multidimensional scaling programme, which takes into account all the responses and plots the aggregate positions on a chart. The resulting map, known as a **perceptual map**, **brand map** or **position map**, shows how close to or how far away the brands are from each other (hence the reason why these maps are sometimes referred to as **space maps**) (see Exhibit 4.13). A modified approach to this would be to use **dyadic comparisons** in which the brands are compared in pairs and a judgement made as to how similar each pair is by allocating a score. All combinations of pairs are considered and, again, a computer multidimensional scaling programme is used to plot the resulting map. The map at this stage would not have any axes. These are added by the researcher using judgement to guess what are the major underlying dimensions or attributes that account for the respondents' perceptions. In Exhibit 4.13, the differentiating attributes appear to be the deodorizing and moisturizing qualities of the soaps.

perceptual map
results from the perceptual mapping process and shows brands' relative positions (also called a brand map, position map or space map)

exhibit 4.13

A possible perceptual map for soaps

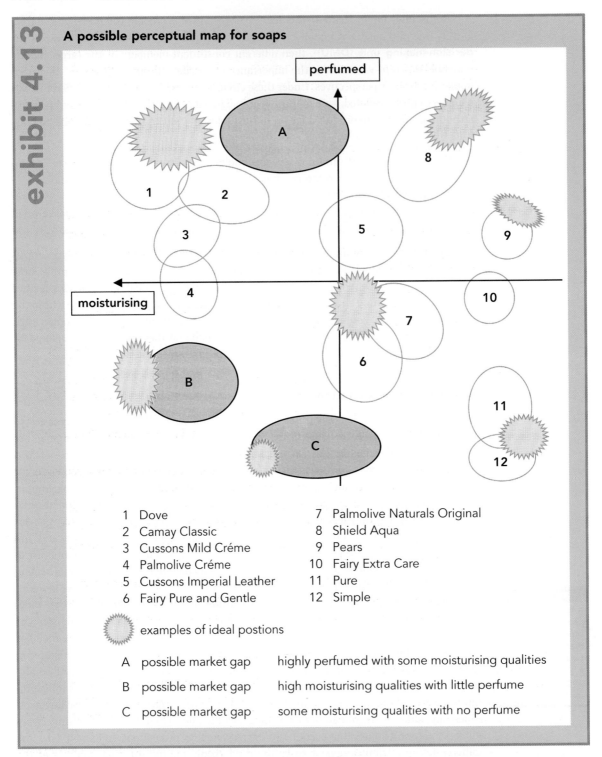

1 Dove	7 Palmolive Naturals Original
2 Camay Classic	8 Shield Aqua
3 Cussons Mild Créme	9 Pears
4 Palmolive Créme	10 Fairy Extra Care
5 Cussons Imperial Leather	11 Pure
6 Fairy Pure and Gentle	12 Simple

examples of ideal postions

A   possible market gap   highly perfumed with some moisturising qualities

B   possible market gap   high moisturising qualities with little perfume

C   possible market gap   some moisturising qualities with no perfume

It is also possible to question respondents about their ideal product and plot the different responses to this as well. As might be anticipated, this does not result in a single ideal position but a range of positions according to the different preferences expressed. These preferences will tend to cluster into particular positions and are shown in Exhibit 4.13 by the circles. The larger the size of circle, the more people who have expressed that ideal preference.

For the purposes of this text, the actual mechanisms of how perceptual maps are constructed are not too important. What is important is to recognize that such maps are used and what they represent. By referring to the positioning of competing brands, the closeness of competition can be assessed, as can possible market opportunities, as represented both by ideal positions and by market gaps. The latter are represented by areas on a map left uncovered by any brand. Market opportunities can be filled by launching a new brand or by repositioning an existing brand. Repositioning can also be considered as an appropriate strategy where two brands appear to be too close together. (Repositioning is considered a little later in this chapter, after 'Positioning strategies'.)

Positioning strategies

A range of different strategies can be considered when positioning a brand against the competition. These strategies are largely to do with the way in which the brand is promoted through advertising and other marketing communications approaches (see Chapter 8), and are outlined below.

▶ *Positioning on attributes/product features.* A common way to position is to differentiate it from other brands by emphasizing its distinctive product feature(s). Head & Shoulders shampoo eliminates dandruff.

▶ *Positioning by price/quality.* For some brands, high price or high quality is featured, others are promoted for their relatively low prices or adequate quality. Stella Artois beer has advertised itself as 'Reassuringly expensive'. Value for money is often emphasized, although this does not always clearly differentiate it well from other offerings. Wal-Mart's ASDA promotes 'ASDA price', Tesco promotes 'Every little helps'.

▶ *Positioning for specific usage occasions.* After Eight mints have consistently been promoted as an after-dinner chocolate.

▶ *Positioning on benefits or needs.* Bold washing powder is a powder and fabric conditioner in one. Some fabric conditioners reduce the need for ironing.

▶ *Positioning by the product user.* Marlboro cigarettes were originally aimed at women, they are now positioned towards men – and specifically feature outdoor ruggedness.

▶ *Positioning against another brand or with respect to a competitor.* 'In tests, our washing powder washes whiter than . . .'

▶ *Positioning with respect to another product class.* Rather than showing a direct comparison against another brand, the positioning can be against a product class. The 'I Can't Believe It's Not Butter' spread clearly compares itself to butter.

activity

Choose a number of different hotel chains (such as Holiday Inn, Travelodge, Great Western, Hilton, Sheraton) and consider how they each try to position themselves within the market. Write a brief description of the market position of each and discuss your ideas with a colleague or friend.

Repositioning

Repositioning is the marketing process of manoeuvring a brand from its current position to a new one in people's minds relative to competing brands. Repositioning arises out of a need to respond to competitor activity and/or changes in the marketplace. Such repositioning might involve relatively minor shifts in perception or moving into totally new segments.

Hellman's mayonnaise found that sales were decreasing not just through competition with other mayonnaise brands but through competition with other dressings. The market for mayonnaise was being attacked and Hellman's was losing out. Initially, changes to its promotional activities achieved a repositioning of its mayonnaise in relation to other dressings such as salad creams. Mayonnaise sales increased, but not only for Hellman's – it had improved the market for its competitors, too. The company's next task was to position itself favourably compared with its mayonnaise brand rivals, and this it succeeded in doing.

Marlboro cigarettes were originally launched to appeal to women. They were repositioned, with their now familiar rugged brand image, to appeal to 'real men'. The tobacco company introduced Virginia Slims as a more suitable brand for women smokers.

Johnson and Johnson: successful repositioning

Johnson & Johnson's Baby Shampoo brand used to be specifically positioned for baby/infant use. To widen the market, the company successfully repositioned it as an adult, gentle, frequent-use shampoo. It achieved this without sacrificing its original position and now maintains two quite distinct positions within the market. This is not often achieved. So successful was this strategy that the company extended it to its other baby products and enjoys similar success for its Baby Oil and Baby Powder brands.

b2bfocus

From RAP to K3: repositioning on multiple levels – company, product and market

RAP was a successful Swedish-owned rubber and plastics supplier and manufacturer, selling its products to large DIY chains such as B&Q. Its repositioning transformation since 2000 has been miraculous. At corporate level, it has acquired new businesses and it is selling off others. It is completely moving out of its original business and into computing software. At this corporate level, the approach is best described as moving into different markets rather than repositioning. The company has bought out Kewill's enterprise software business, which itself started life in the form of computerized

▶ production and stock control systems, and is repositioning this as a total enterprise resource planning (ERP) business with the inclusion of customer relationship management (crm) capabilities. It has fully updated the software from a DOS to the more modern Windows operating environment. It has renamed the company K3.

This total repositioning has required both corporate and product changes, a move from one customer base to others, and from one competitive environment to another. The original RAP business has been sold off and the old Kewill business has been 'revamped' with product and image updates under the newly named K3. Existing Kewill customers, who could have become 'disenfranchized' with the company and product changes, have remained loyal (now to K3) and are responding well to new product developments. New customers are coming online. Kewill competitors are now experiencing stronger competition in their target markets under K3. Software products and services within the K3 range have been modified and repositioned as integrated systems solutions.

Coffee on the move

When starting out, branded coffee retail chains such as Starbucks, Costa Coffee and Coffee Republic focused their marketing efforts and resources on the gourmet coffee drinking segments of the entire coffee drinking market. As coffee drinking and the wish for better coffees have increased, the nature of the market has moved on, creating new opportunities and growth. These chains have become the new cafés. It is no longer the gourmet drinkers who frequent them. Tastes for quality coffee have spread throughout the market and the nature of the segments within the market have changed. Don't ever presume that segments and targets are fixed. Changes in consumer tastes and competitive activities can fundamentally affect otherwise stable market environments.

THE FIVE-STAGE PROCESS FROM MARKET SEGMENTATION TO POSITIONING

By considering all the relevant points above, we can identify a step-by-step process in which companies can move from an early understanding of the total market through to finally determining their own brand positions. Dibb (2000) refers to this as the STP of market segmentation: segmentation, targeting and positioning. Exhibit 4.14 shows the full five-stage process.

There is a logical progression from one stage to another. The total potential market is analysed and market segments are identified. Through an understanding of the market segments, the market attractiveness of each can be determined and one or more segments can be targeted. Further analysis can reveal an understanding of the perceptions of the potential customers and consumers in the target(s), and the relative positions of competing products (brands) can be assessed. The complete analysis can then be used as a foundation for selecting appropriate marketing strategies and tactics, leading to the implementation of specific marketing activities and actions.

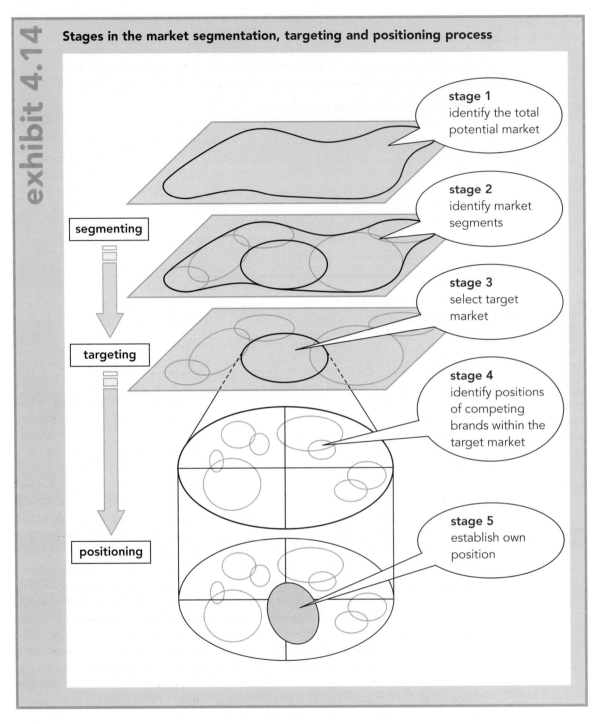

exhibit 4.14

Stages in the market segmentation, targeting and positioning process

segmenting

targeting

positioning

stage 1
identify the total
potential market

stage 2
identify market
segments

stage 3
select target
market

stage 4
identify positions
of competing
brands within the
target market

stage 5
establish own
position

SUMMARY

Market selection is one of the most fundamental aspects of marketing. The choice will be affected by what market opportunities seem to be available matched against a company's objectives, its resources and an assessment of its general business environment, which can be undertaken through the use of PRESTCOM analysis.

Markets consist of customers and consumers, whether they are b2c or b2b markets, but no single company can fulfil the needs of all and so careful attention to defining customer and consumer requirements is vital. While individuals are different, people do share similarities in terms of some of their habits, lifestyles, preferences, where they are located or, in the case of b2b, what type of business they are in, etc. An understanding of these similarities can be used to divide a total market into subgroups such that each consists of buyers and users who share similar characteristics that are different from those of the other subgroups. This process is called market segmentation.

There are many ways to segment markets and this chapter has briefly described the use of geographic, demographic, geo-demographic, psychographic, mediagraphic and behavioural segmentation in the case of consumer markets and macro- and microsegmentation approaches in the case of b2b markets. It is up to marketers to decide which of the segments are attractive enough to target for special attention. This is the process of targeting or target marketing.

In this chapter, a number of different targeting strategies have been described; these range from the general to the specific. These have been identified as undifferentiated marketing, differentiated marketing, concentrated marketing, niche marketing and customized marketing. A useful way to think of them is as a continuum from undifferentiated, where there is no targeting and the product is available to all, to totally customized, in which the product is provided on a totally individual basis.

Having identified one or more potential target markets, an understanding of customer/consumer perceptions of the competing brands in those target(s) is necessary so that the most appropriate marketing activities can be determined. This is the process of positioning and is achieved by, first, carrying out a detailed analysis of the target market(s) so that an appreciation of competing offerings and where one's own brand might fit into the market can be developed. Positioning is very much about understanding customer and consumer perceptions of the brands on offer. These can be plotted on a perceptual (brand) map. With an understanding of the brands competing in the target market(s), a range of positioning strategies is possible. For most products that are already in the marketplace rather than just being launched, a regular check on their perceived positions is something that marketers should carry out as this provides an ongoing assessment of a brand's competitive position. If necessary, repositioning should be considered to reduce or eliminate head-on competition.

The chapter ends by summarizing the total segmentation-to-positioning procedure as a five-stage process, which starts by identifying the total potential market and then goes on to the identification of market segments, the selection of target market(s) and the identification of the positions of competing brands within the target market(s), and finishes by establishing one's own position within the target market(s).

Challenges reviewed

Now that you have finished reading the chapter, look back at the challenges you were set at the beginning. Do you have a clearer idea of what's involved?
Hints:

▶ targeting strategies

▶ differentiated or undifferentiated?

▶ segmentation bases.

READING AROUND

websites
www.upmystreet.com
book chapters
David Pickton and Amanda Broderick (2004) Chapter 17 in *Integrated Marketing Communications* (2nd edn), FT Prentice Hall.
books
S. Dibb and L. Simkin (1996) *The Market Segmentation Workbook: Target Marketing for Managers*, Routledge.

SELF-REVIEW QUESTIONS

1. Broadly speaking, it is suggested that marketers should address three areas of concern when assessing market attractiveness. What are they? (see page 92)

2. What is the difference between market segmentation and target marketing? (see page 92)

3. What are the main criteria for assessing how good a market segment might be? (see page 96)

4. What are the main bases that can be used for segmenting consumer markets? (see page 97)

5. What is social grading and how is it measured? Is it the same as social class? (see page 100)

6. What is geo-demographic segmentation? (see page 101)

7. Why are lifestyles useful for segmentation purposes? Identify an example of lifestyle segmentation. (see page 101)

8. Why is behavioural segmentation a useful approach for marketers? Identify some examples of behavioural segmentation variables. (see page 103)

9. What are the main bases that can be used for segmenting business markets? (see page 106)

10. Why should macrovariables be used before analysing microvariables in business markets? (see page 107)

11. What is the difference between targeting and positioning? (see page 110)

12. What is the difference between mass marketing and niche marketing? (see pages 113–14)

13. Under what conditions is mass marketing an appropriate marketing strategy? (see page 113)

14. What is the five-stage process from market segmentation to positioning? (see page121)

MINI CASE STUDY

Read the questions, then the case material, then answer the questions.

Questions

1. Marketing has to do with matching product offerings with customer/consumer demands. Review the benefits that Peter's product provides, reappraise his definition of the product and identify as many possible uses for the product as you can (a garage door-opening device is just one possibility, and some uses may be in industrial and commercial situations).

2. For each use you have identified, what segmentation variables would you use to segment the market?

3. Consider Auto-Tecnic's situation and resources. What target market or target markets would you advise the company to focus on?

Auto-Tecnic GmbH

Auto-Tecnic is a small German company founded and run by a clever electronics engineer, Peter Schnider. He has built his successful, though small, business over the past five years by undertaking subcontract work for large electronics companies. The work has mainly involved producing small control devices (automatic switches, timers, etc.) in response to his business customers' requests. Peter's expertise is valued by the organizations with which he has dealt.

Having returned from trips outside Germany, Peter noticed an increase in the number of homes making use of automatic garage doors. Drivers would either press a button on a device kept in the car, which activated a switch in a door-opening mechanism fitted to the garage door, or a device would be fixed in the car that automatically triggered a sensor as the car approached, which then operated the garage door-opening mechanism.

With his electronics expertise, Peter designed a better electronic system than the ones he had seen on his trips. His system contains extra security features that ensure constantly changing but synchronized coding between the transmitter (fixed in the car) and the receiver (fixed on the garage door). In other words, other people should not be able to activate the opening switch. In Peter's system, the garage door would automatically open as the car approached the receiving sensor. Peter has arranged for his system to be patented.

Peter recognizes his limited understanding of marketing; his skills lie in technical electronic product development. He is convinced, however, that his new product idea will be profitable. As a first stage, he has asked you, as marketing consultant, to advise him how to define his market – just who would be interested in buying and using his product? He realizes that, as with any product, his system is unlikely to have universal appeal.

REFERENCES

Crittenden, V.L., Crittenden, W.F. and Muzyka, D.F. (2002) Segmenting the business-to-business marketplace by product attributes and the decision process, *Journal of Strategic Marketing* 10(1), 3–20.

Dibb, S. (2000) Market segmentation, in Blois, K. (ed.) *The Oxford Textbook of Marketing*, Oxford University Press.

Dibb, S. and Simkin, L. (1996) *The Market Segmentation Workbook: Target Marketing for Managers*, Routledge.

Dibb, S. and Wensley, R. (2002) Segmentation analysis for industrial markets: problems of integrating customer requirements into operations strategy, *European Journal of Marketing* 36(1/2), 231–51.

Duncan, T. (2002) *IMC: Using Advertising and Promotion to Build Brands*, McGraw-Hill Irwin.

Lindgren Jr, J.H. and Shimp, T.A. (1996) *Marketing: An Interactive Learning System*, The Dryden Press.

Louden, D.L. and Della Bitta, A.J. (1993) *Consumer Behaviour* (4th edn), McGraw-Hill.

Pickton, D.W. and Broderick, A. (2001) *Integrated Marketing Communications*, FT Prentice Hall.

Rothschild, M.L. (1987) *Marketing Communications*, DC Heath.

Shapiro, B.P. and Bonoma, T.V. (1984) How to segment industrial markets, *Harvard Business Review* (May–Jun), 104–10.

CHAPTER 5

BUYER BEHAVIOUR

BY TONY GARRY

BUYER BEHAVIOUR CHALLENGES

The following are illustrations of the types of decision that marketers have to take or issues they face. *You aren't expected to know how to deal with the challenges now*; just bear them in mind as you read the chapter and see what you can find that helps.

▶ You are the marketing manager for a toy manufacturer. The company is planning to produce a range of toys for children under three years old. How do people decide to buy such toys? Who purchases these types of toys? Who influences the purchase and what do they consider when purchasing such toys?

▶ You have developed a brand new product that is a technological breakthrough: a teleporter. It will make most other forms of transport redundant. Which type of person is most likely to be the first to use such a product and how would you persuade them to do so?

▶ I was brought up in a quiet village in the north-west of Scotland. As a child I loved the Scottish countryside. However, I subsequently went to university and now have a yuppie job with a blue-chip company in the City. I miss Scotland and frequently visit home. You are product development manager for a brewery. What type of drink would appeal to me and why?

▶ You are attempting to sell a computer system to a large governmental department. You have to give a presentation to the end users of the computer system, the head of department, the IT manager and an accountant. What criteria do you think they will use to assess the suitability of your computer? Who else should you target within the organization and who do you think has the most influence?

KEY CONCEPTS

decision-making process
internal influences
external influences
types of buying decision
levels of involvement
product adoption process
organizational buying process

CHAPTER OVERVIEW

INTRODUCTION

The previous chapter focused on markets as groups, or **segments**, consisting of buyers or users who share similar characteristics. The first part of this chapter focuses on the **consumer** as an individual within a market. It explores how consumers purchase products in terms of the decisions they make and the various stages they may go through in reaching a purchase decision. It subsequently examines what influences them in terms of internal factors (such as their personality) and external factors (such as friends and family, see Exhibit 5.1). The second part of the chapter does the same, but from an organizational perspective.

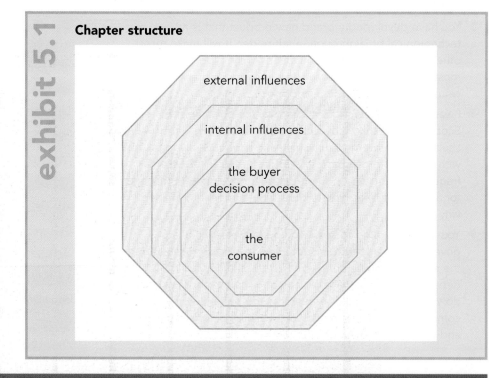

exhibit 5.1

Chapter structure

external influences

internal influences

the buyer decision process

the consumer

THE CONSUMER BUYER DECISION PROCESS

consumer models

representations of consumer buying behaviour, usually as diagrams

Marketers spend large amounts of time and money attempting to find out how consumers respond to different elements of the **marketing mix**. There have been many attempts to portray these responses through the creation of **consumer models** of buyer behaviour. These aim to provide frameworks for explaining the stages that consumers pass through in their decisions on whether or not to purchase a product or service.

Engel, Blackwell and Miniard's (1995) model (see Exhibit 5.2) is a well-known example.

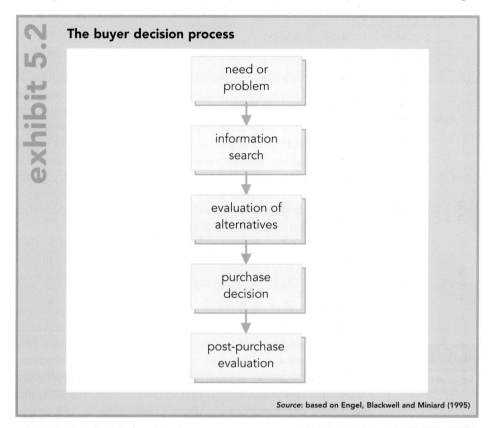

exhibit 5.2

The buyer decision process

need or problem

↓

information search

↓

evaluation of alternatives

↓

purchase decision

↓

post-purchase evaluation

Source: based on Engel, Blackwell and Miniard (1995)

Need/problem recognition: sweets at a supermarket checkout are designed to be external triggers to stimulate need

The exhibit shows the key stages that a consumer passes through to reach the decision as to whether or not to buy a product. Although particularly relevant to new or difficult purchases, the model is useful because it shows all the factors facing a consumer when considering purchases. The next part of this chapter will look at these stages in more detail.

Need/problem recognition

The buyer decision process begins with need/problem recognition. The consumer will recognize that there is a difference between their current (or actual) state and their desired state (see Exhibit 5.3). The trigger for this may be internal factors (such as being hungry or thirsty), or it may come from an external source. External sources are outside of the consumer and include factors such as **point of sale** promotion or advertising.

So, for example, imagine a scenario where you are watching TV and an advert for crisps appears. This may stimulate a desire for a snack even though you are not hungry. There is a discrepancy between your actual state (having the munchies) and your desired state (having a packet of crisps to munch on), and you recognize there is a need that requires satisfying (you just fancy a packet of crisps).

Sometimes the recognition of a need or problem is not as obvious as this. It may be based on vague feelings. Imagine a scenario where you do not do as well in an exam or piece of coursework as you had hoped. On the way home you decide to treat yourself to a large bar of chocolate.

The amount of effort that consumers are prepared to make to solve the need or problem depends on how large the difference is between their current and their desired state, and the relative importance of that need to the individual consumer. This is known as the **level of involvement** and is discussed in more detail later in this chapter.

Marketers must be aware of the needs that consumers have so that they can be in a position to offer products or services that will satisfy these. Marketers must also be aware of the factors that may generate and influence those needs so they are able to develop the right marketing mix.

level of involvement

the extent to which the purchase is important to the purchaser

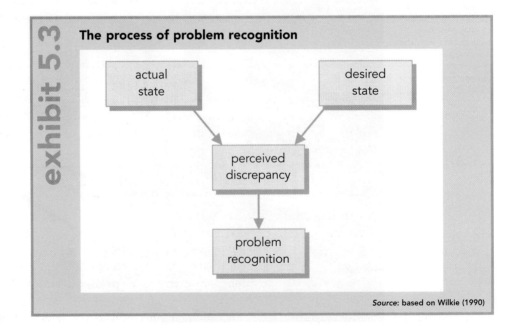

exhibit 5.3

The process of problem recognition

actual state → perceived discrepancy ← desired state

perceived discrepancy → problem recognition

Source: based on Wilkie (1990)

Information search

Once consumers have recognized that they have a need, the next stage of the buyer decision process begins: the **information search**. The information search involves identifying the various ways the need or problem can be satisfied. The information search may be internal or external.

An internal search revolves around accessing your memory and using previous experience. So, for example, if you had been peckish before, and a particular brand of crisps had solved the problem, then you might buy them again. However, if no satisfactory solution is found, then an external search may begin. This may involve some or all of the following external sources of information:

▶ personal sources such as family, friends and other students

▶ commercial sources such as shop assistants and adverts (imagine you are considering buying a new CD player, you become more receptive to (or notice more) adverts for CD players)

▶ third-party reports such as magazine comments, newspaper editorials, Watchdog reports or websites.

@

e-focus

e-information

The Internet may have a significant impact on the buying process. With no central management or ownership, users are able to browse the web to obtain or share information, or interact with other users. Potential buyers of products are now able to access official company websites, impartial consumer watchdog websites (such as *Which?*) and Internet chat rooms and websites where information and opinions are available from other users about the product or service, or the organization supplying them. Potential buyers are no longer reliant upon official sources.

awareness set

range of products or brands that may satisfy the need or provide a solution to the problem

This information will be used to build up an **awareness set**. The awareness set is the range of products or brands that may satisfy the need or provide a solution to the problem. It is similar to a list.

Marketers design their marketing mixes in order to make consumers aware of their products (i.e. to get them in the consumer's awareness set) and to provide consumers with the information they need to make a decision. A product cannot be in the consumer's awareness set if the consumer does not know it exists. Marketers need to be aware of the various information sources that consumers within their target market use, and their relative importance to the consumer. From this, marketers are in a position to target their resources more effectively.

Evaluation of alternatives

Once the consumer has built up their awareness set, the next stage in the process is to evaluate the alternatives, i.e. to assess the different products or brands now within the awareness set. Consumers evaluate these products in a number of ways.

activity

List the attributes you consider important when you are deciding which film to see at the cinema. Get a friend to do the same, and compare notes. Would you be choosing the same film?

Because the consumer is attempting to satisfy a need, they will be examining the benefits of the product's features (product attributes). Different consumers will attach different degrees of importance to different attributes. Salient attributes are those attributes a consumer considers are important and associates with a product when they think of it.

The way consumers evaluate the products in their awareness set depends upon the individual consumer and the specific buying situation. The consumer narrows down the number of products in the awareness set by assessing the products' salient features against their choice criteria.

The shortlist of remaining products is known as the evoked set and the consumer will make a final choice from this shortlist. A number of formal and informal criteria may be used in the final choice. These may include price, reliability and service, as well as more subjective criteria such as status and image (see Exhibit 5.4).

exhibit 5.4

Criteria for evaluating alternatives

criteria	includes
performance related	reliability quality longevity specification style comfort taste
financial	actual price price of extras value for money credit terms running costs depreciation
social	status reputation perceived image social acceptability
personal	self-image level of risk ethics emotional appeal

Having evaluated the alternatives, the next stage in the buyer decision process is the purchase decision.

Purchase decision

purchase decision
the selection of the preferred product to buy

Products in the **evoked set** are ranked in order of preference (according to the consumer's choice criteria). Next, the consumer makes a **purchase decision**, i.e. they select their preferred product or brand. This may happen, for example, in a shop, on the Internet or over the telephone. There are, however, a number of influences that may affect the consumer's purchase decision (see Exhibit 5.5):

▶ the attitude of friends, family, partners etc. may influence the purchase intention; consider a situation where a young teenager goes shopping for new clothes with his or her parents – they may consider price and reliability to be more important criteria than the teenager's status or self-image

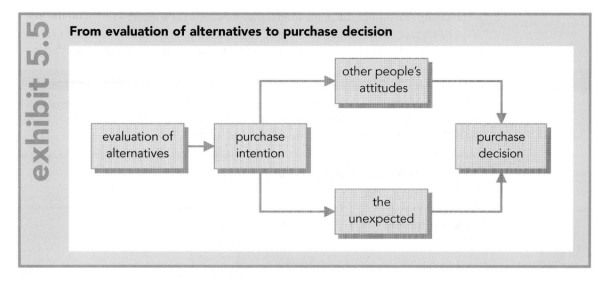

exhibit 5.5

From evaluation of alternatives to purchase decision

- when a consumer is about to make the purchase, unexpected situational factors may intervene; for example, a particular product size or colour may be sold out and so the consumer is forced to make a re-evaluation.

Post-purchase evaluation

The post-purchase stage of the decision process is particularly important to marketers as it will determine whether the consumer will repurchase the product and how they will influence other people in terms of purchasing the product. Smith (1993) suggests consumers tell up to eleven people of a bad experience but only three or four of a good one.

Whenever a product is purchased by a consumer, they evaluate the product in terms of what was promised (in the adverts or by sales assistants in shops, for example) before they purchased it and how it actually performed after they purchased it. There are three common outcomes of this:

1. disappointment – the consumer is unlikely to repurchase the product

2. satisfaction

3. delight – the consumer is likely to repurchase the product, will talk favourably to others about the product, and will pay less attention to competing brands when watching adverts (and will not feel the need to try them).

Sometimes, when the consumer has invested a lot of time, effort and money into the purchase decision, or where there are many similar alternatives available, the consumer may experience feelings of doubt about whether they have made the right decision. You can probably think of examples where you have purchased a product and your friends have questioned your decision: 'How much did you pay for that? I could have got you it for half the price.'

This is called **cognitive dissonance** (Festinger, 1957) and means that the consumer may be psychologically uncomfortable with their purchase. Consumers will attempt to reduce this feeling of doubt in a number of ways:

**cognitive
dissonance**

when a consumer is
psychologically
uncomfortable
about their purchase

- ignoring information that undermines their choice
- paying more attention to information that supports their choice.

Marketers can minimize cognitive dissonance is a number of ways:

- ensuring advertising does not exaggerate the product features (over-promise)

▶ providing reassurance through advertising and after-sales support

▶ allowing consumers to sample or test the goods prior to purchase.

TYPES OF CONSUMER BUYING DECISION

So far, the buyer decision model suggests that consumers will regimentally pass through all the stages for everything they purchase, but this is clearly not the case. Sometimes stages are missed or worked through in a different order. A major factor affecting the flow and formality of the decision-making process is the buying situation. There are three main types of buying situation (see Exhibit 5.6).

exhibit 5.6

Types of buying situation

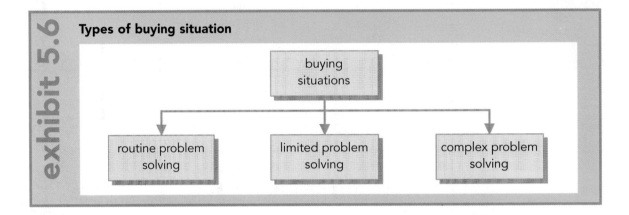

Routine problem solving is where the consumer buys the product on a regular basis and there is no lengthy decision-making process. Packets of crisps and bars of chocolate are routine purchases. There is little financial risk associated with the purchase of these products and so the consumer does not usually think too much about them.

With *limited problem solving*, the product is purchased less frequently and the goods are likely to be more expensive and expected to last longer. Typical examples of limited problem solving products are electrical products such as TVs and hi-fis. These types of product usually involve more deliberate decision-making.

Infrequently purchased expensive items, such as houses and cars, call for *extended problem solving*. It is important to the consumer to make the right choice and so there is a high level of information search and evaluation of alternatives.

LEVELS OF INVOLVEMENT

level of involvement

the extent to which the purchase is important to the purchaser

Related to the purchase situation is the **level of involvement** the consumer has related to the product.

When the purchase is of high involvement to the consumer, they are more likely to carry out a complex decision-making process. However, when the purchase is of a low involvement, or is of no or limited interest, consumers will often use choice tactics or short cuts to reduce the time and effort they expend in the decision-making process (see Exhibit 5.7).

Research suggests there are four factors that affect the level of involvement that a consumer has with a product (see Exhibit 5.8).

1. *Self-image*: where the consumer thinks that a product will affect their self-image (e.g., cars and clothes) then involvement levels are likely to be higher.

2. *Perceived risk*: where the consumer thinks there are risks in making a wrong choice

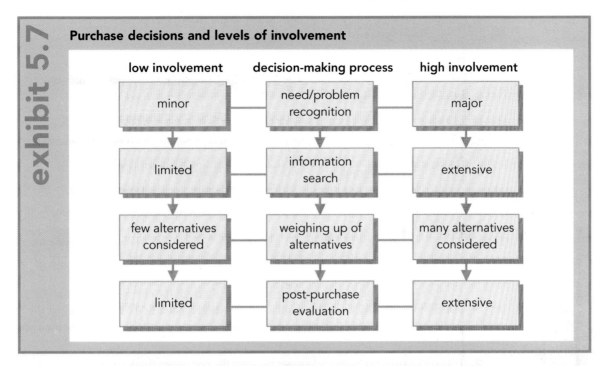

exhibit 5.7

Purchase decisions and levels of involvement

low involvement	decision-making process	high involvement
minor	need/problem recognition	major
limited	information search	extensive
few alternatives considered	weighing up of alternatives	many alternatives considered
limited	post-purchase evaluation	extensive

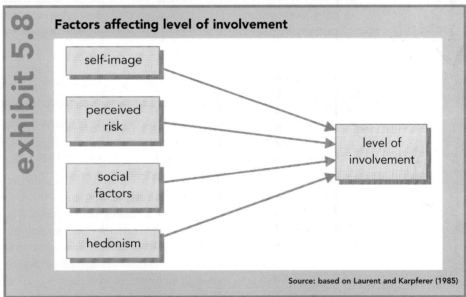

exhibit 5.8

Factors affecting level of involvement

self-image → level of involvement
perceived risk → level of involvement
social factors → level of involvement
hedonism → level of involvement

Source: based on Laurent and Karpferer (1985)

(usually financial risks because the product is expensive) then involvement levels are likely to be higher.

3. *Social factors*: where the consumer thinks that a purchase may affect their social acceptability to others, for example being seen in the right nightclub, then involvement levels are likely to be higher.

4. *Hedonism*: where the consumer thinks that the purchase may be capable of delivering a high degree of pleasure (e.g., a holiday), then involvement levels are likely to be higher.

Thus the buying situation, level of involvement and perceived differences between products will all impact on the type of buying behaviour. Four major types of buyer behaviour may be seen in Exhibit 5.9. These are outlined below.

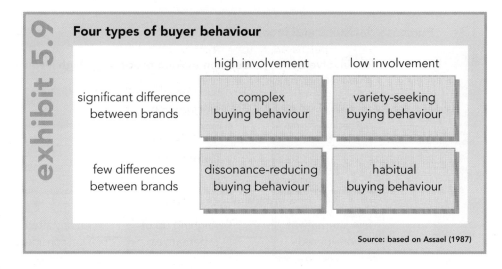

exhibit 5.9

Four types of buyer behaviour

	high involvement	low involvement
significant difference between brands	complex buying behaviour	variety-seeking buying behaviour
few differences between brands	dissonance-reducing buying behaviour	habitual buying behaviour

Source: based on Assael (1987)

1. *Complex buying behaviour*: consumers will move through the complex decision-making process by collecting knowledge and learning (covered later in the chapter) about the product category; from this, they develop beliefs, and then attitudes, about the product type before making a decision to purchase.

2. *Dissonance-reducing buying behaviour*: because the consumer thinks there is little differences between brands, consumers will collect information about a product category by shopping around to reduce post-purchase dissonance, but are likely to make a decision to purchase relatively quickly.

3. *Variety-seeking buying behaviour*: marketers attempt to encourage variety seeking in terms of attempting to get the consumer to switch to their product through lower prices and sales promotion (e.g. free samples through your letterbox).

4. *Habitual buying behaviour*: market leaders will try to stimulate consistent repeat purchases by dominating shelf space in supermarkets and avoiding substitution (i.e., consumers buying alternatives) because of stock-outs (e.g., salt, pepper, sugar).

Marketers need to be aware of the level of involvement that consumers generally have in relation to their products. With high-involvement products, marketers need to understand how consumers gather and evaluate information. Consumers will be actively searching for lots of information, and marketers need to provide it in a format that these consumers can study at their own pace (e.g., newspapers, magazine adverts).

With low-involvement products, consumers are often passive in their information search. They do not actively search for information in these types of situations, so marketers attempt to create, and increase, awareness of their product and to reinforce its positive attributes. Television is often used to advertise low-involvement products because of the opportunity this provides for repetition and reinforcement, and because of the large amount of people who, potentially, will see the advert (think about how many people watch, say, *Coronation Street*).

Think of three items from each of the following categories that you have purchased, or used, recently:

▶ a food or snack item that you purchase regularly

▶ an expensive item such as a TV or CD player

▶ an emergency or distress purchase.

For each of these, make notes on the following:

▶ How did the need arise?

▶ How long did it take to make a decision?

▶ How many alternatives did you consider?

▶ How did you choose between them?

▶ Was it the sort of purchase or consumption your friends would make?

▶ Would you say the purchase was a high- or low-involvement product? Why?

INFLUENCES ON CONSUMER BUYER BEHAVIOUR

Having looked at the consumer buyer decision process, and the different types of consumer buying decisions, the next section of this chapter will look at the internal and external factors that may influence these. First, internal factors will be looked at.

Internal influences

Marketers recognize that, although there are discernible segments, or groups, of customers with common features, these are made up of individuals with their own, unique characteristics. The next section of this chapter looks at what these characteristics are and how they affect individuals.

Personality

Personality is a person's distinguishing psychological characteristics, which lead them to respond in particular ways. Personality consists of all the features, behaviours and experience that make individuals unique and distinctive. It is often described in terms of personality traits, such as dominance, sociability, introvert or extrovert.

Therefore, marketers attempt to identify and define personality traits in terms of target segments through lifestyle or **psychographic segmentation**. For example, personality is often related to self-image or concept. One of the fundamentals of self-image is that a person's possessions (e.g., clothes, books, CDs) reflect their identity. Think of the number of times you have looked at a person's CD collection or browsed their bookshelf and then formed an opinion of that individual.

Very often, brands are described in terms of their **brand personality**. If the following brands were people, what personality would you associate with them?

▶ Nike

▶ Inland Revenue

▶ Virgin Airlines

▶ Next

▶ Gap

These girls almost certainly share certain personality traits and belong to a particular social group

Perception

Two people seeing the same advertisement may react to it differently because they perceive the situation differently. Even the same individual may perceive the same advertisement differently at different times. Imagine how you would react to an advert for a snack when you are hungry and compare that to when you have just eaten.

perception
the process by which people select, organize and interpret sensory stimulation (sounds, visions, smell, touch) into a meaningful picture of the world

Perception, therefore, is the process by which people select, organize and interpret sensory stimulation (sounds, visions, smell, touch) into a meaningful picture of the world. There are three main processes that lead to the formation of individual perceptions.

Selective attention is the process by which stimuli are assessed and non-meaningful stimuli, or those that are inconsistent with our beliefs or experiences, are screened out. This has major implications from a marketing perspective. For example, it is estimated that the average person is exposed to 1500 advertisements per day. Only 5–25 per cent of these advertisements catch the attention of the individual, the rest are screened out. Marketers use various techniques (such as colours, contrasting backgrounds and foregrounds, centre of vision) to ensure their advertisements are given attention.

Selective distortion occurs when consumers distort or change the information they receive to suit their beliefs and attitudes. **Information framing** refers to the ways in which information is presented to people to ensure selective distortion does, or does not, happen. For example, in most of Europe we associate blue with cool and red with hot. Packaging takes advantage of our selective distortion in its use of these colours (think about different flavours of tortilla chips). A famous cat food advert stated that 8 out of 10 cat owners preferred a particular brand. The impact of this is greater than the statement that 2 out of 10 cat owners did not prefer it.

Selective retention refers to the way consumers retain only a small number of messages in their memory. Consumers tend to remember messages that support their existing beliefs and attitudes.

Thus perception and memory are closely associated with learning.

Learning

Learning relates to changes in an individual's behaviour arising from their experiences. Marketers are keen for consumers to learn from promotion so that they know which product to buy and why. Learning can take place in a number of ways (see Exhibit 5.10).

exhibit 5.10

Types of learning

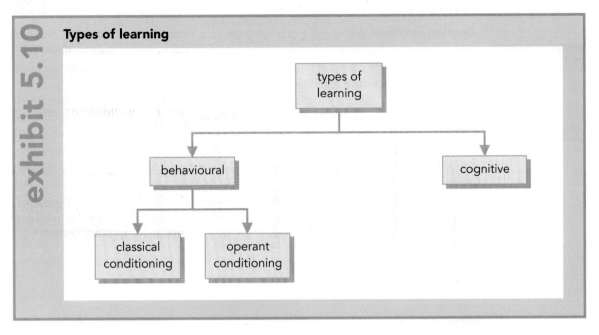

insight

Pavlov's dogs

At the dogs' mealtimes, Pavlov rang a bell. The dogs learnt to associate the bell (the stimulus) with food. Their response was to salivate. After a while, they always salivated on hearing the bell – even if no food was forthcoming. At a more sophisticated level, marketers often use humour in advertising as humour evokes pleasure and the advertisers are hoping this will be associated with their products. An example of this would be the 'Lynx Effect' (see Exhibit 5.11).

exhibit 5.11

The classical conditioning approach to influencing product attitudes

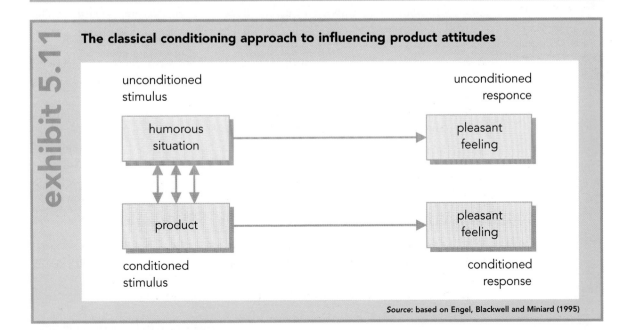

Source: based on Engel, Blackwell and Miniard (1995)

Classical conditioning is the process of using an established relationship between a **stimulus** and a **response** to evoke or teach the same response to a different stimulus. This was famously demonstrated by the experiment carried out by Pavlov on his dogs (see 'insight').

Operant or instrumental conditioning

operant conditioning

(instrumental conditioning) the learner's response produces a reinforcing stimulus

Operant conditioning also requires a link between a **stimulus** and a **response**. However, with operant conditioning, the stimulus that results in the highest reward is the stimulus that is learnt. There are ways to increase the likelihood of a specific response and such things are termed positive reinforcement.

While classical conditioning is useful in explaining how consumers may learn simple kinds of behaviour, operant conditioning is much more useful in determining more complex, goal desired behaviour.

For example, the *Financial Times* (*FT*) sells its paper to students for 20p instead of 85p. The reduced-rate *FT*s are distributed on campus and, because it is at a reduced rate, students purchase it (desired response) and because it has desirable properties (i.e., may help with their studies) it is thought useful (positive reinforcement) and the likelihood of it being purchased again increases (see the first diagram in Exhibit 5.12). Likewise, negative reinforcement and punishment may also be used.

exhibit 5.12

Three types of operant conditioning

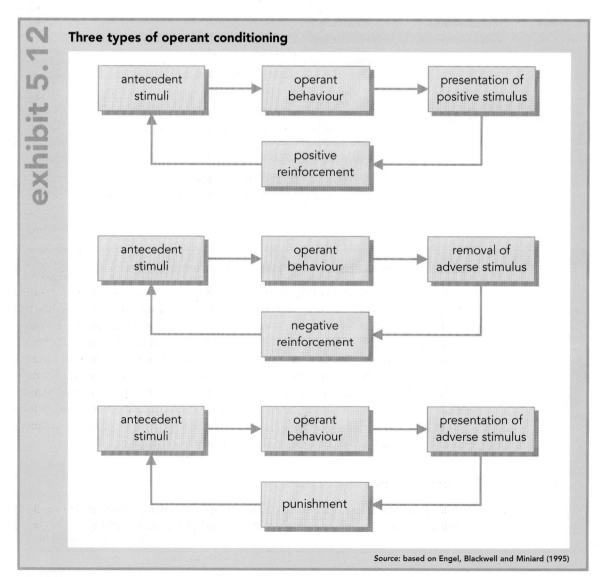

Source: based on Engel, Blackwell and Miniard (1995)

cognitive learning

active learning using complex mental processing of information

Cognitive learning involves the complex mental processing of information rather than emphasizing the importance of external reward and repetition. It may include rote learning (where two concepts are associated with each other without conditioning) or vicarious learning, which involves learning from others without direct experiences or reward.

Motivation and values

Motivation is about the complex relationship between needs, drives and goals. A motive is a need that is sufficiently pressing to direct the person to seek satisfaction of that need. According to Maslow, these needs can be placed in a hierarchy in terms of their relative importance (see Exhibit 5.13).

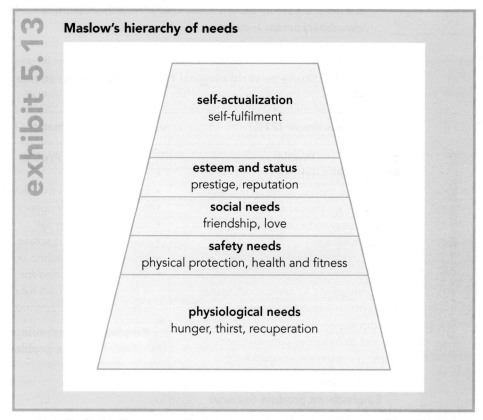

exhibit 5.13

Maslow's hierarchy of needs

self-actualization
self-fulfilment

esteem and status
prestige, reputation

social needs
friendship, love

safety needs
physical protection, health and fitness

physiological needs
hunger, thirst, recuperation

An individual will try to satisfy the most important needs of survival first (the bottom row). When these needs are met, they will stop being a motivator and the individual will then try to satisfy the next most important need represented by the next level in the hierarchy. For example, an individual who is starving will have no interest in designer clothes.

An understanding of the motives that drive consumers to purchase products is important because those motives determine the criteria by which consumers choose which products, or brands, to purchase, and thus how the market may be segmented. For example, consider the purchase of a mobile phone. While some people's primary motive may be to be contactable in an emergency, others may consider it an important tool for socializing or even a status symbol. Advertising would need to take this into account.

Attitudes and beliefs

Attitudes and beliefs are acquired through the experience of doing things and the resultant learning process. A **belief** is a thought that a person holds about something, usually based on knowledge, opinion or faith. Beliefs are important to marketers because beliefs about certain products or brands may affect a consumer's choice criteria.

An **attitude** describes a person's consistently favourable or unfavourable evaluation, feelings and tendencies towards an object or idea. From a marketing perspective, this attitude may be directed at a product or brand (i.e. the object) and thus will be reflected in their behaviour (i.e., whether they purchase the product or not).

Williams (1981) suggests attitude comprises three components: cognitive, affective and conative. The cognitive attitude relates to beliefs about a product; the affective attitude relates to positive and negative feelings associated with the product; the conative attitude relates to the link with behaviour (thus attitude X is likely to lead to behaviour Y). It is this link between attitude and behaviour that is of prime interest to the marketer. The example in Exhibit 5.14 is an illustration of this. It relates marketing strategy to people's attitudes towards technological change.

exhibit 5.14

An example of attitude to technological change and proposed marketing strategy based on this

Embracer (27%)	Pragmatist (22%)
Profile	**Profile**
• usually thirtysomething	• caring
• goes to the gym and live sports events	• keeps an eye on the elderly neighbours
• reads lifestyle magazines	• organizes charity collections
• rarely does own housework or goes to the supermarket	• no time to watch TV
• rarely cares about other people's feelings	• concerned about screen violence
• *uses technology as fashion accessory*	• *does not flash technology credentials*
• *fills trendy warehouse flat with gadgets and gizmos*	• *the Internet is good for jam recipes and a computer is good for organizing the accounts for the community hall*
• *the first to have the palmtop, wide-screen TV, satellite navigation*	
• *regularly surfs the Internet*	**Emphasis on technology as a tool to solve problems**
Emphasis on product features	
Traditionalist (15%)	Resistor (36%)
Profile	**Profile**
• adheres to old-fashioned values	• watches TV and videos
• believes everyone should put something back into the community	• likely to smoke
• spends weekends in museums	• reads tabloids
• happy and self-confident	• likely to lead a non-healthy lifestyle (does not like 'foreign food')
• *sees little need for gizmos and gadgets*	• little time for charities
Emphasis on reinforcing traditional values such as how technology can be used to stay in touch with friends and families	• *refuses to believe that new technology should or could change his/her life patterns*
	Do not target!

Source: a survey conducted by Leeds University and Ogilvy & Mather Market Research Agents

External influences

Having examined how the consumer buyer decision process may be influenced by internal factors, this section looks at the external factors that may influence this process.

Culture

culture

the set of basic values, perceptions, wants and behaviour learnt by a member of society from family and other institutions

Culture manifests itself through art, language, literature, music and religion. As a child grows up in a society, he or she is provided with a framework within which he or she is able to develop society's beliefs, value systems and cultural norms (see Exhibit 5.15).

exhibit 5.15

Elements of culture

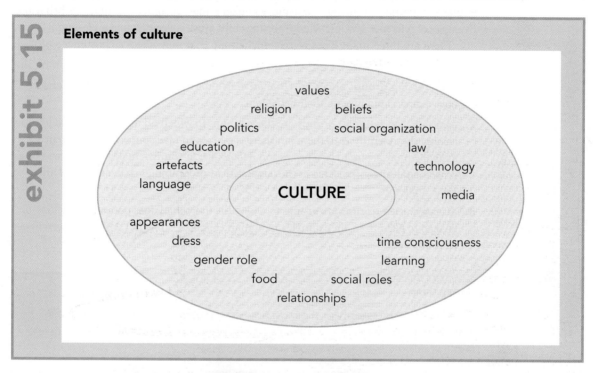

CULTURE

values
religion   beliefs
politics   social organization
education   law
artefacts   technology
language
                         media
appearances
dress   time consciousness
gender role   learning
food   social roles
relationships

Reference groups: *Friends* are an aspirant group for many

Within a culture, there will be subcultures. A subculture is a group of people with shared value systems based on common life experiences and situations. These shared value systems may be based on ethnic origin, geographic areas and religion. Subcultures often form very important market segments.

For example, MTV has a global format that appeals to youth culture whether the young people are watching the station in the UK, Hong Kong, India or the USA.

Reference groups

Reference groups are the groups that an individual belongs to or aspires to. These may be formal or informal groupings, and may influence the consumer's attitude to behaviour. Examples of reference groups include sporting clubs, work colleagues and professional bodies.

There are three main types of reference group that may affect a consumer's attitude and purchasing behaviour:

1. **membership groups** are groups that an individual already belongs to and therefore have a direct influence on their behaviour

2. **aspirant (aspirational) groups** are those groups to which an individual would like to belong; they identify with them but there is no face-to-face contact – an amateur footballer may aspire to be a professional footballer, a young female may aspire to be a professional singer (reflected in the popularity of programmes such as *Pop Idol* and *Fame Academy*)

3. **disassociative groups** are groups to which the individual does not want to belong or be seen to belong; so, for example, an upmarket shopper may not wish to be seen in a discount store.

---

crmfocus

Harley riders

A Harley-Davidson is perhaps the most distinctive motorcycle in the world – and it inspires extreme devotion. If you own a Harley, you are a member of an elite club and this is a feeling the company recognizes and fosters.

Visits its website (www.harley-davidson.com or www.harley-davidson.co.uk) or one of its other international sites, and see how it builds that community feeling. The first page is the 'Harley-Davidson experience', which includes welcoming information and tips for new riders. There are sections where you can post your own photos – even build up an online photo album of you, your friends and, of course, your bikes. You can join HOG (the Harley Owners Group) and so get access to special information and invitations to join in at special events.

Harley owners, and would-be owners, are a privileged group.

Reference groups may influence consumers in at least three ways:

1. they expose the consumer to new behaviours and lifestyles (remember freshers' week!)

2. they may influence the consumer's self-concept (e.g. they want to be accepted and fit in with a particular group)

3. they may create pressures to conform that may impact on product or brand choice.

How important a reference group is to a consumer will vary depending on the nature of the product. It tends to be most important for **conspicuous purchases**. A product is conspicuous if:

▶ it is exclusive and therefore noticeable; many designer brands will fall into this product category (e.g. Rolex, La Coste)

▶ it is consumed in the public domain and other consumers may see it; for example, drinking a particular brand of bottled beer in a nightclub.

Exhibit 5.16 shows how group influence may affect brand choice for four types of product.

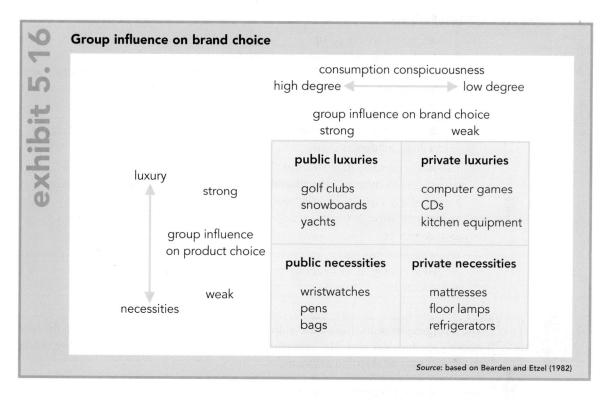

exhibit 5.16

Group influence on brand choice

consumption conspicuousness
high degree ←——————→ low degree

group influence on brand choice
strong   weak

	strong	**weak**
public luxuries	**private luxuries**
golf clubs	computer games
snowboards	CDs
yachts	kitchen equipment
public necessities	**private necessities**
wristwatches	mattresses
pens	floor lamps
bags	refrigerators

luxury
strong

group influence
on product choice

weak
necessities

Source: based on Bearden and Etzel (1982)

Family

The influence of family members – whether nuclear or extended, single- or two-parent – may strongly influence a buyer's behaviour over a whole lifetime. Family influence can generally be divided into one of two categories: family orientation influence and family procreation influence.

Family orientation influence is the influence parents exert over their children even when there is no longer any interaction. This may be at a general level in terms of values and attributes towards product types (e.g. whether you view a car as a status symbol or as a functional product to get you from A to B), or at a more specific level (e.g. continuing to purchase the same brand of coffee as your parents did).

Family procreation influence consists of the more direct influences on daily buying behaviour that family members exert upon one another. This is continually changing with changing social conditions and working patterns. For example, the increase in the number of working mothers has meant the evolution of 'latchkey kids' (i.e. children who arrive home from school before their parents arrive home from work and who prepare a snack or tea for themselves).

Consumer buying roles

Within groups such as families, or even student households, there is often a combination of individuals and roles that make up the **decision-making unit (DMU)** (see Exhibit 5.17). A consumer may fulfil one or more roles in terms of the purchase decision.

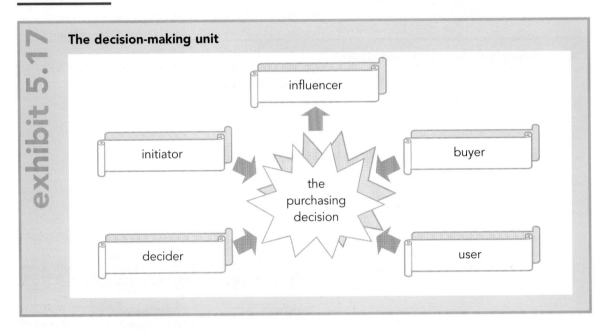

exhibit 5.17

The decision-making unit

The DMU may be defined as all the individuals who participate in and influence the consumer's purchase decision. The individual roles (although an individual may have one or more roles) may be identified as follows.

▶ The *initiator* is the person who initially suggests, or thinks of, the idea of buying a particular product. It may be a friend, parent or work colleague. For example, a child may suggest a trip to Disneyland, Paris.

▶ The *influencer* is the person who influences the buyer by offering advice or an opinion. Again, it may be a friend or relative or it may be a salesperson. For example, Dad's feelings about France may influence the trip.

▶ The *decider* is the person who actually makes the decision whether to buy the product. Mum's vacation time may be limited by her schedule as a lawyer so she decides when, and where, the family goes.

▶ The *buyer* is the person who actually makes the purchase. For example, Dad may telephone the reservations office at Disneyland, Paris.

▶ The *user* is the person who actually uses or consumes the product. For example, the whole family would consume the Disneyland, Paris, experience.

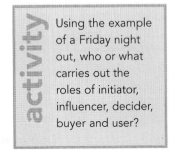

activity

Using the example of a Friday night out, who or what carries out the roles of initiator, influencer, decider, buyer and user?

Pester power

The pre-school market is estimated to be worth a round £4.3 billion a year and, if you add those areas where children influence their parents' purchases the most (areas such as clothing, food, leisure activities, holidays, etc.) that estimate rises to up to £30 billion a year. The Advertising Code of Practice has been tightened in an attempt to prevent advertisers from directly encouraging children to ask for things. However, think about the number of collectable toys, usually based on cartoon films, that are offered by fast-food restaurants, or tins of spaghetti in the shape of children's favourite characters such as the Tweenies or Postman Pat. The Market Research Panel suggests that the five biggest causes of pester power are:

1. TV advertising

2. free promotional gifts

3. attractive packaging

4. licensed characters (e.g. Postman Pat)

5. in-store samples.

THE CONSUMER BUYER DECISION PROCESS FOR NEW PRODUCTS

Having examined the stages buyers go through when purchasing products, and who and what may influence them, we will now explore how consumers approach the purchase of new products or services.

A new product or service may be defined as a good, service or idea that is perceived by potential customers as being new (see also Chapter 7). Consumers go through a mental process (see Exhibit 5.18) in deciding whether to adopt or use a new product.

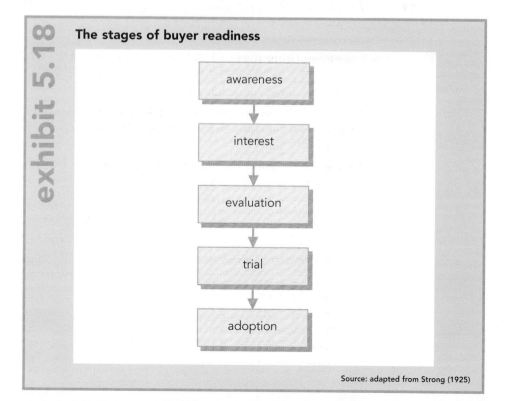

exhibit 5.18

The stages of buyer readiness

awareness

interest

evaluation

trial

adoption

Source: adapted from Strong (1925)

▶ *Awareness*: the consumer becomes aware of the product but does not have any information about it.

▶ *Interest*: the consumer actively seeks information about the new product if they think it may be of use to them.

▶ *Evaluation*: the consumer decides whether or not they should try the new product.

▶ *Trial*: the consumer tries the new product on a small scale to judge its value.

▶ *Adoption*: the consumer decides to make full and regular use of the new product.

Marketers need to plan how they can aid potential consumers to move through the various steps by, for example, providing information or having a trial or testing plan.

Individual differences and new products

Individuals differ in their willingness to try new products. How willing individuals are to try new products also varies according to the nature of the new product. For example, while some people may be willing to try new food they may not be so willing to adopt broadband or even Internet usage. This has led marketers to classify consumers into a number of product adoption categories according to a **product adopters model** (see Exhibit 5.19), as follows.

▶ *Innovators* (2.5 per cent) are consumption pioneers who are prepared to try new ideas.

▶ *Early adopters* (13.5 per cent) are often opinion leaders within their reference groups. Opinion leaders are those individuals who have special skills, knowledge, personality or other characteristics, and exert influence on others (e.g. DJs in the club scene),

▶ The *early majority* (34 per cent) are quite adventurous in their decision-making and, as a result, adopt new ideas before the average person.

▶ The *late majority* (34 per cent) are more sceptical. They adopt new products only after most have tried them.

▶ *Laggards* (16 per cent) are conservative and suspicious of change. They adopt a new product only when it has become something of a tradition in itself.

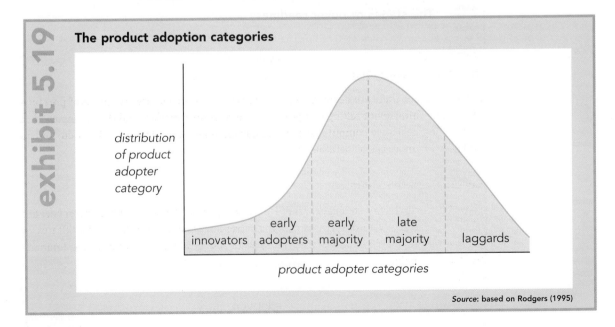

exhibit 5.19

The product adoption categories

distribution of product adopter category

innovators | early adopters | early majority | late majority | laggards

product adopter categories

Source: based on Rodgers (1995)

Marketers need to research and identify the characteristics of the various groups and tailor their marketing mix and, in particular, the message accordingly.

Having looked at consumer markets, the next section will look at the way organizations purchase products.

TYPES OF ORGANIZATION AND THE PRODUCTS THEY PURCHASE

The business to business (b2b) market is far larger than the business to consumer (b2c) market. Consider the purchase of a car: the b2c transaction is only the final stage of a number of b2b purchases that make up the **supply chain** involved in producing and distributing the product (see Chapter 9 for examples).

Although there are many similarities between the b2c and b2b markets, there are also a number of key differences. This section of the chapter looks at organizational customers and how their buying decisions are made, who may be involved and what criteria they may use.

Organizations purchase a diverse and complex range of goods and services. These include:

▶ utility services (such as water, electricity, gas)

▶ raw materials

▶ component parts

▶ capital items (such as buildings and machines)

▶ MRO goods (maintenance, repair and operations materials)

▶ professional services (such legal and financial advice).

(See Chapter 2 for more on organization types and the markets they serve.)

CHARACTERISTICS OF ORGANIZATIONAL MARKETS

There are many similarities between business markets and consumer markets. However, there are a number of key differences between the two types of market. These are now explored in more detail.

Market structure

Industrial concentration

In b2b markets, there are normally fewer buyers but they are far larger in terms of purchasing power. Think about selling computers to the consumer market, and then compare that with selling dedicated computer systems to car manufacturers. There are fewer customers and they are more easily identifiable.

Geographical concentration

Some industries have a strong geographical concentration. These may have arisen because of the availability of resources (for example, steel manufacturing in Sheffield), because of political incentives (for example, EU grants) or for historical reasons (for example, financial services in London).

Nature of demand

Derived demand

All business demand is derived demand – that is, demand that ultimately comes from (or is derived from) the demand for the final product. The demand for steel panels is derived from the demand for cars, which ultimately comes from the end consumer.

Joint demand

Joint demand is demand that is linked with the demand for other organizational products. So, the demand for tyres is linked to the demand for cars.

Inelastic demand

Many organizations have inelastic demand. Inelastic demand is where the total demand for a product is largely unaffected by price changes, especially in the short run. For example, the tyres on a jumbo jet's wheels are one small component of the overall cost of the finished product. A fall in the price of tyres will not affect the overall demand for jumbo jets.

Fluctuating demand

Demand for goods and services tends to fluctuate more rapidly in b2b markets.

The complexity of the buying process

Business purchases are often more complex than those of consumers. They often involve:

▶ larger sums of money
▶ more complex technical specifications
▶ more people at different levels, from different functions within different organizations.

For this reason, the business buying process tends to be more formalized and often involves professional purchasers who adopt sophisticated purchasing systems. Very often, organizations will have policies and guidelines (e.g. a purchasing policy) as to whether purchasing should be centralized or decentralized, and from a single supplier (single sourcing) or a number of suppliers (multiple sourcing). All these policies will have advantages and disadvantages.

ORGANIZATIONAL BUYING SITUATIONS

There are three main types of buying situation. These may be viewed on a continuum ranging from a straight rebuy, through modified rebuy, to new task at the other end of the scale (see Exhibit 5.20)

▶ **Straight rebuy** is where the buyer routinely reorders a product or service without any change to the order whatsoever to the extent that, in some cases, there may be an automatic (perhaps computerized) reordering system. These products are usually low risk, frequently purchased and inexpensive items (for example, products such as electricity or gas).

▶ **Modified rebuy** is where the buyer wants to modify an element of the rebuy. This may be the product specification (such as colour, size or technical specification) or the price or the terms (such as delivery time) of the purchase.

exhibit 5.20

Types of organizational buying situations

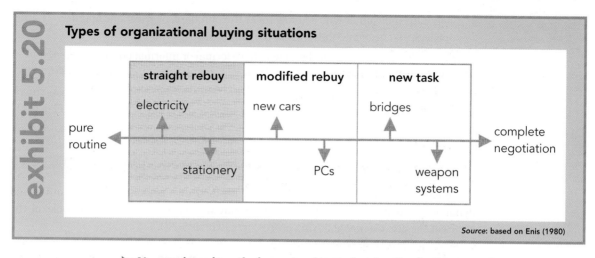

Source: based on Enis (1980)

▶ **New task** is where the buyer purchases a product for the first time. This is the most complex category of purchase. Examples of this may include infrequently purchased, high-risk, expensive products such as computer systems or the sourcing of a new raw material supplier.

THE BUYING CENTRE

Similar to the consumer DMU (decision-making unit) the **buying centre** comprises all the individuals that participate in the business buying decision process. The buying centre will vary depending on the nature of the purchase.

The individuals within the buying centre may fulfil one or more roles (see Exhibit 5.21), as outlined below.

exhibit 5.21

The organizational buying centre

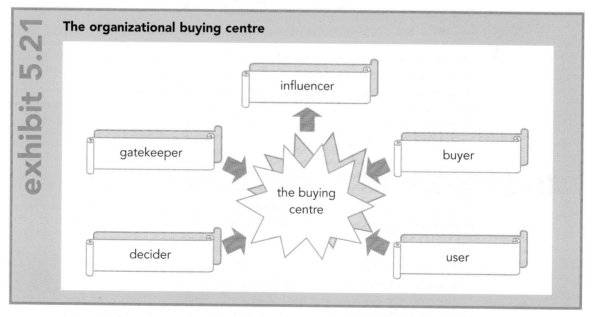

▶ *Users*: members of the organization who will actually use the purchase. For example, machine operators or secretaries using computers.

▶ *Influencers*: individuals whose opinions may contribute to the final choice of purchase. Their influence may be related to their expertise (e.g. an IT specialist) or it could be of a more informal and/or personal nature.

▶ *Buyers*: the individuals who actually make the purchase, or select and approve suppliers, and negotiate the terms of the purchase.

▶ *Deciders*: individuals (e.g. the boss) who have formal or informal powers to select or approve the final suppliers.

▶ *Gatekeepers*: individuals who have some control over the decision-making process thus helping the flow of information. These may include buyers, technical personnel (e.g. IT experts) or secretaries.

THE ORGANIZATIONAL BUYING PROCESS

The buying process will involve individuals with their own personal agenda, motives and dynamics. Now it has been established who may take part, the next section looks at the stages of the organizational buying process (see Exhibit 5.22).

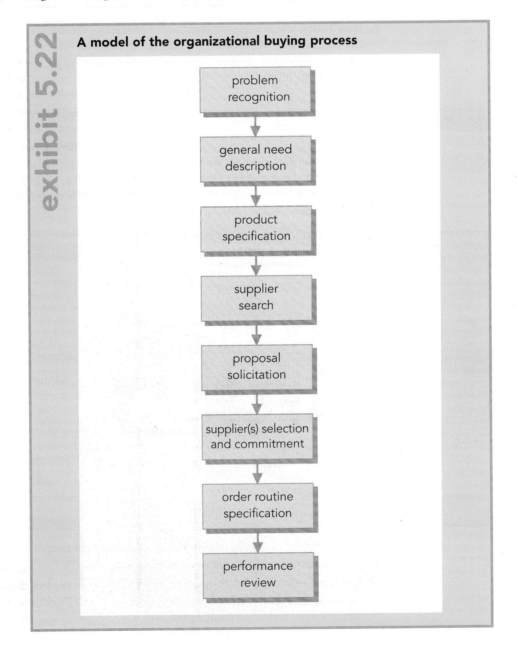

exhibit 5.22

A model of the organizational buying process

problem recognition

↓

general need description

↓

product specification

↓

supplier search

↓

proposal solicitation

↓

supplier(s) selection and commitment

↓

order routine specification

↓

performance review

Problem recognition

An individual, or group, identifies a problem or need that may be satisfied by acquiring a specific good or service. This may be an entirely routine operation, such as reordering stationery, or a much more complex operation, such as purchasing a capital item.

For example, if an organization decides to launch a new product, then it may require new manufacturing systems or new component parts for it. External factors may come from the trade press, exhibitions or a sales representative from a supplier's competitor.

General need description

Having identified a need, the organization describes the general characteristics and qualities of the required product or service. This may require external assistance from, for example, consultants if the product is of a technical nature.

Product specification

The buying organization selects and specifies the attributes that the technical product should have. This is very different to consumer markets, where much of the enjoyment of shopping is not knowing what is required. The product specification will often incorporate aspects such as colour, material quality, performance levels and its compatibility with other components.

Supplier search

The buyer organization searches for the best vendor (selling organization) to supply the product to the specification requested. This may be done using trade directives or brochures kept on file, exhibitions or, increasingly, the Internet.

Many business customers visit trade exhibitions to find new products or suppliers

Proposal solicitation

The next stage is for the buyer to invite suitable prospective suppliers to submit proposals. These proposals may range from catalogues to formal presentations and substantial written proposals.

Supplier(s) selection and commitment

The buying organization will then review the proposals from the prospective vendors and, based on specified criteria, select one to deliver the product or service. The selection criteria usually revolve around attributes such as delivery times, product quality, prices, and possibly even honest corporate behaviour. Companies have, historically, used a number of suppliers as this enables them to obtain price concessions. Increasingly, companies are working more closely with a smaller number of suppliers and, as a result, expecting preferential treatment (see the section on relationship marketing in Chapter 1).

Order routine specification

The buying organization finalizes the order in terms of product specification, quantities, delivery times, price, etc., and forwards it to the supplying organization(s).

Performance review

The buying organization assesses the performance of the supplying organization against specific criteria, and decides whether to continue using them as a supplier.

ORGANIZATIONAL PURCHASE CRITERIA

Organizational buyer behaviour criteria are much more rational, functional and objective than consumer criteria. Criteria such as price, conformity to product specification, quality, reliability and customer service levels, and continuity of supply are likely to be used. However, organizations are composed of individuals who have their own personal goals and motives. Therefore, more intangible, or implicit, criteria may be important. Such criteria may include preferential treatment. This in turn may lead to professional relationships between individuals within, and between, organizations.

crmfocus

Developing a relationship

In recent years, much emphasis has been placed on the importance of buyer–seller relationships and how these may be a source of competitive advantage. The emphasis is on long-term, collaborative relationships between a small number of suppliers and customers. Building trust between organizations is essential to maintaining such relationships.

Ford (1980) proposed the following model of relationship development:

▶ *Pre-relationship stage*: this stage involves the buyer evaluating potential new suppliers.

▶ *Early stage*: potential suppliers are in contact with buyers to negotiate trial deliveries.

crmfocus

▶ *Development stage*: deliveries of the product increase as trust and understanding develops between the buyer and the seller.

▶ *Long-term stage*: the buyer and seller are mutually dependent.

▶ *Final stage*: the relationship has become 'institutionalized'.

Decisions need to be made as to the level of relational development required, since it is clearly a waste of valuable resources to invest in unwanted or unprofitable relationships. Technical support, increased access to expertise, better service levels and risk reduction are some of the benefits to the two organizations that need to be considered.

SUMMARY

Markets are made up of individual people and organizations. In consumer markets (b2c), these people vary enormously in terms of gender, age, income, education, personality, perceptions and attitudes, and many other factors. Marketers need to understand the processes that consumers go through when making purchase decisions: the stages they go through and the criteria they may use. These purchase decisions are influenced by internal factors, such as motivation, attitude and perception, as well as external factors such as family, friends and culture.

Organizational (b2b) buying is much larger and more complex than b2c buying. Organizations vary in terms of size, culture, purchasing policy and many other factors. Organizational buying tends to be much more objective and rational than consumer decision-making to the extent that it may be over-bureaucratic. It is important for marketers to understand the processes that businesses go through and who is involved in purchase decisions.

Before developing a marketing strategy, all these factors must be understood and taken into account. Without this understanding, the marketing organization is unlikely to exert as much influence as it might have during its customers' decision-making processes.

Challenges reviewed

Now that you have finished reading the chapter, look back at the challenges you were set at the beginning. Do you have a clearer idea of what's involved?

Hints:

▶ roles within the decision-making unit (DMU)

▶ product adoption categories

▶ influences on consumer buying behaviour

▶ organizational decision-making unit (buying centre)

▶ organizational buying process.

READING AROUND

website
Mintel provides a range of market research reports, many libraries subscribe to www.mintel.co.uk.
books
Pick out areas of interest in Hanna, N. and Wozniak, R. (2001) *Consumer Behaviour: An Applied Approach*, Prentice Hall.
For more on b2b, see Ford, D. (ed.) (2002) *The Business Marketing Course, Managing in Complex Networks*, John Wiley & Sons.

SELF-REVIEW QUESTIONS

1. What are the main stages of the consumer decision-making process? (see page 129)

2. List the three main types of buying situation and the types of product that might be included in each of them. (see page 134)

3. What are the four main types of consumer buyer behaviour? (see page 136)

4. What are the main types of learning processes? (see page 139)

5. Name the stages of Maslow's hierarchy of needs. (see page 141)

6. What is the difference between an attitude and a belief? (see pages 141–2)

7. List the key roles in the decision-making unit. (see page 146)

8. What are the main stages of the product adoption process? (see page 148)

9. What are the main organizational buyer types? (see page 150)

10. What are the main characteristics of organizational markets? (see page 149)

11. What are three main types of organizational buying situation? (see page 152)

12. What are the main stages of the organizational buying process? (see page 152)

MINI CASE STUDY

Read the questions, then the case material, then answer the questions.

Questions

1. What sources of information do children access in the 'information search' stage of the buyer decision process, and how can marketers optimize their roles in this while maintaining a morally correct position?

2. Who influences children?

3. How may the concept of the decision-making unit be applied to this article?

Seen and not heard?

The way children are influenced by what they see has been the subject of debate for some time. However, criticisms are not just restricted to TV sex and violence any more – parents, consumer associations and the EU are increasingly concerned about the impact that marketing may have on children. To quote Rowan Williams, the Archbishop of Canterbury, 'What can we say about a marketing culture that so openly feeds and colludes with obsession?'

The pre-school market alone is estimated to be worth around £4.3 billion a year and if you add those areas where children influence their parents' purchases (clothing, food, leisure activities, holidays, etc.), the estimate goes up to around £30 billion a year.

Marketers argue that children are more sophisticated media consumers than adults realize, and that many adults are out of touch with the lives their children lead. One term used for this is kids getting older younger (KGOY).

Dan Salem, commercial director for a media sales house, states, 'Children's media consumption is huge but children are fickle – that's the one constant thing. If you want to market to them you have to add value and you have to empower them. It's getting much harder to please them, and you have to be able to react quickly to cash in on what's cool.'

Source: based on Croft, (2003)

REFERENCES

Assael, H. (1987) *Consumer Behaviour and Marketing* (6th edn), Kent Publishing Company.

Bearden, O. and Etzel, M. (1982) Reference group influence on product and purchase decisions, *Journal of Consumer Research* 9, 185.

Croft, M. (2003) Seen and not heard, *Marketing Week* (30 Jan.), 33–5.

Enis, B.M. (1980) *Marketing Principles* (3rd edn), Scott, Foresman & Co.

Engel, J., Blackwell, R. and Miniard, P. (1995) *Consumer Behaviour*, The Dryden Press, 153.

Festinger, L. (1957) A theory of cognitive dissonance, in Sheth, J., Mittal, B. and Newman, B. (1999) *Customer Behavior: Consumer Behavior and Beyond*, The Dryden Press.

Ford, D. (1980) The development of buyer–seller relationships in industrial markets, *European Journal of Marketing* 14(516), 339–54.

Laurent, G. and Kapferer, J. (1985) Measuring consumer involvement profiles, *Journal of Marketing Research* 12 (Feb.), 41–53.

Rodgers, E.M. (1995) *Diffusion of Innovations* (4th edn), Free Press.

Smith, P.R. (1993) *Marketing Communications: An Integrated Approach*, Kogan Page.

Strong, E.K. (1925) *The Psychology of Selling*, McGraw-Hill.

Wilkie, W. (1990) *Consumer Behavior*, John Wiley & Sons.

Williams, K.C. (1981) *Behavioural Aspects of Marketing*, Heinemann Professional Publishing.

MARKETING RESEARCH

BY LEN TIU WRIGHT

MARKETING RESEARCH CHALLENGES

The following are illustrations of the types of decision that marketers have to take or issues they face. *You aren't expected to know how to deal with the challenges now*; just bear them in mind as you read the chapter and see what you can find that helps.

▶ You run a travel agency. You have found a fabulous hotel in the Swiss Alps that you have never used before. However, the hotel wants to know how many rooms to reserve for you next season. What information do you need to work this out, and how will you collect it?

▶ Your company's skateboard sales have been falling steadily over the last two years. How would you make a case to a sceptical managing director that the expense of research into the causes of the fall would be worthwhile?

▶ The editor of *Marketing for Men*, a monthly magazine read by men and women (e.g. the men's wives and girlfriends), has invited you to research the attitudes of readers to its contents. How would you do this?

▶ Your company is hoping to launch a new beer and wants to find out what would be popular across Europe. This is difficult because different European countries traditionally drink different types of beer. However, recently you have seen an Italian drinking British beer, a British man drinking French beer and a Swede drinking German beer. You need to get views from a huge number of beer drinkers to be sure you get the complete picture. It is not practical to interview every beer drinker in Europe. What could you do?

KEY CONCEPTS

market research
qualitative research
quantitative research
sampling
secondary (desk) research
marketing research process
primary (field) research
market segmentation (see Chapter 4)
targeting (see Chapter 4)
positioning (see Chapter 4)
environmental scanning (see Chapter 3)

CHAPTER OVERVIEW

- ▶ Introduction
- ▶ Types of marketing research
- ▶ Secondary (desk) research
- ▶ Primary (field) research
- ▶ Two approaches to research: qualitative and quantitative
- ▶ Commercially available research
- ▶ Quality of marketing information

- ▶ Research methods and techniques
- ▶ Forecasting and trends
- ▶ Summary
- ▶ Challenges reviewed
- ▶ Reading around
- ▶ Self-review questions
- ▶ Mini case study
- ▶ References

INTRODUCTION

Marketing research covers a broad range of activities. This is shown by the following definitions from the American Marketing Association (AMA) and the Market Research Society (MRS).

The AMA's view of marketing research is that it is an objective and systematic process (Anon. 1985; 1987). The customer is placed at the heart of marketing actions. The research process, by collecting, recording and analysing data, results in the identification and refinement of information about customers and the public that is important for marketing decisions.

66 Marketing research is the function which links the consumer, customer, and public to the market through information ... to identify and define marketing opportunities and problems; generate, refine, and evaluate marketing actions; monitor marketing performance; and improve understanding of marketing as a process ... Marketing research is the systematic gathering, recording and analyzing of data about problems relating to the marketing of goods and services. 99

(American Marketing Association)

The MRS, in the UK's definition, embraces all types of data gathering and investigations for market and social research (MRS, 1998):

66 Research is the collection and analysis of data from a sample of individuals or organisations relating to their characteristics, behaviour, attitudes, opinions or possessions ... such as consumer and industrial surveys, psychological investigations, observational and panel studies. 99

(Marketing Research Society)

Research is a planned activity. It is carried out methodically so that the results are seen as impartial and can be supported by evidence that can be validated by others. This is crucial because of the need to maintain trust and confidence between the clients (buyers of research) and agencies (providers of research studies).

TYPES OF MARKETING RESEARCH

Marketing research activities can be grouped under the following headings: product research; services research; customer research; pricing research, advertising and promotions research; sales and distribution research; and business-to-business (b2b) research.

Market research or marketing research?

What is the difference between market research and marketing research?

The phrase 'market research' is a familiar one. It has connotations of people with clipboards stopping others on the street and asking questions. Market research is usually about solving marketing problems – for example, finding out the existing and future product needs of customers. How do people use certain products and services? When they do, what are their attitudes and preferences? What are their backgrounds and lifestyle characteristics? For example, a footwear brand manufacturer might want to find out what the most popular types of shoes are and what colours people want. The company might also want to know if its type of trainers is still considered to be fashionable streetwear.

Marketing research has evolved to cover the activities of market research. It is a broad term that covers the whole body of theories and processes of research that are carried out by governments, public corporations, private-sector companies and individuals concerning what works, or does not work, with industries, organizations and customers in markets. Marketers want information to help them refine the whole of the **marketing mix**. With reference to the example of a footwear brand manufacturer, marketing research into the marketing mix will cover: competitors' prices; locations of shoe shops, which types of shoes the shops specialize in, what their footfall (number of passing customers) is; how memorable the manufacturer's latest advertising campaign is and how much a teenage customer is prepared to pay for a pair of high-fashion shoes.

This chapter is, therefore, called 'Marketing research'.

Product research

Much of product research is about testing the design concept, performance, ease of use, reliability, special features, appearance and packaging of products. Research about brand superiority in terms of qualities, higher prices and snobbery/image appeal to create unique selling propositions (USPs) with customers is important. This is because customers develop strong brand loyalties to products and their manufacturers' trading names. There are many examples of products we use daily that have been tested with customers by market researchers. Customers are asked about their preferences concerning design features for products they use daily, e.g. **consumer durables** such as cars and **FMCG** products such as toothpaste and soap. Products, or parts of products, can be evaluated through **pre-testing** and **post-testing**. Market research has helped to create new industries such as mobile phones, flat-screen monitors and games machines. Food and drinks products (see Exhibit 6.1) consistently top the list of most marketing research being commissioned, or paid for, by businesses.

post-testing
evaluating the effectiveness of a proposed marketing communication with its target audience *after* release

pre-testing
evaluating the effectiveness of a proposed marketing communication with its target audience *before* release

Services research

Services research shares many of the aspects of product research. The expansion of service industries (e.g. financial services, travel, tourism and leisure, media, public services and utilities) has generated considerable work for marketing researchers (see Exhibit 6.1). Marketing research has helped insurance companies and banks such as EGG (insurance) and First Direct (bank) to provide new services and products online (on websites) and offline (by telephone and mail). In the travel sector low-cost flights have tempted many holiday-makers from traditional large carriers to the new, lower-cost operating airlines such as easyJet, Ryanair and BMI. Customers are regularly asked for their opinions on a range of services from beauty care and therapy to second-hand book sales.

exhibit 6.1

Commissioned research

Commissioned research from client sectors	1996 (% change compared to 1995)
Food and non-alcoholic drinks	£61.3m (+12%)
Media	£39.6m (+9%)
Public services and utilities	£35.0m (+9%)
Financial services	£31.5m (+10%)
Pharmaceutical companies	£30.3m (+9%)
Health and beauty	£29.4m (+12%)
Vehicles	£27.5m (+6%)
Business and industrial	£25.9m (+17%)
Retailers	£25.9m (+40%)
Government and public bodies	£20.8m (+13%)
Household products	£16.4m (−2%)
Alcoholic drinks	£16.2m (−2%)
Travel and tourism	£14.2m (+1%)

Source: adapted from AMSO, 1997; Wright and Crimp, 2000
(Note: the Association of Market Survey Organizations (AMSO) and the Association of British Market Research Companies (ABMRC) were dissolved to form a joint body in 1998 called the British Market Research Association (BMRA)).

activity

Log on to www.amazon.co.uk (or your local Amazon site) and pick a book to buy. Find one where Amazon offers you a cheaper second-hand edition. Click through. Look at the seller ratings. What purpose do they serve? How are they arrived at? (Note: there is no need to buy anything to view these ratings. As long as you do not enter a credit card number you will not be charged.)

Customer research

Customer research is central to understanding what determines customer buying behaviour and customers' decision-making processes. Why do some customers buy and others don't? Why do some choose certain suppliers and others remain loyal to one supplier? Analysing customer behaviour and their purchasing intentions has led to a large body of knowledge, spawning the growth of consumer **lobby** groups and consumer associations with their resultant publications. Customer research includes investigating customer attitudes and preferences (i.e. how they make decisions to buy or to change to alternative products) and establishing repurchase patterns. Such customer studies are used to advise profit, and non-profit, organizations about what customers want (e.g. what products and services to provide, what innovative features to develop and how to keep customers loyal given competition from other companies). Much of customer research finds its way into academic publications and is then used by other researchers on consumer projects. These publications (e.g. the *Journal of Consumer Research* and the *Journal of Qualitative Market Research*) and commercial reports, such as Keynote and Mintel, are usually available from university libraries.

Pricing research

elasticity
a significant
response to changes
in a marketing
variable, most
commonly price;
quantity demanded
changes by a
greater percentage
than the percentage
change in price (i.e.
if the price rises, the
revenue falls)

Sales of some product types (e.g. most grocery products), are highly sensitive to price move-ments and so pricing research is important to many firms. Research tests customers' reac-tions to price changes, in-store discounts, price promotions, seasonal prices, and differences in expected price bands for different sizes, packaging and quantities. Even prestige, branded products, such as Gucci and Calvin Klein, are susceptible to price competition when there are reasonably priced quality **substitutes** available. Demand can be **elastic** when there is choice, as there is with many household cleaning products (see Chapter 10 for an expla-nation of elasticity). For many products, the manipulation of prices can be risky as a result of the competitive forces in play, so pricing research is done to establish just how much cus-tomers would be prepared to pay.

Advertising research

Advertising and promoting big brands such as Nike and Reebok is very expensive. Marketing research helps to reduce the risks and costs involved. Marketing research about customers not only uncovers the desires and needs of customers, it also provides valuable databases of customers' details, which companies such as Kaleidoscope and Sears use to **target** their mail-order offerings. Crucial marketing decisions will concern which **market segments** (see Chapter 4) they wish to reach and how best to appeal to them.

market segments
distinct parts of a
larger market –
customers and
consumers in each
segment share
similar characteristics

Sales and distribution research

supply chain
network of
businesses and
organizations
through which
goods pass to get to
their final
destination

There may be many intermediaries in a **supply chain** (e.g., in the food chain, from 'farm' to 'fork'). Sales and distribution research can discover where companies could improve their selling functions or increase the selling effectiveness of their distribution outlets, perhaps by helping distributors with promotions or providing training in the use of products. Sales and distribution research can be carried out by manufacturing companies and producers into their use of intermediaries (warehouse operators, wholesalers, insurance and financial bro-kers and agencies, retail store outlets) to find out how to get the best service for customers. Even small rural businesses, selling what they produce directly to customers, need to know how competitive their markets are and where they can make the most impact. In short, many firms require information to assist them with decisions such as: the kinds of outlets to sell through; which territories to sell in; what field supervision and training are required; and what sales information to provide. For retailers, research about sales and **distribution** is crucial to help with management decisions about siting new stores, in-store layouts, car parking, stock quantities, deliveries, etc. So companies appoint research agencies to investi-gate their selling activities and the effectiveness of sales outlets and distribution networks.

Business-to-business research

In business markets products and services are bought either for use and consumption or for resale in the commercial, industrial and/or **public sector**. This is a vast area because it involves all organizations that buy and sell from each other, from one-person companies to huge **multinationals** and government corporations (see Exhibit 6.1 for the amount of rev-enue earned by research agencies). Business-to-business (b2b) research, as the name sug-gests, involves not only commercial and industrial research, but also government institutions such as local authorities and hospitals, which are large buyers and users of goods and serv-ices. Former public utilities that were privatized, e.g. the gas and electricity companies, frequently conduct b2b research with their industrial and commercial customers. Business-to-business research has continued to grow as these sectors have expanded.

The scope of world research activity is estimated by the European Society for Opinion and Market Research (ESOMAR, 1998) to have been worth more than €10.4 billion in 1997. The 15 EU countries accounted for a sales turnover of over €4.314 million, against a total European figure of €4.688 million. The USA tops the list as the country with the greatest spend in market research, with Japan in fifth place (see Exhibit 6.2).

exhibit 6.2

Value of market research data expenditure (in millions of US dollars)

Top six largest markets	1998
United States	4935.1
United Kingdom	1525.0
Germany	1326.1
France	906.1
Japan	893.7
Italy	414.7

Source: *Marketing News*

SECONDARY (DESK) RESEARCH

Desk research is the search for good-quality **secondary data** that have been validated and are now published for use by others. Such information is freely accessible in libraries or can be purchased from the publishers. Researchers have to be careful in acknowledging the sources used and in gaining permission from the publishers of such sources if any data are to be reproduced in their marketing research reports. The terms desk research and **secondary research** have become interchangeable so, for the purposes of this chapter, the term 'secondary research' will be used to embrace 'desk research' as well.

secondary data

data previously collected for other purposes that could be used in the current research task

Information about past events, and the dates they occurred, can be helpful in establishing the background of significant product and market developments. Research is about revisiting studies or topics and building on past knowledge. Desk research is important in establishing what has already been achieved so that researchers can build on information already known. There is no need to reinvent the wheel. Researchers can also use this information to help forecast future patterns or trends (assuming past and current assumptions hold). Secondary data usage has expanded as there is more and more information added year after year.

Secondary or desk research is the search for published data that are available and pertinent to the research problem at hand. The starting point is usually the internal records of market and customer information held by an organization. When there is a lack of specific data for a new market, or new types of customer, or where we need to understand the reasons for changes in the **marketing environment**, researchers will then look for alternative data sources that are external to the organizations they work for.

Researching at the British Library

crmfocus

Drowning in data

There's a story popular with marketing folk, that when Tesco first introduced its now familiar Clubcard, it produced so much more data than envisaged, it just didn't know what to do with it. This may, of course, not really be true of Tesco, but it has surely happened somewhere to some unsuspecting but enthusiastic loyalty schemer.

Over 70 per cent of Tesco's customers now have a Clubcard. Every time they use it they provide Tesco with a breakdown of their shopping – and not just Tesco shopping – the card is taken at a number of outlets including the optician, Dollond & Aitchinson. The more recently launched Nectar card is taken by an even wider range of retailers and so builds an even more complete picture. Combine this data with the **demographic** information supplied on the card application form, and you can build a detailed profile of shoppers.

The possibilities are enormous. A well-managed loyalty scheme can help a company do so much more than just promote repeat sales (important though that is). Armed with that kind of information, firms can manage the way they interact with their customers and so increase customer satisfaction and long-term profitability. For example, if Tesco has a regular customer who has the right profile for Internet shopping but who does not do it, it might want to find out why. If it can fix the issue, then it can encourage them into a better shopping pattern and, as it is unlikely that this issue is unique, it will probably pick up other new online shoppers too.

They know us so well.

External data collection involves examining books and printed materials in libraries, conducting searches by computer through databases created by other organizations (e.g. large publishers, companies, government institutions and international bodies) or buying information already collected about markets, products and customers from firms such as Mintel and the British Market Research Bureau. There is a wealth of information that can be accessed free or at least quite cheaply. For instance, anyone can carry out secondary or desk research for the names of firms in specific industries using directories such as those produced by Kompass or Dun & Bradstreet. They can access World Bank and UNESCO statistics concerning developing-world poverty, aid or wealth distribution figures in terms of per capita income levels.

Secondary data collection has its attractions:

▶ it is non-reactive – that is, it can be carried out without alerting any organization or business

▶ it is unobtrusive because it only seeks out what is already available

▶ the issue of confidentiality in the use of materials is not usually a problem (so long as copyright permission has been obtained)

▶ accountability is rarely a problem either because such published data have been vetted by previous research and reviewers; so the data collected could be used to back up one's own opinions and statements about what is known about the research problem at hand

▶ it is an economical method whose costs (e.g. travel and access) are usually known very quickly

▶ it is a speedy research method, finding existing information so that only what is not available is uncovered by the more expensive form of **field research**.

field research

(primary research) carried out specifically for the research task in question

Exhibit 6.3 gives an account of the types of data collection from internal and external sources for secondary and primary research. The provision of information from secondary (desk) research and primary (field) research underpins the activities of marketing research.

However, there are limitations to secondary data collection. Secondary data have been compiled both within and outside organizations to collect records for their own purposes. So the data collected are relevant to those organizations and might not be applicable to independent studies currently being conducted by others. The secondary data might also be out of date, depending on how many years ago they were collected. Therefore, the limitations of secondary research to find data that is relevant, up to date and easily available makes the choice of field research an appropriate one. The terms 'field research' and 'primary research' are now used interchangeably.

exhibit 6.3

Comparison of secondary and primary data collection

	Internal sources	External sources
Secondary data collection	Customer records Sales reports Retail outlet/dealer's feedback Financial figures about customers, suppliers and dealers Research and development studies Production and technical records Management reviews Marketing intelligence assessments	Newspapers and media reviews Periodicals, journals and magazines Commercial and industrial reports Government publications Trade association reports Other companies' reports
Primary data collection	Current customer feedback Current customer complaints Sales interviews and daily feedback Current delivery situation Current state of stock turnover Current feedback from marketing, discounts and promotional activity State of current production levels to keep pace with dealer and customer demand Current research and development activity to give competitive edge	Observing behaviour: – observing behaviour and situations – surveillance by electronic means Questioning respondents: – asking questions in personal interviews – asking questions by telephone – using mailed questionnaires – using computer-assisted interviewing – using video links to ask questions Carrying out experiments – carrying out product trials in a laboratory setting – carrying out trials in the field, e.g. with a sample of respondents trying a product at home or in a public place within a specified period

PRIMARY (FIELD) RESEARCH

When relevant **secondary data** are not available, information has to be gathered in the field, directly from individuals. This is known as **primary research**. Researchers always begin with secondary research as this is cheaper and usually quicker. Primary research is then used to fill in the gaps or examine findings in greater detail.

primary data

first-hand data gathered to solve a particular problem or to exploit a current opportunity

External primary research may involve dealers, suppliers, customers, trade associations, industry groups and government institutions. The information (**primary data**) gathered is useful in building up a picture of the level of satisfaction of such groups with the products and services, or of their general attitudes towards the particular organization.

There are three major forms of primary research: watching how people behave (**observation**); asking questions (**survey**); and testing (**experimentation**). Before computers were in general use, all questions were asked in person, by telephone, by fax or by post, and then recorded by hand. This was a time-consuming process. Advances in computing have made gathering, recording and analysing information much easier and quicker.

TWO APPROACHES TO RESEARCH: QUALITATIVE AND QUANTITATIVE

quantitative research

seeks numerical answers, e.g. how many people have similar characteristics and views

qualitative research

investigates people's feelings, opinions and attitudes, often using unstructured, in-depth methods

The two broad approaches to research, **quantitative** and **qualitative**, should be seen as mutually supportive. There are core strengths in both approaches that benefit research clients in terms of problem-solving and decision-making.

Qualitative research

Qualitative research allows researchers to offer their clients new or different ways of looking at problems. Unlike quantitative research, it consists of a body of research techniques that 'do not attempt to make measurements, [but] seek insights through a less structured, more flexible approach' (Birn *et al.*, 1990). It is used to 'increase understanding, expand knowledge, clarify the real issues, identify distinct behavioural groups' (Gordon and Langmaid, 1988). Qualitative research is about finding out what people think and feel. It can be **exploratory**, i.e. an attempt to find out the particular circumstances of a market and its customers. It can be unstructured, e.g. in an interview situation where the interviewees can discuss answers freely and so unearth a greater wealth of information for the researchers. It can be descriptive, as in the narratives offered in **biographical** or **phenomenological** research.

In marketing research there are many good examples of qualitative work. The most common qualitative research methods are **in-depth interviews**, **focus groups** and **consumer panels** (see below). Qualitative work takes place in most markets, including b2b, consumer, youth, financial, industrial, fast moving consumer goods (**FMCG**), pharmaceutical, retail, international, leisure, tourism and travel, and across a range of disciplines – for example, advertising, branding, customer care, design, idea generation, media, new media, new product development, and social and organizational studies (Wright and Crimp, 2000).

Creswell (1998) offers five useful views of qualitative research traditions: biography, phenomenology, **grounded theory**, **ethnography** and the **case study**.

Biography

This is the story of an individual and his or her experiences as told to a researcher or as found in documents and archived materials. The biographical tradition includes autobiographies, or life histories, and the turning points in particular individuals' lives, which are retold and assessed. Researchers will explore meanings from the recollections of individuals.

Phenomenology

This describes the lived experiences of individuals concerning a specific phenomenon or occurrence. Researchers will explore the consciousness of the human experience, i.e. how individuals have lived these experiences, in order to construct social acts or outcomes, and to find meanings from such individual experiences.

Grounded theory

This starts from the intention to generate, or to discover, a theory by studying how people interact in response to a particular phenomenon. Theoretical propositions are developed from interview data and field research. Grounded theory is often about looking at how people react in a visual way and for signs or cues in their group behaviour. It is about defining and refining categories, and revisiting the questions arising from the research repeatedly until specific, tenable propositions arise. These propositions are then developed for further research.

Ethnography

Ethnography is the description, or interpretation, of the observable and learned patterns of behaviour in a social group or setting. The researcher will immerse him/herself in a variety of ways into the culture of the group to be studied. For example, he or she might live with the community, experiencing its day-to-day life and/or pursuing one-to-one interviews with members of the group. By doing this, researchers can experience at first hand how the subjects of the study are living, working and behaving.

Case study

A case study could be about an event, an activity or individuals. A case study contains detailed in-depth information using multiple sources of information to build up a picture of individuals and their contributions to a particular situation.

Quantitative research

Quantitative research requires much larger numbers of respondents than qualitative research. Its aim is to find out how many people have similar or specific characteristics and views. If there are large numbers of respondents, a quantitative survey is used to collect the data. It would be too time consuming and costly to cover a large number of respondents with a qualitative approach. The questionnaires may be posted, faxed or e-mailed and the answers are then subjected to **multivariate analyses** using statistical computing software (e.g. **SPSS** or **Minitab**).

multivariate analysis
two or more variables are analysed at the same time

The largest type of quantitative study, and the most complete way of collecting data, is to conduct a full-scale census of the entire population. Full-scale census surveys are used by governments all over the world as aids to planning and forecasting. Each census provides a large amount of information that gives reliable statistical data about population characteristics. The heads of households, or chief income earners, in each household have to fill in the census questionnaire. The process is expensive and time consuming so population censuses are only conducted every 10 years in the UK.

It is impossible for market research organizations to draw data from every member of the country's population in the way a census does. Respondents do not have to cooperate and, anyway, the costs involved would be huge. Therefore, they question a sample of the population. Each member of that sample group represents hundreds, or even thousands, of people. It is therefore vital to choose your sample carefully to ensure you have the same balance of characteristics (sex, age, background, etc.) that are representative of the **population** that is being studied.

population
a complete group of people, cases or objects that share similarities that could be studied in a survey

Quantitative research is usually regarded as valid and reliable because the results are based on precise calculations by computer. It is a good way to test hypotheses as the data is subjected to statistically rigorous analyses.

hypothesis
a proposition put
forward for testing

A **hypothesis** is a proposition that is tested to find out if the statement made is tenable. It is an informed assumption about a problem or a given set of circumstances (an educated guess). The data is collected and tested statistically to give a result or a set of results that will prove or disprove the hypothesis or proposition.

For example, you might be doing a study into brand loyalty in the household cleaning market. You want to find out how people choose their washing powder. Here are some examples of hypotheses to be tested:

▶ H1 – people tend to buy the same washing powder that their parents bought

▶ H2 – people tend to buy the cheapest powder available

▶ H3 – people try at least one new brand of powder each year.

A limitation of quantitative research is that it focuses on what the situation is now – that is, what respondents know now and what they have already done. So it is a snapshot of today and yesterday – not tomorrow. The strength of quantitative research lies in the way the science of mathematical analysis and modelling is used to explain marketing phenomena. Marketers can base their decisions on statistically proven facts with known margins of error. The development of computer-aided simulations and database applications has greatly enhanced the ability of marketing researchers to build customer characteristics from ***geo-demographic*** data (see Chapter 4 for more information on market segmentation and ACORN geo-demographics) and purchasing records to build up more accurate customer profiles.

ethicalfocus

The Experiment – reality TV

The original 'experiment' was in 1971 (the 'Stanford Prison Experiment'). A psychologist divided 18 student volunteers into guards and prisoners. The study was about oppression and the conditions under which people would accept it. Within six days the guards' behaviour had become so brutal that the experiment was stopped. The researcher in charge was shocked and went on record to say that such an experiment should never be repeated. Then, in 2001, the BBC made a copycat TV programme entitled *The Experiment*.

It asked for volunteers to take part in a 'university-based social science experiment to be shown on TV'. The ad didn't give too many details other than there was nothing to win, no reward for taking part. The successful candidates were warned that they would face tough exercise, hardship, hunger, solitude and anger.

Reactions to the original experiment were so strong that many researchers have worried that it has made later experiments too tame, that people are too frightened of repeating the mistakes made and that this has restricted research topics and methods unfairly. The additional worry in 2001, though, was the televising of the study. How could that be justified?

In the event, the critics' fears were not realized. The British prison guards tended to prefer modern management techniques to brutality and at least one prisoner refused the offer of promotion to the position of guard. However, their behaviour was still worrying enough that this experiment was stopped early too.

Quantitative research can be criticized for its inflexibility and the impersonal nature of the collection of data through large-scale surveys. That is, quantitative work may be limited as it fails to fully understand respondents' attitudes, motivations and behaviour.

However, quantitative research has the reliability of numbers and statistically proven large-scale results.

For example, quantitative research might be used to find out how much of a product is bought, when it is bought and where. This information shows marketing managers how and what customers have purchased, from which they can deduce what customers are likely to consume in the near future. However, should the marketing team want to know *why* people buy what they do, numbers alone will not suffice. A qualitative approach is better at discovering such customers' purchase intentions by interviewing them and probing for in-depth answers.

The two broad approaches of qualitative and quantitative research should be seen as mutually supportive. For instance, as quantitative surveys taking in large numbers of people are expensive to conduct, a smaller-scale exploratory qualitative study is useful to find out whether its results would support the taking on of the quantitative survey. If the exploratory study unearths only very limited demand for a new product, then the need for an expensive quantitative survey is questionable.

COMMERCIALLY AVAILABLE RESEARCH

There are commercial organizations (such as Mintel and Keynote) that conduct research and publish substantial reports which other researchers can then purchase. These have often been gathered from **omnibus surveys** (see below) and from **syndicated data services**. Syndicated data is combined data collected by responses to questions on various topics put together. For example, long questionnaires with over 45 pages, such as the British Market Research Bureau's (BMRB's) Target Group Index (TGI) questionnaire, are sent out to representative consumers (**consumer panels**). Individual members of each consumer panel, usually in their own homes, will answer a battery of questions or have small tasks to perform. Each member, without knowing who the other members of the consumer panel are, will then record and return their responses to the research agency concerned. In this way information is obtained about respondents' general purchasing habits, lifestyles and needs. The surveys cover a comprehensive range of topics, such as brands consumed, levels of income and expenditure. Information collected in this way can be sold to businesses that are interested in any of these consumer topics. As another example, the Broadcaster's Audience Research Board (BARB) collects information on a regular basis on what television programmes are watched. These data are sold to television stations and media buyers, and used to compile the 'most popular programme' lists often published in magazines.

ACNielsen Worldwide, and other research agencies, provide data about the total sales of retailers' and manufacturers' brands in many product categories. A product's barcode contains information such as contents, manufacturer, price and country of origin. Each product is scanned at the store's checkout and this information can then be used by marketing research agencies to compile **retail audits**. Retail companies use computer technology for their retail audits to measure retail sales, to implement electronic stock ordering to replenish their stores, and to keep and analyse large amounts of their customers' personal and financial data.

Agencies such as ACNielsen also have many consumer panels, covering supermarkets, grocery stores, chemists, CTNs (cigarette sellers, tobacconists and newsagents), as well as different panels (for fashion goods, etc.). There are panels of consumers who scan in their retail purchases at home and transmit details of these to the research agency. There are other types of consumer panels, such as those that collect readership or television viewing data.

activity

Go to the library and find a recent market research report. Look for Mintel or Keynote. Can you find out how much the report would cost to buy?

The research agency can sell the data collected from these panels to retailers and manufacturers interested in market trends, brand shares and price movements. Such information is directly relevant to all those who have an interest in brands and the retailing industry, and is, therefore, bought by a large cross-section of businesses. Research agencies (e.g. Research International) also carry out many specific brand investigations commissioned by their own clients. Retail audits and consumer panel data can also be linked to geo-demographic analyses about individuals and where they live. Two leading names in this field in the UK are CACI with its ACORN (A Classification Of Residential Neighbourhoods) system and Experian with MOSAIC.

The different types of commercially available research are too extensive to be listed in full here. Some well-known examples are Mintel, The Times 1000, Fortune Weekly and Keynote Publications. All these sources publish reports from collected data they have updated on a regular basis and sell on to organizations and members. The *Economist* and the *Financial Times* sell surveys about countries, industries and markets compiled from their previous publications or undertaken anew as commissioned by organizations.

Most industries (for example, automobile and electronics) have trade associations. These associations also publish commercial reports about their industries. The MRS publishes a yearbook and a directory of research with a list of members and their firms to help clients select research agencies. The Emerald Database, provided by MCB University Press, gives much free information about journal contents and activities, as well as selling the licences needed to have such databases on-site to libraries, government bodies and businesses worldwide. Library retrieval databases contain indices of periodicals stored on computer from publishers such as ISI and ABI Inform. Virtually every publisher (e.g. Dun & Bradstreet and Kompass) will sell market and business reports, and directories listing names of firms and their activities. Also commercially available are publications such as BIP's two-volume reference books, which give detailed and comprehensive listings of books by publishers, as well as listed in order of subject, title and author. Government departments, by collecting and publishing information and statistics, also generate revenue through publishing this information, which is put on sale or bought through the government's HMSO retail outlets.

QUALITY OF MARKETING INFORMATION

Accuracy

It is important that marketing information is accurate, reliable and timely. Accuracy, or precision, in research estimates, and the outcomes of findings based upon good response rates and properly conducted marketing research, will help those in marketing management to take the most appropriate or the best decisions.

Reliability

The reliability of research is based upon whether the results or findings could be **extrapolated** to the larger **population** of consumers. For instance, focus group members should be representative of the targeted groups of consumers. However, if one were to repeat the topics of the focus group discussions, with a new set of participants, would the findings be the same? It is harder to prove reliability in **qualitative** research because people are different. It is easier to prove in **quantitative** research by asking the same structured questions, in the same format, to new members where they have less flexibility (as in answering yes/no questions). The reliability of research methods in both the quantitative and qualitative approaches is ultimately down to the integrity of the researchers concerned. The work should be unbiased. When entrusting the researchers with their projects and their money, client organizations need to know that they can depend upon the findings when making crucial managerial decisions about their marketing strategies and their markets.

Timeliness

The research should be finished according to the timescale scheduled in the research brief given by the client to its marketing research agency. Timeliness is important as research might have been commissioned by clients to feed into their marketing planning procedures at a pre-specified date. Moreover, research needs to be timely in delivering outcomes as the marketing environment is constantly evolving and changing.

There are different time factors in conducting and evaluating research work. The outcomes expected through the systematic application of research work, and those unexpected, such as needing client approval for higher costs involved and a greater than planned drop-out of respondents in a sample, will affect the timeframe in which the research is expected to be delivered.

Response rates

Response rates will vary depending on the ability of researchers to encourage participation or to offer incentives to respondents to aid their investigations. As noted in Exhibit 6.3, the impersonal forms (e.g. postal questionnaires) are more likely to have low response rates when compared to the more personal forms of in-depth interviewing or moderator-led focus-group sessions.

As an example, the effectiveness of the personal approach in focus-group sessions can be seen in the description given in a research study for Halford's Motor Oils in May 1995 (Kirkup et al., 2000) to probe consumer reactions to the company's new design concepts. The research method chosen was a series of seven extended focus groups that included only one all-female group to contrast with male responses. The research confirmed confusion and lack of understanding among consumers when purchasing motor oils. Factors influencing the choice of brand and grade included the degree of assurance the consumers needed, perceived quality (created by brand or retailer reputation), price and convenience. The research suggested there was limited brand loyalty, and many of those few who did regularly buy a similar brand appeared to do it out of habit rather than a belief that their choice was superior or ideal for their car.

RESEARCH METHODS AND TECHNIQUES

insight

Simply Software

As an illustration of how primary research might work, let us consider the case of Simply Software Ltd. The firm is considering an option of offering hardware maintenance services. It might start by sending an e-mail to its entire salesforce asking how many customers have enquired about such services. Then it might ask a sales team to sound out its customers next time they visit. Additionally, it could write to all local members of the Computer Users' Association.

Having established that there is some interest in the new service, it would want to make sure that it designed it in the most appealing way. To find out what would appeal to customers, it could invite a group to come in and talk about their current hardware service arrangements: what's good and what's not; what extra services they would like; and what they would be prepared to pay.

This scenario makes use of electronic questionnaires, focus groups, face-to-face interviews and a postal survey. But which is which?

Surveys

A **census** is a survey that includes all members of a population. National governments conduct population censuses in their countries to find out about socio-economic and demographic trends, household and work changes, and so on, in order to plan ahead to provide resources for education, health, transport, etc. In the UK a national census is conducted every 10 years, as in 1991 and 2001.

globalfocus

Elusive data

Marketing research in less developed countries (LDCs) can present particular problems. Often, there is very little secondary data available – and what there is may be out of date or unreliable. Population censuses are expensive and so poorer countries are unlikely to do these often, if at all. Few houses, especially in rural areas, may have phones and so the telephone directory will be a slim volume. (In many LDCs, people in remote areas are more likely to have mobile phones than land-line telephones.)

This lack of secondary data also affects primary research as it is hard to obtain an accurate **sampling frame**. As a consequence, **convenience samples** are often used.

The very collection of primary data can also be difficult in itself. In some countries, women still play a subservient role to their menfolk and would not be permitted to talk to a strange man – certainly not alone. So who do you send to do the interview? The obvious answer would be a woman. But how will you find a trained female market researcher in a country where women do not work outside the family? In such countries, people can also be reluctant to talk to strangers at all, especially about personal matters.

On the other hand, countries that have not always enjoyed the privilege of free speech (such as China) may prove a researcher's dream. Response rates to surveys can be very high – though whether this is because people are accustomed to cooperating with official enquiries, or just because they find being asked their opinion on consumer products a novelty, is as yet unclear.

A census is not practical for organizational and market research studies as a full census is too expensive and too time consuming for their limited resources. In marketing research, a survey with a **sample** of respondents is taken to get a general view that is informed and based upon shared characteristics.

For example, a survey drawn from a sample of car buyers would seek to discover their intentions to buy. Questions would be asked about their needs, wants and preferences concerning types of car, manufacturers and their pricing polices, product quality, and their sales and after-sales services. The questions should also include the sampled respondents' current and future personal finances, expectations about their employment and how much they would be prepared to pay for the cars they want, in order to assess their financial status or ability to buy.

sample

a smaller number of people, or cases, drawn from a population and representative of it in every significant characteristic

sampling frame

a list of the actual members of a population from which a sample is then chosen

Omnibus surveys

Research agencies can collect information on behalf of their business clients by using omnibus surveys. Clients can pay to have a series of questions put on a larger questionnaire.

The identities of clients are not divulged to respondents. Such a questionnaire will contain different sections relating to lifestyles, consumption habits, financial circumstances, ownership of motor vehicles, etc. In the motor car and financial services industries, where manufacturers and institutions are very protective of their corporate reputations, omnibus surveys are useful in helping to hide from the respondents the purposes for which the answers to the questionnaire are sought.

Focus groups

A focus group is where a number of respondents (between six and twelve people) meet and where leadership of the group is provided by a moderator. The researcher/moderator will start by asking questions or prompting individuals to respond to the words, sights, sounds and touch of visual images, or the actual products themselves, in order to get the group discussion flowing freely about the subjects or objects. By observing the interactions and recording the discussions, the moderator can gain useful insights about the group's intentions and feelings towards the subjects or objects. Research agencies have consumer panels in different regions of a country.

Focus groups can give useful insights into people's views and feelings

Interviews

In an in-depth interview the interviewer will usually start off by asking a few questions or putting up a problem situation or case scenario. Each interviewer will vary in his or her approach to a respondent, but the main idea is to create a situation where the respondent will feel at ease and can talk freely about the subject, thereby generating more information and insights for the interviewer. Interviews are time consuming and can take from one to several hours.

exhibit 6.4

Comparison of main primary research methods

	Advantages	**Disadvantages**
Postal survey	Low cost per interview. Avoids cost of travel. A large number can be surveyed.	Limited to short questionnaire to avoid non-response. Non-personal so there is inflexibility in probing respondents. Problem of low response rates.
Telephone	Cost limited to time spent on the phone. Allows probing. Avoids cost of travel. CATI can speed up automated data collection.	Intrusive into privacy. Development of call centres with resulting increase in calls to homes can make people less willing to answer questions. Can be time consuming. CATI is more expensive to set up than using phone.
Personal interview	Flexibility – visual materials and any other aids can be used to test respondents' reactions. Allows probing. Trust can be built up to get more reliable data. CAPI is faster and more accurate, to handle multivariate data analysis.	More expensive (e.g. travel, time taken). Have to set up individual interviews on an appointment basis, which could be cancelled at short notice. CAPI is more expensive to set up. Greater staff training required.
Focus groups	More flexibility – visual materials and other products can be used to test/probe respondents' reactions. Flow of discussion encourages greater intensity of ideas and participation of individuals.	More expensive and time consuming. Needs good control by the 'moderator' otherwise group dynamics can take over, with loss of direction. Can be problematic in getting a truly representative sample of individuals.
Consumer panels	Flexibility and participation – consumer can do product testing or give responses from home. Diaries are filled in and/or use of recording devices with computer link.	Expensive and time consuming to set up. Can be problematic in getting a truly representative sample of individuals.
E-mail	Very cheap compared to above methods. No international boundaries. Words, images and sounds can be sent. Versatile and very quick.	Incomplete directories of names. Poor lists are unrepresentative of sample. Brevity of e-mail responses can be a problem.

	Advantages	Disadvantages
Electronic sites	Intranet is free and accessible to a ready-made population within an organization. Internet websites give ready access to freely available information and to potential respondents. Have similar advantages to e-mail.	Respondents select themselves. Little control over sample. Limited to those with access to computers. Reliance on people to find and visit a website. Problems of differences – much diversity in website provision.
Use of observational equipment and recorders	Cameras and CCTV can be left for long periods to gather evidence in everyday or test/experimenting situations. Audience ratings can be measured by leaving videos recording in respondents' homes.	Much information is useless. Time consuming to sort out required details. Monitoring of respondents needed in test situations – more researcher time needed.

Sampling

To sample means to choose a smaller number of respondents to represent the **population** characteristics that are of interest to marketing managers. The objective of sampling is to allow researchers to draw accurate inferences, from the estimates or measurements of the sample, about the larger population.

First, the **sampling frame**, from which the sample is drawn, is identified. The frame might be a telephone directory, an electoral register, a list of members of a club, or any other list. The list should contain records of the entire, statistical population. Second, the sampling unit is selected, i.e. which respondents display which representative characteristics? Third, the sampling size should be determined – how many people should be sampled? Fourth, which sampling method is most appropriate?

insight

Sampling

Let us imagine that you want to find out how children spend their time. Clearly you cannot question *all* the children in the country, so you will try to find a representative sample. Then you can ask this subset of children and scale up to get a close approximation of the picture across the whole country. You establish (perhaps through a smaller qualitative study) that the key influencers of what children buy are:

▶ their gender (boy or girl), and

▶ their age.

The country's child population breaks down as follows:

▶ 52 per cent are girls

▶ 20 per cent are 0–3 years

▶ 20 per cent are 4–6 years

▶ 30 per cent are 7–12 years

▶ 30 per cent are 13–15 years.

The names you select for your survey (perhaps 1000 names from the total million or so), should also be: 52 per cent girls, 20 per cent 0–3, etc. Then you should have a representative sample of the whole.

There are several, popular sampling methods, as shown in Exhibit 6.5.

exhibit 6.5

Sampling methods

Random (probability) sampling	Non-random (non-probability) sampling
Simple random	Convenience
Stratified random	Purposive
Area or cluster sample	Quota (judgemental)

Simple random sampling

In **simple random sampling**, every member of the **population** should have an equal or known chance of being selected. It is important that the characteristics of the sample should be as close to those of the population as possible, as the sample is meant to be representative of the population from which it is drawn.

Each individual on the list is identified by means of a number and the numbers are drawn at random until the sample has been filled. This is a simple **random sample**. For example, a telephone directory can provide a convenient sampling frame. Every seventh name can be picked out of the directory. If the **survey** population is of any size, we may decide to adopt a systematic procedure. This is called **systematic random sampling**.

Stratified random sampling

In this type of sampling the population is divided into mutually exclusive groups and random samples are drawn from each group. For example, we can stratify the population by social class group and then by age group. These **demographic** variables are used for **market segmentation** purposes. Be aware, though, that classifying people according to social classes has always been one of the most dubious areas of market research investigation, although it is still one of the most widely used classification systems.

In another example, let's suppose we need to draw 500 individuals from a survey population of 5000, so the sample members will amount to one-tenth of the survey population. We could draw it manually, but that would be slow, so we use a computer to draw each number ending in a 5 until the sample is filled. This will result in a list of the individuals numbered 15, 25, 35, and so on. We have to be sure that the names recorded on the sampling frame in the first place are in a sufficiently random order, though.

Area or cluster sampling

This is taken when the population can be divided into mutually exclusive groups (e.g. geographical region) so that a random sample of the groups can be selected. Where the population sample can be drawn from mutually exclusive groups, blocks or tracts it is useful to conduct cluster sampling.

Take, for example, electoral polling. The decision as to how many constituencies to draw, and then how many polling districts to select, is based on informed judgement. If we were using a postcode file as a sampling frame, we would have to find out how many postcode areas there were. Then we select the sectors within these postcode areas to draw. So, in the UK, this cluster sampling could, for example, be concentrated in 200 out of over 630 voting constituencies.

Convenience sampling

A **convenience sample** is picked on the basis of convenience to the researcher. Organizations sometimes use their own employees to evaluate new products or prototypes that their research and development departments have come up with. Universities and colleges carry out market research surveys based on convenience samples of students and visitors to their campuses.

Convenience sampling lends itself to **qualitative research**, where consumer information can be obtained fairly quickly, inexpensively and effectively from convenient respondents who are close to hand. The rationale is to select the most accessible members of the population from which to conveniently draw the sample. Unless the members of the population are reasonably uniform (e.g. in expectations, socio-demographic make-up, etc.), there can be problems of the sample not being representative of the population. In such a case a **judgemental sample** (see below) would be a better method.

Purposive sampling

This is a non-probability sampling method, where every member of the population does not have an equal chance of being picked. For example, if it is known who the experts are within a particular industry this method of purposive sampling is simply to pick these people to represent the expertise of the industry. So knowledge gleaned from these people would be more useful than picking from a larger sample of people who are less expert in the particular field. In another example, if we wanted to investigate the market for a product used by people above the age of 65 years we could start by using a list of residential homes for the elderly as a sampling frame. We would then interview a given number of people in these homes until we have enough information with which to form conclusions about product usage by those over the age of 65. In a further example, we know that there are a vast number of retail outlets selling food in Britain, but the leading food stores that have control of the national chains of supermarkets are few (Tesco, Wal-mart/ASDA, Sainsbury's, Safeway and Gateway). So a purposive sample of large retail firms would include these stores.

Quota

In marketing research it is common practice to use **quota samples**. What this means is that we put a prescribed figure or a number of the members of the population in each of several categories or quotas. For instance, in industrial and trade research we may be interested in sampling output or sales turnover. Our base for sample design is, therefore, the output or turnover and not the number of establishments or shops in a particular industry. We would, therefore, include a quota or selected number of firms based upon output and turnover for our study.

As another example, a survey of the manufacturers of paints should include a selected number or quota of the large companies such as ICI Paints. Judgement is involved in selecting the quota because when we draw these firms to sample they should be representative of the paints industry. Quota samples should include members of the population who are good prospects from which to draw this accurate data. In consumer studies we can set quotas based upon socio-economic and demographic characteristics such as age, race, gender and education attained.

Testing

Pre-testing and post-testing

Consumer responses to a product launch are affected by how it is introduced as well as how it is priced, packaged and finally presented to the market. A planned programme of pre-testing and post-testing can be expensive, but the results can yield useful data for marketers.

Pre-testing can be carried out on a range of products, packaging and prices. For instance, groups of respondents can be asked for their views on a range of products (product research) or be shown different pack sizes (for packaging research) or asked about what they would be prepared to pay for a product given high/moderate/low prices (for pricing research). Without divulging either the product name or producer identity for the product that is being researched along with the other known brands, marketing researchers can find out valuable information to help the producer to refine its product prior to market launch.

Post-testing with the same sample of respondents, or varied by the inclusion of new respondent samples, can provide further observations about the final price, pack, taste and advertisement effects. For example, we can pre-test the effects of marketing communications by showing advertising material in advance and observing the effects that changes to the material have on respondents. We can then test the after-effects of the actual advertising programme. Thus, an experimental group can be used to observe changes in its members' individual responses to various marketing communications in pre-testing. Then the same experimental group can be used to assess the differences in responses to the after-effects of post-testing when the actual communication is rolled out to introduce the new product into the marketplace. (Further explanation is provided in the later section on 'Recognition and recall'.)

Tracking studies

In the marketing research industry **tracking studies** are often used to monitor and evaluate the performances of brands and the effects of advertisements. Information from tracking studies is often sold as **syndicated research data** by market research agencies. Usage and attitude studies can establish what brands are being used by respondents. When collecting brand image data it is important in the first place to get right which brands particular respondents are using, or have used, and which other brands they are aware of.

Tracking studies are used as inputs to market models such as those used for diagnosing the effects of marketing mix elements (e.g. the contribution of new advertising spend on improving brand share). An example of the benefits of tracking audience responses to viewers' understanding and recall of television advertisements is provided in the case study about quantifying the cost benefits of television pre-tests conducted by the research company Millward Brown for the Direct Line insurance company (Ashman and Kent, 2000).

Statistical tests

A sample **survey** draws data from only a part of the **population**. We lose some accuracy when we sample, so there are statistical methods for adjusting bias or errors given the uncertainties in the data. For example, in marketing research we would normally settle for a level of risk of 1 in 20 of being wrong (often referred to as the 5 per cent level of significance, i.e. 5 per cent probability of being wrong). This means we would normally settle for a 95 per cent confidence of being right. A truly representative sample should have the same distribution of relevant characteristics as a **census** and this will reduce the margin for error.

Statistical tests using a computer involve many complex calculations and formulae. Basic statistical tests include working out the **standard error** and **level of confidence** of an estimate. The range of uncertainty surrounding a measurement from a **sample** is indicated by the standard error of that measurement. This would be worked out from calculating the arithmetic mean (average), standard deviation (spread of data) and the variance (square root of the standard deviation).

level of confidence
the degree to which the researchers are sure that data are accurate

standard error
average amount of error introduced through the sampling process

Test marketing

A test market is a mini-market – a smaller version of the whole market, in which new products, services or promotions can be tried out. If the product, or campaign, is successful in the test market, then it can be rolled out to the real market with more confidence; there is less risk of it proving an expensive failure. In the UK, television advertising campaigns are often tested in one of the television regions (e.g. Granada, Grampian); however, not all European countries have regionalized television (Germany, for instance, does not), so TV adverts are more difficult to test.

Where new markets and new products or services are concerned, there could well be a lack of information or misconceptions about the needs and wants of consumer groups, or about how they base their buying decisions. Therefore, test marketing is conducted for concept testing (i.e. testing the design concept of a product with new consumers in the market and for new product launches).

Although test markets are cheaper to manage than whole markets, they can still prove expensive exercises. That is why some companies run simulations of test markets. There are benefits in simulating test markets, as follows:

▶ speed of both market penetration and repeat buying

▶ provisions for extensive diagnostic questioning

▶ no dependence on attitude measurement scores or the availability of trend data

▶ no need for much of the hitherto necessary separate testing of elements such as advertising, pack and product.

Respondents can be tested conveniently in the following locations:

▶ in-hall, where there is greater interviewer control of product presentation and sample

▶ in-home, where respondents can consume the product according to their normal daily routine

▶ on-site, on business premises such as pubs, wine bars and working men's clubs.

Recognition and recall

In marketing research, say at the **pre-test** stage (i.e. before the campaign begins), the most commonly used measures of creative effectiveness are:

▶ recognition of what is tested, i.e. the product or advertisement

▶ recall, unaided and aided, about the advertisement

▶ effect on attitude towards the product or brand

▶ intention to buy.

Questions about a respondent's buying habits will often help to determine whether the respondent is a suitable participant in the test. These questions will also contribute to the interpretation of answers to recognition, recall, attitude and intention-to-buy questions.

Once the campaign is out in the world **recognition** is an important measure. If members of the **target audience** recognize elements of the campaign, then it is reaching them and being noticed. Awareness and campaign penetration are other terms used when discussing advertising research. Awareness covers a range of responses from mere recognition to unaided **recall** of the attributes the advertising seeks to associate with the brand. Campaign penetration measures help to establish whether the **opportunities to see (OTS)**, view or hear, as offered in the media schedule, are in fact being taken by respondents consciously or unconsciously.

Questionnaire design

The **questionnaire** is a very useful, flexible and far-reaching tool for the market researcher, who can use it to obtain important information about consumer behaviour, attitudes and awareness of product and service offerings. In **quantitative research** standardized questionnaires are common as survey instruments to be used with a large **sample** of several hundreds or thousands of respondents. Such questionnaires normally contain structured questions for ease of coding and statistical analysis.

There are three basic types of questionnaire:

1. fully structured with **closed questions** and no comments invited

2. a compromise form of semi-structured questionnaire with mixed question types and room for comments

3. completely unstructured with **open-ended questions** seeking to discover or explore the respondents' minds.

Face-to-face interviewing in the street

exhibit 6.6

Examples of ways of asking questions

(Please tick or circle as appropriate.)

• *Closed questions*
'What is your age?'   16–25 ___   26–35___
'Do you have a bank account?'   Yes/No
'Do you like cheese?'   Like/Dislike

• *Semi-structured questions*
These can use a mixture of attitude scales and rank order types, followed by room on the questionnaire for 'comments'.

(a) **Likert scale**
Do you agree with speed limits?

☐	☐	☐	☐	☐
strongly agree	slightly agree	neither agree nor disagree	slightly disagree	strongly disagree

Comments: _____

(b) **Semantic differential scale**
Was Rosannica Restaurant's service:

Good	_ _ _ _ _ _	Poor
Reliable	_ _ _ _ _ _	Unreliable
Fast	_ _ _ _ _ _	Slow
Expensive	_ _ _ _ _ _	Cheap?

Comments: _____

Please rank in order of importance: 1 = very important, 5 = least important, in the boxes.
In your opinion, how important is your university's provision of the following facilities to your studies?

Sports facilities   ☐
Medical centre facilities ☐
Library facilities   ☐
Parking facilities   ☐
Restaurant facilities   ☐

Comments: _____

• *Open-ended questions*
'What did you enjoy about the play last night?' or 'Describe your feelings concerning the news about . . .' or 'What do you think the level of competition will be like in the next five years?'

Comments: _____

Structured questionnaire

The order in which questions are asked, together with their exact wording, is laid down. The interviewer must not alter or explain questions. Many questions are *closed* and the possible answers to most questions are pre-coded so that all the interviewer has to do is to ring round a code number or tick a box.

Semi-structured questionnaire

This usually constitutes a mixture of closed or fixed-response questions (yes/no), quick response ranking (e.g. 1 = highest-ranked favourite, 10 = lowest-ranked favourite) or rating scales (e.g. 1 = most wanted, 7 = least wanted) for measuring attitudes to organizations and their products. There are also open-ended questions or spaces for respondents to fill in their comments. Semi-structured questionnaires are useful in enabling the interviewer to stage-manage the interview by making sure that all questions are covered, with room for the interviewee (respondent) to add comments to the specific questions already asked.

Unstructured questionnaire

Most of the questions are open-ended. The interviewer is free to change the order of asking questions and to explain them. The questionnaire may take the form of a checklist for discussion. The unstructured questionnaire is used in **in-depth interviews**, group discussions and in non-domestic surveys. The interview may be respondent-led, particularly if the interviewee is an expert in the field, so that the observations and expertise of the respondent can be taken account of fully.

e-focus

e-questions

Nowadays, researchers often use e-mail to send out their questionnaires. This means that information can be collected much faster and physical distance is no obstacle. With e-mail it is no more expensive to contact people on the other side of the world than it is to talk to people in the next office. So researchers ask questions internally, via a company's own intranet, or externally, using the Internet and websites.

They can also collect primary information electronically to find out what competitors are providing so that comparisons can be made. Researchers can also sit respondents down at computer terminals and ask them to answer questions – for example, visitors to exhibitions might be approached. Computerized questionnaires have significant advantages over their old-fashioned paper counterparts. The computer does away with that tedious (and confusing) business of 'if you ticked yes, now go to question 44b, otherwise go to question 16'. Each answer can determine what the next question will be.

The information collected from all the respondents is then downloaded to a central computer to be processed (collated), statistically analysed, cross-related and systematically grouped into the types of categories that will allow researchers to make meaningful statements to their clients about the findings. This type of computer-assisted personal interviewing (CAPI) is effective by saving the researcher time. It frees the researcher from having to take each respondent through the questionnaire step by step. Computer-assisted telephone interviewing (CATI) works on the same principle, by allowing responses on the telephone to be recorded on to the computer and computer-generated analyses to be carried out speedily and impartially.

▶ **e-focus**

Further examples are small digital handheld cameras, traffic sensor devices and closed-circuit television (CCTV) equipment used in stores and shopping precincts to observe and record the sounds, movement and behaviour of customers. Information can be collected by experimenting using computers to record and to analyse what was said by respondents or answered by respondents on questionnaires in their testing of a new shaver or a cosmetic cream over a specified period of time.

FORECASTING AND TRENDS

Forecasting can be defined as the estimation of the future value of a variable (most commonly sales). A key assumption is that a relationship must exist between the variable being forecast (the dependent variable) and the other one or more variables that are being measured against (the independent variable/variables). For example, the growth in sales, as the dependent variable, can be measured against some other independent variable, such as advertising, income or price.

Marketers need to have some forecast of the value a new product can generate in sales revenues. An agreed forecast is an agreed basis for a plan of marketing activity – for instance, in planning new advertising and salesforce activities, stock inventories and price reductions for retail outlets. Spreadsheets are used on a computer in order to plot trends and compounded growth rates. The purpose of forecasting is to provide the basis for management's expectations of the future, e.g. expectations of sales levels, and to offer an understanding of potential alternative courses of action.

Forecasting, then, has several purposes:

▶ to relate informed opinions (judgements) about markets to forecast expectations (from marketing research) of what the markets will bring

▶ to plot regularities of trends (e.g. time series, showing observations of sales over a specified period of months) or in economic behaviour (effects of rises in incomes and expenditures) that will carry over into the future

▶ to relate occurrences or turning points (e.g. in stages in a product's life cycle) relevant to management decision-making over a time period

▶ to create models of the interactions between specified key variables (e.g. sales, profits and cash flow within a specified market scenario).

The decision to develop a new product or enter a new market will bring new risks, not just in terms of whether customers would want the new product, but also as to what competitors' retaliatory strategies might be. A costly failure could mean much loss of revenue and could be disastrous for an organization.

insight

Producer risks

OnDigital's venture into a new market to compete with BSkyB not only ended in failure, it also brought about the demise of the company and the loss of investors' money. Its forecast sales of its new set-top receivers failed to materialize in the early 1990s. OnDigital had used cable technology to provide 30 channels, which compared with the 150 channels on offer from the British Sky Broadcasting Corporation (BSkyB). BSkyB emerged as the winner, thanks to its coverage, aggressive sales promotions and pricing tactics.

SUMMARY

Marketing research is crucial to understanding customer attitudes and in soliciting facts. Its results are valuable to the objectives and successes of both profit and not-for-profit organizations. The procedures used are well-established forms of collecting, analysing and conveying information about people and markets. Markets can be described and analysed in detail so that opportunities can be taken, the performances of organizations assessed and competitors' activities tracked. Marketing research is, therefore, indispensable for the marketing intelligence purposes of organizations and in helping them to develop their marketing strategies.

Challenges reviewed

Now that you have finished reading the chapter, look back at the challenges you were set at the beginning. Do you have a clearer idea of what's involved?

Hints:

▶ sources of secondary information

▶ objectives of research

▶ consider appropriate qualitative research methods

▶ sampling.

READING AROUND

journal articles

M. Earls (2003) Advertising to the herd, *International Journal of Market Research* 45(3), 311–36.

C. Nancarrow, A. Barker and L.T. Wright (2001) Engaging the right mindset in qualitative marketing research, *Marketing Intelligence & Planning* 19(4), 236–44.

B. Tarran (2003) The birth of an idea, *Research* (the magazine of the Market Research Society), August, 22–4. (See also the blank image on the front cover of *Research* (same issue), 'Editor's apology'.)

SELF-REVIEW QUESTIONS

1. Why is marketing research sometimes referred to as market research? (see page 161)

2. If marketing managers know about their customers from past purchases why do they need to conduct marketing research? (see page 161)

3. What are retail audits and consumer panels? (see page 170)

4. What is meant by defining a research problem and a hypothesis? (see page 169)

5. What is random, quota and stratified or area sampling? (see pages 177–8)

6. What are the advantages of secondary data over primary data? (see page 165)

7. What is qualitative research? (see page 167)

8. What is the difference between simple random sampling and stratified ramdom sampling? (see page 177)

MINI CASE STUDY

Read the questions, then the case material, then answer the questions.

Questions

1. Now that you have been recruited to the post of marketing research manager for Alcofizz Ltd you will need to 'define the problem' for the company.

2. Using the information and trends in Exhibits 6.7–6.9 comment on the usefulness of the information given. What other information would you need?

3. Choose and justify the research method you would adopt to find out consumer attitudes and preferences to your company's brands if you were to rebrand one of the company's products.

Alcofizz Ltd

Alcofizz Ltd is a family-owned/managed firm that has recruited you to conduct market research in the alcoholic wine market. Alcofizz specializes in importing wines from Latin America and Australasia, which it bottles and then sells on to retailers under its own labels. Imported wine is its principal business, but the wine market is a mature one and price sensitive. The company is, therefore, facing severe competition in the marketplace and is looking at ways of rejuvenating its brands or rebranding to make them more appealing to consumers.

Alcofizz Ltd was started in 1978 when its founder left a well-known wine company to form his own wine importing and distributing business. Its founder, Adrian Rose, had observed that the various government campaigns to stop motorists driving while under the influence of alcohol had not decreased sales of wines in retail outlets or in public places (see Exhibit 6.7).

The changing demographics in the UK (see Exhibit 6.8), higher standards of living, changes in

exhibit 6.7

UK Wine Market at current prices (£m) and forecast UK wine market at current prices (£m)

Year	Light wines	Fortified wines	Year	Light wines	Fortified wines
1995	4990	485	2000	6950	420
1996	5450	470	2001	7350	400
1997	5800	460	2002	7700	400
1998	6350	450	2003	8100	380
1999	6800	440	2004	8200	380

exhibit 6.8

Demographic changes in UK age groups 18+

Age category	1996	2001 (estimated)	2005 (projection)
18–24	5,123,000	5,157,000	5,423,000
25–34	9,420,000	8,604,000	7,861,000
35–44	8,093,000	9,189,000	9,561,000
45–54	7,596,000	7,867,000	7,861,000

exhibit 6.9

Preferred places for drinks consumption (base 66.2% of all adults, 1999)

	At home	Public house/ club/restaurant	Neither/would not drink it
White wine	48	26	24
Red wine	39	19	42
Whisk(e)y	25	15	59
Gin	18	16	65
Lager	17	40	43
Vodka	14	28	58
Bitter or ale	6	35	59

Source: the exhibits in this case study have been adapted from information derived from Mintel, 2001; Strathclyde University Department of Marketing, n/d

consumer attitudes, with a willingness to try new products, more retail outlets prepared to stock increased numbers of drinks products, a greater number of younger and older teenagers prepared to consume alcohol and more female drinkers mean that wine consumption is on the rise.

Consumers are also becoming more discerning as they are less willing to settle for inferior products and are inclined to drink socially at home and in public houses, wine bars, restaurants and clubs (see Exhibit 6.9).

REFERENCES

AMSO (1997) *Annual Report*, 7–29.

Anon. (1985) AMA Board approves new marketing definitions, *Marketing News* (1 March), 1.

Anon. (1987) New marketing research definitions approved, *Marketing News* (2 January), 1, 14.

Ashman, S. and Clarke, K. (2000) Optimising advertising effectiveness for Direct Line: quantifying major benefits of painstaking television pre-tests, in Wright, L.T. and Crimp, M., *The Marketing Research Process* (5th edn), FT Pearson, 360–72.

Birn, R., Hayne, P. and Vangelder, P. (1990) *A Handbook of Market Research Techniques*, Kogan Page.

Cresswell, J. (1998) *Qualitative Inquiry and Research Design*, Sage Publications Ltd, 47–68.

ESOMAR (1998) Annual Study on the Market Research Industry, 1–4.

Gordon, W. and Langmaid, R. (1988) *Qualitative Research – A Practitioner's and Buyer's Guide*, Gower.

Kirkup, M., Walley, P. and Temperley, J. (2000) Hanford's Motor Oils: research and own brand development, in Wright, L.T. and Crimp, M., The *Marketing Research Process* (5th edn), FT Pearson, 287–91.

Marketing Research Society (MRS) (1998) ICC/ESOMAR Code of Marketing and Social Research Practice (Code of Conduct), April, 11.

Mintel (2001) Flavoured alcoholic beverages, at http://Mintel.com.

Strathclyde University Department of Marketing (n/d) *Strathclyde Vintners*, marketing teaching case study.

Wright, L.T. and Crimp, M. (2000) *The Marketing Research Process* (5th edn), FT Pearson, 14, 18.

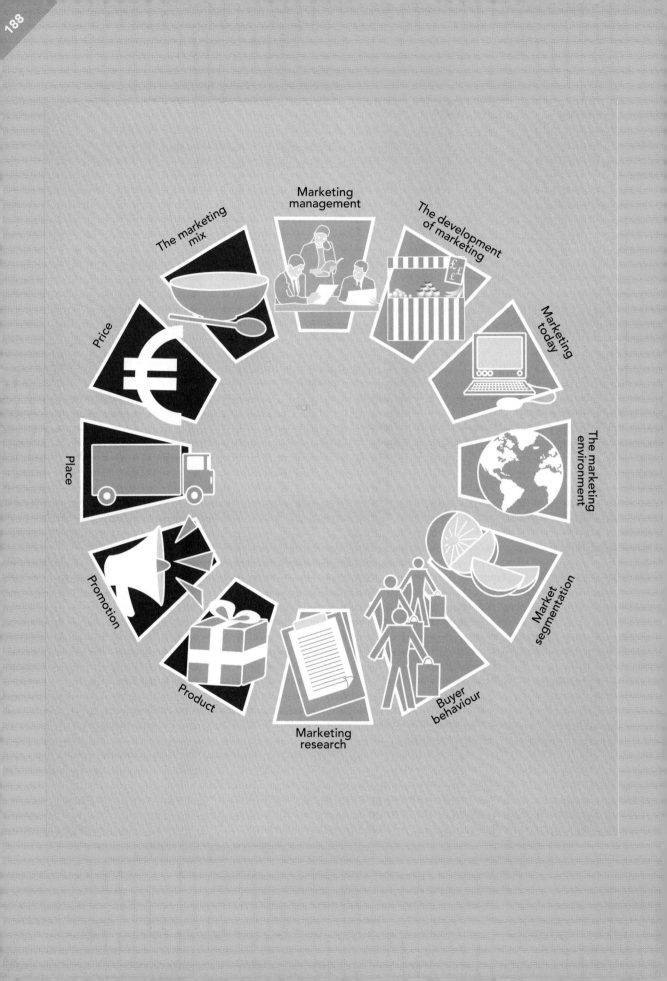

Marketing management

The development of marketing

Marketing today

The marketing environment

Market segmentation

Buyer behaviour

Marketing research

Product

Promotion

Place

Price

The marketing mix

MARKETING TOOLS

WHAT THIS PART IS ABOUT:

Armed with an understanding of their customers and the surrounding environmental forces, marketers make plans. The backbone of these plans is a set of tools known as the marketing mix. This part considers each element of the marketing mix separately and then combines them (along with a few additional elements) in its final chapter.

If you prefer, you can read Chapter 11 first as an overview, followed by the more detailed chapters on the individual elements of the marketing mix.

PRODUCT

BY KIT JACKSON

PRODUCT CHALLENGES

The following are illustrations of the types of decision that marketers have to take or issues they face. *You aren't expected to know how to deal with the challenges now*; just bear them in mind as you read the chapter – and see what you can find that helps.

▶ You are a manager at Cadbury's and feel the time is right to launch a new chocolate bar. How are you going to make sure it sells well without taking too many sales away from other Cadbury's bars?

▶ You are the marketing director of Peugeot. The finance director wants to cut the product development budget. She cannot see why you need to keep launching new models so often. Can you convince her that this is necessary?

▶ You are given the task of managing a well-known and long-established brand of jeans. The brand is showing its age and is suffering from a gradual decline in sales. What might you do to halt the decline and revitalize the brand?

▶ You are a salesperson at an electronics retailer. You stock the same PCs as everyone else and cannot change the basic product itself. How can you make it more attractive for customers to come to your store rather than go to your rivals?

KEY CONCEPTS

product types
basic product
total product
innovation
core benefit
product development
product life cycle
product range
product portfolio analysis
product management
brands
branding strategies
services
market segmentation (see Chapter 4)
product adoption (see Chapter 5)

CHAPTER OVERVIEW

INTRODUCTION

product life cycle

a product analysis tool based on the idea that a product has life stages: introduction, growth, maturity, decline, deletion

Boston Consulting Group (BCG) matrix

a portfolio analysis tool involving classifying products, or SBUs, according to their market share and market growth rate, as stars, cash cows, problem children or dogs

branding

the process of building a brand

The product may be as touchable, or tangible, as a tin of beans or as untouchable, or intangible, as an insurance policy. Whichever type of product it is, marketing managers need to understand every detail of how it is constructed and how it appears to the customer; they should also be clear as to how well it satisfies customers' needs.

In this chapter we will consider what makes a product a success in the marketplace. We will follow its progress from original idea to eventual deletion.

Most companies sell more than one product; they have a range of products available. The entire range must be managed so that individual products contribute to the success of the whole. **Product managers** have a number of tools that they can use to help them do this, and we will consider some of those, notably the **product life cycle** and the **Boston Consulting Group (BCG) matrix**.

There is more to the idea of a product than just an item that you pick up, touch, smell, taste. No product is purely physical, all have a service element to them, e.g. after-sales service, warranties, guarantees, installation assistance. Equally, very few **services** are pure service, most have a physical element to them. When you have your hair done, the hairdresser uses shampoo etc. When you travel by train, you get a ticket. When you eat in a restaurant, you get food. Product providers often use the service aspects of their products to differentiate them from the competition, whereas service providers may try to use the **physical evidence** of their services to do this.

Whether it be primarily a product or a service, it can be branded. **Branding** was perhaps the primary competitive weapon of the 1990s and we will look at its role in building product sales. First, though, let's be clear on what makes up a product.

WHAT IS A PRODUCT?

A product has been described as a bundle of attributes. A loaf of bread may be large, sliced and wholemeal – these are its physical attributes. Some, equally valuable, attributes of that loaf are intangible. For example, it may also be good for you and provide good value for money. All these things are features and qualities of the loaf but its primary purpose is to satisfy hunger. A product is really a means by which people can satisfy needs. A watch can be seen as satisfying the need to know the time. A car satisfies the need to travel from one place to another, and washing powder satisfies the need for clean clothes.

From earliest times, and certainly before any thoughts of commercial manufacture, human beings satisfied their needs through their own problem-solving activities. If they did not know how to do something themselves, they persuaded someone else to help them, often by offering them something of an agreed equal value. It would not be unreasonable to imagine that the earliest cavemen might have done a deal along the lines of swapping a spear for a good helping of mammoth meat.

This early specialization of the spear-maker and the hunter, who derived value from each other's efforts and skills, has become ever more sophisticated over the millennia. However, the principle remains that the satisfaction of a perceived need by someone else deserves to have a value. The only relevant debate is over the precise value each party places on the transaction.

Products are at the heart of most organizations. The customer judges the value of a firm's offering by the product and all its components. Whether or not an **exchange** will take place depends upon the customer's judgement of that value. The perceived value and the actual or intrinsic value of a product are very often widely different and depend upon the effective use of all the elements of the **marketing mix**. The way in which the marketing mix is constructed should have the effect of creating an offering that matches the customer's expectations and needs. This coming together of all the marketing mix elements is called the **total product**. The total product may have to satisfy a range of needs, e.g. Diet Pepsi is required to quench thirst, taste good, be low calorie and convey a suitable image. Needs range from the simple (e.g. quench thirst) to the elaborate (e.g. convey suitable image).

What, then, is this crucial thing that we call a product, without which the exchange of value could not take place and the organization would have no reason for existence? In order to glimpse the power and potential of the product, we should examine its make-up and unravel the processes by which we can control and manage it.

ethicalfocus

Playing with lives

In October 2003, Channel 4 transmitted a stunt featuring the illusionist Derren Brown. The stunt was Russian roulette – with a real bullet. The programme was billed as going out live but, in actual fact, there was a slight delay in the transmission just in case something went wrong and he actually did kill himself.

On the night there was indeed a hitch, but fortunately only in that Derren mistook a blank bullet for a live one and fired it into the waiting sandbag rather than his head.

The show was not universally popular. Parents' groups and police criticized it on the grounds that it might inspire youngsters to copy it. There were also complaints that, in a week when there had been a number of shootings and gun crime was a hot topic in all the papers, the programme was in bad taste. Channel 4 defended the show by pointing out that it contained a number of warnings of the dangers, and explanations that the game was enacted within a controlled environment and under the supervision of firearms experts.

Did you watch it? Was this programme an ethically sound product?

Core benefits

The core benefit is what is left when all other parts of the product have been stripped away. We are left with the simplest possible answer to an expressed need: no frills, no fancy **branding** and packaging, no warranties and service promises, just the bare bones. It is also true to say (surprisingly perhaps) that there is no such thing as a new need, just new or different ways of solving a problem. For example, the horse was an improvement over walking from one place to another, the train replaced the horse, the car has largely supplanted the train, and the aeroplane has, in many types of journey, replaced trains and boats. The transport problem is being solved in new and different ways. Electric light replaced gas for lighting, which in turn had replaced paraffin and candles, which in turn had replaced tallow wicks as a way of extending the day. In this idea lies a law of nature which dictates that all that follows, however complex, high- or low-tech the product might appear, is still essentially a solution to a basic human need.

This is important if we are to understand how, and with what, ever more demanding customers are going to be satisfied. It is necessary to be positive that what is offered satisfies a need in its most basic sense and that, should it fail to do this, then it fails completely. For example, it would be an uphill task for Rolex to attempt to sell watches that are not accurate. No matter how much in the way of precious metals and jewels might come with the offering, timekeeping of a high order is the basic, core satisfaction demanded of a watch, however expensive. Probably the more expensive the watch, the more accurate it must be. Likewise, no matter how cheap, a washing powder that fails to clean clothes has little chance of success, since it does not deliver the basic satisfaction it claims.

The marketing manager must keep focused on the problem to be solved: understanding it well, addressing it precisely and directly, and placing this solution at the core of the total product. This need satisfaction may be upfront or may be concealed within the complete product, but it must be there as it is central to the perception the customer has of its ultimate value.

To own a watch is one thing, to own a piece of jewellery is another, and to create a watch that is a piece of jewellery is yet another. If the watch does not keep good time, it is not satisfactory, and if the diamonds are not real and the gold is not gold, then it is not a jewel. The lack of either element is fatal to the integrity of the product and will destroy its capacity to satisfy; the lack of both will probably be the subject of legal action!

core product

the minimum benefits a product should confer, e.g. a pen must write, a car must go

Once you are sure what the **core product** is, it is possible to consider how the offering can be improved to appeal to customers' individual characteristics. This requires a much deeper understanding of what it is that particular customers want (see Chapter 6). It is also vital to be aware of what is already being offered to proposed, or existing, customers by the competition.

In a **monopoly** situation, where there is only one provider of the means to satisfy needs, the provider may just offer the bare minimum. With no available choice, the customer has to satisfy their requirements as best they can with whatever is available, however unsuited the product may be. Fortunately monopolies are increasingly rare and wherever they do exist they are usually subject to substantial monitoring and control systems to secure the best for the public.

globalfocus

I'll have the usual please

Unfortunately, you may not be able to get your usual product abroad. There is an ever increasing number of global brands available but, although they may look the same as the ones at home, there are sometimes subtle differences.

Take Coca-Cola, for example: the US drink is not quite the same as the one you can buy in parts of Asia where it has more sugar added. McDonald's? Well, you can hardly sell hamburgers in India where the cow is sacred, so those burgers are made of lamb instead. Then there's the strange story of the Mars bar.

Mars was founded in the USA – and Britain. The first company was the US one, which was so successful that its founder could see no reason to change. However, as is the way of the world, his son wanted to make improvements. Frustrated by his father's blocking, the son emigrated to England where he set up his own company.

Mr Mars Senior's bestselling line in the USA was Milky Way. The new British company started with the same product but called it the Mars bar instead. Eventually father and son, and the two companies, were reunited. However, the Mars bar and Milky Way are still confused – if you know someone who is going to the States, ask them to bring you a Mars bar and see what you get.

THE TOTAL PRODUCT (THE OFFERING)

Without monopoly we have competition and with competition comes choice. With choice comes the opportunity for customers to express their individuality in the way they make this choice. They will choose the products and services that have value to them. An understanding of how the customer sees value gives the organization a chance of making an offering that matches the preferences of the customer.

exhibit 7.1

The total product

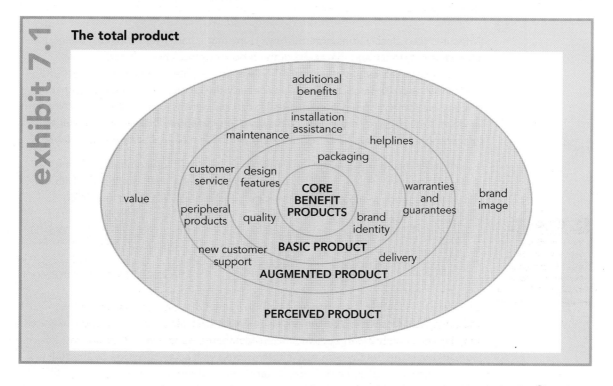

The core benefit that the product must provide is central. A pen must write. A chocolate must taste good. Medicine must make us better.

The basic level of product incorporates all those things that are taken away by the buyer. These include its features (how fast, how loud, how many tasks, etc.), **brand name**, quality level, design and packaging. All these are separate from the core benefit but complete the product in the eyes of the customer. These attributes attract the eye and the interest of the customer, and are often the first things used to judge the product against the competitor's offering.

The next level out contains supporting features. Among these are guarantees, service network, delivery, after-sales service and credit facilities. Again these can be an important source of differentiation from the competition. They provide ways to enhance the offering and can be used to counter objections or resolve doubts in the customer's mind: 'You can't afford it? We'll lend you the money!' 'How do I get it home and what can I do with my old one?' 'Don't worry, madam, we will deliver and install the new one and take away your old one. All at no extra charge.'

Since such extras are not physically part of the product, they can often be changed without modifying the basic product itself. For example, in 2003 Fiat was offering a 12-year anti-perforation warranty on the bodywork of its cars, together with 0 per cent finance deals. Its offers may well be different now but the cars themselves may not have changed. There may be actual costs incurred in this augmentation process that must be borne by someone; either by the supplier or by the customer, or both. A balance still needs to be struck between cost and perceived value.

brand name

the product's, or product line's, given name

crmfocus

Towards a learning organization

By the close of the twentieth century, the UK manufacturing industry was in a bad way. One of the worst-hit sectors was textiles, where high-cost Western firms were having trouble competing with manufacturers from the low-wage economies of the East. It became clear to one small (130 employees) Leicestershire textile components manufacturer that, if it was to survive, it needed to find new ways to improve long-term profits.

When it looked closely at its order history, it saw that it had a variety of customers, both large and small, and that many of them bought products made to their own specifications. The obvious course of action was to cut out the smaller customers and reduce the range of products offered – especially the bespoke ones. However, that's a strategy that cannot be repeated endlessly and, anyway, the company was reluctant to let down loyal customers who had stuck with it. So it decided that it would prefer to understand its customers better, and serve their needs more precisely and profitably.

It discovered that its local university, De Montfort, ran 'teaching company' schemes. A postgraduate student, supervised by experienced university staff, would work with the company to introduce more modern management techniques. During the initial business analysis process, it was realized that many people within the company had areas of specialist knowledge (e.g. ways to improve knitting quality), which they did not share with their colleagues – or customers. Such expertise was not usually deliberately withheld, it was just the way things worked. Procedures had not changed very much in a long time. It was time they did.

The company identified a computer database system that would integrate all the information sources within the business (sales records, product details, contact reports, etc.) together with outside sources (databases, suppliers' information, journals, etc.). This new system was initially viewed with some suspicion by the staff but, after training and some practice, it was wisely realized that more came back to the individual than the individual gave.

This improved access to better-quality information means that the firm can serve its existing customers better and has greatly improved relationships, as well as helping forge relationships with new customers. By sharing knowledge throughout the company, and with customers, striking results have been achieved. The total product offering has been improved immeasurably. Sales revenues are up and, most importantly, profits are increasing.

activity

Ask some friends to describe a well-known branded product – for example, the Big Mac, Marks & Spencer underwear, Nike shoes, Bounty chocolate bars. It is likely that they will have different views. They will each perceive that product differently.

The outer ring (see Exhibit 7.1) is the perceived product. This is a far less certain thing as customers' perceptions will vary. **Perception** is the way we interpret our world, and each of us does it differently.

Our perceptions are built from our life experiences and our personalities. We have different likes and dislikes, different tastes – that is largely why suppliers offer us a choice of products. One of the big challenges of marketing is to ensure that customers perceive a product in the way that is intended. If there is a mismatch of customer perception and supplier intention, then there is a problem. For example, when Sunny Delight was launched, it was **positioned** as a healthy drink for children; one that children would like the taste of

brand

the essence of a product, what it is (physical characteristics) and what people believe it to be and expect from it

brand identity

all the outward trappings of the brand, e.g. logo, name, colours, strap line and packaging

brand image

people's perception of the brand

and parents would feel was doing them good. Children did like the taste but parents did not share Procter & Gamble's view of the product's healthy qualities. There was a rethink, a redesign and a relaunch.

Products confer benefits aside from the core. You may buy a car primarily so that you can travel to other places with relative ease. However, which car you buy will depend upon its features and the additional benefits they provide. You may want a fast car, a safe car, a car that keeps you cool. In a competitive market, the customer's perception of the product is very important as it is the main determinant of their choice.

Branding spans two levels in our total product diagram. As **brand identity**, it is a part of the basic product, giving it a name and signalling its level of quality. **Brand image** is also an important part of the customer's perception of the product (see below for further explanation of branding).

activity

There are a number of coffee shops in most shopping areas (e.g. Starbucks, Costa Coffee). Visit two, or more, of them and observe how they try to differentiate themselves from their competitors. This may be by service, quality, product range, surroundings, and so on. How well do they do it?

PRODUCT TYPES

All products are not the same. They may differ in the way they do things, the way they are used, the way they are distributed and who they are aimed at. The successful management of a product, brand, or group of products and brands, depends to a great extent on an understanding of the type or types of products and brands with which we are dealing. Clarity in this enables the selection of the most appropriate way in which to design and communicate a properly integrated and focused set of images, messages and customer relationship activities. Products can be grouped with others of broadly similar requirements and need satisfaction.

exhibit 7.2   **Product types**

consumer products	examples
durable	fridges, bicycles
non-durable	fresh food, toiletries
services	theatre seats, haircuts
convenience products:	
impulse buys	snacks, flowers
staples	bread, washing-up liquid
emergency	headache pills, tissues
shopping products	stereos, cars
speciality goods	antiques, sports cars
b2b/industrial products	
capital goods	fork-lift trucks, computers
accessories	screwdrivers, hard hats
raw materials	flour, steel
subassemblies/components	engine, wheels
supplies	stationery, serviettes
services	cleaning, accountancy

Consumer products

Durable goods

These products are expected to last a considerable length of time. They are not used up all at once but can be used repeatedly. A washing machine, for example, is expected to perform a large number of washes, a car a large number of journeys.

Non-durable goods

These products are used up in the process of consumption. They do not last. Fruit is eaten. The powder in the washing powder box dwindles rapidly.

Service products

Services cannot be stored at all. Normally they are used there and then. You watch a film and are left with only a memory (and possibly a ticket stub). You get off the bus and have no further claim on it. Services present marketers with particular challenges and will be discussed in more depth later in this chapter.

User-based products

This is a different way of categorizing products. Grouping them by customer behavioural characteristics can be helpful when devising marketing plans.

Convenience goods

These are products that customers buy frequently and think little about. They are of little value and have many close **substitutes** so they need strong **branding**, and eye-catching colours and designs to make them stand out from the rest. There are a number of categories.

▶ **Impulse goods**: spur-of-the-moment purchases that have no advance planning (e.g. an ice cream because you're standing in a queue and you fancy one). Customers are not usually prepared to pay too high a price for such purchases.

▶ **Staple goods** (essential goods): **staple goods** are purchased regularly, perhaps always kept in the cupboard (e.g. coffee, milk, shampoo). Customers usually look for good value.

▶ **Emergency goods**: **emergency goods** are infrequently purchased but needed at short notice (e.g. rain capes, sun hats, plasters). Such products may be location-specific (rain capes sell well at Disney World and Wimbledon) and have a high value to customers at that time, so their prices can be higher.

Fast moving consumer goods (FMCG) are a form of convenience good, but in this case looked at from the retailer's point of view. They are the products that move off the shelves quickly and so need frequent restocking.

Shopping goods

Shopping goods carry a higher associated risk than do convenience products. They may be higher priced or it may be that the cost of product failure is high.

Customers are likely to *shop around* to find the right car, stereo, furniture, necklace or lawn mower for them (hence the name 'shopping goods'). For many, shopping for such things is an enjoyable leisure activity in its own right. Customers are likely to spend some time over the decision-making process, assessing the options, seeking information and opinions, trying things out. These products are therefore sometimes referred to as **high-involvement purchases**, (i.e. the customer gets very involved in the decision-making). (For more on decision-making, see Chapter 5.)

Speciality goods

Speciality goods are unusual, probably quite pricey, products, which are commonly sold in **niche markets**. They are often high-risk products and customers may need extensive emotional support and encouragement from the supplier. This often means that they are sold through limited outlets (see 'Exclusive distribution' in Chapter 9) by highly trained staff. Examples of speciality goods include model aeroplanes, health foods, wedding clothes, horses and classic cars.

Product failure

Ways in which products may fail to live up to consumer expectations include the following.

▶ **Non-performance**: the product may not deliver the core benefit required. It may not meet the basic need for which it is being bought (i.e. it may not work). The car may not start, the CD may not play. There are degrees of non-performance. The product may meet the core benefit but not deliver all the additional benefits anticipated (e.g. the car works but there is a strange squeak coming from somewhere), or it may be too complicated (e.g. the car radio has 'too many' functions) or, at the extreme, it may turn out to be physically dangerous (e.g. the car's brakes do not work).

▶ **Not me**: the product may not suit the customer after all. They get it home and do not feel good about it.

▶ **Social disapproval**: the customer's friends and family may not like the product.

▶ **Poor value**: there are several elements to this. The customer may wonder whether he or she could have got the product cheaper, or it may turn out to be of lower quality or lower spec than anticipated. Alternatively, it may take up too much time, either in the purchasing or in the installation, learning curve, or ongoing use.

▶ **Non-delivery**: the product may never arrive. This is a common fear of Internet shoppers.

B2b/industrial products

Capital goods

Capital goods are **durable products** such as machinery and buildings. They have to be in place for production to happen. They are usually high cost, bought infrequently and carry high potential risk. Consequently great care is normally taken over these purchases.

Accessories

These are smaller capital items, e.g. hand tools, chairs, shelving. They support the production process.

Raw materials

Raw materials are goods that are processed, and added to, by the manufacturing process. Together they become the finished article. For example, cotton is knitted into socks, crude oil is refined and becomes petrol (and a number of other products), water, hops and yeast are brewed into beer. At this level it may be difficult to distinguish one supplier's products from another since, by their nature, raw materials may be similar. They are often generic products. However, service, delivery terms, technical assistance and many other aspects can be exploited to make the organization different and the preferred supplier (see the **total product** diagram in Exhibit 7.1).

Subassemblies, components and parts

These products have already been manufactured but are not finished goods. They are bought by businesses to incorporate into their own products. For example, Levi's buys denim fabric to make into jeans, Nokia buys microchips to incorporate into its mobile phones, Siemens buys condensers to put into its fridges.

Supplies

Numerous minor items are used in the production process; they are important in the smooth running of the whole process. Companies depend on such things as lubricating oil, stationery, pens, copier paper and floppy disks. These are not **capital goods**. They are non-durable (i.e. they are used up relatively quickly rather than being reused over and over).

Services

Manufacturing businesses rely on efficient machinery, so maintenance and repair services are important to them. All workplaces need regular cleaning. Buildings must be maintained. In addition, there are a large number of business services, such as consultancy, accountancy, legal advice and IT support. The special nature of services is discussed later in this chapter.

There are many different ways to categorize products. Different markets have their own preferred descriptors. Products and services fit into several different categories. Many are bought both by businesses and by consumers (though the specs may be different). For example, floppy disks may be b2b supplies and bought in bulk, or a consumer staple, bought in single packs.

These product types refer to basic products. However, most of the products we buy today are not generic products – they are branded.

SERVICES

Many of the more developed economies rely upon **services** for the bulk of their wealth. The most developed countries (MDCs), e.g. many EU countries and North America, have moved to the next stage and are said to be **knowledge-based economies**. These countries make the bulk of their wealth from the sale of knowledge and skills. Their advanced computer and communications technologies enable this trade.

So Europe has become a continent of consultants, financiers, computer technicians and lawyers, who are paid for their expertise while other countries, with cheaper labour costs, do the manufacturing. Current thinking is that it is a company's intellectual capital that is its most valuable asset, not the more tangible things it owns. This, as Charles Handy (2002) points out, can cause a problem because companies do not actually *own* their employees. They are not slaves. They are free to leave and take their expertise with them. Handy quotes a story about Maurice Saatchi, one of the founders of the advertising agency Saatchi & Saatchi. The board fired Maurice Saatchi, who duly left, taking major clients and some of the agency's best staff with him. These things did not belong to the company or its shareholders.

One of Britain's main foreign currency earners is the City of London where banks, insurance companies and other financial institutions carry out their business. However, tourism also brings huge amounts of money into most European capitals as well as to the beach towns of southern Europe. So, more traditional services still have their part to play.

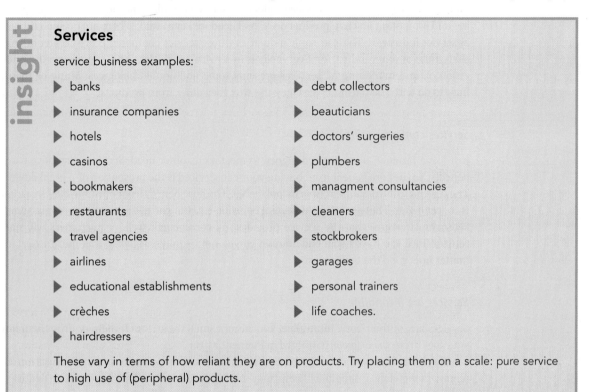

insight

Services

service business examples:

▶ banks	▶ debt collectors
▶ insurance companies	▶ beauticians
▶ hotels	▶ doctors' surgeries
▶ casinos	▶ plumbers
▶ bookmakers	▶ managment consultancies
▶ restaurants	▶ cleaners
▶ travel agencies	▶ stockbrokers
▶ airlines	▶ garages
▶ educational establishments	▶ personal trainers
▶ crèches	▶ life coaches.
▶ hairdressers	

These vary in terms of how reliant they are on products. Try placing them on a scale: pure service to high use of (peripheral) products.

Today, many products have a strong service element, which may be their source of **competitive advantage**. Electrical goods are sold with warranties. Computer software may come with a helpdesk service. Technical equipment needs operator training.

Equally, many services have a product element. A cut and blow dry needs shampoo. A car service needs filters. A consultancy project produces a report. Software comes on CD and has a manual (unless downloaded from the Internet, of course, in which case it may be one of the few examples of a pure service). The degree to which the offerings we are concerned with fall into one end or the other of this spectrum will materially affect the ways in which we choose to create our offering. Service products can use physical elements within the offering to reinforce the experience, and physical products can use service elements to add to the satisfaction provided by the product.

Characteristics of services

services
intangible products

A service is an activity that is carried out for someone else's benefit. There are many other definitions of the term service but most marketers agree that **services** have the following characteristics:

▶ the customer gains some benefit from them
▶ they are intangible
▶ they are time and place dependent (i.e. they cannot be stored or transported)
▶ the service provider is part of the service itself

▶ they are inconsistent

▶ there is no resultant ownership of anything.

Throughout much of this book, products and services have been treated similarly. Many marketers even refer to the 'service product'. A service is really a product and it needs pricing and promoting just as a product does. As Theodore Levitt said, 'There are no such things as service industries. There are only industries whose service components are greater or less than those of other industries. Everybody is in service' (in Kotler, 2003). However, the provision of, and marketing of, services presents some additional challenges. Many of these have to do with the nature of services: the way they differ from products.

Services confer benefits

Just like a product, a service is designed to meet a customer need. Services also have core benefits. So the core benefit from having your car serviced is the prevention of a breakdown. The core benefit from a haircut is to look better. The core benefit from most medical services is to feel better. There may be additional benefits, e.g. the car being worth more, but marketers must ensure that the service provides the core benefit well, or customers will not return. Once you have had a bad haircut, you do not usually go back to that hairdresser no matter how good the coffee was.

Services are intangible

Services are, at their core, intangible. You cannot smell them, touch them or drop them on your foot (from *the Economist*, quoted in Palmer, 2001).

Some services are more intangible than others. For example, a dental check-up is almost completely intangible. There may be no products involved beyond the dentist's instruments. The essence of the service lies in the dentist's skill and that has to be taken on trust. On the other hand, a meal in a restaurant has a lot of tangible things associated with it; in particular, the food. This intangibility makes services harder to market than most products. Potential customers feel more confident buying something that they can see and feel – and take back if necessary. So one of the key challenges for marketers is to make services appear more tangible, often by emphasizing the **peripheral products** used in carrying out the service. Restaurants usually try to convince potential diners that the food is really good. Beauticians stress the properties of the products they use.

Services cannot be stored or transported

This means that they happen at a specific time and place. There are two elements to this. First, you cannot buy a service to keep in the cupboard and use at your convenience like you might a tin of soup or a bottle of shampoo. Few services can be administered long distance. A hotel room cannot be moved; you must sleep in the hotel. A play is not performed whenever and wherever you want; it must be at the theatre and at a scheduled performance time.

Second, just as the consumer cannot store the service, nor can the service provider. A sunglasses manufacturer might well make extra products in advance of the summer and then store them in a warehouse until they are needed, but a hairdresser cannot get ahead by doing extra haircuts.

There are significant managerial implications for service providers. For example, customers who are late for appointments cause serious scheduling problems, and the management of peaks and troughs of demand becomes harder and more important.

The service provider is part of the service

For many services, particularly personal ones such as hairdressing, chiropody and dentistry, the service provider must be at the same place as the customer. The service provider (e.g. the hairdresser, chiropodist, financial adviser, estate agent) is an intrinsic part of the service. The quality of that service is largely dependent upon their skills and so the quality of the people who provide a service is even more important than the quality and skills of those who make products. Faulty products may be caught by quality control before they leave the factory but there are no second chances here. It is not possible to rewind and start again (e.g. uncut someone's hair).

So one bad **service encounter** is a serious thing that may lead to a significant loss of custom. Consequently, **service recovery** is very important. If the service does go wrong, then the customer's complaint must be handled with great care. Good customer relationships are even more important to services businesses. A complaint should be looked at as an opportunity to provide great service. It is possible to turn the situation around and impress the customer after all. Restaurants may apologize profusely and take things off the bill or offer free drinks. Airlines may upgrade seats to first class or offer free tickets for another flight.

service encounter
the time during which a customer is the recipient of a service, e.g. the duration of a meal in a restaurant

service recovery
trying to retrieve a situation caused by a bad product or poor service encounter

e-focus

Internet banking

New technologies have overcome some of the difficulties normally found in the marketing of services. In particular, technology has helped address the issues of inconsistency and inseparability.

In the virutal world, a service product may be intangible but consumption can take place without both provider and customer being in the same place, and be delivered consistently. This has a major advantage in terms of opening hours. Internet banking, for example, is available 24/7 without staff having to be there.

First Direct, now a division of HSBC, was a pioneer of telephone banking and was also among the first to move into Internet banking. Customers can manage most aspects of their accounts online: view balances and statements, transfer money, pay bills and set up direct debits. First Direct has no branches, which means it makes considerable cost savings.

The website helps First Direct in other ways too. The technology provides a more consistent service delivery than a person would, imagery and branding are more tightly controlled and a record of transactions is created automatically.

On the other hand, customers are at the mercy of the unpredictability of the Internet service itself and this may affect their perception of First Direct's service. Also an Internet service is quite easy to mimic, making it harder for brands to differentiate themselves from the competition.

Services are inconsistent

Products aim for consistency in quality, packaging and features. Services, however, are dependent upon humans, and humans are not always consistent. It is rare that two haircuts would be exactly the same. In a restaurant, you might order the same food as before but it is unlikely that it will be prepared and served by the same staff – and, even if it was, it could still be a little different.

Consistency is something that many services strive for, but few deliver. It is more important for some services, e.g. financial ones, than it is for others. Lawyers and accountants rely upon documentation to try to provide consistent services. The Internet has been of great assistance here. Services provided online are made consistent by the constraints of the technology. However, it could be argued that with this consistency comes an inflexibility that does not always provide the service that customers actually want.

Services cannot be owned

This is largely a function of the intangibility of the service. There is nothing to actually own. A client pays for the beautician's skill (and the lotions and potions applied) but at the end of the treatment has nothing more than a good feeling (and possibly better skin) to take home. Services clients are paying for expertise, experience, advice, skills, knowledge and the benefits these bring. The benefits may last, but the service itself is of limited duration.

BRANDING

Branding is 'a strategy to differentiate products and companies, and to build economic value for both the consumer and the brand owner' (Pickton and Broderick, 2001). This section will discuss how it is possible to create and build value into a product by means of a **brand**.

What is a brand?

A brand is 'designed to enable customers to identify products or services which promise specific benefits' (Wilson et al., 1995). From the earliest times, people have marked their possessions in order to differentiate them from other people's. It is not unreasonable to suppose that early man would have scratched a symbol on an axe-shaft to indicate ownership.

Moving forward in time, we can readily identify with the idea of branding one's cattle to show that these particular animals belong to your ranch. Anyone who has watched a cowboy film will have seen the good ol' cowpoke wrestling the calf to the ground and marking it with a red-hot branding iron. Each iron was unique and formed an indelible identifying mark. The possession of such a mark by a beast was an assurance that it was not stolen and that the quality of the beef was likely to be as good as the reputation of the particular ranch.

Although the process is now more sophisticated, the idea of applying an organization's mark, or brand, to products remains the same. The growth of value in the branding activity sprang from the realization that a particular craftsman made especially good tools or leather, or that a particular cattle ranch produced cattle of an above-average quality, which therefore could be sold at a higher price than the others. Now the application of a brand to a product brings with it a wealth of quality, value and high performance cues, which are there for the customer to interpret without the firm having to say a word.

---

activity

What do these marques say to you?

Go to:
http://www.mercedes.co.uk
http://www.rolls-royce.com/
http://www.ferrari.com/
http://www.ford.co.uk

1. What do these car marques say to you?

2. What values to you associate with each of the brands?

3. How does Ford's logo compare to Rolls-Royce? What do the differences convey about each brand identity?

The idea of branding has developed alongside marketing as a managerial process. In its modern form, it can be traced back to the start of the twentieth century, although some company names exist from even before this time, for example Sunlight Soap, Swan Vesta matches, Daimler motor cars, His Master's Voice records (HMV), Boots the Chemists, and many more.

globalfocus

What's in a name?

Increasingly, manufacturers are trying to use the same name for their products worldwide. In Britain, Jif cleaning cream has become Cif to match the rest of Europe. Marathon became Snickers and Oil of Ulay, rather oddly, became Oil of Olay. The UK won on Twix, though, that used to be called Raider elsewhere, but now it's Twix to everyone.

Those name changes were made as part of global branding exercises. Having the same name helps to standardize brand positioning, promotes global recognition and, of course, it's cheaper in terms of packaging, support literature and promotion. Sometimes, though, the name changes because it has to. The existing name just will not do in other languages. For example, Vauxhall used to make a car called the Nova. Ask someone who speaks Spanish what that means and you'll see why they changed it. In China, Coca-Cola translated as 'bite the wax tadpole'. The Jolly Green Giant turned into 'Intimidating Green Ogre' in its Arabic translation.

Here are some products that never made it in English-speaking countries:

▶ Pocari Sweat (soft drink, Japan)

▶ Pipi (orangeade, Yugoslavia)

▶ Pschitt! (soft drink, France)

▶ Skinababe (baby cleanser, Japan)

▶ Krapp (toilet paper, Sweden).

Branding as a marketing tool

Hand in hand with the growing understanding of how and why branding works, has come a change in emphasis within organizations. Companies used to be centred on making or producing things. They then expected customers to beat the doors down to force money into their hands. Next came a time when forceful salesmen would drive sales by persuading customers to buy their product, often quite aggressively. Now we accept the achievement of customer satisfaction as being more crucial to success than production or selling (see Chapter 2). This, of course, has not necessarily been the result of companies being seized with compassion for their customers, but rather the result of ever increasing competition, and the realization that the one who achieves most nearly what the customer wants is the one who will win out. The development of faster and better methods of manufacture has led to the vastly increased level of choice being offered to the customer. This change from a supply-dominated marketplace to one where customers demand certain things and are prepared to look for what they want comes from the certain knowledge that it will be available from one of the many possible sources now competing for their business.

A good brand name helps a firm achieve a premium price for its products. Without it, the likelihood is that the firm will have to settle for a commodity position in the market where price (inferring cheapest) is the only driver for sales. This can, of course, be a perfectly honourable strategy and position to adopt, but not one that sits comfortably when considering marketing as a series of complex management tasks that will lead to greater future success for the organization. This is more particularly so since the modern world – and all its complexities in communication and distribution of goods and services nationally, internationally and globally – presents vast choice to customers. The challenge is to obtain a customer in the first place, and to hang on to them in the future. Branding aims to do this. The appearance of the brand on a product simplifies the shopping or **adoption** process, short-circuiting a lot of the searching that the customer might otherwise expect to undertake.

If a particular brand has served the customer well in the past, they will assume that it can be expected to do so in the future. This can simplify the process of introducing new products to the market as customers are more likely to trust a new product from a known name. They feel safe in the knowledge that if there is a problem with the product, the company will stand behind it and resolve the problem.

From this it can be seen that good experience of a brand equals a happy customer who continues to purchase and that, conversely, a bad experience can lead to an unhappy customer who may very well reject future offerings bearing this brand, no matter how attractive the offering. Worse still, they may tell their friends, family and acquaintances of their bad experience, influencing them against the brand. Attraction and retention are the key words when thinking about the development of a brand.

Brand strength is important and so maintaining and building this strength is an essential part of managing a brand. However, bearing in mind the insubstantial nature of a brand (how we cannot touch, taste, hear or smell it), how can we get to grips with the successful management of this mystery? The practical way of thinking through this process is to consider the rationale behind the brand while remembering that its characteristics are entirely dependent on the customer's feelings towards it.

Behind the brand

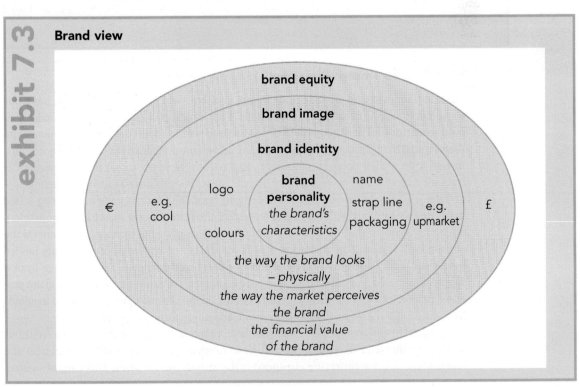

exhibit 7.3

Brand view

brand equity

brand image

brand identity

logo   **brand**   name
        personality
e.g.   *the brand's*   strap line
cool   *characteristics*   packaging   e.g.
colours   upmarket

€   £

*the way the brand looks
– physically
the way the market perceives
the brand
the financial value
of the brand*

Branding has spawned a host of terms that are often used slightly differently in different texts. At the heart of a brand is its **brand personality**. A brand can have the same traits as a person or, at least, it can be described in the same way. Brands may be young (e.g. Barbie), mature (e.g. Saga), rebellious (e.g. Virgin), understated (e.g. Liberty), classy (e.g. Aston Martin), forceful (e.g. Nike), caring (e.g. BUPA) – the list goes on. Marketers endow their brands with a personality, which may be articulated in a brand personality statement. However, deciding you want your brand to be fun is a different thing to getting other people to see it that way.

The brand's personality has to be put across to the outside world and this is done by means of the **brand identity**. This consists of all the outward trappings of the brand, e.g. **logo**, name, colours, **strap line** and packaging.

Cadbury has a strong brand identity

However, messages are not always received as intended (see Chapter 8). The **target audience**'s perception of the brand may be different to that which was intended. This audience perception of the brand is called the **brand image** and it is this that really matters. This is what people really think of the brand.

To sum up, the **brand personality** is put across through symbols known as the brand identity and these create a brand image in the minds of the target audience.

Brand image has a value. You know this. You know that branded goods cost more than unbranded ones. If it is a strong, desirable, brand, then it will cost a lot more. Compare the prices of lesser-known brands of sportswear with those of Nike and Adidas. This value is known as **brand equity**, and it is notoriously difficult to calculate. One way to do it is to examine takeover bids. Companies usually have to pay more than the value of a firm's physical assets in order to buy it. They pay for goodwill (ongoing business prospects) and, in a consumer goods firm, that is largely down to the strength of the firm's brands. In the early 1990s, Nestlé paid an additional £1.5 billion (€2.1 billion) for Rowntree's in a deal that gave it rights to one of the biggest-selling chocolate snacks of all time: KitKat. An alternative way to value a brand is to ascertain how much extra customers are prepared to pay for the branded good rather than an unbranded one. So, how much more would you pay for a KitKat than for an unheard-of chocolate wafer biscuit? That **price premium** can then be multiplied by the number of bars sold (say in a year) to arrive at the brand equity. Neither these, nor the many other valuation methods tried, are entirely satisfactory. However, it is generally agreed that strong brands do have value – we are just not sure how much.

The brand–customer relationship

Central to any effort to establish or grow a brand is the strength of the relationship developed between the customer and the brand, sometimes not necessarily with the brand owner. For example, Diageo is the owner of a large number of drinks brands (Smirnoff, Bailey's, Guinness, Johnny Walker, Captain Morgan) and yet few customers realize this when buying these drinks in a bar. Their relationship is with the brand and not the brand owner.

The product itself is providing the reinforcement and increasing the brand value perceived by the customer.

This, of course, is a very personal value and may be arrived at independently of any marketing proposals that may be made. The realization that this is the case has led companies to engage in relationship-building activities whereby a line of communication is established with the customer so that a two-way flow of information can take place. Examples of this activity in practice include: club memberships, loyalty card schemes, registration of warranties and website activities.

Brand loyalty

The driver behind the effort to establish brand value in the mind of the consumer is **brand loyalty**. The achievement of brand loyalty in the customer, when the customer will consistently choose your brand over another, is the ultimate goal. This loyalty can help to achieve premium status and prices for our products. However, loyalty can be destroyed much more quickly than it can be established. Quality considerations are crucial, both in the product itself, and in the quality of service. Have you ever tried to resolve a home computer problem by using the much-heralded helplines? The experience can be traumatic, and will certainly lead to doubts about the wisdom of purchasing another product from the company involved.

| **brand manager** |
| similar to a product manager, markets a particular brand |

The pursuit of brand strength forms a major part of any **brand manager**'s activity. A strong brand will survive and grow in a competitive environment, providing customer satisfaction through differentiation from competing brands. This is a function of the perceived value placed on it by the consumer. Tied in with this is the process of building brand loyalty by establishing, through excellent performance and service, a willingness on the part of the customer to continue using the brand in spite of persuasive attempts by other, similar suppliers.

Much of what we consider to be brand loyalty can be considered as an emotional reaction on the part of the customer, an emotional bond that can be very personal and powerful, and is largely the result of past experience. Consider the reaction in America when Coca-Cola launched New Coke. The product had been extensively blind taste-tested in the marketplace and had been almost universally described as having a superior taste to original Coke. However, when the new version replaced the old, public reaction was violent. Street protests took place and the demand was for the old version to be brought back. The emotional involvement with the product, and all that it meant personally to customers, was so deep that any tampering with it tested customer loyalty to its extreme. The cynics among us might wonder how a brown fizzy liquid could excite such emotions, but emotions are fickle and can be troublesome to influence and control.

The great value in building these emotional linkages, and hence loyalty, is that, economically, it is far more expensive to obtain a new customer than to retain an existing customer. Indeed some corporations calculate the lifetime value of a customer, making the argument that it is therefore worth paying great attention to customer retention as an activity, since the loss of a customer will destroy the remainder of that lifetime value. Burger King has, for example, placed a lifetime value on a regular purchaser of approaching £2500 (€3500). This therefore leads into considerations of how to retain a customer rather than how to achieve the one-off sale. The stressing of mutual added benefits between the customer and the organization as the result of a continuing relationship plays a great part in this process.

Brand types

exhibit 7.4

Brand types

corporate umbrella brands	all products use corporate name	e.g. Heinz, Next
family umbrella brands	the organization uses a different name for its products	e.g. St Michael (Marks & Spencer), Jonelle (John Lewis)
range brands	groups of products share a brand name	e.g. Taste the Difference (Sainsbury's), Lean Cuisine (Nestlé)
individual brands	each product has its own brand name	e.g. Twix (Mars), Bold (Procter & Gamble)
own-label (private)	products bear the retailer's name	eg Tesco, Safeway

There are a number of different types of brand in the marketplace today (see Exhibit 7.4). Each of these brand types has advantages and disadvantages but most companies use the type of brand name they do for historical reasons. Companies often start out with the owner's name (e.g. Mars, Cadbury's, Guinness, Ford, Mercedes, Marks & Spencer), this remains the corporate brand as it is known and people make associations with it. Later, the company may add further names, either individual names, family names or range names. Most of Cadbury's products have an individual name as well as the corporate name. The Cadbury's name is the badge of quality, the individual name is an identifier for a particular recipe of confectionery. A purely descriptive name for a Cadbury's Flake would be too long and would not differentiate the product from the competition. Heinz traditionally sticks to descriptors, e.g. Heinz baked beans, Heinz tomato ketchup, relying on its own name to establish the **brand image**. More recently, however, it has introduced, or acquired, some range brands (e.g. Weight Watchers and Linda McCartney).

Own-label brands are a relatively new phenomenon. They are popular with retailers (and some wholesalers) because they enable them to earn better profits. These products are not manufactured by the retailers, just badged. The advantage to the manufacturer is that it can use up spare capacity this way. However, these brands can be the cause of friction in the **supply chain** if the manufacturer believes that the own-label product is too similar to its own (see 'ethical focus' box).

own-label
products that bear a retailer's brand name, e.g. Tesco (also known as 'private brands')

ethicalfocus

The lookalikes

Over the last few years, a number of manufacturers have taken retailers to court over own-label brands that just look too much like the real thing. The complaint may be about the make-up of the product itself or it may be about the packaging – an infringement of the brand is protentially even more damaging than a rip-off of the product itself.

▶ United Biscuits, makers of the much-loved Penguin, sued ASDA over its Puffin bars.

▶ Coca-Cola's objection to Sainsbury's Classic Cola can resulted in a redesign.

> ▶
> > ▶ Kellogg's has complained about the package design of Tesco's breakfast cereals.
>
> > ▶ ASDA was in trouble again, this time over the appearance of its own-label versions of popular spirits such as Archers and Malibu.
>
> The original manufacturers have put millions into brand development and don't see why these retailers should cash in. It is difficult to decide where to draw the line – when is it a product inspired by the original, and when is it a cheap imitation?

Branding strategies

The choice of brand type could almost be said to be a strategy in itself. It certainly has far-reaching consequences for the company's marketing. However, there are some specific strategies that relate to branding.

Co-branding is when two companies' brand names appear together, as on PCs when the brand name of the chip manufacturer appears alongside the PC maker (e.g. 'Intel inside'). Either or both brands should benefit from this as the good image of one rubs off on the other.

Multibranding is a strategy employed by companies that have multiple products within the same category. This gives the customer the illusion of choice. They can **brand-switch**, but still be buying from the same supplier. For example, Procter & Gamble has many different brands of washing powder: Ace, Dreft, Bold (Bolt), Ariel, Dash, Fairy, Daz, Bonus, Vizir and Tide. These are not all available in all countries, and each lays claim to slightly different properties, but they all clean clothes.

The above are ongoing strategies. However, one of the great advantages of a strong brand is that it can be used to launch new products with a far greater chance of success. According to Kotler (2003), there are three ways to introduce more products under the auspices of an existing brand:

1. **line extension** – using the brand name on products within the same category

2. **brand extension** – using the brand name on products in a new category but within the same, broadly defined market

3. **brand stretching** – using the name on products in a different market.

For example, when Robinsons launched a new summer fruits drink flavour, that was a line extension. When Mars started making ice cream bars, that was a brand extension. The king of the brand stretch is Richard Branson of Virgin. Taking a brand name originally chosen for the music industry and launching it into airlines, drinks, trains, radio, cosmetics, mobile phones, etc. – that's brand stretching.

These new product strategies carry different levels of risk. The lowest risk would appear to be the line extension. It can be anticipated that existing, loyal customers will try a new variant of a product they already buy. However, all that is happening here is that they are substituting the new version for the old. There is no overall increase in sales. Line extension does have a role to play, though. In fact, it is essential to many brands that new versions be introduced or the line will become stale. Chocolate manufacturers launch new bars. Perfumiers introduce new scents or packaging. Drinks companies try out new flavours. New versions of products replace those that have reached the end of their lives and no longer sell well. A good brand manager anticipates that decline, and has the new variant ready in advance of it (see 'The **product life cycle**', below).

Brand extension carries a higher risk of failure. People loved Mars ice cream. It was such a success that other chocolate manufacturers followed suit. Would you buy any kind of food from Mars? How about frozen ready meals? Baked beans? Breakfast cereal? Unilever successfully extended its Lynx brand. The original Lynx was just a deodorant but now a wide range of grooming products are available under that brand name. Sometimes a brand carries with it associations that would be unhelpful to the new product. Companies may then actively try to disassociate the two. So Levi's didn't go for Levi's cotton; it called its cotton trousers Dockers. Sometimes, a company opts for a new **family brand** name, perhaps coupled with the **corporate brand** (e.g. Tesco Finest).

The riskiest of these three strategies is brand stretching. Often, the stretched brand breaks. Xerox computers were never as popular as the company's copiers and printers. *Cosmopolitan*'s move into the health food sector (with a range of low-fat dairy products) did not work, nor did its Cosmo Spirit Cafés (Anonymous, 2003). The strategy does work for some, however, even without a new family brand name. Yamaha successfully added musical instruments, home audio/video equipment, computer peripherals and sports equipment to its motorcycle range. Many retailers have successfully moved into financial services, offering credit cards, loans and insurance. Usually they do not run these services themselves, of course; they license others to do so, lending their name to the enterprise.

insight

Boots march on

It used to be called Boots the Chemist but that may not be appropriate for much longer. The high street retailer long ago extended its range of products beyond medicines. In a Boots store today, you can have your eyes tested and get films developed, as well as buy cosmetics, toiletries, baby clothes, gifts and sandwiches. However, the electrical goods and kitchen utensils have gone. The brand has already successfully stretched into health services. There are Boots dentists and laser eye clinics. Its most recent addition is fitness equipment – a complementary product for its West London gym.

Whatever brand type or strategy is adopted, it is important that the idea of the brand is not limited to the actual product. It should be part of the whole experience. A **brand promise** is made to the customer. Fulfilling that promise, hopefully even exceeding it, is a key part of brand management.

PRODUCT DEVELOPMENT

New products are the lifeblood of a company. Competitors improve their product offerings all the time and customers will switch brands to a newer, better offering if there is one. Would you buy a typewriter, or a dedicated word processor, when you could have the latest PC with the latest word-processing package? Do you want last year's fashion? Without successful innovation, companies die.

New products do not have to be new inventions. Most new products are modifications of previous offerings rather than new-to-the-world products. It is as legitimate to describe changing the colour of the packaging of a washing powder as product development as it is to describe the invention of the electric light or the Dyson cleaner. The essence of any product is that it satisfies a real customer need or want. Remember that there are no new needs, only new ways of serving them.

The importance of innovation

New products can be used to:

▶ increase or defend market share by offering more choice within the range, or by updating older products (e.g. Ford has developed people carrier versions of most of its models)

- appeal to a different **market segment** (e.g. Guinness bitter, Häagen-Dazs frozen yoghurt)
- maintain reputation as a leading-edge company (e.g. Apple computers)
- diversify into new markets and thereby spread risk (e.g. Virgin Cola/Vodka)
- improve relationships within **distribution channels** (e.g. Allied Domecq offering its Baskin-Robbins franchisees further franchise opportunities in Dunkin' Donuts and Togo's)
- make better use of resources such as production capacity (e.g. some chocolate bars can be made on the same production machinery)
- even out peaks and troughs in demand (e.g. ice cream parlours selling baked potatoes; Father's Day was invented by greetings card companies).

The Dyson vacuum cleaner was an innovative new product

Types of new product

Types of new product are as follows.

- **Innovative product**: this is a really new product, probably a technological or medical breakthrough, e.g. DVD (although this could be said to be a replacement for CD), the Internet, text messaging, laser eye surgery. There are relatively few of these types of new-to-the-market products and services.
- **Replacement product**: these are more common than innovative ones, e.g. the CD (more or less) replaced LPs, the Ford Focus replaced the Ford Escort.
- **Variant product**: many companies frequently introduce new, related products to their ranges, these may be temporary or more permanent additions, e.g. KitKat Chunky (long term), Ford Fiesta Flame (special edition).
- **Me-too product**: these are imitations of products already on the market, e.g. Wrigley's Extramints, Trebor 24/7 chewing gum. It makes sense to let others do the costly market research and development first. Innovative new products may be protected by a patent, requiring imitators to obtain a licence to produce their version or risk being sued.
- **Relaunched product**: this is not really a new product at all, the physical characteristics of the basic product may not be altered (or only slightly) but the **total**

product offering has changed. There will be a different marketing strategy, perhaps changing the emphasis on product benefits, e.g. in 2003, the magazine *Inside Soap* was relaunched as a weekly, rather than a fortnightly, publication.

Marketers must manage and control the total product offering so that maximum customer satisfaction can be had. It is therefore essential to devise a process that brings forward the right new products.

Top management should believe in and provide active support for the constant development and improvement of existing offerings, as well as providing for their replacement. This process can take a number of forms. It may range from an informal exercise in bringing ideas forward, up to a formal structured approach that has its own staff and facilities, and that is charged with the requirement to bring forward new offerings that match the ever changing demands of the consumer. The better the product offering matches this demand, the more likely it is to achieve consumer satisfaction – and success in the marketplace.

It may be seen, then, that a vital component in the construction and management of the product is an understanding of what consumers want. This changes with time and experience: consumption changes the consumer. No matter how excellent, innovatory and leading edge a product might be, once the consumer has experienced it, that experience becomes the base acceptable standard. Anything less in the future will be regarded as inferior and therefore of less value. For example, imagine you go to a restaurant and buy a burger and fries. The meal comes with a relish tray and a side order of onion rings. This is what you expect if you decide to eat at that restaurant again. If the next time you go, the burger is smaller or less tasty, or there are no onion rings or relish tray, then you will be disappointed and unlikely to return to the restaurant.

The new product development process

The following is an idealized model of the process of product development and places into context the various activities which it is suggested are necessary when trying to achieve effective product development, preferably on a continuous basis.

exhibit 7.5

New product development

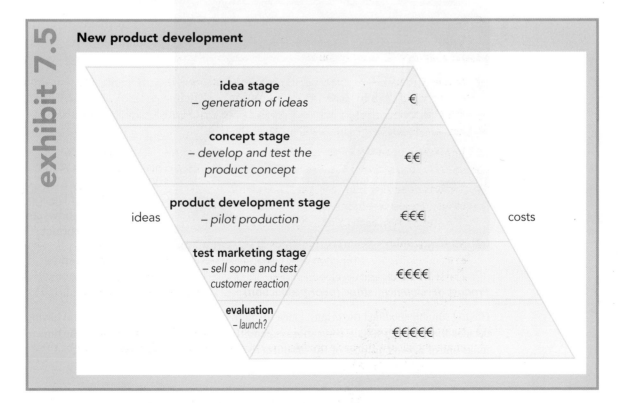

idea stage
– generation of ideas
€

concept stage
– develop and test the product concept
€€

ideas

product development stage
– pilot production
€€€

costs

test marketing stage
– sell some and test customer reaction
€€€€

evaluation
– launch?
€€€€€

Constant monitoring and evaluation are indispensable requirements in this product development process. The aim is to bring forward only the right products, and to dispose of those that have little or no chance of success as early as possible.

Idea stage (generation of ideas)

There are many ways to bring forward new ideas: from brainstorming to establishing original research facilities. Brainstorming is the collection of ideas from a group of people who are given a free hand. At first, nothing is barred and no idea is disregarded.

For example, 3M (the makers of Scotch Tape and Post-it Notes) expects all of its employees to devote a certain percentage of their time to thinking up new ideas, and the company also has sophisticated research facilities. Any source of new ideas is acceptable just so long as everyone involved accepts that many such ideas will be discarded, sometimes very early in the process of monitoring and evaluation.

Concept stage (develop and test the product concept)

This stage involves the production of drawings, descriptions and theoretical models to see whether an idea works. At this stage the concept should be examined to see that it fits in with the strategic plans of the organization.

For example, in the motor industry many ideas are floated but get rejected quickly. Those that still have merit are passed to the design studio where the proposed car is mocked up, perhaps even as a full-size clay model that can be seen in three dimensions. Individuals, both inside and outside the organization, are then shown the model and their opinions sought.

At this stage the concept should be examined to see whether or not it fits in with the strategic plans of the organization. Is it, in fact, the sort of product that will add to and complement the company's range of products? Success here will lead to the next stage.

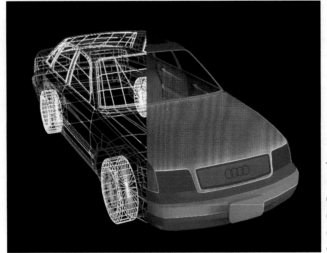

This image of an Audi 100 car made by a Computer Aided Design (CAD) package shows an early stage of product development

Photo credit: Alfred Pasieka/Science Photo Library

Product development stage (pilot production)

Having suitably modified the original idea through the concept-testing process, and having decided that the idea still deserves more expenditure of time and money, now is the time to make one or a small number of the products to evaluate production capabilities.

A full-size, working product should be made to see whether any so far unforeseen problems arise. These may be manufacturing difficulties, or not being able to achieve costing or profit targets.

These initial pilot runs may involve making the product entirely by hand, looking for production pitfalls. Critical evaluation can now take place, assessing the fitness of the product in its approximately finished form, after testing its effectiveness and potential profitability. In short, does it work at all levels? Is it something people will buy and can we make a profit doing it?

A crucial judgement will probably be made now as to how this proposed product will fit in with the other products in the organization's portfolio or range of products. Does it add to, or enhance, the range, or does it have the potential to take business away from the firm's other products?

Test marketing stage (sell some and test customer reaction)

Ideas that have overcome all the previous hurdles and are products which, it is believed, are ready for sale, could now be the subject of a limited production run, to be sold to a small, selected market. By choosing a marketplace in miniature, which market research shows reflects the real world, the new product can be tried out to see if it performs as well as expected.

This trial should comprise not only the product itself but also all the related marketing mix activities. For example, a particular geographic area may be selected for the trial or test market, and all the advertising and promotional activities selected for the product – for example, local television and radio stations, newspapers, and so on, together with any billboard advertising and in-shop promotions.

Using a discrete area to test market the product enables the monitoring and evaluation of the effectiveness of all parts of the offering and its associated marketing mix. If this proves successful it may be decided, in the case particularly of **FMCG (fast moving consumer goods)**, to roll out the launch immediately. It may also be that the test-marketing exercise leads to a decision to withdraw the product for modification or even withdraw it completely. Hopefully the monitoring and evaluation activities undertaken so far will not have let a product so fatally flawed get to this stage

It is obvious, however, that test marketing is a vastly expensive and time-consuming exercise, which apart from costing a lot of money may reveal product secrets to the competition before the organization is ready to take them on. It may also be that the new product is a simple modification of an existing one, the market is well known and understood, and any reaction one way or the other is likely to be minimal. Test marketing should not be thought of as an indispensable part of the development exercise. It should be used with caution and as appropriate.

Evaluation (to launch or not to launch?)

Mention has been made of evaluation at each stage in the product development process. This is a crucial activity that seeks to eliminate those ideas that do not pass the tests as early as possible, and certainly before the embarrassment and expense of a failed product. The idea should be looked at critically to see whether it fits the organization's requirements as well as those of the potential customer.

However, when assessing a product idea, it should not be forgotten that sometimes there is a potential need for a product that has not yet been identified by the consumer. It is not really possible to assess customer reaction accurately, before we show them the finished item. Take, for example, electric light. We take it for granted now, but 100 years ago people were

---

FMCG (fast moving consumer goods)

low-value items, frequently bought, e.g. toothpaste

quite happy with gaslight. They liked the greenish glow it gave and appreciated the extra warmth in winter. Yet Thomas Edison knew that electric light would sweep civilization. He was greeted with scepticism at first, and had to give many demonstrations, including lighting the streets of New York by building at his own expense the generating stations necessary and installing the lamps free of charge. Indeed in the early days of domestic electricity the electricity companies had to offer to wire up houses free of charge to encourage use.

The same principles apply today. The ISP AOL provide 50 days' free trial in the hope that the public will adopt its service. Mobile phones have been offered free of charge if customers will sign up for a monthly contract.

insight

Clockwork power

As the pace of technological change gathers speed, there are, apparently, fewer and fewer areas where customers might be surprised by new-to-the-world ideas. New and wonderful electronic gizmos, both for entertainment and for more serious applications, are everywhere and have become the norm. Yet it is still possible to be surprised. Take, for example, the Bayliss wind-up radio, which exploited old clockwork technology, applied modern techniques and produced a fully portable power source that is now being exploited elsewhere – for example, in powering laptop computers, satellite navigation systems and even for recharging mobile phones by use of a device included in a pair of hiking boots (every step generates power for the user's phone).

Initially, Trevor Bayliss found it next to impossible to find a manufacturer prepared to back him. They were unable to envisage the potential of his radical idea.

Development continues apace. New products are launched regularly, and indeed the continued existence of many large high-tech corporations hangs on the successful launch of their next new product. Just look at the battles between the producers of computer games and their associated equipment. Where is Sega now? Miss the target and billions of pounds' worth of sales can slip into the hands of competitors. So much depends on the effectiveness with which target markets have been researched, and expectations matched, when the new product is launched.

Having developed a new product offering, the manager must now get to grips with how it performs in the real marketplace. One of the tools available to aid the planning and management process is the product life cycle concept.

THE PRODUCT LIFE CYCLE

The **product life cycle** concept is one that has many opponents and many supporters. On the one hand it has limited usefulness as a management tool, since it provides no absolute answers. On the other hand it has great utility by providing guidance as to future activity, and the mere action of creating such a model stimulates the generation of considerable comparative market analysis. With such analysis comes a greater understanding of the product's commercial environment. Assessing the position in the life cycle attained by an individual product can clarify the manager's thoughts as to the status of each individual product in the range, and what reasonable expectations can be placed on them.

This plotting process gives a clearer view of what has gone before and what might happen in the future. With this knowledge, the marketing manager is able to plan for the best return for the organization.

This must, of course, be qualified. The life cycle position of any product is going to be largely a matter of opinion rather than absolute scientific fact. Any recommended management action can be just that, a matter of opinion, based on past experience. The balancing and weighing of material facts, experience and theoretical advice is the basis of all management, which still retains elements of skill, experience and craft.

The plotted position of the product in the model can provide a solid indication as to the balance of our use of the various marketing tools. Did they work? Are they working? How might they work in the future? Should thought be given, for example, to changing the emphasis of the promotional activities from educational to more deliberate sales encouragement? Has the time come to re-examine the position of the product in the market, and should we try to find other groups of customers?

The model (as shown in Exhibit 7.6) illustrates how products move through a series of stages in their progress from introduction to a market to their final replacement with another product, offering, or solution to the expressed problem. This process is likened to the path we take as human beings, from our birth, through growing up, reaching maturity, then old age, and finally into decline and ultimately death.

The big difference, though, is that a product has no natural life except that which we choose to give it by managing its existence. We can terminate it, or extend its life at will, we can change aspects of its character to help it adjust to changing market conditions, and indeed renew it at will. The benefit of the product life cycle model as a tool is that it enables us to understand in general how a product is performing in the real world, how it has performed in the past and how we might anticipate it to perform in the future. In particular, it gives us a guide as to the actions that are most appropriate when thinking about how we use the marketing tools available to us.

This model can be related (though not precisely) to the stages of **product adoption** (see Chapter 5).

Introduction

At the introduction stage, clearly the product has no **market share**; the customers may in fact never even have heard that such a thing is available. The challenge is to educate the market, tell people about the product and where it can be acquired.

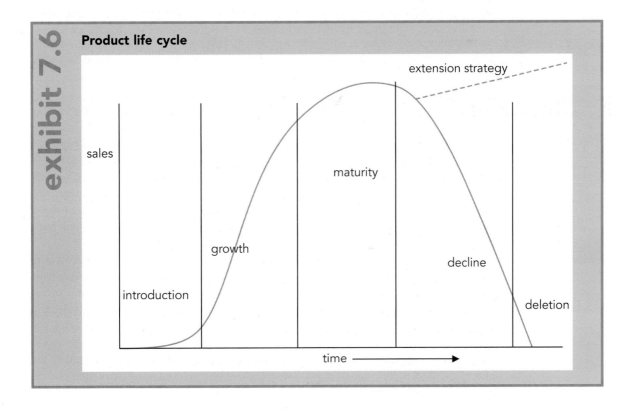

exhibit 7.6

Product life cycle

Growth

The growth stage reflects the increasing sales, adoption, and understanding and appreciation of the product. Marketing activity will centre upon aiming to reach the anticipated sales and profit forecasts that were the principle basis for the decision to launch the product. We strive to achieve the market share that reflects the main target achievement. This stage is characterized by an increasing share of a growing market and, more than likely, the appearance of me-too competitors.

Maturity

The maturity stage of the life cycle represents the achievement of the desired share of the market and is characterized by gradually decreasing growth in sales, a relatively stable market, and probably a falling-away of weaker or less committed competitors. The effort will possibly be to find new market segments to serve, or new uses for the product in order to drive volume growth. This is the stage at which the greatest profit may be had since we have paid for all the development and launch costs, and have achieved the proposed standing in the market. Our promotional spending will have reduced, being principally arranged to support and remind customers about the product, and to achieve the greatest level of satisfaction through our service and performance. We will do everything we can to maintain this position for as long as possible, by whatever means are available to us. Refreshing the appearance of the product and augmenting the offering with perhaps extended warranties and accessories may be activities that can extend the profitable life of the product.

Decline

The decline stage, which we have attempted to delay for as long as practically possible, will be signposted by stagnating sales in a declining market. There are no longer any options left open to revitalize the product since the market itself is shrinking. This may not be as catastrophic as it at first appears, since many examples exist of products being well managed in their decline, producing very satisfactory profits, and preparing the market for the successful introduction of the new replacement. Little promotional spending is incurred, as well as little in the way of improvement expenditure on service, production or distribution.

Deletion

The final activity is the deletion stage, when the decision is taken to withdraw the product from the range, usually indicated by evidence that the product is costing more to maintain and support than it garners in profit. It is costing money to retain it. Signs to look for are a stagnant, or shrinking, market. This may be indicated by falling sales in spite of the best efforts of the management team, declining profits, the existence of new, alternative ways of satisfying customer needs and wants, and the necessity to expend ever increasing amounts of money on supporting promotional activities.

Ra-ra skirts, hula-hoops (the plastic toys, not the snack), yo-yos and typewriters have one thing in common. They are all products that experienced invention, growth and decline, and no longer hold any significant commercial value (although hula-hoops and yo-yos make sporadic reappearances as novelty items). They all went through their life cycles and were replaced by other products that better reflected customers' perceptions of being the right thing.

In spite of life cycle theory, however, there are some products that appear to defy the idea of eventual decline and deletion. Examples may be given of Coca-Cola, which goes on and on, Mars bars, Morgan cars, Levi's jeans, and many others.

Of course, when we look more closely we see that, in fact, these products are brands, which are being constantly refreshed and renewed. Coca-Cola comes in vanilla flavour, different-size bottles and from different outlets. There are Mars bars ice creams and miniatures, Morgan updates (the Plus 8 supercar, for example) and Twisted jeans from Levi's. Nothing remains static as markets and customers continuously change and evolve. Products and offerings must change as well; the skilful manager understands this and is constantly adapting the offering to suit changing conditions and demands. **Extension strategies** may be used, for instance, which enable the product to reach a wider audience, or indeed persuade the existing customer base to use more of the product. Perhaps in different combinations with other products, or by using the product in a different way (100 uses for WD40, or Rice Crispies made into a chocolate confection for children's parties). It may be an option to change the **positioning** of the product to bring in a whole new set of customers. Lucozade, for example, was known for many years as a drink best used by invalids in order to increase their energy levels. Being ill was made more bearable by the sight of the orange film-wrapped bottle. The product's owners then repositioned the drink to be an energy booster for sportspeople, and it assumed a much more youthful, 'isotonic' personality, aimed especially at young people. The **brand personality** has been changed yet again to become a mixture of a health drink and an energy drink. Each change has been to target different **market segments**, extending usage of the product and thereby its life. However, for the most part products have a life span that eventually leads to decline.

> **extension strategies**
>
> means of prolonging the product life cycle

Eventually, the decision may be reached that the product is no longer viable and the firm should consider deleting it from the range offered. However, deciding and doing are two different things. Consideration must be given to all the surrounding circumstances.

What effect, for instance, might the deletion have on the rest of the range? Would the whole offering become incomplete? Could we risk losing business all round because of this? How is this going to appear to the customers, some of whom may have great loyalty to us? What residual problems may we be left with (for instance, warranties and service expectations)?

Take, for example, an airline that decided to delete a particular service to a particular destination. Frequent users of this service had accumulated a substantial number of Air Miles, which they were now no longer able to use. The airline has to continue to show these as something it owes to its customers until they are used and would therefore be showing a large debt in its books. Since the Air Miles had no expiry date this debt could apparently have existed for ever. The airline solved the conundrum by converting the value of the Air Miles into shopping vouchers, which the customers could spend at home.

Critique

The product life cycle model is not without its critics. Its very simplicity ensures that many will say it cannot possibly adequately represent the situation in a complex and dynamic marketplace. Not all products follow this pattern, of course. Some just never seem to die (e.g. KitKat). Others, of course, never actually grow to maturity. It is estimated that at least 50 per cent of new products fail within a year of their launch: they die before they have lived. So the product life cycle is a model of a successful product, not a failure.

PRODUCT PORTFOLIO MANAGEMENT

Few companies sell just one product; some sell thousands. Their products are collectively referred to as the **product portfolio**, and this needs careful management.

> **product portfolio**
>
> all a company's, or SBU's, products

The number of **product lines** a company sells is referred to as **product breadth**. Within each line, there will be several products (**product depth**). For example, the Ford

product manager

responsible for the
marketing of a
specific product or
product line

Fiesta is a product line. It contains a number of models (Finesse, LX, Zetec, Ghia, etc.), which may have different engines and other features. That is its depth. The **product manager** will lay down guidelines for the consistency required within each line, both in terms of product features and in terms of marketing activities. Products may be introduced, dropped, modified, replaced. Sufficient resources must be allocated (e.g. budgets for advertising, research, customer support). The manager must also agree what contribution to profits the product can reasonably be expected to make. The company must have enough cash-generating products to support the cash eaters.

A number of management tools have been developed to help managers to manage their product portfolios. These help to judge how individual products and **brands**, or ranges of products and brands, are performing. They can also be used to judge the performance of **strategic business units (SBUs)**. Then decisions can be taken on the products' futures.

There are a number of different **product portfolio analysis** tools and, even though they appear simple, all require considerable effort if they are to prove genuinely useful. The **Boston Consulting Group matrix (BCG matrix)** is one such tool (see Exhibit 7.7). This model looks at the growth of the market and the relative share the company has of that market.

Star

Star products and services are in rapidly growing **markets** in which the company has a high relative **market share** (e.g. Sony's desktop video-cam, HSBC's First Direct Internet banking service). They are good investments as they have high earning potential both at the present time and in the future. That investment is likely to be needed if the company wants to retain its market position, as competitors will be measuring themselves against the star.

Cash cow

This product is in a less dynamic, or even a static, market in which the company has a high relative market share. Many cash cows (e.g. KitKat, Levi's 501s) are the cream of the crop. They require little promotion although under-investment can turn them into dogs (see below) so they should not be taken for granted. The object is to hold the position in order to

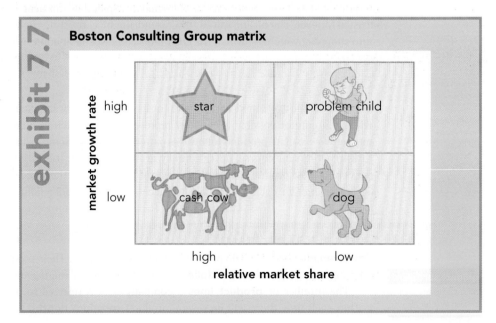

exhibit 7.7   **Boston Consulting Group matrix**

return on investment (ROI)

profit expressed as a percentage of the capital invested

obtain maximum **return on investment (ROI)**. The profits from cash cows can be used to invest in stars or problem children.

Problem child

Products in this quadrant are those in a rapidly growing market but in which the company has a somewhat lower relative market share (e.g. parts of BMW's Rover range). They are sometimes called **question marks** or **wild cats**. The market looks attractive (as long as it keeps growing). Just maintaining current market share will increase sales as the company would have the same percentage but of a bigger market. However, the company may be unsure how the market will develop or whether it can generate or acquire enough customers from competitors to make investment here worthwhile. Small companies often suffer by having too many problem children in their portfolios. Problem children will require heavy investment and a successful **marketing mix** if they are to develop but, if they prove to be too much of a drain on resources, it may be prudent to sell them off, if possible.

Dog

Dogs are in stagnant or slow-growing markets in which the company has low relative market share. A number of smaller European firms have found themselves in this position. When a dog gets old it may be kindest to put it to sleep but, from a company's perspective, there may be sound reasons to keep it alive. It might be an effective **loss leader** or barrier to market entry by competitors. It can be quite difficult to judge just when a product has reached the end of its useful life and, ideally, rather than just phase it out, it is often worth trying to sell it on to another company. One company's dog could well be another's cash cow, or even a star if they are operating in different markets or **market segments**.

Here is a saying that may help you to remember how to use the BCG matrix:

Milk the cow, to feed the problem child in the hope that it will grow to be a star. And shoot the old dog.

The BCG matrix is sometimes related to the **product life cycle**. Stars are often still in the growth stage, cash cows are generally mature products and dogs are in old age (decline), although this is not necessarily always the case.

Another classic marketing analysis tool is the **McKinsey/General Electric matrix** (market attractiveness, market share matrix). This tool is used to look at the relative attractiveness of a **market** and the position of the company in that market (see Exhibit 7.8). Attractiveness will be defined in a number of ways depending on the particular circumstances of the company, for example:

McKinsey/General Electric matrix

a portfolio analysis tool developed by McKinsey & Co and GE involving classifying product lines or SBUs according to their competitive position and market attractiveness

- market size
- market growth rate
- ease of market entry
- competition
- profitability
- social and environmental impact
- technological requirements
- legal implications
- energy and other resource requirements.

exhibit 7.8

McKinsey/General Electric business screen matrix

	strong	**medium**	**weak**
high	invest for growth	invest for growth or to hold position	develop or hold or harvest
medium	invest for growth or to hold position	develop or hold or harvest	harvest or divest
low	build on strengths to hold position	harvest	divest

market attractiveness (vertical axis)

competitive position

The business's competitive position may be calculated by assessing its:

▶ **market share**

▶ market share growth rate

▶ the skills and competences of its management team

▶ product quality

▶ brand strength

▶ distribution channels

▶ promotional effectiveness

▶ production capacity

▶ production efficiency

▶ **unit costs**

▶ research and development success.

These criteria are then weighted according to their relative importance to the company and the market.

The strategic options are as follows.

▶ Grow: these **SBUs** are equivalent to **stars** in the **BCG matrix** and so warrant investment.

▶ Hold: these are equivalent to **cash cows**, they are good earners and should be protected.

▶ In the middle sectors, there are hard choices to make between developing, holding and harvesting; these are the **problem children**.

stars
a category within the Boston Consulting Group matrix, products or SBUs with relatively high market share in a high-growth market

cash cows
a category within the Boston Consulting Group matrix, products or SBUs with relatively high market share in low-growth markets

problem children
a category within the Boston Consulting Group matrix, products or SBUs with relatively low market share in high-growth markets

dogs

a category within the Boston Consulting Group matrix, products or SBUs with relatively low market share in low-growth markets

▶ Harvest: these products can be managed to produce steady cash flow.

▶ Divest (i.e. get rid of them) the **dogs**.

It has often been argued that **portfolio analysis** tools oversimplify what are actually complex situations. Ironically, some of these tools have now grown so complex that they cannot meaningfully be applied in real life. Some of the criticisms are briefly outlined below.

First, they merely provide a snapshot of the company's portfolio at a single point in time. The next day, things may have changed. Also, they ignore products in development that have yet to be launched into the market.

Second, consider how market share is calculated. At best, it is a guesstimate, often based on knowledge of one's own business and estimates of competitors' sales, sometimes informed by industry analysts (and often only then when the stock market has a keen interest). How, then, is it possible to compare the relative growth of one market to another in order to map the company's portfolio? Furthermore, is market growth the best criterion for analysis; surely profitability is more important?

Third, these tools fail to recognize any interdependencies between elements of the company's **product portfolio**; for example, a dog may be supporting a cash cow.

This is not to say these tools are not useful in principle as a systematic approach to market analysis and, indeed, the potential flexibility of the GE matrix in particular does make it more helpful because it enables companies to choose relevant criteria. They may be useful for resource allocation in an established business, but it is important to recognize their general limitations (Lancaster and Massingham, 2001).

SUMMARY

total product

the complete product offering, including all marketing mix elements

In this chapter we have attempted to look at products and services from all angles. There are many different types of product, each has particular characteristics that influence its marketing, but all are designed to deliver a core benefit. However, **competitive advantage** often comes through differentiating aspects of the **total product**, rather than its core. The service elements of a product can be a key selling point as can the product elements of a service. Both products and services can be **branded** and this is often at the heart of the customer's choice. Again, there are a number of brand types and strategies to consider.

Management of a **product portfolio** is a huge marketing challenge. Products are launched, build sales and eventually die. There are a number of **portfolio analysis** tools which can help managers to judge a product's contribution to the overall portfolio and to decide what course of action to take next. In this chapter we have briefly considered two of them: the **Boston Consulting Group matrix** and the **McKinsey/General Electric matrix**. There are criticisms to be made of these tools, as there are of the **product life cycle** concept, but they still provide useful insights to help manage the product offering.

Challenges reviewed

Now that you have finished reading the chapter, look back at the challenges you were set at the beginning. Do you have a clearer idea of what's involved?

Hints:

▶ product portfolio management

▶ importance of innovation

▶ product life cycle – extension strategies

▶ total product concept – augmented and perceived product.

READING AROUND

book chapters

David Aaker (1996) What is a strong brand? Chapter 1 in *Building Strong Brands*, Free Press Business.

Adrian Palmer (1999) The marketing of services, in Michael Baker, *The Marketing Book* (4th edn), Butterworth Heinemann.

websites

www.healthfinder.gov and www.bullying.co.uk for pure online service examples.

SELF-REVIEW QUESTIONS

1. Define a product. (see page 192)

2. What is meant by the term core product? (see page 194)

3. What are the distinguishing characteristics of services? (see page 201)

4. What is the relationship between brand personality and brand image? (see page 207)

5. Which usually attracts higher customer involvement, convenience goods or shopping goods? (see page 198)

6. What does FMCG mean? (see page 215)

7. List five different brand types and give an example of each. (see page 209)

8. Draw the product life cycle diagram. (see page 217)

9. What is an extension strategy? Give two examples. (see page 219)

10. Draw the BCG matrix. (see page 220)

11. What should you do with a dog? (see page 221)

12. Why might that be the wrong decision? (see page 221)

MINI CASE STUDY

Read the questions, then the case material, then answer the questions.

Questions

1. Why would Volkswagen delete the vehicle on which its reputation was founded?

2. Why would the company replace the original with a lookalike product?

3. Does Volkswagen's brand image give the company the opportunity to introduce other non-car products, and what might these be?

The original VW Beetle

In the aftermath of the Second World War, a British officer serving in the Allied occupying force discovered the remains of a car manufacturing plant that was about to be dismantled. He considered that there was considerable potential in this and halted the destruction of the factory. The designs, machinery, press tools, spare parts and so on were offered to both Austin and Morris in England, who at the time were the fourth and fifth biggest volume car manufacturers in the world. Neither was interested, so the officer worked tirelessly to restart production. The car produced was the Volkswagen Beetle; it ultimately became the biggest-selling single car ever built, next to the Model T Ford.

The final Beetle rolled off the last existing production line, in Brazil, in July 2003, having had a life of nearly 50 years.

Much of the image of Volkswagen is as a result of the success of the Beetle, and its replacement, although completely new in all respects, has a marked similarity in appearance to the original vehicle.

225

REFERENCES

Anonymous (2003) Cosmo forced to scrap branded cafe project, *Marketing Week* (7 August).

Handy, C. (2002) *The Elephant and the Flea*, Arrow.

Kotler, P. (2003) *Marketing insights from A to Z: 80 Concepts Every Manager Needs to Know*, John Wiley & Sons.

Lancaster, G. and Massingham, L. (2001) *Marketing Management*, McGraw-Hill.

Palmer, A. (2001) *Principles of Services Marketing*, McGraw-Hill.

Pickton, D. and Broderick, A. (2001) *Integrated Marketing Communications*, FT Prentice Hall.

Wilson, R., Gilligan, C. and Pearson D.J. (1995) *Strategic Marketing Management*, Butterworth Heinemann.

CHAPTER 8

PROMOTION

BY LYNN STAINSBY

PROMOTION CHALLENGES

The following are illustrations of the types of decision that marketers have to take or issues they face. *You aren't expected to know how to deal with the challenges now*; just bear them in mind as you read the chapter and see what you can find that helps.

▶ You are a marketing manager responsible for a new range of chilled fruit drinks. What budget would be appropriate for the launch?

▶ There are so many different media today: newspapers, magazines, TV, iTV, radio, Internet, mobile phones. How can you choose the best combination for your advertising?

▶ You believe that your new manager has an unusual sense of humour. He wants to incorporate some of his jokes into a television advertising campaign for your long-established brand of mid-market, male footwear and he wants your views. His idea doesn't make you laugh but you're not sure how your customers will react. What will you do?

▶ Disaster! You are the public relations manager for a major airline. The check-in staff and baggage handlers have gone on strike, leaving thousands of passengers stranded at an international airport. They are angry and frustrated. What will you do now? What will you do later, when the crisis has passed?

KEY CONCEPTS

marketing communications
promotion
marketing mix
promotion mix
advertising
public relations (PR)
sales promotion
personal selling
sponsorship
direct marketing
direct sales
target audience
audience profiling (see also Chapter 4)
message
media
new media
creative execution
attitude change (see Chapter 5)
decision-making process (see Chapter 5)
branding (see Chapter 7)
push and pull strategies

INTRODUCTION

4Ps

a mnemonic (memory aid) for the marketing mix: product, promotion, place, price

The term **marketing communications** encompasses a variety of different promotional strategies and techniques at both the corporate and **brand** level. This chapter will examine the reasons why it is necessary for organizations to communicate, who they communicate with and how they can get their message across.

Promotion, another term for marketing communications, is one of the **4Ps** of the **marketing mix**. It is an essential part of the **total product** offering. No matter how good your product is, if people do not *know* it is good, then they will not buy it. Equally, no matter how good your promotion is, if your product is poor, then people will not continue to buy it. Some form of promotion, or marketing communication, is necessary to make customers aware of the existence of the product, help create its brand identity and persuade them to try it.

There are many potential promotional tools or activities and the traditional way of categorizing all of them is as the **promotion mix**, which comprises:

▶ advertising

▶ public relations (PR)

▶ sales promotions

▶ personal selling.

There are other ways of classifying the promotion mix but we'll stick with this simple one.

What comes to mind when you think of **advertising**? Do you enjoy it? Are you irritated by it? Advertising includes any paid form of non-personal presentation of ideas, goods and services by an identified advertiser. It is paid-for promotional messages carried by the **mass media** (TV, radio, press, cinema, posters, the Internet).

What comes to mind when you think of **public relations**? Does the word 'spin' feature? That really is not the whole story. PR uses different activities designed to promote goodwill between an organization and the outside world. These activities may include placing stories in the media, running events, sponsorship, and building relationships with influential individuals and groups.

point of sale (POS)

promotion – the general term for any type of promotion found where the sale takes place. Most usually associated with retail outlets

merchandising

selection and display of products within a retail environment

Sales promotions are special offers and other added-value activities intended to induce buyers to buy, or try, a product. Such offers include two for the price of one, money-off coupons and instant wins. This also includes **point of sale** (POS) promotions and **merchandising**.

Personal selling, as the name suggests, is the most personal of the promotional tools. It involves persuading customers of the benefits of products and services, usually on a one-to-one basis. Such personal communication is costly; imagine sending a salesperson out to sell single bottles of shampoo to individuals. Consequently, it is an approach favoured in **b2b** sales where the order quantities are higher. Similarly, it would be a waste of television advertising if it was used to sell ball bearings as the vast majority of those who saw the ad would not be interested. There is not a **mass market** for such things and so it would be more efficient to send sales representatives to the few companies that might be interested.

Different techniques are needed in different markets, in different situations and to achieve different ends. This chapter will examine those techniques and their effective use.

Each category of the promotion mix has certain strengths that will be outlined below. Some organizations – e.g. Nike, Cadbury and Volkswagen – emphasize advertising and public relations efforts in their promotional mixes. Others, especially those engaged in business to business (b2b) marketing, choose personal selling as a significant promotion mix ingredient. Smith & Nephew, Johnson & Johnson and 3M market healthcare products to hospitals and all tend to favour personal selling in these situations. This is, in part, because of the complex nature of the decision-making units involved (see Chapter 5) and the need to identify and nurture different **stakeholders**.

> **activity**
>
> Collect or identify as many examples of promotional material from one organization as you can. How do they differ? Why do you think they differ? Who are the audiences?

Marketing communications or promotion?

These two terms mean the same thing; promotion is the older name and fits within the mnemonic the '4Ps'. In this chapter (as in life), the two terms will be used interchangeably.

Promotion defined

In its broadest sense, promotion means to move forwards. Think about the term in relation to a promotion to a higher grade or more senior position at work. Over time, this meaning has evolved so that, in marketing, promotion refers to communication designed and implemented to persuade others to accept ideas, concepts or things; to motivate customers and consumers to take action.

PROMOTION MANAGEMENT

Promotion management is the practice of coordinating the various promotion mix elements, setting objectives for what the elements are intended to accomplish, establishing budgets that are sufficient to support the objectives, designing specific programmes (for example, advertising campaigns) to accomplish objectives, evaluating performance and taking corrective action when results are not in accordance with objectives.

Campaigns

When planning promotional campaigns, many decisions need to be taken. These include: what emphasis to put on interpersonal versus mass communication, whether to select a **push strategy** or a **pull strategy**, and how much importance to place on each of the different promotion mix elements. A promotional campaign is a series of promotional activities aimed at achieving a specific objective or set of objectives. Fundamentally, the objective(s) set indicate(s) what the organization wants the promotional strategy to achieve. For example, the task of introducing a new product requires a promotional campaign considerably different from one intended to maintain the competitive position of an established or widely recognized product. A campaign intended to raise awareness or develop a brand image is very different from one intended to generate sales. An organization's campaigns should form part of its overall strategy.

PROMOTIONAL STRATEGY

There is no one clear definition of the term strategy. Over the years strategy has acquired a number of meanings, and academics and practitioners are not in total agreement. Broadly speaking, Engel *et al.* (1994) use the term promotional strategy to refer to a controlled, integrated programme of communication methods designed to present an organization and its products or services to prospective customers; to communicate need-satisfying attributes; to facilitate sales, and thus to contribute to long-run profit performance. Pickton and Broderick (2004) emphasize the need to consider a range of target audiences when determining strategy and not just focus on customers.

Promotion serves four basic purposes. An acronym to help remember the purposes of marketing communications is DRIP. That is, the purposes are to:

▶ **differentiate** – it is widely accepted that marketing communications can act as a differentiator of products, especially in markets where there are many similar products

▶ **remind** – promotional messages may be aimed at reminding people who already buy a product of reasons why they should continue to do so; as well as product or service quality, reasons could include some form of reward for loyalty, such as a price discount, or even a free prize draw

▶ **inform** – promotion provides a great deal of factual information about products and places of business such as where a shop is located; in the UK, for example, multiples such as Tesco and Budgens, as well as franchises, such as Londis, often advertise in local newspapers and produce **flyer** inserts in local free papers giving information about special price promotions and special buys – plus directions

▶ **persuade** – persuasion is a primary goal of promotion and encourages purchases or changes in attitude; in fact, many people regard promotion as persuasive communication; think again about the contents of the supermarket flyers – what might they contain that would induce or urge you to visit and buy from them?

The importance of objectives

A strategy is the means by which a firm tries to achieve its objectives. Objectives are fundamental in providing direction for an organization so long as they are clearly stated, are compatible with each other and known, understood and followed (Pickton and Broderick, 2004). A marketing manager must set the promotion objectives before deciding on the optimal promotion mix. Objectives should be **SMART**:

Specific	i.e. no vague terms or ambiguity
Measurable	i.e. capable of being assessed/the firm should be able to *know* it has achieved the objective
Achievable	i.e. possible within resource constraints
Relevant	i.e. contribute to corporate objectives
Timed	i.e. have timings associated

One of the major advantages of stating objectives in measurable terms is that this allows the organization to assess the effectiveness of its promotion mix. If the promotion mix is not effective, the manager can begin to alter certain aspects of it and then monitor the change to see if promotional effectiveness is improved.

In order to set realistic promotional objectives, the firm needs a clear statement of its **target market**. However, a promotional campaign may not be aimed at the entire market; it may even be aimed at people who are not part of the market at all. Promotional campaigns reach out to **target audiences**.

Target audience or target market?

target audience
the people, or organizations, that are selected to receive communications

Target markets are customers (i.e. the people who buy goods and services). The term is also used to refer to **consumers**. However, in **marketing communications**, everyone involved in the purchase decision, not just the customer, needs to be understood and targeted. These people are **target audiences** or **publics** and may include members of the trade, opinion leaders, members of the media, employees, clubs and associations, present and potential shareholders – anybody who influences the purchase decision.

A good deal of marketing has international dimensions, though not all organizations are global yet. Many audiences are worldwide and major brands try to maintain consistency in their worldwide positioning. How disappointing to visit a foreign country and find that your favourite designer is considered downmarket, or that your beer is looked down on. Some beers that are 'reassuringly expensive' in the UK might not have quite the same image elsewhere. Many marketers have to take a varied international audience into account when designing their marketing communications strategies.

globalfocus

Happy 25th birthday, Garfield

He's fat, he's lazy, he's rude and he's possibly the only cat in the world who would gladly give up his nine lives for a plate of lasagne. For 25 years Garfield has been scratching, chewing and wise-cracking his way into the affections of readers around the world with his unique brand of comic nastiness.

Whether he's mocking his owner Jon, or annoying Jon's long-suffering dog Odie, or Squeak the mouse, or just trying to eat and sleep more, the *Daily Express*'s resident cat never tires of grumbling or gluttony. After 25 years and 9125 strips, age has not wearied this fat cat – nor has it done much to temper his sarcastic tongue.

With such a disagreeable personality, some might be surprised that the feisty feline has become as well loved as he is. Garfield, who made his debut in 1975, has become a worldwide phenomenon. The comic strip is now seen in 2570 publications around the world and its estimated daily readership of 263 million makes it the most widely syndicated cartoon strip on Earth.

Garfield's licensing arm, Paws Inc., operates in 111 countries, his books have sold in the region of 140 million copies and, along with promotional websites and TV shows, he has generated mountains of coffee mugs, fluffy toys and other assorted **merchandise**.

Why the global interest? According to the cat's creator, Jim Davis, we can all identify with Garfield's character: 'We all eat, we all sleep and, let's face it, we'd probably all be lazy and selfish if we could get away with it!'

Put simply, 'Everyone can relate to Garfield in some way because most of the humour is about things we all do – and most people can relate to the pet–owner relationship.'

Source: adapted from the *Daily Express*, Saturday 7 June 2003

Push and pull strategies

One way of understanding the different promotional emphases of various organizations is to think of them as **push** and **pull strategies**. Who is the customer? Who is the prime or secondary target of a promotional strategy? In some companies, marketing efforts and tactics are aimed primarily at the trade, such as **wholesalers**, distributors and **retailers**. In this case advertising and sales promotion, selling effort, as well as pricing strategies, are aimed at generating trade interest and demand for the company's products. This promotional focus is designed to push a product into, and through, the distribution channel by aiming promotional efforts at members of the **distribution channel**. Push strategies are common in the industrial sector and also the field of medicine. Medical sales representatives from companies such as Astra-Zenica promote (push) products very strongly to general practitioners and support this push with promotional material from the marketing department. This promotional material may include brochures and special sales promotions. Next time you visit your doctor observe the different promotional materials in the surgery, such as posters, post-its, pens and mouse mats.

Conversely, a pull strategy focuses a company's marketing efforts on the final customer or **consumer**. The objective of this strategy is to generate sufficient consumer interest and demand for the company's products to be pulled through the distribution channels. The goal is to generate demand at the retail level in the belief that such demand will encourage retailers and wholesalers to stock the product.

Although we see push and pull as distinctive strategies, it is usually not a case of deciding between one or the other, but more of determining where the balance should be. An effective marketing communications strategy often uses a combination of push and pull.

The strategy is implemented through the marketing communications mix, which is considered in more detail later.

SETTING THE PROMOTIONAL BUDGET

Marketing communications should be seen as an investment. It can, however, be quite expensive and so attention should be paid to getting the budget right. However, setting the promotional budget is not an exact science. Various techniques are used by organizations, the five most popular ones being:

1. arbitrary method
2. affordable method
3. competitive parity method
4. objective and task method
5. percentage of sales method.

Budgeting methods between organizations vary in popularity, although the percentage of sales method is reputed to be a favoured approach in larger organizations. However, it is believed that small businesses are more likely to use arbitrary or affordable approaches.

Arbitrary method

Rather than a method, this is an approach to arriving at a budget figure. It is more a judgement that seems right at the time. It is unlikely to be based on any significant criteria and is more likely to be based on gut feel or intuition. It is an educated guess – but, remember, it may have been made by a very experienced marketing director.

Affordable method

In essence this means that the company will spend on promotion what it thinks is reasonable and can afford – although organizations using this approach, like the arbitrary approach, are more likely to reflect a view that marketing communications are an expense rather than an investment.

The affordable method causes problems with long-range planning. The company cannot guess the funds that will be available in the future to spend on promotion. Also, in times of recession or hardship, very little will be spent on promotion, and yet this is most likely to be the time when extra spending would be of benefit.

Competitive parity method

A budget is set that matches, exceeds or is in proportion to competitors' budgets. Care has to be taken in applying this method. For example, not all companies have the same objectives. Some may want to become the market leader (market share objective), while others may wish to become more profitable (profitability objective). A company's nearest competitor may be much bigger or much smaller than it is. Simply matching expenditure in this situation would not be sensible where setting the budget as an appropriate proportion would be a better approach.

Objective and task approach

The objective and task method determines a budget based on what the various communications activities need to achieve. In essence, objectives are set and then the marketing communications tasks to achieve the objectives are decided upon. By calculating the costs of those tasks, a budget is set.

Although this method may appear to be the best, it is a method that is rarely applied in its entirety. Difficulties in implementing this approach include:

▶ the company may not be able to afford the budget arrived at

▶ it is time consuming (and therefore expensive to prepare)

▶ the task may not actually achieve the objective anyway, e.g. the planned PR campaign may not raise the company's credibility as intended.

Percentage of sales method

The percentage of sales method is probably the most popular method – the classical approach – partly because it is easy to calculate. It links marketing communications expenditure directly to levels of sales by allocating a fixed percentage of **turnover** to marketing communications.

However, there are difficulties. What percentage should be used and how should the turnover be determined? The percentage may be based on previous practice, on competitor allocations or on industry averages. Turnover could be based on historic sales, last year's sales or sales averaged over a number of years. It could be based on current sales levels, or it could be based on forecast sales (which may, of course, be wrong).

Perhaps unsurprisingly, in practice most organizations use a combination of all these approaches to set their budgets.

THE MARKETING COMMUNICATIONS PROCESS

An understanding of the communications theory that underpins the marketing communications process is helpful in ensuring that messages arrive safely. Schramm (1955) is attributed with first modelling the communications process and the model presented in Exhibit 8.1 is based on his initial, simple model.

exhibit 8.1

Simple communications model – after Schramm

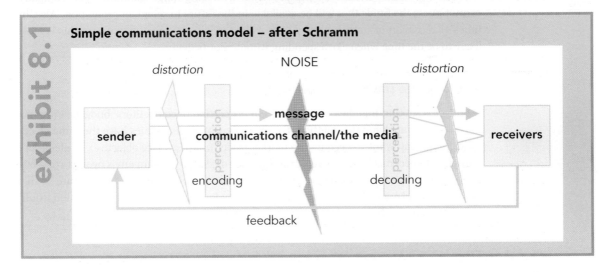

There are two principal participants (or sets of participants) in the communications process.

1. The sender is the originator or source of the message. This is widely regarded as the company which is doing the advertising, such as BT or Coca-Cola. In practice, agents or consultants may actually do a lot of the work on behalf of the sender.

2. Receivers are the people to whom the message is sent, the **target audience**(s).

Advertising will be used for the purposes of this explanation; however, the model is applicable to all forms of **marketing communications**. The advertiser wishes to communicate with a chosen target audience; the *message* is the actual information and impressions it wishes to send. This message is coded into an advert by the agency's **creative team** (they make the ad). It can then be sent: the *media/channels* are the means used to carry the message, e.g. in the case of advertising this may be by television, radio, cinema, etc.

The challenge of marketing communications is to ensure that this process communicates the right message, in the right way, to the right people, in the right place, at the right time. Communication only actually takes place when the receiver understands the message and, ideally, acts upon it. This may not be a physical action; it may be a change of attitude (a frequent objective of advertising), but something happens to the receiver as a result of receiving the message – even if it is only an increase in knowledge.

Senders are not usually telepathic. They cannot transmit pure thought so they have to put the message across through a commonly understood code, such as words, pictures, symbols and/or actions: senders *encode* messages, using their skills and resources (e.g. film studios or printers). Encoding is the first step in the communications process. Ideally, the sender's intended message is transmitted, although in reality this does not always occur. Have you ever tried, unsuccessfully, to express an idea? You know what you intended to say, but the words that came out of your mouth failed to reflect your thoughts? Media advertising is an expensive business. An advert that does not come across well to its target audience is a major waste of time and money. That is why agencies, and their clients, put so much into getting them right. See the insight box for an example of what can go wrong.

Smoke without fire

Some years ago, an anti-smoking organization commissioned an advertising campaign to be shown on television. Television is an expensive medium and so this represented a major investment. The organization needed good returns and so was delighted when its groundbreaking campaign won a raft of industry awards.

The ads depicted two situations in which parents who smoked in front of their children were seen to be encouraging the children to smoke themselves. In the first advert, a smartly dressed woman is sitting beside the bed of a small girl, reading a bedtime story. The woman is smoking a cigarette. At the end of the story she puts down the book and says to the girl, 'So, do you see the moral of the tale, darling?' The little girl puts her hand to her mouth, mimicking her mother's smoking, and says, 'Yes, Mummy.'

The second advert featured a father and son fixing a bicycle on the kitchen table. The father is smoking a cigarette. The son is holding a pencil. When the bike is mended, the father leans back and draws on his cigarette. 'So, do you see how it's done, son?' he says. 'Yes, Daddy,' replies the boy as he puts the pencil to his mouth and sucks.

Unfortunately, these ads were not **pre-tested** (probably to save costs), i.e. no one tried them out on smokers to see if the message was received correctly. They were, however, **post-tested** (i.e. after the campaign) on two groups of parents who smoked; one group of ABs (higher income, educated professionals) and one of CDs (lower income, less well educated). The results were surprising.

In the case of the first ad, the ABs found the message positive. Reading stories to children is constructive and educational. The CDs, however, found it scandalous. They assumed that the woman was going out (as she was dressed up) and that she was reading the story because she felt guilty about leaving the child alone.

The second ad fared no better. The CD group thought this was positive, encouraging fathers to do more with their sons. The ABs were horrified: 'dirty working-class habit, putting bikes on the kitchen table!'

None of them noticed the cigarettes and the intended point of the ads was missed.

Messages that are encoded badly get distorted and are not received correctly: **distortion** is a coding problem, a lack of skill either on the part of the sender (who encodes) or the receiver (who decodes).

The message may get distorted at either end of the channel. For example, there might be technical problems, such as a poorly reproduced newspaper advertisement or a weak radio or television signal, or the problem may lie with the poor language skills of the receiver. In **marketing communications**, it is up to the sender to try to ensure that the way the message is coded is suitable for the intended target audience.

Decoding happens at the other end of the channel and consists of the receiver's receipt and interpretation of the message transmitted. The sender hopes that the message received is identical to the one transmitted, but this is not always the case.

Distortion is not the only **barrier to communication**. There are a number of other things that may get in the message's way: poor television reception, graffiti on a poster, a computer going down, crackle on a telephone line, the receiver having a headache – this is all 'noise'.

However, levels of coding skill are easier to deal with than the distortion that comes from perceptual problems. **Perception** is how we see the world. Our perception is built up over the

perception
the process by which people select, organize and interpret sensory stimulation (sounds, visions, smell, touch) into a meaningful picture of the world

years through all of our experiences. Without it, we would be unable to interpret the world around us. Think of a newborn baby. It knows nothing and may well misinterpret its world. How puzzling those new shiny toys must be – especially the ones that make its mother shout when it reaches for them. There is no understanding, no ability to interpret external stimuli, without learning and experience. As no two people's lives are exactly the same, then their perceptions will not be the same either, and this can cause communications problems.

Individual perceptions are influenced by **selective attention** and **selective distortion** (see Chapter 5).

After the decoding process, the receiver responds to the message. The receiver may show interest in the message and may accept everything that is communicated without question. However, the receiver may also react unfavourably to the communication or may totally ignore it. From the marketer's perspective, the message will not be effective unless it elicits the desired response. This may be covert, such as a favourable attitude change towards a product or increased awareness or knowledge of a product. Sometimes the response is overt, such as redeeming a coupon, or returning a form to order a product or to receive more information. The sender needs to know that the message has been understood: *feedback* is the response from a receiver back to the sender.

Feedback can sometimes, especially with advertising, be hard to pick up. The change in the receiver may be slight, e.g. an increased awareness of the shampoo on offer. The original Schramm model portrayed one-way communications, where there was no feedback. This is no longer accepted as correct. Communication must be two-way. It should be a dialogue, not a monologue.

This two-way communication may be asymmetric or symmetric. In two-way asymmetric communication, there is communication from a sender to a receiver with little or delayed feedback, producing a non-direct dialogue, such as in most advertising. In two-way symmetric communication, which according to Pickton and Broderick (2004) is the richest form, there is a direct dialogue between the sender and the audience. Traditionally, personal selling activities have provided this major benefit. However, new technologies are creating new opportunities for interactivity and near immediate response. Interactive and direct response television, the Internet and telephone call centres are aiding this process.

The more comprehensive models of the communications process regard communication as an exchange process in which thoughts or ideas are the things exchanged.

INFLUENCING CUSTOMERS (AUDIENCES)

Influencing and encouraging buyers to accept or adopt goods, services and ideas are among the key objectives of marketing communications. In fact, some argue that the ultimate effectiveness of promotion is determined by the degree to which it causes **product adoption** among potential buyers or increases the frequency of current buyers' purchases. Rarely can a single promotional activity cause an individual to buy a previously unfamiliar product. To have realistic expectations about what promotion can do, product adoption should be viewed not as a one-stop process, but as a multi-stage process.

In Chapter 5, five stages of the consumer buying process were listed as:

1. need or problem recognition
2. information search
3. evaluation of alternatives
4. purchase decision
5. post-purchase evaluation.

Throughout this process the consumer deliberately, or unconsciously, adopts various attitudes, or has various mind-states, in relation to the product/service offer. The nature and objectives of marketing communications need to alter to take account of these in order to encourage the correct purchase, or repurchase, decision.

Several models, known as **hierarchy of effects models**, have been developed to illustrate the activities required to take a consumer from the state of unawareness to one of willingness to purchase the product or service.

A simple model, commonly used by marketing professionals, is **AIDA**. According to this model, potential buyers go through a psychological or behavioural process before purchasing a product. AIDA, is an acronym for:

Attention

Interest

Desire

Action.

It incorporates various psychological processes. That is, attention or awareness is a cognitive process. It relates to how and what we think and believe. Interest and desire are affective processes; they relate to our emotions, how we feel about something. Finally, action takes the form of manifest behaviour – we buy the product or tell others about it.

AIDA and setting promotional objectives

Although a simple model, AIDA is very helpful when setting promotional objectives.

Attention

At the awareness or attention stage, the promotion objective is to get the product seen and, ideally, talked about by the **target audience**. For example, an effective advertisement must grab attention from the very first viewing or hearing. If the target audience's attention has not been caught, then whatever follows will be of little use.

Interest

After attention has been gained, interest must be aroused. This is achieved by creating an understanding of the benefits of the product in relation to the personal need(s) of customers, and focusing the message on how the product or service being advertised actually meets these needs. Thus, the objective of the interest stage is to motivate individuals to want information about the product's features, uses, advantages, disadvantages, price and location, etc.

Desire

At this stage, a company tries to appeal to the target customer's wish to fill some need. Interest in, and desire for, the product may be established in nearly simultaneous steps.

Action

As the name suggests, the action stage aims to get individuals to do something such as purchase the product or service. This is often helped by making it easier for the target customer to take action. This can be done by giving a phone number, an Internet address or closing with a note saying that credit cards are accepted.

hierarchy of effects models

describe the stages individuals go through when making a purchase, or consumption, decision

AIDA and the promotion mix

Think for a moment about the sequential nature of AIDA. It comprises a number of stages that are ordered sequentially. However, it is not always necessary for organizations to start promotional campaigns at the top of the hierarchy, at the attention or awareness stage. The product may have been around for a while and everyone has already heard of it.

The choice of promotion mix will depend on where in the response hierarchy the organization wishes to direct its promotional effort. For example, if the firm's primary objective is to create awareness, then advertising is often the most effective promotional tool. Advertising is also, generally, most effective at creating and holding interest, and at reinforcing positive aspects of the product to develop post-purchase satisfaction. Personal selling tends to be effective at creating desire and motivating purchasing behaviour. Sales promotion can also be very effective in getting a customer to try something new. For example, a half-price offer reduces the risk associated with trying a new hair gel.

Exhibit 8.2 illustrates the use of the various promotional tools. Hierarchical models such as AIDA describe the step-by-step process through which individuals move when exposed to marketing communications; these encompass the cognitive (thinking), affective (feeling) and conative (doing) steps.

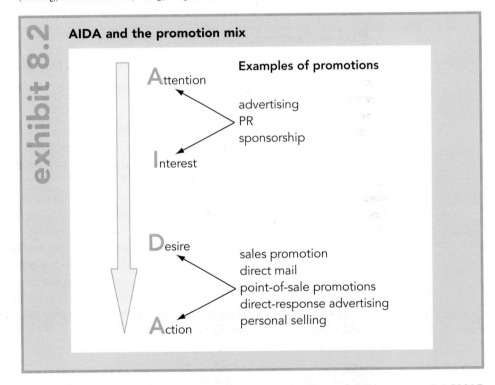

exhibit 8.2

AIDA and the promotion mix

Attention

Interest

Desire

Action

Examples of promotions

advertising
PR
sponsorship

sales promotion
direct mail
point-of-sale promotions
direct-response advertising
personal selling

Russell Colley (1961) developed a hierarchy of effects model known as **DAGMAR** (Define Advertising Goals for Measured Advertising Results). In this he stressed the importance of setting objectives against each element within the hierarchy (or at least those that were relevant to the promotional campaign being devised). Although his focus was on advertising objectives, his propositions are equally appropriate for consideration across all marketing communication tools (see Exhibit 8.3).

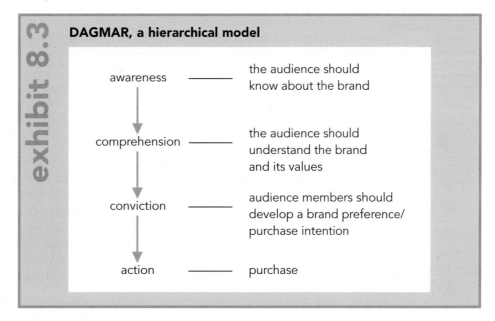

exhibit 8.3

DAGMAR, a hierarchical model

awareness ——— the audience should know about the brand

↓

comprehension ——— the audience should understand the brand and its values

↓

conviction ——— audience members should develop a brand preference/ purchase intention

↓

action ——— purchase

DRIP communication

DRIP is an acronym that helps us to remember the four main purposes of marketing communication (these were described in the earlier section on promotional strategy). In influencing customers and other target audience members it is useful to keep DRIP in mind. We may want to concentrate promotional effort on ensuring we *differentiate* our product from the competitors (e.g. car advertising). Our product may be well known but we may wish to *remind* and ensure continued positive associations (e.g. Coca-Cola). Our principal purpose may be to pass on *information*, such as through company financial reports. Finally, we may wish to be much more *persuasive* in our promotions.

A large number of messages that reach the respondent's senses do so as a result of persuasive communication. This type of communication is intended to affect the individual's learning and alter his or her responses and the overall perceptions, cognitions and motivations that predispose him or her to behave in a certain way. Effective persuasive communications are those that generate greater attention or willingness to attend, and create a more positive state of conviction regarding some object or situation.

THE MARKETING COMMUNICATIONS MIX

To achieve the communications objectives, various promotional techniques are used. As identified earlier, historically these tools, or techniques, have been organized into four broad categories: **advertising**, **public relations**, **sales promotion** and **personal selling**. This is known as the **promotion mix** (or marketing communications mix). However, increasingly, other categories are being added that either do not fit neatly into these four or that some people feel deserve their own category heading. Examples include **direct marketing**, **sponsorship** and packaging. Whichever classification is used, what is most important is to recognize the vast array of promotional activities that is available to marketers.

These promotional tools involve either direct (i.e. personal) communication, usually on a face-to-face basis or on the telephone (and, perhaps, through videoconferencing), or indirect (i.e. non-personal) communication via some medium such as television, magazines or radio, or through packaging, leaflets, etc. It is the responsibility of the marketer to determine which approach is best for each situation.

promotion mix

traditionally,
advertising, PR, sales
promotion and
personal selling

Whichever element, or elements, of the promotion mix organizations choose, the purpose is to communicate a **message** to an appropriate **target audience** in order to elicit a favourable response, such as purchasing a product or changing an attitude. The term **integrated marketing communication** is used to emphasize that all elements of the promotion mix should be coordinated and systematically planned to complement each other.

The separate elements of the promotion mix will now be discussed in more depth.

b2bfocus

Talking shop

Although much of marketing and marketing communications theory focuses on consumer goods, particularly fast moving consumer goods (FMCG), a significant amount of marketing communications is conducted between businesses. Interestingly, the big FMCG manufacturers' primary contact is with the trade, not end customers. Managing trade contacts (e.g. wholesalers and retailers) is quite different from dealing with end customers and consumers. For example, whereas a consumer might want one bottle of wine, a retailer may want many cases of different types.

Such major sales warrant a different approach. The supplier may well send a sales representative cold-calling or use techniques such as telesales, direct mail (post, fax or e-mail) or trade exhibitions either to make sales or to set up appointments for the rep to call.

ADVERTISING

Advertising includes any paid form of non-personal presentation of ideas, goods and services by an identified advertiser. Communication by advertising is transmitted to a **target audience** through what is known as the **mass media**, which include television, radio, cinema, press, posters and the Internet.

The major benefit of media advertising is its ability to communicate to a large number of people all at once, e.g. all the existing and potential consumers for McDonald's fast food.

frequency

the number of times
that an average
member of the
target audience is
exposed to an
advert during a
campaign

As advertising is indirect and non-personal, it allows marketers to send a uniform message with great **frequency**. However, it does have several disadvantages. Even though, for example, the cost per person reached by the advertising may be relatively low, the total financial outlay can be extremely high – especially for commercials shown during popular television programmes such as *Coronation Street*. These high costs can limit, and sometimes prevent, the use of this type of advertising in a promotional mix. It should be remembered that not all companies have huge marketing communications budgets like Nike or Coca-Cola (and even these aim for effectiveness and efficiency in using their companies' budgets). By contrast, regional advertising can reduce the costs of television advertising, and the use of other mass media need not be outside the budgets of many firms. Another disadvantage is that advertising rarely provides rapid **feedback**. However, with the development of interactive television this limitation may well be overcome, to a certain extent, in the near future.

Advertising objectives

John Bartle, managing director of advertising agency Bartle Bogle Hegarty, believes that although advertising may set out to create a basic awareness of a brand, ensure improved knowledge of a brand and its attributes, create a more favourable image, stimulate positive attitudes, and so on, the ultimate function is to sustain a brand as a profitable entity: 'Although advertising can be, and is used in a variety of different ways, its prime contribution is in helping to build and sustain brands for commercial benefit, often leading this process.'

This means that advertising fulfils a number of roles and has a number of aims. Some of the more common ones concern creating awareness, reminding consumers, and changing or reinforcing the attitudes, perceptions and beliefs of the customers and/or consumers.

exhibit 8.4

Typical advertising objectives

awareness	usually for a new product
recognition	a form of awareness, appropriate where the purchase decision is made at the point of purchase, e.g. anything sold in a supermarket
recall	another form of awareness, the ability to remember the product rather than just to recognize it, useful where decisions are made in advance of purchase, e.g. seeing a film at the cinema
remind	for established products that may be being overlooked
reposition	altering the way the brand is viewed by the target audience, e.g. Baileys is an anytime drink, not just an after-dinner liqueur
differentiate	making the brand stand out from the competition
inform	telling the audience something about the brand, e.g. that it has new features
change image	a form of repositioning, altering the market's perception of the brand, e.g. a Skoda is a top-quality car
educate	tell the audience what the product is for, or how to use it – especially new products
obtain information	direct-response advertising provides audience information back to the advertiser
change attitudes	change a negative to a positive, e.g. 'Volvos are not for me' to 'That's a cool car'
reinforce attitudes	encourage positive attitudes, e.g. 'I like brand x'
correct a misconception	e.g. 'I can't afford a new car' to 'That's cheaper than I thought'
stimulate trial	if a person never tries your product, then they can never become a regular purchaser
sales	purchase

Marketers use advertising in a number of ways. You may relate more readily to product advertising, which focuses on the uses, features, images and benefits of goods and services. However, there are other forms. For example, institutional advertising promotes the images and ideas of organizations, as well as political issues.

The underlying objective of almost all adverts is to sell things. However, as we have seen above, customers go through a number of stages when making their decisions to buy, and advertising is rarely the best tool for closing a deal. So advertising objectives tend to relate to the early stages of AIDA.

The problem with trying to measure advertising's effectiveness on sales alone is that it is hard to prove that the advert really did cause the increase in sales. Of course, there is a lot of anecdotal evidence to suggest that advertising has a positive effect on sales. Sales do tend to rise during an advertising campaign – and then to fall off soon after. However, that is not conclusive proof. There could be any number of other reasons why the sales rose, e.g. a competitor was short of stock, there was a price reduction at major retailers, a journalist wrote a good review. Conversely, it might be unfair to judge the advertising as bad just because sales do not rise. It may not be the advertising's fault. Many companies today advertise just to keep up. It is not so much a question of trying to increase sales, but of protecting their **market share**. If they stop advertising, they hand an advantage to the competition.

So we need to take a balanced view of advertising and measure it against some truly **SMART** objectives.

SMART
objectives are: specific, measurable, achievable, relevant, timed

The essentials of advertising

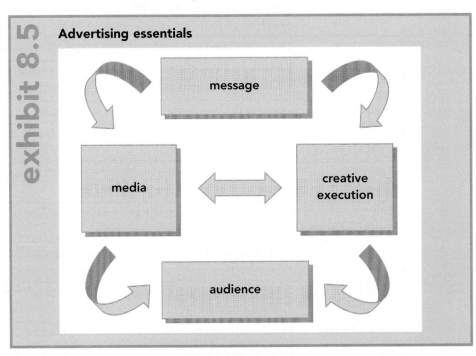

exhibit 8.5

Advertising essentials

- message
- media
- creative execution
- audience

Audience

Get the right message to the right audience and you have a good ad. It sounds simple, but unfortunately it is not. Advertising agencies put a lot of time and effort into understanding audiences and into developing **audience profiles**. If you want to communicate effectively with someone, it helps to know them well. (See Exhibit 8.6 for an example of an audience profile.)

Remember that a target audience is not the same as a target market. The audience for an advert is the people at whom the message of the ad is aimed. They may be part, or all, of the target market, or they may not. Sometimes adverts are deliberately aimed at influencers rather than actual purchasers, e.g. many toy ads are (rather controversially) aimed at toy consumers (children) rather than customers (parents). In the past, anti-smoking campaigners have also aimed at children, urging them to nag their parents into giving up. Trade audiences are often wider. Take, for example, an advert in a trade magazine for cars. It could be aimed at the fleet manager (who manages the company's car fleet), professional buyers (who negotiate terms of purchase), the company owner or the finance director (who may make the ultimate decision), the people who have cars (who may push for new ones) or the PR department (which guards the company's image) – in fact at any member of the **decision-making unit (DMU)** (see Chapter 5).

audience profile
a detailed description of audience characteristics used by communicators to tailor their promotional efforts

b2bfocus

exhibit 8.6

Independent readers

This is an example of an audience profile. 'Cover %' refers to the percentage of people in that category who read the newspaper, e.g. 2.3 per cent of 25–34-year-olds read the *Independent*. 'Profile %' refers to the percentage of the overall *Independent* readership that falls into that category.

Independent newspaper audience demographic profile

Audience's demographic profile for the *Independent* newspaper

Source: NRS Oct 02–Mar 03	Readership 000's	Cover %	Profile %
All adults	666	1.4	100.0
Men	377	1.7	56.6
Women	289	1.2	43.4
Age			
15–24	118	1.6	17.7
25–34	181	2.3	27.2
35–44	118	1.3	17.7
45–54	124	1.7	18.6
55–64	77	1.2	11.6
65+	47	0.5	7.1
Social class			
AB adults	428	3.6	64.3
ABC1 adults	559	2.2	83.9
ABC1C2 adults	614	1.8	92.2
C1 adults	132	1.0	19.8
C2 adults	54	0.6	8.1
DE adults	52	0.4	7.8
AB men	241	3.9	36.2
ABC1 men	310	2.5	46.6
ABC1C2 men	337	1.9	50.6
C1 men	69	1.1	10.4
C2 men	27	0.5	4.1
DE men	39	0.7	5.9
AB women	187	3.3	28.1
ABC1 women	249	1.9	37.4
ABC1C2 women	276	1.6	41.4
C1 women	63	0.9	9.5
C2 women	27	0.6	4.1
DE women	13	0.2	2.0

b2bfocus

exhibit 8.6

Source: NRS Oct 02–Mar 03	Readership 000's	Cover %	Profile %
ITV region			
Anglia	43	0.9	6.5
Border	2	0.3	0.3
London	328	2.9	49.3
Central	83	0.9	12.5
Wales & West	61	1.2	9.2
Grampian	11	1.1	1.7
Yorkshire	38	0.7	5.7
West Country	29	1.7	4.4
Meridian	109	1.9	16.4
Granada	32	0.5	4.8
Tyne Tees	18	0.7	2.7
Central Scotland	16	0.5	2.4

Source: Newspaper Marketing Association

Message

Once the advertisers have established exactly who it is they want to talk to, they can develop the correct message to achieve their advertising objectives. A message is what the advertising should say and the impression it should create, but it is not necessarily phrased in the way that the ad will say it. For example, the message that this is a fun beer that enhances sociability while also providing refreshment might result in the slogan 'refreshes the parts other beers cannot reach'. The slogan is the clever, catchy form of words that goes into the actual ad. It is part of the creative work and is written by a **copywriter** (**copy** just means text, i.e. the words in an ad).

Creative

The message is not normally put across through words alone, there are visual elements to most advertising that assist its transmission: a picture, a scene, colours, designs. There may also be music, other sound effects, acting – all of these form part of the **creative execution**.

creative execution
the way an advert is designed in order to put the message across

This is the heart of the advert. Advertisers appeal either to our emotions (e.g. through humour or sex) or to our rational side (e.g. through value for money or product features), in order to interest us in their products and services. There are a number of common execution approaches including those below. Look out for these and others as you see and listen to advertisements.

▶ Slice of life: a real, everyday situation shows the product in normal use, e.g. a little boy plays his separated parents off against each other and persuades them both to take him to McDonald's.

▶ Animation: cartoon characters can liven up a dull product or deal with an embarrassing subject, e.g. the Tetley tea folk.

▶ Testimonial: uses supposed experts, or past users, to verify the merits of the product, e.g. 'my washing has never been so white'.

▶ News style: common in press adverts, makes the advert look more like part of the publication.

▶ Fantasy: catches the imagination, particularly useful when the product cannot be shown in use, e.g. Smirnoff ads.

▶ Spoof: catches attention through humour, e.g. a woman sends her lover to the fridge for more Häagen-Dazs but he spots the Fosters lager and takes it with him to watch TV rather than return to the bedroom.

▶ Guarantees: reassure prospective purchasers, e.g. 'a closer shave or I'll give you your money back'.

▶ Demonstrations: show how the product works, e.g. how Flash can clean up so quickly.

▶ Celebrity endorsement: attracts attention and gives the product credibility, e.g. Sharon and Tracy from *Birds of a Feather* fight over the Surf.

▶ Problem solution: lends a helping hand, e.g. the *Yellow Pages* ads.

globalfocus

Famous Grouse woos Canadians

Arguably Scotland's best-known bird, the Famous Grouse, as featured in the TV whisky ads, has been given a makeover for the benefit of Canadian drinkers. For the first time the computer-generated bird will be wearing a kilt and – according to its designers – sticking to the tradition of wearing nothing beneath the tartan!

The kilted grouse is spearheading a marketing campaign in French-speaking Quebec, one of the top 20 export markets for Famous Grouse.

'It's nice to know that Grouse still appreciates the merits of tradition – as well it should. It has been making "dram" fine whisky for more than 100 years,' said a spokesman.   Source: adapted from the *Daily Express*, Wednesday 7 May 2003

Media

The final essential of advertising is the media: the carriers of the message. Without media, no one will ever hear or see it. The right choice of media is essential to the effectiveness of a campaign. It has to be appropriate to the **target audience** and to the **message**.

There is little point in advertising in *Cosmopolitan* if you are trying to reach elderly men (though there may be some point if you are trying to reach younger men as, apparently, a large number of them read it; they do not buy it, just read their girlfriends' copies). It is important to establish the readership/viewership profile of media vehicles and match this to your audience profile. Newspapers, TV channels, etc., provide guides to assist with this and to help sell their advertising space.

The choice of media also affects how the message comes across. If your message is a complex, informative one, perhaps explaining the technical advantages of a new computer system, then a 30-second TV ad just will not do. You need the space and copy possibilities of **press**. However, if you want your new jeans to catch the eye of the younger generation, then the creative scope offered by a cinema ad may be the best thing (and then you can cut it down to show on TV as well).

exhibit 8.7

Examples of advertising media

terrestrial TV	cinema	buses/taxis/trains
cable/satellite TV	posters	tickets
video	newspapers	mobile phones
CD/DVD	magazines	e-mail
radio	trade journals	Teletext
Internet	directories	

media class

or media category, type of media, e.g. television, press, posters, cinema

media vehicle

the actual newspaper, magazine, poster site, etc. where adverts appear

Advertisers must choose a **media class** (the **inter-media decision**) and then a **media vehicle** (the **intra-media decision**). This decision is based on the creative scope a medium offers and its audience profile. For example, a TV advert aired during *Big Brother* would allow the advertisers to use colour, sound and movement (actors, props and/or animation) to create an impact on a young audience.

Exhibit 8.7 lists examples of the media available although, as new ones are added all the time, you can probably add to the list. Of the traditional **mass media**, press advertising takes in the most money despite being a less expensive medium than TV – there is just so much more of it. The picture is constantly changing, though. New satellite and cable channels keep opening up. These are cheaper vehicles than terrestrial television and can be targeted more closely as many channels are very specialist and so appeal to clearly defined audiences, e.g. a home improvement channel is clearly a good place to advertise DIY equipment. In the UK in August 2003, the cable and satellite channels' combined audience was larger than that of BBC1 for the first time, and the popularity of these channels, largely driven by increased interest in digital television, looks set to grow.

insight

Zipping and zapping

Television advertising just isn't as effective as it used to be. There are so many adverts that audiences just tune out – sometimes literally. They record programmes on video, then zip through the adverts to carry on watching the programme. If viewing a programme as aired, they use the remote control to zap and channel hop to a station where there are no ads.

There is a silver lining here for advertisers and it comes in the form of TV sponsorship. Think about it. When you're zapping through the ads on the video, what are you looking out for so that you know when to stop?

The traditional mass **media classes** are still commonly used; however, other media types are becoming increasingly popular, e.g. **new media** and **ambient media**.

The Internet, along with other digital technologies such as **iTV** and mobile phones, is referred to as the **new media**. The technology behind new media has a number of advantages:

▶ interactivity

▶ faster response times

▶ more direct communications

▶ the ability to put the message across in a more sophisticated way.

Sirens calling

Lever Fabergé used the interactivity of new media along with the impact of ambient media to launch Siren, a fragrance in the Impulse body spray range.

The campaign was targeted at 16- to 24-year-old females. Posters displayed photos of nine, supposedly missing, male models alongside the strapline, 'Where have all the men gone?' The ambient media campaign was supported by a website, SMS voting, a text message advice line and **viral marketing**.

Visitors to the website were encouraged to vote by text or e-mail for their favourite man. Voting entered them into a prize draw where they could win an invitation to an exclusive Siren party.

Lever Fabergé's campaign for Siren

---

noise
a barrier to communication, usually from an external source

viral marketing
modern form of word-of-mouth advertising, often uses new media (e.g. e-mail and texting)

Ambient media is a relatively new term and was originally applied to unusual outdoor media. It is becoming more widely used now to describe any outdoor media, though some ambient media may be indoors. Used in this broader way, the original, and still the biggest, ambient media are poster sites. Advertising is getting everywhere today and the discovery of new media possibilities is a great source of differentiation and a way to cut the **noise** created by communications overload. More unusual ambient media include cars, laser light shows, people, tickets, stairs, postcards, balloons and skywriting.

The final medium to mention is **word of mouth**. This is probably the most pervasive of all. When friends and relatives talk positively about a product or service, it sounds so much more convincing than when the words come from an actor on television who has been paid. Some adverts are deliberately designed to stimulate word of mouth, to get people talking. Budweiser's 'Wassup?' – remember that? Did you ever say it yourself? Budweiser's budget reached many more members of its audience thanks to the creative excellence of that campaign.

> **activity**
> Take a walk around your local high street. Note down the different types of ambient media you find.

Direct marketing

As identified earlier, it is not always easy to fit all the elements of the marketing communications mix into four broad categories. Where to put direct marketing (or more accurately in the context of promotions, direct marketing communication) is one such problem, as it can make use of advertising as well as sales promotions and personal selling. However, for our purposes, it has been included here.

Most promotional tools are aimed at mass audiences but there are weaknesses with the mass approach. Since the early 1990s, some companies have adopted a more direct approach to their markets. They are motivated not just by cost advantages but also by opportunities to improve quality and service provision.

Direct marketing establishes direct contact with prospects and customers to encourage a direct response. Early direct marketing focused on providing a telephone number or a response card in advertisements (i.e. **direct-response advertising**). Today, **direct mail**, telemarketing and door-to-door activities are among the main response media used, although with the onset of digital technology it is expected that mobile phones, television and radio will become even more important direct response media in the future.

Direct marketing has outgrown its early roots and has become a sophisticated marketing tool used for building relationships with customers. Direct-response advertising is now only a part of the huge direct marketing industry. The Institute of Direct Marketing (IDM) emphasizes the importance of building customer relationships through direct marketing efforts, and highlights the roles of 'planned recording, analysis and tracking of individual customers' responses and transactions for the purpose of developing and prolonging mutually profitable customer relationships'. The primary objectives of direct marketing are to build and sustain a mutually rewarding relationship with individual customers, to reduce media cost and to improve the effectiveness of marketing communications and the measurement of results.

Undoubtedly, direct marketing has grown and developed because of rapid advances in computing and communications technology, transportation and changing market conditions. Technology has facilitated the collection, storage, analysis and retrieval of customer data. It has increased opportunities for direct communication even on an individual basis to millions of people. It offers a solution to the fragmentation of the marketplace. It can also create problems of unwanted communications.

direct marketing
all activities that make it possible to offer goods or services or to transmit other messages to a segment of the population by post, telephone, e-mail or other direct means (according to the CIM)

direct mail
advertising material delivered by post

e-focus

Spam spam spam

An explosion of unwanted e-mails, or **spam**, has sent orders for SurfControl's filtering software up 43 per cent in the past three months.

The company's chief executive, Steve Purdham, said that the surge in demand meant that profit targets for the year to the end of June would be met and would be even better for the next year.

'The amount of spam has grown tenfold in the past six months,' he said. 'Spammers make about $50 to $100 for every half a million e-mails they send out, so the fact they are making billions of dollars a day gives you an idea of the billions of e-mails they are sending.'

Source: adapted from the *Daily Express*, Wednesday 9 June 2003

Direct-response advertising

Direct-response advertising is, according to the IDM *Direct Marketing Guide*, 'advertising or selling through any medium inviting the consumer to respond to the advertiser'. As with all advertising, it requires good audience profiling, creativity and wise media choice. Direct marketers make good use of database technology to build up information on customers and **prospects** (see Chapter 2 for more on **database marketing**). Using this, they can compile **mailing lists**, or lists suitable for other media, and so reach their **target audiences**.

Media choice

While most media can be used for direct communications, Exhibit 8.8 outlines the main media choices open to direct marketers.

exhibit 8.8

Direct response advertising media

display advertising (press)	door to door
classified advertising (press)	websites
mail	Internet advertising (e.g. banners)
telephone	Internet pop-ups and instant messages
SMS	e-mail
TV	inserts in magazines/papers
iTV	flyers
radio	posters

Factors affecting media choice in direct marketing communications

No one medium always achieves the highest response at the lowest cost, and it is generally true that those media that elicit a higher response also tend to be the most expensive. For example, telephone responses are potentially the highest of any media, but the costs are also the highest.

To assess the media for a direct marketing campaign, the framework AIMRITE can be used as a decision-making aid (Pickton and Broderick, 2004).

▶ **Audience**: does the media reach the desired target audience?

▶ **Impact**: does the media have sufficient impact to ensure the message has a chance of getting through the clutter?

▶ **Message**: does it help ensure the message is clearly communicated?

▶ **Response**: does it make responding easy?

▶ **Internal management**: does it enhance the efficient management of the campaign?

▶ **The End result**: what are the costs and projected likely revenues? Taking the above into account, and looking at the average response rates for the chosen media, how likely are you to hit target for the campaign?

Obtain a direct-response press or magazine advertisement or a piece of direct mail. Critically appraise the media choice made, using the AIMRITE framework (although you are not likely to be able to assess the end result).

PUBLIC RELATIONS (PR)

public relations (PR)
planned activities designed to promote goodwill between an organization and its publics

publics
the groups of people that the organization communicates with

Traditionally, PR was perceived to be a function of **corporate image** rather than product or **brand image**. Nowadays, there are a number of types of PR, and marketing communications has embraced and adapted the various elements of the discipline in a positive and productive way. Creating and maintaining goodwill for corporations is just as relevant to product brands as it is to corporations as a whole.

Raising the visibility of organizations and encouraging interest in them and goodwill towards them is an important function of marketing communications. In recent times **public relations** has assumed a greater significance at both the corporate level and within the promotion mix.

What is public relations?

According to the Institute of Public Relations, 'Public relations is the planned and sustained effort to establish and maintain goodwill and mutual understanding between an organisation and its publics.' Reflecting on this definition, the words *planning, sustained effort* and *mutual understanding* need emphasizing. Good public relations involves conducting planned programmes with clear objectives, so that results can be assessed and understood. Good public relations involves sustained activity over time. The objectives of creating and maintaining goodwill are not achieved by short-term activities alone (although such activities will be part of a sustained programme). Finally, good public relations requires mutual understanding between the organization and its various publics. In public relations, the organization receives as well as transmits information, listens as well as speaks (Jefkins, 1989).

The scope of public relations

Public relations can raise awareness, inform, interest, excite, educate, generate understanding, build trust, encourage loyalty and even help generate sales (Pickton and Broderick, 2004). PR can raise visibility and also help develop corporate and product credibility in ways that other promotional tools cannot. It can also be used to enhance the effectiveness of advertising. Any solid management planning relies on research and analysis and PR is no exception. The planning and management of PR is a systematic process of identifying PR tasks, setting objectives, defining **publics**, integrating PR within the promotion, or marketing communications mix, scheduling, managing the implementation of PR techniques and assessing their effectiveness.

PR techniques

Media relations/publicity

Good media relations encourage media coverage and favourable, positive publicity. Conversely, they discourage negative coverage. This is an important function of professional public relations specialists and involves developing positive personal relationships with editors and journalists. Publicity is gained through the dissemination of press and other media releases. These contain positive information about the organization and its products or brands in the hope of obtaining positive editorial coverage. **Publicity** may use the same mass media as advertising. However, unlike advertising, the media costs are not paid for directly by the company, nor does it identify itself as coming directly from the company. Publicity can be described as stimulation of demand for goods, or services, by generating news about them in the mass media. This is done by means of **press releases**, **press conferences** and events or **publicity stunts** (e.g. Richard Branson flying across the Atlantic in a hot-air balloon to get the Virgin name in the news).

> **activity**
>
> Press releases are often written as articles suitable for publication. Time-strapped editors sometimes print them with little or no amendment. Browse through a newspaper or magazine and try to find stories that may have been placed by a commercial company (the weekend glossies are often the best source). Are these stories favourable or unfavourable?

Publicity can be an impressive and effective promotional tool. However, as it involves a third party, such as a newspaper reporter or editor, who has the power to determine the nature of the message, a firm has little control over its timing and content. An extreme example of this is the publicity, good, bad or indifferent, a company's products get in *Which?* magazine. *Which?* regularly evaluates products and services, and publishes the results of the tests. Companies have no control over the tests or the resultant publicity.

insight

Families at war are good for ratings

In 2003, Channel 4 screened a programme called *Masters and Servants*. It was the latest in a line of reality TV shows and featured two families, one playing the role of masters while the members of the other family became servants. The Rose and Mills families fell out so spectacularly that it led to press speculation that the whole thing might have been staged. The extensive media coverage attracted an additional 300,000 viewers to the next programme in the series.

Publications

The PR department or agency is usually responsible for this important task, although advertising agencies and others also offer the service. A variety of publications are produced – for example, employee newsletters, financial reports, consumer magazines, brochures and media packs. Such publications are the mainstay of much organizational PR.

Corporate communications

Aspects of corporate communications that fall into the category of PR include corporate identity programmes, corporate image management, corporate advertising, some internal communications and some communications with other publics or stakeholder groups.

Public affairs and community relations

This involves contact with the government and government agencies, special interest and professional groups, as well as the local community, with a view to building and maintaining local, national and international relations.

Lobbying

An approach associated with public affairs and media relations. It aims to build and maintain positive relations with, for example, group leaders, legislators and officials, through negotiation and persuasion.

Sponsorship

sponsorship
giving financial aid, or other resources, to an individual, organization (usually non-profitmaking) or event in return for a positive association with them

A business relationship in which one organization provides funds or other resources/services to another organization (or an individual) and gains commercial advantage through being linked to them. It may be on a relatively small scale directed at a local activity, or involve millions of pounds.

Product placement

This is another promotional tool that is growing in importance. How many times have you rented a video or DVD and zapped through the adverts to the start of the film itself? The marketing communications industry is aware that adverts, whether on television or in other media, can irritate some of the audience. This, as well as clutter in the marketplace, was the impetus behind product placement. Today, a wide variety of brands is directly placed in television programmes and films. The brands are seen being used (and thus, by implication, endorsed) although the audience is not always fully aware that this is taking place. The communications process is quite subtle.

Sponsorship: a rising star

Should the Notting Hill Carnival or school lessons and sport be sponsored? These, and many similar questions are being hotly debated by various publics. But why has sponsorship assumed such an important role in marketing communications, and gained such mistrust among many different publics?

The Queen's Club international tennis tournament is better known as? (See picture for clue)

Sponsorship is an effective and valuable marketing communications tool. The sponsorship of events, activities and organizations will continue to grow because it affords access to specific target audiences and enhances the sponsor's corporate image.

Sponsorship really took off as a communications tool in the early 1990s. According to Meenaghan (1991) the key reasons are: national and European policies on tobacco and alcohol, the spiralling costs of advertising media, the proven ability of sponsorship, new opportunities due to increased leisure activity, greater media coverage of sponsored events, and the recognition of the inefficiencies associated with the traditional media.

Certain activities have attracted sponsorship more than others; these are: sports, programmes and broadcasts, the arts and other areas that encompass activities such as wildlife/conservation and education.

Events management

This is the staging of events. These may be one-off events or conferences, or something that occurs regularly. If a new product is to be launched, there may be internal announcement meetings. External events may be staged to attract, hopefully, favourable publicity and extensive media coverage.

Crisis management

Dealing with unforeseen events is an important facet of PR and is often referred to as damage limitation. It may involve product recall, such as in the now famous Perrier case, or dealing with major ecological disasters, such as the *Exxon Valdez* oil spillage, or a scandal such as a football manager being overheard insulting his club's fans.

Visit an exhibition. Observe and evaluate all the activities that are going on. Consider the organization of the exhibition as a whole – the number of stands, layout, visitor attendance, exhibitor attendance, promotional/ informational materials, atmosphere and all the supporting services.

▶ Evaluate the whole event from a visitor's perspective.

▶ Evaluate the event from an exhibitor's perspective.

What recommendations would you make for future exhibitions?

SALES PROMOTION

Most people, it seems, like to think that they have got something for nothing. It could be free conditioner with a brand of shampoo, or money off a badly wanted DVD. The term **sales promotion** refers to promotional activities intended to induce buyers to purchase, or try, a product, or to stimulate the effectiveness of channel members. Sales promotions can add value to the product offering or create an incentive for certain behaviour.

Sales promotion is a very effective promotional tool that has grown enormously in its usage since the 1980s. More money is spent on sales promotion than on advertising. The Institute of Sales Promotion (ISP), the body that represents all the major sales promotion practitioners in the UK, gives this definition of sales promotion:

> Sales promotion comprises that range of techniques used to attain sales/marketing objectives in a cost-effective manner by adding value to a product or service, either to intermediaries or end-users, normally, but not exclusively, within a defined time period.

According to Cummins (1989), there are six main reasons why sales promotions appeal to the organization and the customer.

1. They work. Companies use sales promotions to the extent that they work because they have daily proof of their effectiveness.

2. Their effectiveness is easily measurable. A sales promotion is normally available for a specified period, and it is easy to measure its sales volume and profit consequences. For example, money-off coupons have to be handed in, so they can be counted.

3. They can be closely targeted. Thanks to computer databases, a special offer can be directed at specific groups of people within particular market segments. For example, online retailers might send out incentives to people who have registered but never bought.

4. They fit with niche marketing. **Niche markets** often do not justify the level of spending needed for successful advertising. Sales promotion is usually cheaper.

5. They are quick acting. The fortunes of brands and companies are increasingly volatile. Sales promotions can be devised and implemented, and take effect far more quickly than other forms of promotion.

6. They create interest. Sales promotion brings in an element of novelty, excitement and humour, which customers enjoy, and, more importantly, respond to.

Many marketing managers believe that sales promotion will go on taking a rising share of their marketing budgets. The changes that are taking place in society are giving greater weight to this view. For example, the fragmenting TV audience is making this medium more expensive to use, the decline in community identity at a local level is making it more difficult to reach particular groups (such as the young) through local papers and, contentiously, the growth in the number of competing brands and products is leading people to switch off from the many messages beamed at them.

Sales promotion objectives

Sales promotion is usually used to achieve short-term objectives such as to:

▶ introduce a new product
▶ encourage greater usage
▶ combat or offset competitors' marketing efforts
▶ stimulate product trial.

However, it should be fully integrated with other promotional tools to form a cohesive plan that supports the organization's long-term objectives. Many sales promotions are seen as downmarket and therefore are unsuited to campaigns that are promoting an upmarket image. Also, some types of promotion would be too expensive to fund if extended to high-priced goods, and so bogof promotions, for example, tend to be found on low-priced products such as toiletries, food and drinks. Sales promotion is at its most effective in the latter stages of the buying process. Promotions are good at prompting action.

There are three categories of sales promotion: consumer, trade and salesforce.

Consumer promotions

Trial is regarded as the most important action objective for almost every brand. In **FMCG**, getting a customer to buy for the first time is harder than getting repeat purchases. Customers making **high-involvement purchases** may also want to try them out, e.g. test driving a car. Sales promotions are a good way to stimulate trial, to add value and to reassure.

Consumer promotions are generally one of three types: save, win or free. Some examples of consumer promotions are:

▶ samples – standard or trial size giveaways

▶ coupons, e.g. 25p off your next purchase

▶ premiums – an extra, free item, e.g. **bogof**

▶ special offers, e.g. half price this week

▶ bonus packs – extra quantity or larger product, e.g. 25 per cent bigger bar

▶ multipacks – cheaper than buying separately

▶ competitions, e.g. answer the following questions . . .

▶ prize draws, e.g. check the number by ringing/writing in

▶ instant wins, e.g. KitKat's 'Win a Million' promotion

▶ points to collect, e.g. Air Miles or Nectar card points

▶ tie-ins – giving a different product away, e.g. cereal gifts

▶ cause-related promotions – the seller gives a donation to a worthy cause for every product sold, e.g. Pizza Express donates to the Venice in Peril Fund every time one of its Veneziana pizzas is sold

▶ **self-liquidating special offers**, e.g. a cereal company offering a set of breakfast bowls in return for £10 and four tokens.

sales promotion
a short-term special offer

self-liquidating special offer
a sales promotion that pays for itself (usually because the company making the offer has bought the promotional items in vast quantities and so obtained a substantial discount)

Consumer sales promotion programmes may be paid for by the retailer but are commonly financed by the manufacturer. They are often supported by advertising, point of sale (POS) promotions and merchandising activities within retail outlets.

Trade promotions

Consumer goods suppliers spend a great deal on trade promotions to distributors, including retailers, as part of their **push strategy**.

Promotions by manufacturers to their distributors, generally called trade promotions, are most often some form of price promotion because the main factor motivating distributors is their reseller profit margin.

Price promotions are used most often to gain trial, i.e. an initial stocking of the product or offering of the service by the distributor. There are three main types of **trade trial promotions**, as described opposite.

1. New line fees (slotting allowances): these are cash payments or a proportion of the shipment (consignment of goods) donated free, which amounts to a price inducement, in return for stocking a new product or offering a new service for a specified period of time.

2. Price-offs: these are straight reductions in the selling price to the distributor and are sometimes called off-invoice promotions.

3. Returns: the manufacturer agrees to buy back unsold quantities of the product. An extreme form of this is something called distributing on consignment, whereby the distributor pays nothing to the manufacturer until the product is sold (also known as sale or return).

Price promotions are also important in encouraging repeat purchase by the distributor. There are four types, as described below.

1. Price-offs: as described above, but on the understanding that part of the discount will be passed to the end customer or consumer, or that the distributor will provide extra display, advertising or both.

2. Joint promotions: these are agreements by which the manufacturer and distributor both contribute funds towards promotional expenditure. The proportion of contribution may vary.

3. Sales contests: competitions in which retailers, or other trade partners, can win attractive prizes.

4. Sales education: this is applicable mainly to industrial products and services, or to the more technical types of consumer durables. Manufacturers train the retailer's or wholesaler's staff and all parties benefit from the increased sales.

Salesforce promotions

Manufacturers have a salesforce to motivate. Salesforce promotions include monetary rewards, such as bonuses, and non-monetary rewards, such as prizes, training programmes, motivational meetings and selling aids.

What can go wrong?

Sales promotions must be very carefully planned. There is a code of practice to abide by, and laws on gambling and competitions to be obeyed. For example, if someone has to pay to enter, then that is gambling and, in the UK, a licence is required to run gambling games. Hence that familiar phrase 'no purchase necessary'. There is a thriving sales promotion industry in the UK and, as the details of promotions can get quite complex, it is usually advisable to enlist expert help for anything but the simplest of offers. Some of the scenarios that might arise are outlined below.

▶ Over-redemption
  – bad promotion design: for example, the classic case of the Hoover flights promotion; Hoover offered a free flight to New York with every vacuum cleaner purchase; unfortunately, the vacuum cleaner was cheaper than the flight and people flocked to electrical appliance stores instead of to travel agents; that promotion is reported to have cost £48 million.
  – error in administration: for example, Pepsi's Philippine subsidiary promised one million pesos (about £25,000) for bottle caps bearing the winning number 349; when Pepsi had paid out £8 million, it realized something was amiss – there were far too many winners. The withdrawal of the offer provoked riots.

▶ Misredemption: one of the advantages of sales promotion is the accuracy of its targeting. You can send a coupon to precisely the person you want to redeem it – but can you prevent it from being passed on to someone else?

▶ Malredemption: the likely number of winners for any promotion is carefully worked out and budgets set. Lottery syndicates are encouraged but, if a promotion requires the collecting of a set of something, beware: joint efforts (and swaps arranged through newspaper columns or on the Internet) could blow the budget.

▶ Faulty pack design: some sales promotions require a special pack design to disguise which one is the winning pack. This packaging must be designed with great care. If someone swallows a prize notification ticket when upending a packet of crisps into their mouth (as has happened), then trouble will ensue.

▶ Pilfering: if the pack design is not good enough to disguise a winner, the chances are it will never make it out of the shop. Bored sales assistants enjoy trying to spot a winning pack.

▶ Lost in the post: many samples fail to reach the right target; they may arrive but be picked up by another member of the household. Recently there have been complaints that some of the promotional items that land on doormats are dangerous to young children who may think that they are toys or sweets, when they are not.

Sales promotions need careful, worst-case scenario planning – and professional indemnity insurance.

PERSONAL SELLING

There is talk of outlawing door-to-door selling in the UK. This will be good news for many people who feel threatened and coerced by such salespeople, and bad news for the unprofessional sales organizations whose behaviour has prompted the ban. Putting to one side the ethical problems associated with extreme forms of personal selling, it has a major role to play in the promotion mix of many companies. **Personal selling** is an oral presentation, in a conversation with one or more prospective purchasers, for the purpose of making sales.

Personal selling involves informing customers of the benefits of products and services, and persuading them to buy through personal communication in a potential exchange situation. It includes such things as a salesperson explaining a product's features, a technician demonstrating a new MRI scanner to relevant hospital personnel, and even the person at the supermarket who gives you a free sample of a new luxury ice cream while telling you something about it.

Personal selling differs from other forms of communication in that messages flow from a sender to a receiver directly (often face to face). This direct and interpersonal communication lets the sender receive and evaluate feedback from the receiver immediately. This communications process, known as **dyadic** communication (between two people or groups), allows the message to be tailored more specifically to the needs of the sender and receiver than do many of the other media.

Reaching a limited number of people through personal selling efforts costs, proportionately, a considerable amount more than it does through advertising. However, in many situations it is thought to be worth it because of the immediate feedback and its greater persuasive impact on customers.

Salespeople

To develop a salesforce, a marketing manager needs to decide what kind of salesperson will sell the firm's products most effectively. Various authors classify sales roles in different ways. Some classify sales jobs into two broad categories: service selling (which concentrates on getting sales from the existing customer base) and developmental selling (which aims to convert prospects into customers). Others refer to three basic roles: order taking, order supporting and order getting. From reading the above, you understand that there are many sales roles and, in reality, these roles may not be discrete. Salespeople now have to perform many tasks and activities daily (not just selling), which involve numerous skills, such as:

▶ buyer/seller team coordinator
▶ customer service provider
▶ buyer behaviour expert
▶ information gatherer
▶ market analyst and planner
▶ sales forecaster
▶ market cost analyst
▶ technologist.

Stages of selling

A number of sequential steps go into making a sale, as illustrated in Exhibit 8.9.

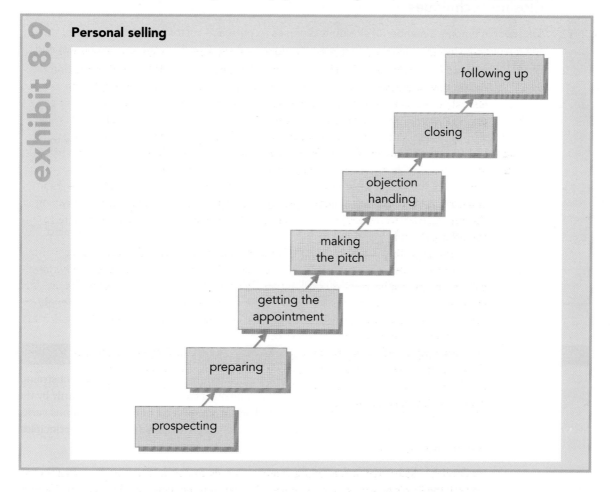

exhibit 8.9

Personal selling

- prospecting
- preparing
- getting the appointment
- making the pitch
- objection handling
- closing
- following up

Prospecting is about finding potential customers. Exhibitions are good sources of prospects, as are direct-response promotions. It is important that a salesperson should prepare before approaching a prospect. They need to know what kind of person they are dealing with, why they might want the product/service and what their likely 'hot buttons' are. The next step is to get the appointment. This may be arranged in advance (e.g. over the phone) or the salesperson may **cold-call**. The next step is a big one. Although, on Exhibit 8.9, it is labelled 'making the pitch', there is more to it than that. First, the salesperson should find out what the customer wants, then he or she can draw attention to the most appropriate products and their benefits. The best salespeople are good listeners. It is unlikely that the product will fit the customer's needs perfectly; there will be some objections raised (e.g. it is too expensive, it is the wrong colour, it has no cover). The salesperson must address these concerns honestly, and perhaps convince the customer that the things the product lacks are unimportant. Now comes the close. This is the part that many salespeople find the hardest: they just have to ask for the order. Finally, there is the follow-up: making sure the product is delivered, that it works properly and, of course, checking if the customer needs anything else. This could be the start of a long and profitable relationship.

Not all steps are used in all sales situations. The retail sales assistant, for example, will be in a very different situation to a key accounts salesperson who works for a manufacturer of heavy industrial equipment.

insight

Closing techniques

Salespeople employ a number of closing techniques to persuade customers to place orders, some more effective than others, some less ethical than others. Good salespeople are honest and straightforward. If customers like and trust them, they are far more likely to buy from them.

Some examples of closing techniques are:

▶ the straight close, e.g. 'So would you like one?' followed by silence

▶ the deadline, e.g. 'There is only the one left in stock and I don't know when we'll be able to get more'

▶ the assumptive close, e.g. 'So I'll get it delivered next week then'

▶ the alternative close, e.g. 'Would you like the blue or the green?'

▶ the no problem close, e.g. 'Order it now and you can cancel it later if you change your mind'

▶ the sympathy close, e.g. 'I just need one more order to make my **sales quota** this month.'

Look out for these next time you're out shopping. You may even be able to add to the list.

REGULATIONS

Throughout Europe and elsewhere, marketing communications are subject to constraints and regulations. Some controls are set by law and others are self-imposed voluntarily by the marketing communications industry itself. The balance of legal and self-regulations varies from country to country. Collectively, the regulations seek to uphold four guiding principles. Promotions should be:

▶ legal

▶ decent

▶ honest, and

▶ truthful.

These principles are used to produce a series of codes of practice covering different media and types of promotions. An example of these codes can be seen on the web at www.cap.org.uk.

Despite attempts to ensure that these principles are maintained, there are examples of some dubious practices. Regulatory bodies police the industry and, where necessary, require that promotions are withdrawn if they contravene the principles above. Legal action can be taken in extreme cases. Where infringements do occur, it is more likely to be because of issues of decency, or moral, ethical or misrepresentation concerns, rather than outright lack of honesty or a deliberate attempt to mislead (although these do occur in a minority of cases through false claims and downright illegal practices). Notable examples that have been widely publicized are the poster promotions for Benetton in which the use of imagery has often been deemed to be too shocking to be seen in public places where it might create a degree of offence. In coming to a view on such matters, it is not a question of offending everybody that is the issue but, rather, one of creating what may be considered widespread offence.

In general, it is up to the media owners (TV, radio, cinema, newspaper and magazine owners, etc.) to come to a view as to whether or not an item is likely to contravene the codes of practice, and not accept the promotion where this may happen. In the case of TV and radio, any advertising should be pre-vetted – that is, checked before transmission. But in the case of most other promotions, such pre-vetting is impossible and so checks are made after the promotions have been circulated. Members of the public are encouraged to make complaints, which are subsequently investigated. In the case of the UK, a great deal of voluntary self-regulation is relied on to enhance the legal controls; the Advertising Standards Authority (ASA) is responsible for regulating advertising (other than TV and radio, which have their own regulatory bodies), sales promotions and direct marketing (including the Internet). There are also numerous other professional bodies representing the different elements of marketing communications, which also have their own codes of professional practice. Most other countries have their own similar arrangements although the extent of the control exerted varies significantly.

ethicalfocus

Breaking the code

It's in the nature of human beings to push boundaries to see how far they'll stretch, and advertisers are no different. The ASA and the ITC are there to maintain standards.

For example, in 2003, e-bookers.com fell foul of the code for an advert headlined 'Want Maori for your money?' The ad went on to say, 'New Zealand. Fourteen nights from £319'. However, the offer did not actually include flights – a fact only mentioned in the small print. The ASA upheld a complaint that the ad was misleading.

Over 150 viewers complained about the upsetting and offensive nature of a Gillette TV ad for Right Guard deodorant. In the ad, an office worker was seen running from a building that was being demolished around him. This was ostensibly part of a test to determine whether his deodorant was effective.

Viewers complained that the images were reminiscent of the World Trade Center disaster on 11 September 2001. There were also complaints about the insensitive timing of the campaign, which was close to the second anniversary of the events. The agency, Abbott Mead Vickers, edited the ad to make it clearer that the man was

▶

ethicalfocus

playing a game and took it off air between 7 and 22 September. However, there were still so many objections that the ITC decided the overall theme of the advertisement was likely to upset viewers. It was withdrawn.

The most complained-about press ad of 2002 was one for the British Heart Foundation. It showed a woman with a plastic bag over her head as an illustration of what having heart disease was like. There were concerns that children might imitate this. The ASA Council concluded that, as the ad had appeared in media where children might see it, a small-print warning in the corner of the ad stating that plastic bags should be kept away from children was not enough. It upheld the complaints.

Second and third place in the ASA complaints chart went to the Pot Noodle 'Slag' campaign. Complaints that these ads were offensive were upheld in one instance, but not the other. Visit the ASA website, www.asa.org.uk (go to 'Annual Report'), for the full story and for the rest of the complained-about ads.

SUMMARY

This chapter has introduced some basic concepts and models that will help you to understand how marketing communications decisions are made. The key model to understand is the communications process, since marketing communications, or promotion, is a communication process. This involves an understanding of the sender, the message, the media and the receivers.

Organizations can use a variety of promotional tools to communicate with potential customers, whether consumer or b2b. The major promotional tools are advertising, PR, sales promotion and personal selling. To these can be added direct marketing and sponsorship, together with many other activities such as packaging and exhibitions. Collectively, these are known as the promotion, or marketing communications, mix. Advertising, PR and sponsorship are primarily mass communications, whereas personal selling is interpersonal communication. Sales promotion and direct marketing may be either.

The organization can use its promotion mix to develop both push and pull strategies. With a push strategy the organization directs its promotional efforts at marketing channel members. These then push the product forwards to the final buyer. With a pull strategy the organization directs its promotional efforts at the final buyer to develop a strong demand for the product that is used to pull a product through the marketing channel. Most organizations use a combination of push and pull.

The purpose of all marketing communications is to create a response from potential buyers. One response model, also known as a hierarchy of effects model, is AIDA (Awareness, Interest, Desire and Action). Each promotional tool has different degrees of effectiveness in eliciting these different responses.

One approach does not fit all. There is no single optimal promotion mix and no one accepted scientific approach to determining the promotion mix. Many factors need to be considered, such as: the objectives of the marketing plan; the size and characteristics of the target market/audience and their buying decision process; the type of products being promoted; the objectives of the promotional efforts; and competitors' promotional efforts.

Challenges reviewed

Now that you have finished reading the chapter, look back at the challenges you were set at the beginning. Do you have a clearer idea of what's involved?

Hints:

▶ see 'setting the promotional budget'

▶ media planning

▶ audience profiling and research

▶ time for crisis management; see 'publics' and 'media relations'.

READING AROUND

websites

www.theidm.co.uk – the Institute of Direct Marketing, go to the knowledge centre and browse

www.nmauk.co.uk – the Newspaper Marketing Agency, check out its 'breaking ads' page

www.asa.org.uk – the website for the Advertising Standards Authority

book chapters

Abilasha Meta (1999) Celebrities in advertising, Chapter 17 in John Philip Jones, *The Advertising Business*, Sage Publications.

Pickton, D.W. and Broderick, A. (2004) Chapters 1, 2, 3 and 9 in *Integrated Marketing Communications* (2nd edn), FT Prentice Hall.

video

Minority Report, starring Tom Cruise – look for the possible future of marketing communications

SELF-REVIEW QUESTIONS

1. List and explain the key elements in the communications process model. (see page 234)

2. Identify sources of noise in the communications process. (see page 235)

3. What are the main elements, or tools, of the promotion mix? (see page 228)

4. What are the advantages and disadvantages of mass communication and interpersonal communication? (see page 229)

5. Define push and pull strategies. (see page 232)

6. What are the problems with using 'increase sales' as a promotional objective? (see page 242)

7. How is advertising controlled or regulated in the UK? (see page 258)

8. What is the AIDA model and how can it be used to set promotional objectives? (see page 238)

9. Explain how personal selling is a two-way communications process. (see page 256)

10. Explain and give examples of the major types of consumer sales promotions. (see page 254)

11. What is direct-response advertising? (see page 248)

12. Discuss the strengths and limitations of each budgeting method. (see pages 232–3)

MINI CASE STUDY

Read the questions, then the case material, then answer the questions.

Questions

As marketing consultant to Roy Eddington, you have been asked to develop a post-strike marketing communications campaign. Consider the nature of the problem from a marketing communications perspective. Reflect on the public perception of BA, as indicated in the case study, to assist you with your decision-making. Your campaign suggestions should:

▶ highlight key target audience members

▶ list the objectives your campaign should achieve

▶ identify all the marketing communications activities you would use.

British Airways strike wrecks £6000 honeymoon

Thousands of holidaymakers faced misery in the summer of 2003 when check-in staff, working for British Airways at Heathrow, went on a series of strikes. The troubled company lost an estimated £40 million through the industrial action, and ruined travel for more than 90,000 people, causing some of the worst chaos ever seen at Heathrow.

Chief executive Rod Eddington intervened in a bid to end the biggest crisis in the airline's history, which saw thousands take their custom elsewhere. The unofficial walkout by 250 check-in staff was triggered by the imposition of a swipe-card entry system, which workers felt could lead to new working practices, such as being sent home during quiet periods and called in at busy times.

The union leader, who represents the GMB (the union that many of the check-in staff belong to), said that his union would strike for 'as long as necessary to force BA into a climb-down on its introduction of the controversial swipe-card system for staff' as it was unacceptable. The union leader also said, 'We are not backing down on this. BA must withdraw the swipe-card system or face a series of very damaging strikes. If we wipe out the company's profits as a result, it will have to face that.'

For many BA travellers stranded at the airport, the misery was not over when they did eventually get a flight, as their luggage was still at Heathrow. BA admitted that 18,000 cases had not made it on to the flights and many passengers were not reunited with their possessions until a full week after their flight. Tabloid press in the UK took advantage of the situation and published many stories focusing on how the strike had caused personal misery for stranded customers. One story about newlyweds spending their first day of marriage on the airport floor, rather than at their honeymoon destination, quoted the groom as saying, 'I will definitely never fly with BA again ... BA's managing director can apologize all he wants – but it does not give us our honeymoon back.'

Brand reputation is crucial for an airline such as BA. It argues that, unlike the low-cost flight operators, it offers more than just a cheap seat. It believes its reputation for reliability, comfort and customer service is particularly important and worth paying a little more for.

Since becoming CEO of BA in 2000, Rod Eddington has won praise for his success in steering the airline through an era of unprecedented crisis for the travel industry. The travel and economic downturn following 11 September, the build-up to war in Iraq, and SARS have severely reduced passenger numbers. This, combined with competition from low-cost airlines such as easyJet and Ryanair, has required major changes at BA. However, some commentators doubt that BA's internal culture is well suited to the task of winning back the respect of its customers and restoring good industrial relations after the summer of 2003.

REFERENCES

Colley, R. (1961) *Defining Advertising Goals for Measured Advertising Results*, Association of National Advertisers.

Cummins, J. (1989) *Sales Promotion: How to Create and Implement Campaigns that Really Work*, Kogan Page Limited.

Engel, J.F., Warshaw, M.R. and Kinnear, T.C. (1994) *Promotional Strategy* (8th edn), Richard D. Irwin.

Jefkins, F. (1989) *Public Relations Techniques*, Heinemann Professional Publishing Ltd.

Meenaghan, T. (1991) Sponsorship – legitimising the medium, *European Journal of Marketing* 25(11).

Pickton, D.W. and Broderick, A. (2004) *Integrated Marketing Communications* (2nd edn), FT Prentice Hall.

Schramm, W. (1955) How communication works, in W. Schramm (ed.), *The Process and Effects of Mass Communications*, University of Illinois Press, 3–26.

CHAPTER 9

PLACE

BY PHIL GARTON

PLACE CHALLENGES

The following are illustrations of the types of decision that marketers have to take or issues they face. *You aren't expected to know how to deal with the challenges now;* just bear them in mind as you read the chapter and see what you can find that helps.

▶ Imagine that you work for Reebok. Your objectives are to increase the number of sales made in your home market and to maintain the relative exclusivity of the brand. You could easily do this by increasing the number of stores selling your products. In the longer term, however, this may impact on your brand's image as it might be seen as less exclusive. How can you use the stores to achieve your objectives?

▶ A journalist you know is writing a story about the increase in direct marketing and has come to you, as a marketing consultant, for some advice. You have told her that getting the right product to the customer on time is critically important. In reply, she has asked you to explain why, if it is so important, all manufacturers do not take responsibility for every aspect of deliveries themselves.

▶ You are working for a French wine company. You know that Australian wine producers are seen as more technologically advanced. How can you compete?

▶ Your small furniture company is located in a small industrial estate in Cornwall. You know that your products have great potential if only consumers could see them. Unfortunately the major retailers tell you that you cannot make enough furniture to be worth their while working with you. How can you develop to get around this?

KEY CONCEPTS

distribution
exchange relationships (see
    Chapter 1)
supply chain management
logistics
distribution channels
distribution channel members
length and breadth of channels
exclusive, selective and
    intensive distribution
segmentation, targeting and
    positioning (see Chapter 4)
customer relationship
    management; crm (see
    Chapter 1)
direct marketing (see Chapter 8)
personal selling (see Chapter 8)

CHAPTER OVERVIEW

INTRODUCTION

We start this chapter by asking when and from where did you buy your last T-shirt? Does it have a brand logo? If so, whose? How did it get to the store? You probably answered the first couple of questions fairly easily but what about the last one?

Millions of consumers spend billions on products and services each year. They rarely know the origin of those products. Few people are interested in the plantation that their bananas came from or the factories in which Sony made its televisions. It is the purpose of the **supply chain** to put those products in the right place so that those customers can exchange their money for them. For most customers place simply means the shop that you buy things from. For a marketer, **place** is more complex and creates a number of questions to be answered if success is to be achieved.

> **supply chain**
>
> the network of businesses involved in distributing goods and services

In the marketing mix, place is more than just a shop, it encompasses everything that marketers must get right so that the right goods get to the right customer, at the right time. There is a significant management challenge here: a challenge requiring the management of both time and space.

The customer usually chooses where and when to buy something. If a customer wants farm-fresh fruit and vegetables they go to the farm. This is a fixed, geographic location and so we can see that geography represents the simplest idea of place. Whether you can buy the food that you want depends on the growing season of the product. So another fixed point, that of time, can be added to our idea. In our increasingly technology-driven world, however, the concepts of place and time are more flexible. You can buy products from around the world that could not be grown in your own country. You can sit at home and buy your food via the Internet. There is more to place than physical location. Our concept of place encompasses a range of activities that make the product or service available to potential customers. As we shall see, several of these activities may be crucial to effective **targeting** and creating **differentiation** in the mind of the customer.

This chapter looks at the key elements of the **exchange** relationship. We will discuss the importance of time, space, information, bargaining power and what sellers have to do to match buyers' expectations. By the end of the chapter you will begin to realize just how much work has been done to put those trainers in your local sports shop or to make your next dream holiday a reality.

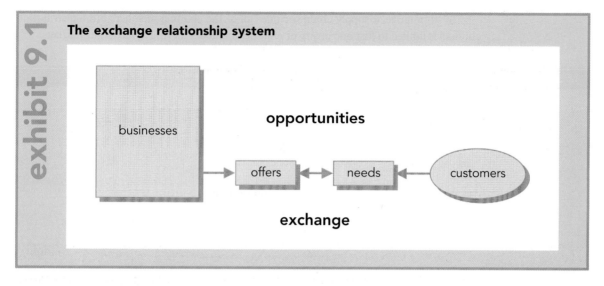

exhibit 9.1

The exchange relationship system

businesses

opportunities

offers ⟷ needs

customers

exchange

GETTING THE PLACE RIGHT

marketing opportunity

a chance to reach a particular group of customers with a product or service offer

physical distribution

the process of moving goods and services between businesses and consumers

All businesses depend on **marketing opportunities** to meet potential customers' needs. They are the primary source of **revenue** and they are what shapes the future of the enterprise. For example, in the 1960s, IBM was the **market leader** for computers. However, it did not write the software programs that ran on them but commissioned other businesses to do this. Early in the development of a new product that would become the personal computer, IBM asked a small company called Microsoft to provide an operating system program. Its head, Bill Gates, spotted a great marketing opportunity. The rest is history. Microsoft's operating system (now called Windows) is still the market leader.

Changes in place can bring new opportunities. For example, the *Financial Times* is able to meet its customers' needs for instantly accessible news and information thanks to advances in Internet technologies.

In a competitive environment, the customer can shop around. It is not generally desirable to be second choice. The tension between consumer needs and business capabilities creates a constant dynamic for change. One of the key roles for marketing management is the creation of attractive opportunities for exchange.

Distribution channels

A **supply chain** is a network of businesses and organizations through which goods pass to get to their final destination. In most developed markets, these networks will be extensive and have many participant businesses. A global business such as the Ford Motor Company has a supply chain that runs through a number of countries. Each of the businesses within that chain is likely to have further international suppliers so that the whole network spans the world. So, Ford buys raw materials and parts from a number of other businesses and sends cars on to a number of resellers.

A **distribution channel** is a specific route through the supply chain. The shape of the distribution channel is affected by the supplier's marketing objectives. For example, Rolex watches target quite a small customer group (the relatively affluent), offer high-quality service and want to project a quality image. Consequently, Rolex generally uses upmarket retail partners with comparatively few stores. This is called **selective distribution** (see 'Designing the supply chain', below).

To summarize, a supply chain includes all of the channel members but a distribution channel is limited to just one group of channel members serving a particular market.

MEMBERS OF THE SUPPLY CHAIN

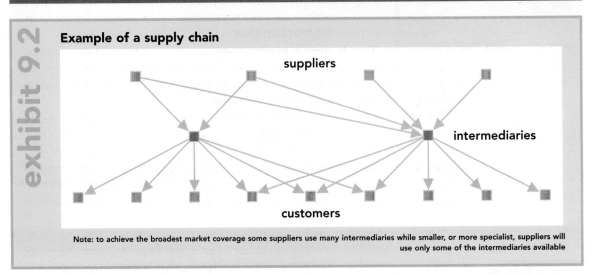

Example of a supply chain

suppliers

intermediaries

customers

Note: to achieve the broadest market coverage some suppliers use many intermediaries while smaller, or more specialist, suppliers will use only some of the intermediaries available

Buyers – consumers, businesses and other organizations

This group is at the end of a supply chain for a product or service. Its members do not sell the product on but buy it to be used by themselves or their organization. (For more on customer types see Chapters 2 and 5.)

Sellers – manufacturers, retailers, wholesalers, resellers

Manufacturers and producers are the major group of sellers. Many of the largest manufacturers achieve global recognition for their products. For example, Hewlett Packard is considered to be one of the world's leading computer printer manufacturers. Its products are sold to customers in different markets through a global network of outlets, some of which are **retailers**, selling to end-user customers, and some are **resellers**, selling the products on.

Products are transformed as they move along the **supply chain**. For example, FAG buys steel and then transforms it into ball bearings, which it then sells to motor manufacturers across the world. The motor manufacturers sell their motors to quarry plant manufacturers, who make equipment to extract material from the earth. The length of this supply chain is determined by the complexity of the final product and its user's needs.

The seller that most consumers engage with is the retailer. The retailer is usually the last member of the supply chain before the end customer. Retailers may operate from a shop, a catalogue, a phone line, a **direct-response advert** in the press or on television, or a website (sometimes a combination, as is the case with, say, Argos). The retailer brings expertise to bear on the selection of goods and services to be offered to the consumer. When this is done well, the retailer thrives, when it is done poorly, the retailer withers.

As businesses, retail organizations come in all sizes. The biggest retailers, such as Wal-Mart and IKEA, are global household names and can offer consumers products from around the world.

The vast majority of products purchased by retailers are also transformed. It is this transformation that enables the buying business to become a selling business. An illustration of this is Sainsbury's transformation of Heinz beans. The retailer will buy millions of cans of beans and these arrive at its distribution depots packed on pallets. The next step is

breaking down
the process of
reducing the
quantity of product
to be moved

wholesalers
buy products in bulk
to sell on to other
businesses in smaller
quantities

breaking down these pallet loads into individual cans that are stacked on the supermarket's shelves. This enables Sainsbury's to sell the individual cans of beans to the final customer. In the Zara case study at the end of this chapter, the breakdown process is done at the distribution centre. In an IKEA store it may be the customer that has to take the product from the stack of products in the warehouse, which directly passes the cost of the work to the customer.

Wholesalers are currently in decline. These businesses are one link further from the final customer than the retailer. They usually buy products to sell on to other members of the supply chain. Their business is to support smaller retailers by holding stock close to the market, thus reducing the delivery time from the manufacturers. Most retail wholesalers also transform the products by breaking down the quantities supplied by the manufacturer. In this respect they are quite similar to the retailer.

This type of business is often found in clothing and food markets because the volume of transactions is high and that helps the wholesaler to reduce the risks involved in holding quantities of stock available for other channel members to buy. The main reason for the decline in the numbers of wholesalers has been the growth of large retail businesses, which generate significant buying economies by buying in bulk direct from the manufacturers. This makes it more difficult for the wholesaler to sell their products at prices that earn sufficient profit.

In business-to-business (b2b) markets, many businesses carry out the breakdown function. They are called resellers – that is, businesses that buy the product from the manufacturer with the purpose of selling it on to another business further down the chain.

Facilitators – agents and logistics services

This group of businesses smooths the flow of products and services through the supply chain. Members of this group usually have specific expertise in a market, or other specialist resources that enable them to undertake tasks more efficiently.

Christian Salvesen are
well-known logistics
contractors

Agents are businesses that represent other businesses in a particular market. Smaller businesses often use locally based agents as a means of entering new or distant markets because the agent has knowledge of the market and access to local facilities. The agent can thus reduce the costs and risks associated with entering the new market. These businesses do not usually buy the products from the manufacturer so they cannot be classed as resellers. They take orders and are paid a commission.

The UK housing market provides a good example of how agents work. In this market, the buyers and sellers tend to be individuals or families with just one house to sell. The estate agency does not take ownership of the house at any point, it brings buyers and sellers together by communicating the property's details to potential buyers and showing them around the house. The agency then charges the seller a commission for any subsequent sale of the property.

The final category of participants is that of the businesses that transport and store products for the various members of the supply chain. These businesses have specialist facilities and knowledge. They are known as **logistics** services, and include warehouses, distribution depots and transport services. Some, for example UPS, have grown to a global scale and can bring products to your market from anywhere around the globe. The vast majority of logistics businesses, however, are much smaller.

The prime purpose in using logistics services is to reduce costs. The logistics businesses generally earn their revenues by bringing individually small, but similar, needs together to create larger units of demand. For example, Christian Salvesen operates a number of cold-storage depots across the country. Manufacturers and retailers that need special conditions to store chilled food products use these depots rather than buying and maintaining these facilities for themselves.

RIGHT SPACE

Space (physical location) and time have a role in **positioning** a business against its competitors. Have you ever stopped to consider how a retail business chooses where to put its stores? It depends on a number of things but, most importantly, its **target market** (McGoldrick, 2003). If a clothing retailer wants to attract the rich and fashionable, then its stores will need to be in more exclusive locations, such as Bond Street in London or the Quadrilatero della Moda in Milan. If, however, the retailer depends on high **sales volumes** to achieve its objectives then it will be better off in London's Oxford Street or in a popular shopping mall. The image of an area indicates the type of customer likely to be found there, and the location of the store reflects this.

There are other factors, apart from image, to be taken into account when choosing a location. For instance, there is volume. Oxford Street is far busier than Bond Street and so is more likely to attract passing trade. Have you noticed that there is nearly always a newsagent's (and a bar) at, or near, railway stations? People want things to read (and sweets to eat) on train journeys. When they miss their train (or it is delayed), then they may want a drink and a snack to while away the time. In the early days, McDonald's used to snap up sites near highway intersections – often in the middle of nowhere. It had realized that the bulk of its customers came by car, usually on their way somewhere else, and could be tempted to take a break by the sight of those famous golden arches. Other fast-food retailers have been known to set up shop anywhere McDonald's did – just because McDonald's was so good at picking locations.

Sometimes a retailer spots a **marketing opportunity**; a high street with no food store, a vacant shop near a school, a residential area with no bars or restaurants (these are retail outlets too), an out-of-town site large enough to take a superstore with parking. The choice may seem ad hoc but these are places where there is little or no competition and where the retailer could reasonably expect to make good profits.

Some areas become known for certain types of shop. For example, London's Tottenham Court Road is full of PC dealers, the Lanes in Brighton is known for antiques, Hatton Garden is the place for jewellery. Clearly these retailers are not trying to avoid the competition, rather they seem to revel in it. So why do they do it? Again, it is about volume of customers. If an area is known for a product type (e.g. PCs), then customers will flock there and not bother to go anywhere else. They know that they have a wide choice in that one place.

Any retail business has to decide whether its strategy will be to take its stores to the customers or to try to attract customers to its stores. Whichever route is chosen shapes all of the business activities back down the **supply chain**.

---

activity

Find a map of your local area. Where would you want to open the following types of retail outlet:

▶ an upmarket restaurant

▶ a bar

▶ a Gap clothing store

▶ a DIY store

▶ a sweet shop?

What problems might you face, i.e. what are the constraints?

RIGHT TIME

To deliver what the customers want exactly when they want it requires flexibility in the supply chain and that usually results in higher operating costs. Think about how food is sold. For millions of people, the superstore has become part of everyday life. These huge buildings frequently offer over 20,000 different products. Millions are spent weekly on food and drink. Some of these stores are open 24 hours a day, six days out of seven. This creates the impression that you can get anything you want at any time. The only thing that stops them being permanently open is government legislation, i.e. the laws limiting the hours of trading on Sundays.

Even this last hurdle can be overcome thanks to modern technology. The large grocery businesses, such as Tesco and Sainsbury's, provide Internet ordering services so that shoppers can order their food and drink at any time to suit their own needs. For a small fee, these products are then brought to the location specified by the shopper at the time specified by the shopper. However, this still will not get you a pint of milk in the middle of the night; available delivery slots are limited to more sociable hours.

e-focus

Tesco Online – getting the goods to the customer

Brian Walker is a Tesco.com delivery driver with a tight schedule to stick to. He and his colleagues manage the day's workload, which can involve handling anything up to 17 deliveries between 9 am and 11 pm, with the help of a computerized scheduling system. The order details, address of destination, expected delivery time and even the most efficient route between drops are all fed through to Walker's local store from a computer system in Dundee.

At the store, 70 pickers work in shifts to collate the orders, and a pool of 12 drivers, with the use of nine vans, is available to transport goods directly to customers' homes.

e-focus

In busy times, the drivers help pickers in the store. 'We are trained to multi-task, so it is very much a team effort,' says Walker.

One of Walker's regular customers – a housewife in Surbiton – has 22 boxes of goods, each box containing three or four bags of produce, delivered every month. 'She has a large, young family and she gets everything delivered by us,' he says. 'A month's worth of nappies can take up a lot of space, and she has told me that she just couldn't handle that amount of shopping by herself.

'We keep hearing how Tesco.com is now the most successful online grocery service in the world. It is great to know you are involved in something that's a success story,' says Walker.   Source: *Retail Week*, 12 December 2002

DIFFERING VIEWS OF PLACE

The consumers' view

Generally speaking, shoppers do not think very much about **place** or the management of the **supply chain**. Shoppers are usually more concerned with the availability of the goods and services that they want. The shoppers' perceptions are thus largely focused on the last link in the supply chain (Piercy, 2002). Just take a moment to think about your daily newspaper. Millions of people take it for granted that their preferred title will be available in a local shop each morning. They don't think about how it gets there or how its components have been brought together. They want the information or entertainment it contains and they will be frustrated if it is not there when they want it. Similarly, when was the last time that you thought about where your trousers came from and the activities that made it possible for you to buy them from the outlet you did? The key management task is to ensure that the right goods are there when and where the customer wants them.

There are a few times when shoppers will be very concerned about the source of the goods. These usually reflect some concern about health or ethical issues. In the first instance shoppers that want organic food will seek reassurance from the retailer that the original source is reliable and truly organic. This is fairly easy for a major grocer to do as the reassurance comes from their own brand and the trust that the shopper has in that reputation. You can see from this example that the provision of relevant information to help the decision-makers is critical to completing the buying process. (For more on branding, see Chapter 7).

In the second instance, there are sometimes ethical issues that excite the shopper. For example, there have been numerous instances of child labour being used to produce products. Many shoppers in developed countries don't like this idea, considering it the exploitation of vulnerable children. Sellers can respond by collectively organizing to reassure shoppers. An example of this would be the Rugmark label. With this, the retailers subscribe to a neutral third-party organization that checks the source to ensure that it does not employ child labour.

Fair Trade

A still from Co-op's TV ad for their Fair Trade chocolate bars

The Fair Trade Foundation, which awards the Fair Trade Mark, is made up of different organizations such as Oxfam, the World Development Movement and Christian Aid. The Fair Trade Mark shows consumers that the farmers that produced the food products guaranteed fair pay for their workers. The farmers have also undertaken to respect the workers' working conditions and to treat their environment with care.

Fair Trade products include many different foods such as cocoa, coffee, tea, sugar, bananas, orange juice and honey. Any product that is awarded the Fair Trade Mark must meet strict conditions of production and the Foundation has independent assessors to check that these conditions are being met.

Through such 'third-party' schemes the concerns of the final consumers are passed back through the supply chain to the original source of the products. The customer can be satisfied that the money paid to the retailer will be passed back to the supplier and then on to the workers. In this way the Fair Trade Mark meets consumers' need to avoid exploiting poorer workers in the developing world.

Unfortunately there will also be events beyond the control of any management, which have a crippling impact on the shoppers' demands. In these cases the effects of the events ripple through all members of the supply chain. A classic example of this was the impact on Perrier of the discovery of benzene in its product. As the news went through the media shoppers dropped the brand immediately and, consequently, **retailers** bought less of the product. It took the company's management several years and significant communications expenditure to regain its number-one position. In a few cases the damage may be more permanent. Another fairly extreme case would be the impact of the BSE crisis on the consumption of British beef. Several years after the crisis the demand for the product has not fully recovered and it is unlikely to do so while there is any indication of a health risk. We can see from these examples that the demands of the consumers directly affect the products sold through the distribution channels.

Clearly the design, and management, of the supply chain is important. The specific design will vary from product to product; we will discuss some of the design issues later in this chapter. What we can say now is that shoppers need more than just products and services. They also need a reassuring environment so that they feel comfortable with their purchases. In this respect they are no different from most businesses. Just like ordinary consumers, businesses need goods and services too.

The organization's view

Does a business see the **supply chain** in the same way as the shopper? The answer is yes and no. It depends on the business, its purpose and the situation. For example, let's consider a local newsagent selling pick'n'mix sweets. This requires small paper bags. Where do these come from? How much effort should the newsagent put in to finding the cheapest source? It is likely that this business will simply add the bags to its shopping list for the next visit to the **wholesaler**. In this respect the business is acting like a typical consumer and will be just as frustrated if the bags are not in stock at the seller's store.

---

insight

Faulty tyres

The Firestone Tyre Company contracted to provide the tyres for the Ford Motor Company's new Explorer truck but it could not have foreseen the consequences. Ford had been the buyer of Firestone's tyres and had sold them on to its customers as part of its product. The exchange relationship between the two companies thus formed part of the supply chain for the Explorer truck.

The tyres did not perform as well as expected. US regulators linked accidents involving Ford Explorers and Firestone tyres to more than 250 deaths and over 800 injuries. The result has been damage claims running into millions of dollars from the relatives of the dead, and personal injury claims against both companies. The claims from the injured represent only part of the total picture. In addition, there are economic loss claims from people seeking compensation for the reduced resale value of their cars, and lost sales as negative publicity impacts on consumers' perceptions of the two manufacturers' products.

The example shows how a defect in one part of the supply chain can have implications for all members of the chain.

---

vendor rating
a vetting process to help buyers identify where there may be potential benefits or difficulties associated with a particular supplier

To ensure that potential sellers are able to meet the organization's needs, many large organizations, both businesses and other groups, engage in a process of **vendor rating**. This means evaluating sellers' performances against a set of predetermined measures. These measures usually include reviews of product range (both current offer and potential for development), product quality, production capability and capacity. For example, DaimlerChrysler, the car manufacturer, uses a vendor rating system that has four broad headings, each with its own importance weighting: quality (40 per cent), delivery (25 per cent), price (25 per cent) and technology (10 per cent). Each of the broad headings has four measures so the overall evaluation considers 16 features of the supply relationship. The systems can be used to assess potential sellers as well as existing sellers. The aim is to ensure that the network of sellers can cover the wide range of needs of the business. By using a process to ensure that the best sellers are used, the company is attempting to ensure that its **supply chain** is as effective and efficient as possible (Lysons and Gillingham, 2003). You can see from the examples in this chapter just how important an effective supply chain is to a business.

The partnership view

It has become normal practice for businesses to organize partnerships with their sellers. This is most evident in the **retail** field. It is now common for the tills in a store to be linked to a head-office computer. This machine checks stock quantities against predetermined levels and produces an order that is transmitted electronically to the seller's computer. The seller then takes responsibility for delivering the order to the store. There is a considerable degree of trust built into such relationships. The retailer benefits from reduced stock risks but pays a higher price for the flexibility that this gives. The seller has to be more flexible in production but receives a higher unit price to cover the increased costs. Thus, with the improved flow of information between the buyer and seller both can benefit.

Buyer and seller organizations need to work together to ensure that their corporate images reflect their actual level of performance. A seller that always delivers the goods on time, with no subsequent problems, at a price that is acceptable to the market creates a reputation for successful operation. This will help it to develop its business beyond its existing set of customers or to strengthen its defences against possible newcomers to the market. For a buyer the benefits are derived from making the business more efficient. If a business treats its sellers well then they can be very supportive in the development of new products or in helping to establish new ways of trading.

PLACE MANAGEMENT

In its simplest form, **place** management is only concerned with the moment at which an exchange of value happens. In reality, however, the moment may be simple but there is usually some preparation needed to make the exchange possible. For example, you might go into a corner shop and buy a bar of chocolate. If the owner of the shop had not previously been out and bought it (usually from a **wholesaler**) then your visit would be a waste of time. This also holds true for the wholesaler, who would have had to purchase the bars from the manufacturer. From this simple example you can see that the supply chain extends away from the final exchange by a series of prior exchanges. If this chain is broken at any stage then the final exchange is at risk. Ensuring that the chain is in place and delivering the expectations of all businesses involved is an important part of the management function.

activity

Think about something important that you bought recently. How did you choose the place that you bought it from? Did you just go somewhere you'd been before, or did something else affect your choice?

In a small business, the buying and selling tasks are likely to be only part of a manager's job. In a larger organization, these functions are likely to be carried out by specialists in a dedicated department. In such departments there are likely to be individuals with significant amounts of product expertise. There will often be a department that is focused on selling the organization's products or services. The department thus has a crucial role in the relationship with potential clients. Having taken the orders and made the delivery promises it is also usual for sales departments to undertake the coordination of the physical delivery of the product to the customer.

Finding, and keeping, the right place for the exchange usually requires the development of successful long-term business partnerships within the **distribution channel**. Only rarely will it benefit a business to change sellers regularly. There is usually much more to be gained from working together. An illustration of how this can deliver substantial gains is given in the b2b focus box.

b2bfocus

We built an oil well!

Before the early 1990s experts had decided that the Andrew oil field in the North Sea would be uneconomic. The potential value of the field meant that BP had to find a new way of tapping the resource. This new way came from a commercial partnership in which all members would gain from the development.

The Andrew Alliance consisted of BP and seven major partners. They agreed to share out any savings made against the target project budget. Thus, they were all working to reduce costs while creating a product that could meet the challenging operational requirements of drilling for oil in the North Sea.

The contractors set about their task with a great deal of commitment and delivered the finished oil platform six months ahead of the target delivery date. Not only did they beat the delivery date but the final cost of its production was £85 million less than its original budget.

The benefits largely came from the **supply chain** members working together to an agreed set of objectives. Each business contributed its skills to help the others achieve the overall goal of the customer's satisfaction. As a consequence, each member of the Alliance received a substantial payback for their investment in the partnership.

The supply chain as a network of partners

Substantial networks, both horizontal and vertical, may be developed in pursuit of the right place. Consider the linkages necessary for a pick-your-own (PYO) fruit farm to reach its market. Initially it might seem that there could not be a simpler form of exchange. After all, customers just take the food from the ground and pay for it. However, there are a considerable number of other participants in the process. For a crop such as strawberries, most PYO farms will buy in the plants from a dedicated nursery that has grown the plants from seeds. The growth of the plants can be further encouraged by the use of fertilizers bought from agricultural merchants. So now we have a crop, but how does the potential customer get to hear about the opportunity? Another relationship is needed to develop the promotional aspects of the business. This may be with a local printer or the local newspaper. The **place** where the **exchange** happens affects all other aspects of marketing function (Michel *et al.*, 2003).

A zero-level supply chain; straight from farmer to customer

insight

Building an airbus

'Part of building a successful aircraft is building up a reliable and proven chain of component sellers. Over the past 30 years, we have sought out sellers of everything from sheet metal to landing gear. As a result, we now have more than 1,500 contractors in over 30 countries who have demonstrated they can deliver the quality we demand within the required time frames.

'**Procurement** is responsible for providing externally sourced goods and services to time, cost and quality as agreed with Programmes and Operations. Procurement implements standards, policies and processes across the whole of Airbus and its **supply chain**. This allows Procurement to manage its relations with sellers, monitor their performance and drive corrective and improvement actions in close collaboration with Manufacturing and Quality.

'The largest single area of sellers is the United States. Over 800 companies in more than 40 states produce hardware for us, ranging from engines to window glass. Airbus also has a host of excellent sellers from all over Europe and in Asia, Africa and Australia, providing aerostructure commodities, materials, equipment systems, propulsion systems as well as company consumables and services or product related services.

'By continuing to build on this chain of highly qualified companies, Airbus pursues the spirit of international co-operation on which the company was founded.' Source: extracted from the Airbus.com website

DESIGNING THE SUPPLY CHAIN

Each of the members in a network has both something to offer and something to receive. In addition, the businesses in a network have customers to whom they address their efforts and for whom they design a product or service offering. The customers and the sellers are involved in a complicated dance routine in which the buyer and the seller adopt particular positions. Finally, the effective construction of the **place** at which this comes together is the result of agreement, and often compromise, between the parties at each stage in this process. The construction of the **supply chain** is an important management task and we will now turn our attention to the issues that managers need to consider.

There are two key words that are important in supply chain design. They are effectiveness and efficiency. These two words shape the objectives for the operation of any supply chain. If the goods are not in the right place at the right time then the exchange is not likely to take place and the supply chain is not effective. If there are too many costs being added to the basic product by the various players, then the final product will be too expensive and the customer may choose to buy from another source. Lack of efficiency at any stage will add to these costs and thus put the whole exchange process at risk. This is the reason why many Western companies now seek low-cost sellers from developing nations. Production in Western economies has become expensive.

The choice of supply chain members depends on the product, the market and the tasks to be undertaken. Where there are many stages in the process of manufacturing the product and engaging the final customer, then the number of members in the supply chain is likely to increase. We have seen in the Airbus example that there can be hundreds of companies involved in the production of the product, but it does not stop at production. The customer for Airbus will be an airline company that needs other services to enable its aircraft to fulfil its role as a passenger carrier. This need for additional services simply adds more businesses to the airline's supply chain. The tasks of partner selection and the maintenance of the relationships are now critical issues for management (Gattorna and Walters, 1996).

Some products might have specific requirements for their handling from manufacturer to final customer, and this can have an influence on the choice of partner. For example,

think about the last time you ate ice cream. For many customers this will have come from their own freezer, but how did it get there? Customers need freezers to store the product and so does every business involved in moving the product from the manufacturer to the retailer's store. There has to be a transport system capable of moving the product in its frozen condition. Not every transport business has such resources and this limits the potential number of partners. The same idea applies to other types of product. For example, specialist transport companies transport industrial gasses in specially designed bulk tankers. The specific needs of the supply chain can thus create **niche** business opportunities.

Mass marketing or selective marketing?

selective distribution

the distribution channel is restricted to a few outlets

The next thing to think about is the nature of the market that the company is trying to reach (Hutt and Speh, 2001). The wider the range of potential customers, the wider the **supply chain**. If there is only one customer, then the relationship between manufacturer and customer is likely to be very direct and leads to the use of a **selective distribution** channel. Exhibit 9.3 illustrates this connection.

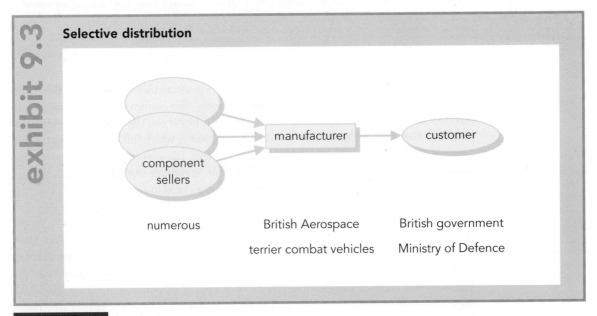

exhibit 9.3

Selective distribution

component sellers → manufacturer → customer

numerous

British Aerospace
terrier combat vehicles

British government
Ministry of Defence

exclusive distribution

the distribution channel has only one or two outlets

In other cases, where there are many different types of customer, perhaps in different locations, then the pattern of connections becomes more complicated. Such a situation is likely to lead to the use of multichannel distribution, in which numerous types of outlet are used.

Exclusive, luxury goods such as designer clothing would normally have the most restricted distribution channels, i.e. **exclusive distribution**. In extreme cases, the designers may only support one or two outlets for their products, often those directly owned by the designer. This allows them to keep very close control over their distribution.

Nike, however, could not have become as large as it has by using selective channels. Nike operates its own stores and has a large number of major retail partners, both specialist sportswear outlets (such as JJB Sports) and clothing stores. The range offered in the general clothing

intensive distribution

products are available at numerous outlets

stores is limited so as not to challenge the specialist sports sector. By using these different channels Nike is engaging in **intensive distribution**. This use of different types of channel to reach the same potential target group is also known as **multichannel distribution** (see Exhibit 9.4).

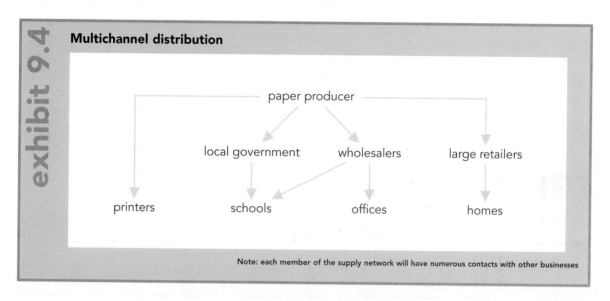

exhibit 9.4

Multichannel distribution

Note: each member of the supply network will have numerous contacts with other businesses

Short, simple chains or long, complicated chains?

Exclusive, **selective** and **intensive** distribution are to do with the breadth of the **distribution channel**, i.e. how many members it has at each level in the channel. When designing a channel, it is also important to think carefully about its depth, i.e. how many levels there will be between the producer and the final customer (see Exhibit 9.5).

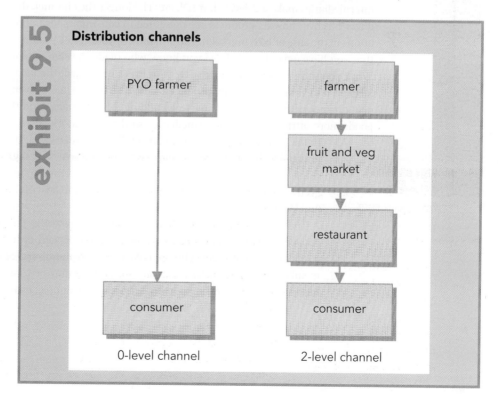

exhibit 9.5

Distribution channels

The simplest distribution channel is the one that connects the producer directly to the consumer. The **supply chain** diagram for our PYO farm (in Exhibit 9.5) does not have any suppliers linked to the farm as we have assumed that the business aims to be self-sufficient in fertilizer (manure) and seeds. Contrast the simplicity of this diagram with the complexity of the supply chain diagrams in Exhibit 9.6.

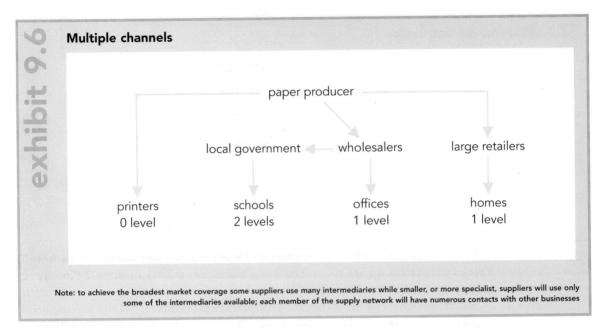

exhibit 9.6

Multiple channels

Note: to achieve the broadest market coverage some suppliers use many intermediaries while smaller, or more specialist, suppliers will use only some of the intermediaries available; each member of the supply network will have numerous contacts with other businesses

The shortest channel has no **intermediaries** at all. The producer sells direct to the end customer. This is called a 0-level channel or direct selling (**direct sales**). If there is one intermediary between the producer and the end customer, we call that a 1-level channel, two intermediaries make a 2-level channel, etc. The longer the channel, the less control the producer has over how its products are presented to consumers (or to final customer organizations in the case of **b2b** markets). You will have in your home products made by companies that you have never heard of. Do you know who made the components in your television? What about the zips in your jeans? Or who grew, or cooked, the food with a supermarket label on it in your fridge? Many producers advertise to consumers even though they do not deal directly with them. This is part of building a brand name and thereby making their goods more attractive to the intermediaries so that they stock them. A company such as Heinz is entirely dependent upon retailers to make sales. It redresses the power imbalance through **marketing communications** campaigns designed to persuade end customers to ask for its products when they go to the shop. In the UK, even the largest of supermarkets would not want to be without Heinz baked beans and ketchup.

There are a number of different ways to create the potential for exchange between customer and business. All channels depend on a number of participants of different types who are called **channel members**. Some of the channel members are manufacturing businesses, others may be retailers and some businesses exist to provide supporting services (for example, transport companies).

Sources of power and conflict in the supply chain

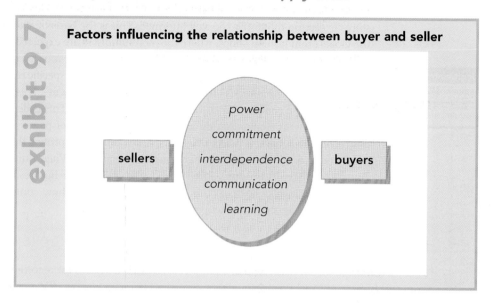

exhibit 9.7

Factors influencing the relationship between buyer and seller

sellers

power
commitment
interdependence
communication
learning

buyers

The different routes to the final customer are known as **distribution channels**. Each business involved is known as a **channel member**. Any **supply chain** is dependent for its success on the individual contributions of its members. These members are selected for their resources and skills. Each member has some power in the particular distribution channel of which it is a part (see Exhibit 9.7). The greater the power the business can exert on the other channel members, the more it can gain from the relationship. Taking a fairly extreme example can show just how important this aspect of the relationship is. By 1996 Marks & Spencer had grown to be the world's fifth largest retailer and was making profits of £1 billion (€1.4 billion) per year. Under the chairmanship of Sir Richard Greenbury, the company was proud to announce that the vast majority of its products came from British sources. Unfortunately the company's financial performance stalled and then collapsed. As profits slumped, Sir Richard was replaced and the management of Marks & Spencer's operations was severely overhauled. One result of these changes was a new approach to buying products. The old 'Buy British' strategy went and, as a result, several of Marks & Spencer's old suppliers then collapsed. In this channel, Marks & Spencer was the dominant player and even had the power to close down other members' businesses.

This example is related here because it illustrates the importance of the relationships between channel members. In most cases businesses recognize that being too dependent on another business is potentially dangerous (in fact, Marks & Spencer did, at one time, have a policy of never allowing a supplier to become dependent upon its orders so as to avoid this situation). Most businesses aim to have a variety of different customers, which spreads the risks and reduces the chance of collapse if one partner fails.

In the example above, Marks & Spencer had power because of its size and consequent financial strength. Most businesses do not have sufficient resources to control the whole supply chain. There are, however, other sources of power that channel members can use to gain advantage in their relationships. The main source of power, outside that of sheer financial influence, is knowledge or expertise (known as **referent power**).

referent power
influence over others gained through superior knowledge or expertise

You can see from the story of the Andrew Alliance (in the b2b focus box on page 276) that partners bring their expertise together to create solutions to business problems. Businesses that are expanding into new areas look for partners that have knowledge of the particular **market**. This knowledge will help to reduce mistakes and to build relationships that may lead to further profitable developments. In the UK, specialist retailers such as Jessops (cameras and other optical instruments) survive because customers come to their stores expecting the staff to be well informed. This is the basis of specialist retailing across the globe. From fashion shops, where the merchandisers are expected to be aware of trends and details, to delicatessens, where staff should know a serrano from a parma.

legitimate power

influence over others
conferred by law or
regulations

A third source of power in the supply chain comes from specific regulations or laws that are used to regulate markets (also known as **legitimate power**). This form of power can be used to increase control over the other channel members. This is definitely the case when one partner owns a patent on the required item. This type of power is commonly found in pharmaceutical markets where drug companies can legally protect their investment in new products for a number of years. No competitor can make Viagra until its legal protection runs out, unless its inventor, Pfizer, decides to allow other businesses to buy production licences. The insight box contains another illustration of how control of a specific technology can bring about market power.

---

insight

Pause

JVC is a Japanese electronics company that invented VHS, a system for recording TV pictures. A few years before JVC patented its invention Sony had launched its own TV recording system, which was known as Betamax. Although the two companies had an agreement to share each other's technologies, both of them wanted to create the dominant system. The stage was set for a global battle between these two Japanese companies and other recording systems such as those invented by Philips and Grundig (two European companies), and RCA in America. The non-Japanese companies did not provide the business support needed for their systems to engage in global marketing and their products gradually disappeared.

Sony had the technically superior system but wanted to maintain control over its distribution and restricted production to a small number of manufacturing sites. JVC, recognizing the technical inferiority of the VHS system, decided to allow many other companies to make VHS-based video recorders. The company now had partners across the world and could thus reduce the costs of manufacture, allowing lower prices for consumers. These two advantages, of price and availability, sped up consumer acceptance of the JVC system. To reach this wider audience Hollywood made more videos in VHS format than in Betamax format, and this gave JVC even more advantage in the market.

Allowing its technology to be used widely did not weaken JVC; instead, it gave it a winning advantage over its rival. Today, Sony makes VHS video recorders for most markets in the world.

Creating a **brand** is another way of gaining legal support for your products. Millions are spent on creating images that **position** the brands in the market. A brand needs to be able to protect its image if it is to be able to charge a **premium price** for the products it offers. The law can be used to protect a brand in a number of ways. There have been cases of retailers virtually copying a manufacturer's branded product and selling it as if it were the retailer's own product. ASDA was found guilty of this when it copied the McVitie's Penguin biscuit bar. The court took the view that such activities were intended to mislead the customer as to the origin of the product, and were therefore unacceptable. This case illustrates the conflict that can arise between channel members when one challenges the power of another's brand. (For more on branding see Chapter 7.)

A well-designed **supply chain** should limit the potential for conflict between the channel members. Any conflict reduces the effectiveness in the supply chain and may ultimately lead to channels being closed off. Failure to resolve conflict between members, without the use of the law courts, should be seen as a failure of the management of the buyer–seller relationship.

MARKETING FUNCTIONS IN THE SUPPLY CHAIN

At every stage in the chain there has to be an ability to create value. Additionally, the pressure to reduce costs is felt at all stages in the supply chain. There are a number of different business functions that **supply chain** members undertake. The following sections identify several of these functions that are directly related to the management of a business's marketing activity.

Stock holding

For a retailer, having stock available is critical to success because it is usual that 'No stock = no sales'. Stock that does not sell is a waste of the retailer's money, so every effort is made to minimize this. This often means putting pressure on sellers to hold stocks away from the retailer's stores but ready to be called in at short notice if required. This **just in time** (JIT) approach reduces the retailer's waste but increases the seller's financial risk if the products do not sell.

Transportation

So you've been on the Internet and bought your CD rewriter but you are at home and it is in the retailer's warehouse. Clearly there needs to be some activity to bring the product to the customer. This job is often is undertaken by businesses outside the buyer–seller relationship. Such businesses are referred to as **logistics** services and they work for one or other of the original parties in the relationship. It is often cheaper to use a specialist logistics company rather than handle deliveries in-house. Imagine that Amazon had to deliver every item it sold. How many lorries and vans would that take? Imagine how much money would be tied up in buying those vehicles and maintaining them.

The simplest form of transportation is the postal service. For bigger items, courier services or small transport companies may be used. If there are vast quantities of products to be moved around, then the logistics business will also need to be a big company.

There are drawbacks to contracting out deliveries. For a mail-order company, the only face-to-face contact with the customer may come at the point of delivery – and then that is not with one of its own employees. The customer service provided by the logistics company is therefore a major determinant of customer satisfaction, but it is not in the seller's control. Apart from the impact this has on customer relationships, there are a number of marketing opportunities lost here. For example, the lorries and packaging may not bear the seller's name. To get around this, many major retailers who contract out their distribution insist that the transportation company paints its vehicles in the retailer's corporate colours. Those Marks & Spencer lorries you see on the motorway actually belong to Exel Logistics and are driven by that company's staff.

For some products the task of transportation is complicated by the nature of the product itself (for example, moving natural gas from the North Sea to homes). The transportation system for this example includes production platforms, pumping stations and thousands of miles of pipeline; without that specialist transportation system this market could not exist.

Information gathering

This is a function that is undertaken by all participants. By information gathering we do not necessarily mean a formal **market research** project. All businesses obtain information on the markets that they serve as the result of their day-to-day operations. Many small businesses fail to recognize the value of this by-product of their work. Successful businesses, however, will analyse the information to shape the ways in which they approach their customers, both current and potential.

In some cases the information is shared with other members of the supply chain. This sharing activity helps to improve the efficiency and effectiveness of the chain as a whole, and is evidence of healthy relationships between the participants.

Communicating

This function helps to develop efficiency in the supply chain. If information can be shared quickly then the costs of operation can be reduced. Most major retail businesses use **EPOS (Electronic Point of Sale)** systems to capture information from their stores. Such systems use the barcodes on products to identify the items and quantities that have been sold. This data is then sent to a head-office computer that adds up all of the individual stores' information. If more stock is needed the central computer can then place an order with the seller's computer using an EDI (electronic data interchange) system; replacement products can thus be ordered without any human effort. These systems can work 24 hours a day 7 days a week and are a major force in the globalization of retailing.

Constantly swapping business partners is inefficient. It leads to additional costs in selecting and evaluating prospective candidates. The development of long-term relationships helps to create trust and facilitates the exchange of information between the partners. In the longer term this reduces the costs in the supply chain and brings financial benefits to all members.

Promoting

All buyers and sellers in the supply chain will promote their products and services to each other. The final consumer does not see the majority of such promotional efforts, but they are vital to the development of the various relationships in the supply chain.

Promotional activities can be very sophisticated and behind the scenes, such as a manufacturer giving the retailer a retrospective discount dependent on the volume of product sold in a particular period of time. Alternatively the effort can be blatant, such as Debenhams' Blue Cross Sale advertisements that announce 20 per cent discounts on specific days (often on Tuesdays to boost sales in the quieter part of the week). Some retailers combine the two forms, such as KwikSave's '£1 off Beefeater Gin' promotion. In this case, the product is a brand of AlliedDomecq, a wine and spirit distribution company. This company sees it as in its own interests to support the retailer in promoting its product in preference to those of its competitors.

The possible objectives and the various methods for these promotional activities are discussed more fully in Chapter 8.

E-CHANNELS

Over the last decade the revolution in communications technology has affected almost all businesses. As we have defined it, the concept of place has two major components: time and space. The Internet has affected both of these. Its impact on the exchange relationships between businesses has been increasing dramatically over the past five years.

For many businesses the ordering process is still paper based. It might depend on a salesperson visiting potential customers to collect orders personally, which are then forwarded to a central sales office. The Internet creates opportunities for customers to send in their orders without any such visits. The customer can choose the time when the ordering will take place and can be shown a much wider variety of products than any sales representative is able to carry.

It is this capacity for carrying information, and for transmitting it so speedily, that makes the Internet so effective as a channel for communication. Buyers can surf the net looking for potential suppliers from anywhere in the world. Similarly, suppliers can also use the net to find potential customers anywhere in the world. Some facilitating businesses exist simply as **portals**, allowing sellers to post their products on the host site (for a fee, of course). This saves the buyers search time and the sellers gain access to a worldwide marketplace. One such business is click2procure, which has over 1000 supplier businesses listed, each paying around €3000 for the privilege. This may seem expensive but the payback comes from the €1 billion worth of contracts that have been arranged via the online trading system. One estimate is that this system has reduced buying costs by up to 25 per cent for some contracts.

For example, the German electronics giant Siemens has set up an EDI system that allows it to communicate directly with its suppliers for a quarter of all its procurement. Although this represents a significant advance, there are still some major drawbacks associated with EDI systems. Most importantly, the initial development costs are high. Then there is a requirement for the suppliers to buy in to the system. Not all members of the distribution channel will have the same systems and this can cause compatibility problems. The Internet helps as it provides a common communications platform. Siemens has recognized the benefits of this type of structure for its operations and has set a target of 50 per cent of all products to be sourced via the Internet by 2008. To give you an idea of the scale of this business, for Siemens this means that products worth around €20 billion will be traded annually over the Internet. As the software available develops into **mass-market** applications, so the number of smaller companies able to take advantage of electronic trading will also grow dramatically and the shape of the **exchange** relationship will alter accordingly.

crmfocus

Web support

In 2003, the British Red Cross ran an online campaign to encourage repeat contributions. The interactive campaign was also designed to provide greater understanding of its supporters.

It employed an e-crm specialist company to analyse the paths that visitors to the website followed. From this it was able to work out what prompts prople to donate online and what aspects of the site visitors found most attractive. Later development was planned to include the ability to monitor individual's donation records. Knowing how much, and how often, people donate will mean that they will know when a request for cash is more likely to be successful and how much to ask for. Charities routinely ask donors for a little more than they gave the last time.

Charities are always looking for ways to reduce the costs of obtaining donors and the new system should help there too. Thanks to digital technology, it will be cheaper for the Red Cross to communicate with donors and so a greater proportion of each pound will go directly towards its work.

Longer term, the organization hopes to provide supporters with personalized information about the campaigns they have contributed to via the website. This, it is hoped, will build on this positive relationship – and encourage people to give more, more often.

One of the biggest changes the Internet has brought to our lives is through electronic distribution. Have you ever played a game through your mobile telephone or listened to music on an MP3 player? If you have, then you have probably downloaded some software from a site that has made such things possible. If you have a computer that has anti-virus protection you can buy an online updating service. You can set up your system so that you do not even have to switch your machine on to receive the latest protection updates. They arrive at your computer (the place) at a time dictated by you (the customer).

activity

Get together with some friends and think about the future of TV programmes and films. How do you think you will be watching them in the future? Will you be watching them at all or will something else have replaced them? What will happen to the businesses that depend upon films? What are the dangers and to whom? What marketing opportunities can you see?

The possibilities are growing almost daily. For example, it is possible to download a complete movie through the Internet but the download takes longer than it does to watch the film! With the spread of new technologies, download speeds are increasing and the quality of transmission is improving so that in the near future businesses will be able to sell you a movie direct into your own home. The Internet offers 24/7 access to services delivered directly to the receiver's PC. This level of convenience is something that store-based retailers cannot match and gives **e-tailers** (using e-distribution) a distinct market advantage.

For the marketer, new technology allows new services to be created and these will need to be distributed to customers. These new opportunities also bring potential dangers. In a digital world it is very difficult to control the distribution of a digital product. If you have an MP3 player then you may be using pirated recordings. Services such as Napster grew from individuals illegally copying CD-based music and making it available through the Internet. With physical products a counterfeiter has to create a manufacturing facility, and that takes resources. With digital products the copying and distribution can be done at the press of a button. In the future marketers will have to pay more attention to protecting the distribution of their digital products if they are to secure the maximum return on their investments.

The Internet's impact in b2b markets has been even more dramatic. One result has been the phenomenon of **disintermediation**. Previously, it was necessary to have shops, often large ones, often chains of them, if you wanted to sell to consumers. Now products can be sold from a website without the need for such expensive investment. This has changed the competitive nature of many markets (for example, booksellers). It is easier for new competitors to enter markets and it is easier for producers to sell direct. Internet retailers are judged by the impression their website makes. It is much cheaper to build an impressive website than an impressive shop, and so smaller companies can compete much more easily with larger ones. This is true throughout the **supply chain**.

There are snags, of course. Manufacturers have little or no experience of dealing with consumers. They still need to break down bulk as consumers will not want to buy a case of mayonnaise, just a jar. Then there is delivery. This is where many of the direct sellers fall down and where they lose the trust of their customers. In the early days, Internet-ordered goods were frequently late, wrong, damaged – or no-shows. It is still vital to get the right goods to the right customer at the right time – and that is not such an easy task.

OUR TECHNOLOGICAL WORLD

The key challenges for global distribution are exactly the same as identified above. How can customers' needs be identified and how can they be satisfied? The first question requires communication and the second requires transportation. The ability to develop new markets in different places depends on solutions to these problems. Until the middle of the nine-teenth century, world trade was fairly limited, and dominated by the countries of 'Old Europe'. Then there was a century of unprecedented change. Transportation technology in particular changed amazingly. The telegraph, the railway and steam-powered shipping all changed the shape of the trading environment. In the twentieth century, two world wars brought developments in radio, air transport and the birth of the electronic computer.

Over the second half of the twentieth century developments in communications have been a significant driving force towards global supply networks. For example, the introduc-tion of the fax machine, using standard telephone lines without any associated software, allowed businesses to send drawings across the world in a matter of minutes. This signifi-cantly reduced response times and opened new markets for manufacturers from the devel-oping world. For example, in the 1970s, domestic European markets were dominated by home-based shoe manufacturers. By the turn of the millennium almost all of the domestic manufacturing businesses had disappeared as the major European retailers were importing from producers in the Far East to reduce costs.

The vast improvements in air travel have also opened up new markets. Look in your local supermarket and see how many products are brought in from tropical countries. These can be provided because air travel makes efficient transportation possible. For example, you could have strawberries from Kenya in the middle of the English winter. The most significant change that air freight has had on distribution is in the reduction of delivery time. Fashion businesses can fly in supplies of successful products from manufacturers around the world. This enables them to reduce the quantity they need to buy initially and releases cash to sup-port the chosen businesses. The Zara case study at the end of this chapter provides another illustration of why it is important to reduce the time taken to get product from design to market.

The Internet crosses borders and provides many new **marketing opportunities**. Modern communications technology improves the efficiency of information exchange. However, unless the product being sold is digital, it does not physically bring the product to the buyer. To understand global marketing opportunities, we need to look at how products are manufactured and transported.

The basic choice facing any seller who wishes to trade internationally is:

▶ make the products at home and export them, or
▶ make the products abroad.

Most firms start by exporting. This is an easier route, with lower financial risks. They find an agent with knowledge of the target market and use them to sell, arrange delivery of, and service products overseas. Larger, or more experienced, firms may handle the export them-selves, sending personnel overseas as required. As business builds and becomes more prof-itable, and as the firm's knowledge of the market grows, it may set up facilities overseas; perhaps a sales or servicing office, an assembly plant, even a fully fledged factory.

In global markets expansion is often crucial to long-term business success. A larger organization can reduce its overall costs (thanks to **economies of scale**). These cost reduc-tions can then be used to increase the business's competitiveness and/or its **profit margins**. The world's biggest retailer, Wal-Mart, has cost reduction as a key objective and although it has not always been successful in its overseas developments it is globally feared by all of its competitors.

To become a global business a company needs to consider carefully the extension of its **supply chain** and the development of the new **distribution channels** needed. In order to grow, it will need suitable partners to help provide the benefits that new customers seek.

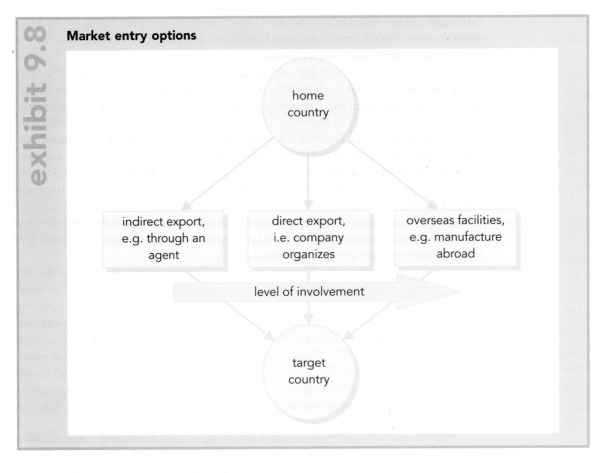

exhibit 9.8

Market entry options

SUMMARY

Throughout this chapter we have seen that effective place management is vitally important to the marketing function. The elements of space and time are combined to create opportunities in which buyers and sellers can come together. At this stage a clear understanding of the buyer's needs, not just from the product but from the exchange itself, helps the seller to shape an offer that maximizes the chances of an exchange.

Most exchanges will use existing **supply chain** networks. These are formed from different types of businesses that are connected by their own exchange relationships. These networks have many forms: from the simple (farmer direct to consumer) to the complex (Boeing building a 747). As the networks become more sophisticated, so there is more likelihood that the members will begin to operate as business partners. These partnerships may be for a particular project, as in the BP Alliance example, or on a long-term basis.

Each business in the supply chain has its own skills and capabilities. These are a source of business power in its relationship with the other members of the network. In most cases there is little open conflict but there is usually some tension because of the opposing profit objectives.

As we enter the twenty-first century, business exchange relationships are increasingly becoming global. We have seen how changes in communications and **physical distribution** have made this growth possible. As the distances between buyers and sellers have increased, the management of the physical movement of goods has become progressively more important and more complex. Over the last two centuries there has been massive technological change, culminating in the establishment of the Internet, and these changes in communication and transportation technology have had a massive impact on our ideas of **place**. As technology continues it rapid development, marketers will need to be open to change if they are to maintain their business's effectiveness.

Successful management of place also requires an understanding of its role in the marketing function. Place offers opportunities for information gathering, for testing new products or services, for trying out promotional techniques and for getting feedback on pricing strategies.

The manager's ability to create, sustain and develop relationships is a fundamental skill in generating business success. To manage place well requires that you manage relationships well. These relationships will be both internal (with other departments that affect the flow of products through the business) and external (with customers and suppliers) (Gadde and Håkansson, 2001).

Getting all the activities that come under the heading 'place' right will set the scene for a successful exchange. For that to happen, marketers must ensure that the right goods get to the right customer in the right time and space.

Challenges reviewed

Now that you have finished reading the chapter, look back at the challenges you were set at the beginning. Do you have a clearer idea of what's involved?

Hints:

- breadth of distribution coverage
- ways in which place can provide competitive edge
- how do the members of the supply chain add value?
- the importance of building relationships through the supply chain.

READING AROUND

directory
If you are in any doubt about the variety of businesses, and the range of different suppliers that they can use, then look no further than your local *Yellow Pages*; the book contains a mass of contacts and information to shape the buyers' search process

newspapers
The big newspapers, such as the *Independent*, often run stories about businesses and their suppliers; you can find more detail on the effects of the conflict between Marks & Spencer and its UK suppliers by looking at 'Dewhirst founding family seeks £113mn buyout' in the *Independent* (11 January 2001)

book chapter
Joseph Alba *et al.* (2001) Interactive home shopping: consumer, retailer and manufacturer incentives to participate in electronic marketplaces, Chapter 3 in P. Richardson, *Internet Marketing Readings and Online Resources*, McGraw-Hill.

SELF-REVIEW QUESTIONS

1. What is a supply chain and what is its purpose? (see page 266)

2. How can a manufacturing business be both a buyer and a seller? (see page 268)

3. What is the main function of an agent? (see page 270)

4. Why do major grocers, such as Tesco and Sainsbury's, have Internet stores when they have invested so much in physical supermarkets? (see page 271)

5. How can a firm use the concept of place to help it position its business against its competitors? (see page 270)

6. Heinz engages in direct marketing communications to the final consumers of its products. Why it is unlikely to engage in direct delivery of its products to those customers? (see page 268)

7. Why would businesses want to create long-term relationships with their suppliers? (see page 274)

8. Why is it important that the supply chain should be responsive to customers' needs? (see page 272)

9. What is vendor rating and in what kind of business would you be most likely to find it? (see page 274)

10. Why is product expertise important to businesses? (see page 281)

11. Give an example of how partners can be used to create a competitive advantage in the marketplace. (see page 276)

12. Why does the physical nature of the product sometimes affect the choice of supply chain participants? (see page 277)

MINI CASE STUDY

Read the questions, then the case material, then answer the questions.

Questions

1. If a major function of managing the supply chain is the reduction of costs, then why is Zara committed to high-cost production methods?

2. Why is effective communication so important to Zara?

3. How does Zara's need for rapid response to market needs affect its suppliers?

Zara – fast fashion

It is half an hour before opening at Zara's flagship store in downtown Madrid, and Esther Gomez is taking stock. Plenty of beige and white, but black, navy blue and garnet are in short supply. Leather items – particularly the short skirts – are selling briskly, so are the tailored jeans and the black sequinned shirts. She spots a black dress and calculates: on Monday she received four, and now, just two days later, only one remains. 'I've got to predict what we are going to sell next week,' she says. 'I'll probably order six to sell between Monday and Thursday.' Thus decided, she pulls out a customized Cassiopeia handheld and, with stylus in hand, taps in an order that's beamed over the Internet to Zara headquarters in the Spanish town of La Coruña.

Deliveries to Zara stores aren't just a bit faster than rivals such as Gap, whose lead time is nine months, they are 12 times faster. Zara can lay a strong claim to owning the most impressive manufacturing and distribution process in the apparel industry. What sets Zara apart is a network that ties the store floors to the designers and in-house factories in the closest thing to real time that exists in retail. It can redesign a pair of jeans in the time it takes a customer to try them on.

While **recession**, and a few **merchandising** mis-steps, have caused some European stores to retrench, Zara continues to expand. Profits at Zara's corporate parent, Inditex, more than tripled between 1996 and 2000 and climbed 31 per cent in 2001 – a year when many clothing chains saw sales and profits collapse. Zara's impact isn't confined to retail, however. For any company in any industry that cares about time to market, customer focus and streamlining business processes, Zara is suddenly an organization to watch.

▶

The Zara model may be unique, but at its heart is a perfectly simple principle. In fashion, nothing is as important as time to market. For decades, apparel companies have farmed out their manufacturing to countries in the developing world in pursuit of lower costs. Zara decided against doing so. In the end, the company reasoned, the ability to respond quickly to shifts in consumer tastes would create far greater efficiencies than outsourcing to sweatshops could. 'The fashion world is in constant flux and is driven not by supply but by customer demand,' says José María Castellano, CEO of Inditex. 'We need to give consumers what they want, and if I go to South America or Asia to make clothes, I simply can't move fast enough.'

Once the company committed itself to having the world's most responsive supply chain, the pieces of its operating model fell logically into place. About half the items Zara sells are made in its own factories. Zara has a twice-a-week delivery schedule that not only restocks old styles but brings in entirely new designs. To make this possible, Zara's prolific design department cranks out more than 10,000 fresh items each year, far more than most of the competition does.

The warehouse is not so much a place to store clothes as a place to move them. The cavernous building is connected to 14 Zara factories through a maze of tunnels, each equipped with a rail that hangs from its ceiling. Along the rails, cables carry bundles of merchandise on a system not unlike a ski gondola. Each bundle is supported by a metal bar that indicates where exactly in the warehouse the bundle must end up.

In the warehouse's distribution centre every Zara store has its own staging area. As soon as a store's order is complete, it is carted directly to a loading dock. There, it is packed along with other stores' shipments, in order of delivery, on to a truck for each European destination. 'The vast majority of the items are in here only a few hours,' says Alba.

According to Zara, the advantages of world-beating time to market more than offset manufacturing costs that run 15 to 20 per cent higher than those of its rivals. Responding so quickly to shifts in customer tastes means, for one thing, that Zara almost never needs to have large-scale **write-downs** to correct merchandising blunders. As a result of this organization and planning, the company maintains steady profit margins of 10 per cent, in line with the best in the industry.

Source: adapted from May 2002 issue © 2003 Business 2.0 Media Inc.

REFERENCES

Gadde, L.E. and Håkansson, H. (2001) *Supply Network Strategies*, Wiley.

Gattorna, J. and Walters, D. (1996) *Managing the Supply Chain: A Strategic Perspective*, Macmillan.

Hutt, M. and Speh, T. (2001) *Business Marketing Management*, Harcourt.

Lysons, K. and Gillingham, M. (2003), *Purchasing and Supply Chain Management*, FT Prentice Hall.

McGoldrick, P. (2003) *Retail Marketing*, McGraw-Hill.

Michel, D., Naudé, P., Salle, R., and Valla, J.P. (2003) *Business-to-Business Marketing*, Palgrave Macmillan.

Piercy, N. (2002) *Market-led Strategic Change*, Butterworth Heinemann.

PRICE

PRICE CHALLENGES

The following are illustrations of the types of decision that marketers have to take or issues they face. *You aren't expected to know how to deal with the challenges now*; just bear them in mind as you read the chapter and see what you can find that helps.

▶ You run a medium-sized business: a second-hand car dealership. A competitor, the showroom on the other side of town, reduces its prices. Should you do the same? What will happen if you don't? If you do?

▶ You have decided that it is a good time for your business to grow. The business is fashion design and just getting known. You need to make more money to fund that growth: to make sample garments for the shows and to give away to celebrities. Could changing prices help at all? Should you put them down, or up?

▶ You have developed a new product. It is brand new, a technological breakthrough: a teleporter. It will make most other forms of transport redundant. How do you know how much to charge for it?

▶ How can we use pricing to gain competitive edge? Imagine that you are a marketing executive in an international firm that is losing business to local firms in Italy and the chief executive has asked you this question. What would you say?

▶ Yours is a multinational company with branches in most countries. Incomes, and currencies, vary. How can you set prices for your televisions that will maximize profits in the richer countries without losing business in the poorer markets?

KEY CONCEPTS

price elasticity of demand
breakeven
cost-based pricing
market-based pricing
price skimming
penetration pricing
price discrimination
prestige pricing
pre-emptive pricing
loss leaders
supply and demand (see Chapter 1)
advertising elasticity
marketing mix (also Chapter 11)
competitive advantage
positioning (see Chapter 4)

CHAPTER OVERVIEW

INTRODUCTION

Pricing is often a seriously undervalued part of the marketing mix. On the one hand, this is a great shame as many companies miss out on the competitive edge that the creative use of pricing brings. On the other hand, it is a good thing for the marketers that do appreciate the finer points of pricing. In the right hands, it can be a devastating competitive weapon.

A recent study found that only 8 per cent of companies base their pricing decisions on serious pricing research. Few companies revise their prices often enough, most thinking that it is good enough to set them once a year, along with the budgets (Cox, 2001). Other common mistakes include not taking into account the rest of the marketing mix and focusing too much on costs.

Price is the odd one out in the marketing mix. The other three elements can be perceived as costs but the price of the goods and services a firm sells is a major determinant of its profit – and most businesses' primary aim is to make high profits. Pricing strategy, therefore, is a key part of a firm's overall marketing strategy.

As an alternative to, or in combination with, another marketing mix element, the firm can use pricing to improve the customer's perception of the product's value. Lowering the price is not the only way to do this; in fact, it might be counterproductive, making the product seem cheap. This is where creativity, and judgement, come in. This chapter will attempt to show how.

There is more to price than the price tag. The price to the customer is everything they have to give up to obtain the product. This includes time, effort and alternative purchases. **Customer value pricing** takes account of these other costs.

Through most of this chapter, price will be used in the simpler sense of the money charged for a product or service (unless otherwise stated), and wherever the word 'product' is used, 'service' is usually just as appropriate.

WHY IT IS SO IMPORTANT TO GET THE PRICE RIGHT

The price of the goods and services a firm sells is a major determinant of its profit – and most businesses' primary aim is to make high profits. Pricing strategy, therefore, is a key part of a firm's overall marketing strategy.

The prices an organization charges have a direct bearing on key corporate and marketing objectives, as described below.

Profit and revenue

It is easy enough to sell a lot of something – just sell it really cheap. Firms that use this technique will lose out on profit of course. So why not set the price really high? Now the firm will not sell anything at all. This much is obvious, but what is not so easy is finding the spot in the middle: the highest price at which the most people will buy. This is the price that will earn the most profit.

---

insight

What is profit?

Profit is what's left over when all the bills have been paid.

   sales revenue − costs = profit

So to make the most profit, you need to get in as much money as possible (revenue):

   sales revenue = **sales volume × selling price**

and pay out as little as possible (costs).

Here's an example of how to work out profit.

Kidzone clothing sells 100 T-shirts at £5.00 each. Each T-shirt costs £1.00 to make and sell.

Sales revenue from the T-shirts is:

   100 (volume) × £5 (price) = £500

The company's profit is:

   £500 (sales revenue) − £100 (total costs) = <u>£400</u>.

---

sales revenue

(turnover) the income a firm receives from the sale of goods and services

costs

a firm's payments to suppliers, etc.

sales volume

how *many* products are sold

(selling) price

how *much* each product is sold for

Generally speaking, marketing focuses on maximizing sales revenue, rather than keeping costs down. However, if the costs are too high for the price, no amount of clever marketing can make up for it.

Finance people have been known to dismiss marketing as an unnecessary cost. The marketers' response is that marketing expenditure is an investment in the firm's future. It is true, however, that pricing is the only part of the marketing mix that does not involve financial outlay.

Image

'Pile it high, sell it cheap' is a motto that has been attributed to various supermarkets. Upmarket or downmarket? The strategy of reducing price, and so selling large volumes, appears a downmarket ploy. Price affects image.

Survival

A sure way to go out of business is to set prices lower than costs. Firms may get away with this in the short term (see '**contribution pricing**' and '**loss leaders**', below) but keeping prices too low, for too long, is a recipe for disaster.

market share

a firm's sales expressed as a percentage of the total sales of that type of product, in the defined market

Market share

If a company wants to increase sales, this is likely to mean taking customers away from a competitor. Any increase in one firm's market share means a decrease in another's. One of the most common ways to do this is by undercutting competitors' prices. (see '**Market pen-etration**' and '**Predatory pricing**', below).

PRICING VIEWPOINTS

What is a price?

A basic definition of price is:

> the money charged for a product or service.

That does sound obvious and there is more to it than that. Think about what you *really* pay for a product, say a computer. There's the price of the PC itself, but then there's other things too: peripherals, software, maybe service agreements. The customer and the salesperson may see the price differently.

A more comprehensive definition is: 'everything that a customer has to give up in order to acquire a product or service'.

This second definition takes account of the added costs associated with the purchase. For example, buying a new pair of shoes takes time: going to the shop, trying them on, maybe taking them back. It costs additional money for transport, maybe for lunch too. Then there may be accessories to buy, such as cleaner, protector, a handbag. It takes effort. It involves giving up alternatives that the money could have bought (**opportunity cost**). It takes an investment of brain power and judgement to ensure you get the right pair. There is also the actual price of the shoes.

To illustrate the complexities of pricing decisions, Lancaster *et al.* (2000) consider three differing perspectives on pricing: the economist's, the accountant's and the marketer's. There is also the customer's view, of course.

The economist's view of pricing

In a free market, a product or service's price would be set by the forces of demand and supply (see Chapter 1). The idea is that the price goes up, and down, until it settles at the point where buyers are prepared to buy just exactly the same amount as sellers are prepared to sell (see Exhibit 10.1).

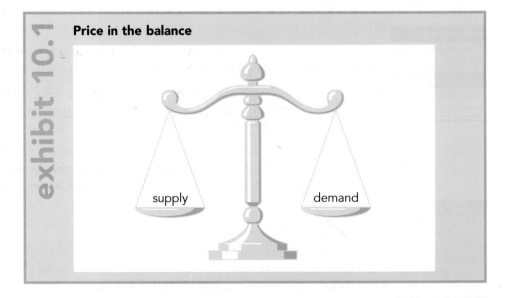

exhibit 10.1

Price in the balance

supply   demand

If there are more buyers than products, the price goes up until enough buyers fall out of the market and demand equals supply again.

Take the example of a fruit and vegetable stall in a market towards the end of the day. The trader shouts out his or her prices, gradually reducing them until he or she attracts customers. At an auction, the potential buyers bid against each other, pushing the price up: the more buyers there are, the higher the price goes. If there is only one potential buyer, then the price stays low.

However, that is not the way business is done in shopping malls. The economist's view is more theoretical than real-world. In practice, shops and suppliers cannot change prices so dynamically. The price is largely fixed in advance. The concept of supply and demand remains useful, though. Clearly, as the price of a product goes up, fewer people will be prepared to buy, and if a firm wants to clear out old stock, then it will usually reduce the price. The consequent increase in sales is evidence of the law of supply and demand.

Drawbacks in the economist's view of pricing include the following.

▶ It assumes that the firm's main objective is to maximize short-term profit. This is not always true, they may want to break into a new market, or they may be a **not for profit** organization, or in an industry where excess profits are unacceptable (e.g. electricity supply). There are many reasons why a firm may choose to make less profit than it could.

▶ Price is not the only thing that influences demand, and it is complicated to work out a demand function using all of the possible variables, e.g. marketing communications (promotion), competitors' prices. Therefore, demand forecasts are never 100 per cent accurate.

insight

Banking bullies?

In Britain in 2002, four banks (Lloyds TSB, Barclays, HSBC, and Royal Bank of Scotland and NatWest), controlled more than 85 per cent of all small business accounts, a situation that was described by the Competition Commission as a 'complex monopoly'. The banks operated very similar charging structures.

Business accounts are usually run differently to personal ones. They attract more charges and they don't pay interest. The Competition Commission inquiry into small business banking found this situation unfair. The banks' argument was that they had to charge small businesses in order to fund their large networks of branches. Many small businesses need easy access to branches (to pay in cash, for instance) and they take up a disproportionate amount of the bank staff's time.

Industry sources claimed that 95 per cent of small business customers got the finance they required, at rates generally cheaper than in other countries.

'If you introduce price regulation, that could have a knock-on effect,' a senior banking executive said. 'It may deter competitors from coming into the market, as has happened with stakeholder pensions.' (The government capped charges for stakeholder pensions to ensure their affordability.)

Meanwhile, smaller banks were moving in and trying to steal market share. Between the government and the new competition small businesses looked set to get a better deal.
                                                              Source: adapted from Treanor and Elliott, 2002

The accountant's view of pricing

Accountants want to make sure that the price of a product or service covers all its costs, so that a profit can be shown (see 'Cost-based pricing', below).

Drawbacks in the accountant's view of pricing include:

▶ it can be hard to work out all the costs involved

▶ focusing solely on the firm's own costs means ignoring the market – and the power of the rest of the marketing mix; people may be prepared to pay more, especially if the brand is strong, or there's been a good advertising campaign, or a firm has shops in better locations – or all the competitive products are twice that price; this could be a missed opportunity for profit.

The customer's view of pricing

Customers usually want the best quality at the lowest price. For a customer, the price has to represent good value:

$$\text{perceived value} = \text{perceived benefits} - \text{price}$$

Drawbacks in the customer's view of pricing include:

▶ quality costs money; there has to be a trade-off between the two; the highest-quality products cannot be sold at the lowest prices

▶ people's perception of the value of a product differs – for example, some people will pay a lot more for branded goods such as Nike, others will not.

The marketer's view of pricing

Marketers see pricing as an opportunity to gain competitive advantage. It is vital to take account of what the market can bear: how much people are prepared to pay, and how much competitors are charging.

Drawbacks in the marketer's view of pricing include:

▶ marketers may set a price that does not actually cover the costs of making a product; clearly, this can only be sustained in the short term, or the firm will make a loss (see 'loss leaders' and 'contribution pricing', below).

PRICING IN THE MIX

Clearly, it is important to have a good product, but a product without a price is a gift. So, marketers must set a price; the question is, how much? The answer must take account of the rest of the mix. The price sends a message, just as the promotion, distribution channels, product and its packaging do. People do not expect Harrods to be cheap, but what about Pricerite? Which is likely to sell the highest-quality goods? The price sends a message about quality. Customers associate a high price, sometimes mistakenly, with high quality.

> **activity**
>
> Visit a local department store (such as John Lewis, Fenwick or House of Fraser), go into the fashion, sport or perfumery department and find examples of expensive, and cheaper, products in the same category (e.g. tennis racquets, football boots, perfume, trainers, shirts). What are the differences in terms of packaging, materials used, presentation? Could you tell which was cheaper before you looked at the price tag?
>
> Now go to a discount store or a chain store (such as Littlewoods or Woolworth) and see if you can find the same brands. If you cannot find them, find the most similar thing you can and compare that with your impression of the more expensive department store brands.

When you're next watching TV, take note of the adverts and see if you can guess the price, or the relative prices (cheaper than X, dearer than Y) of the products advertised.

Certain styles of promotion are associated with cheaper or more expensive products. When prices are rock bottom, the advertisers often shout – literally or through their choice of bold colours. There is more **sales promotion** (money-off coupons, two for the price of one, etc.) at the lower end of the market. Marks & Spencer used to think that all advertising and sales promotion was too downmarket and unnecessary for such a well-known brand. Top fashion brands only advertise in glossy high-fashion magazines such as *Vogue* (if they advertise at all – public relations is more their forte).

PRICING OBJECTIVES

objective
a goal or target

Pricing objectives can be grouped under two main headings:

▶ financial return, e.g. maximizing revenue, recovering an investment made (usually in developing the product)

▶ market orientated, e.g. **positioning**, maintaining **brand image**, building **market share**, enticing customers to the store, rewarding customers for loyalty.

The financial objectives are largely inward looking, while the market-orientated ones look to the external environment. Some of these objectives are really short term, e.g. 'enticing the customer into the store', and some should normally be long term, e.g. 'maximizing revenue'.

There are numerous pricing techniques that are used to meet these objectives.

Pricing techniques

Strategies, tactics and methods

Textbooks and commentators cannot seem to agree on which of the various ways of setting prices are strategies, tactics or methods. Some have apparently given up on categorization altogether.

In this book, a pricing strategy is defined as being medium to long term and having a significant impact on the company's overall marketing strategy, or even corporate strategy. A pricing tactic is defined as a short-term action, or one with limited impact beyond the product being priced. Pricing methods are mechanical ways to set prices. They are a good starting point, or a good way to check that the price arrived at is sane, but, marketers would argue, not a way to set prices in isolation. It is also important to check out the ways price could be used to greater effect via a specific strategy or tactic. Some pricing techniques, e.g. market skimming (see below), could be used as strategies (longer term) or tactics (shorter term).

PRICING METHODS

There are three key elements to price setting: competitors' prices, customers' perceptions of the product's value, and costs.

A business's costs must be covered, but too great an emphasis on costs in a pricing strategy leads to missed opportunities. It is vital to take account of what's going on in the market. What are competitors charging? How much do customers want to pay? Exhibit 10.2 shows the key influencers on the pricing decisions.

In the case of a car manufacturer, there would be substantial costs in buying the materials required to make the cars. In the long run, these must be covered by the pricing of the car or the company will be out of business. Costs of supplies are an important consideration.

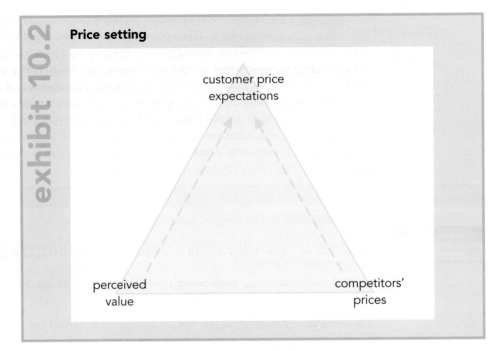

exhibit 10.2

Price setting

customer price
expectations

perceived
value

competitors'
prices

The company buys in engine parts, sheets of metal, mirrors, etc., and then adds value to them by turning them into a functional car. They have to pay wages, rents and other bills in order to do this. So additional cost is incurred here. But then there's the question of value. Is the car only worth the sum of its parts? Of course not, otherwise why bother to put it together at all? It is worth more as a car than as a pile of materials and sub-assemblies, but how much more?

Competitors and customers have a key role to play in determining how much value has been added by turning the parts into a car. Is it a better or worse car than the competition? How much are customers prepared to give up for it?

Most methods of pricing can be classified as either:

▶ market-based pricing (taking account of competitors and/or customers), or

▶ cost-based pricing

MARKET-BASED PRICING

There are a large number of different market-based pricing methods, including:

▶ customer value pricing

▶ psychological price barriers

▶ going-rate pricing

▶ tenders

▶ cartels.

Customer value pricing

A product or service is only worth what someone will pay for it. The price is the company's estimate of the product's value. The customer may place a different value on the product. The trick is to make these two concepts of value balance, so that the firm is paid a fair price and the customer gets a good deal. This is a difficult balancing act. The seller will have invested a great deal of time, money, effort and creativity into its offerings. They have great value. The customer has many choices as to what to buy, and will consider their relative values. The seller can increase the value of its offering in a number of ways – for example, through added features, better quality, a superior brand image, better service, home delivery. Increases in value are usually created through the other elements of the marketing mix – one of the reasons why it is so important to coordinate all marketing mix elements.

In **customer value pricing**, the price is based on what customers value it at, i.e. what it is worth to them, rather than on what it cost the firm to make. If the balance between value and price is right, then customers will see that the price they are being asked to pay is justified even if that price is higher than the competition's.

Psychological price barriers

Many people have a budget in mind before they go out to buy something. They may exceed the budget by a little, but there will be a price beyond which they will not go. That is their **psychological price barrier**. Some marketers set prices by conducting research to establish just where that barrier is. Then they set prices just below it.

---

activity

How much are you prepared to pay for:

▸ lunch

▸ a CD

▸ a jacket

▸ a pair of shoes

▸ a concert ticket?

Work out your own psychological price barriers. Then, the next time you buy such things, see how well the products available match up to your budget.

You are likely to find a range of prices, e.g. lunch can cost anything from a sandwich at less than £1 (€1.4), to a fancy restaurant meal at £50 (€70) plus. Where do you fit in this range? (See also 'Product line pricing', below.)

Psychological pricing is a related concept (see below).

Auctions

Auctions used to be the preserve of art galleries and antique dealers – but the advent of the Internet has changed all that. Now auctions are a way to get products cheaper – online. Bandyopadhyay *et al.* (2001) attribute the success of auctions on the Internet to simplicity, real-time price negotiation and the large number of participants. (For a full explanation of Internet auctions see www.ebay.co.uk.)

Going-rate pricing

Competitors' **prices** have to be taken into account when setting prices. Charge twice as much as the competition and the firm will make no sales; charge half as much and it is missing an opportunity for profit (as well as possibly sending the wrong message about quality).

Some established firms are considered to be **price leaders** (or **price makers**); they set the prices that the others (the **price followers** or **price takers**) follow. Price leaders are often the largest competitors in the market but sometimes a smaller company is recognized as having particular expertise, and even larger firms will follow its lead. Throughout the 1990s, other lenders usually looked to Abbey National to take the lead in raising or lowering mortgage rates.

Going-rate pricing is one of the most common ways of choosing a price. It is especially favoured by new entrants to a market who need to make sure that they set their prices at a realistic level in comparison to the competition, and who have no track record to guide them.

Advantages of going-rate pricing are that it:

▶ avoids **price wars** (see below)

▶ makes use of the expertise of more established firms.

Disadvantages are that it:

▶ assumes that competitors got their sums right and set the best price – they may not have

▶ firms have different cost bases; it is quite possible that Coca-Cola can charge 23p (€0.32) per can and still make a profit, it may cost a new competitor 25p (€0.35) just to make the drink and can it.

> **price war**
>
> two or more firms keep undercutting each other in an attempt to build market share until one or other backs off or goes out of business

Tenders

There are numerous types of **tender**, but the basic premise of all of them is that a number of firms bid for a contract. The contract is awarded to the lowest bidder. This type of pricing is common in government, particularly for public works contracts such as road or bridge building, where the tender system is seen as being open and above reproach.

Tenders may be by sealed bid (when a firm does not know what the others are bidding) or open.

Cartels

A **cartel** is a group of companies that get together and fix prices between them. Cartels are most common in **oligopolistic** markets where they justify their joint price setting by saying that it avoids price wars. When companies get together and choose a mutually acceptable price, it tends to be higher than it would have been had they had to compete with one another. So it is cosy and safe for business, but bad news for consumers.

Probably the most famous cartel is OPEC (the Organization of the Petroleum Exporting Countries). In the 1970s and 1980s, OPEC set the prices for the world's crude oil. Now there are other countries involved, but the 11 OPEC members (Saudi Arabia, Iraq, Kuwait, Venezuela, Nigeria, Algeria, Libya, Iran, Indonesia, the United Arab Emirates and Qatar), still 'voluntarily restrain their crude oil production in order to stabilize the oil market and avoid harmful and unnecessary price fluctuations' (OPEC, 2002).

Cartels are considered an anti-competitive practice and are illegal in the EU. However, that did not stop eight European drugs companies colluding to fix the price of vitamins. In 2001, they were fined €855.2 million (£529.5 million) for what the EU anti-trust chief, Mario Monti, described as the 'most damaging series of cartels the commission has ever investigated' (Anonymous, 2001).

COST-BASED PRICING

Many marketers warn against placing too great an emphasis on costs when setting prices. However, they are important. If a firm does not cover its costs then, sooner or later, it will go out of business. The downside of focusing on covering costs is that the firm may miss out on profit.

Cost plus pricing

Cost and price are different. Costs are monies that a firm has to pay. Prices are what they charge for the products/services they sell. The 35p a customer pays for a chocolate bar is a cost to him or her – but a price to the shop that sells it. Clearly, prices should be higher than costs, at least most of the time.

There are a number of pricing methods that take the costs of making the product, or of delivering the service, and then add an amount on to arrive at a price. It is therefore now necessary to take a slight detour into accounting, and briefly look at various types of costs (see insight box).

---

insight

Types of costs

The different types of costs are:

▶ total costs – the sum of all costs

▶ direct costs – costs that are clearly due to the making of a particular product, e.g. cocoa and sugar are direct costs of Cadbury's Dairy Milk

▶ indirect costs – costs that cannot be attributed to a particular product as they are not directly associated with its production or sale, e.g. the running costs of the chief executive's car

▶ variable costs – costs that go up as production increases, e.g. electricity bills

▶ fixed costs – costs that do not vary with production, e.g. insurance premiums.

Costs will be either fixed or variable *and* either direct or indirect. Examples include:

▶ electricity is usually a variable, indirect cost – it costs more as production increases, but it is hard to work out just how much electricity went into the making of a particular product

▶ raw materials are variable, direct costs – you need more flour to make more cakes, and you still know just how much flour it takes to make a cake

▶ rent is usually a fixed, indirect cost – it does not vary month on month, and contributes to a number of different products/services

▶ highly specialized machinery may be a fixed, direct cost – the nozzle that pipes the perfect star on top of the coffee creams in the chocolate factory, perhaps.

Cost plus pricing methods include:

▶ mark-up pricing
▶ full-cost pricing
▶ contribution pricing.

direct costs

costs that are clearly due to the making of a particular product, e.g. cocoa and sugar are direct costs of Cadbury's Dairy Milk

Mark-up pricing

This pricing method is common in retail as it is a relatively straightforward way for a shop to set prices: calculate the **direct cost** of the product, then add on an amount to cover **indirect costs** and provide a profit. For example, a boutique buys in dresses for £50 each. The £50 is the direct cost, but there are other costs involved in running the shop (heating, lighting, rent, wages, etc.). To price the dresses, it uses a simple formula, perhaps adding on 300 per cent of the direct cost. This should mean that each dress sold covers *all* costs, and makes a profit.

direct cost:	£50.00
mark-up;	£150.00
selling price:	£200.00

Advantages of mark-up pricing are that:

▶ it is a relatively simple way for retailers (and some other businesses) to set their prices

▶ unlike full-cost pricing (see below), mark-up takes account of demand; retailers do not apply the same mark-up to all products – they are usually adept at varying prices to take account of the popularity of products.

Disadvantages are that:

▶ the mark-up may not be high enough to cover all the indirect costs, especially if some products remain unsold

▶ a retailer knows the (direct) cost of products but it is not always so simple; direct cost per unit varies depending upon the level produced, e.g. there may be a discount available for buying a larger quantity, so costs come down (**economies of scale**).

So we need to know the demand for the product before we can set the price, and demand is largely determined by price. What output level shall we pick to get our cost base? It is a vicious circle (see Exhibit 10.3).

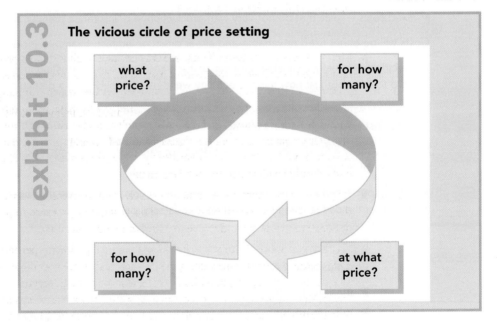

exhibit 10.3

The vicious circle of price setting

what price?

for how many?

for how many?

at what price?

Full-cost pricing

This is also known as absorption costing.

total cost

all product costs, i.e. direct + indirect, or fixed + variable

Full-cost pricing is as it sounds: work out the total unit cost (i.e. the total cost per product) of making the product, then add a further amount, and that's the price. For example, the local pizzeria adds up the costs of all the ingredients on its four seasons pizza, adds in an amount for wages and the running costs of the restaurant, then adds 100 per cent – for profit.

per pizza   direct costs   = £0.75
indirect costs = £1.25
total cost = £2.00
+ 100%   = **£4.00**, so that's the price

Using the full-cost pricing method, work out the price for a box of chocolates when:

fixed costs (rent, etc.)	= £40,000 per month
variable costs (ingredients, etc.)	= £1 per box
sales volume	= 100,000 per month

The accounts department has set 25 per cent as the profit margin.

(The answer is at the end of the chapter, on page 326.)

Advantages of full-cost pricing are that:

profit margin
the difference between cost and price, expressed as a percentage

▶ all production costs are covered by the price

▶ cost increases get passed on to the customer in the form of a price increase, so **profit margins** (in percentage terms) remain the same

▶ it may be the only way to price a job for which the amount of work cannot be predicted, i.e. the price is set retroactively, when all the costs are known, e.g. for a research and development project.

Disadvantages are as follows.

▶ Direct costs, such as ingredients, are easy enough to allocate to a product (a baker knows how much flour was used in each loaf), but if a salesperson sells a range of products, of differing values, how much of his or her salary, company car costs, etc. should be added to the cost of each item? And just imagine how complicated that would be to work out for each of a thousand products sold by a hundred salespeople, all on different salaries. Then there's the other staff, buildings costs, etc. This allocation of costs to a product is often quite arbitrary; what percentage of the chief executive's car costs should be allocated to each Dream bar?

▶ It ignores market forces (demand and supply) and the price sensitivity of customers – they may be prepared to pay more, or they may not be prepared to pay that price at all, in which case a way would have to found to reduce the costs.

▶ If a firm gets more efficient (i.e. fixed costs per unit go down – perhaps because you have installed more modern equipment), then their price goes down too; but if the product was selling well at a higher price, why lower it? In practice, a firm might not lower prices in this circumstance, but that would mean that it was no longer adhering to the firm's cost plus pricing policy and had allowed some market awareness to creep into its price setting.

Contribution pricing

contribution
the amount of money remaining from the sale, when the variable costs have been paid

Mark-up pricing uses direct costs as a basis on which to set the price. Full-cost pricing uses the total cost as a basis. **Contribution pricing** is based on variable costs.

It is being included here with the other cost-based pricing methods, but this one is rather different. Really, within the classifications given earlier in the chapter, contribution pricing is usually used as a pricing tactic. It is something that can only be used in the short term

– usually just for one order. Try to use it all the time, on all products, and the company will rack up the losses and go under. However, it is also a way to price **loss leaders** (see below).

The idea behind contribution pricing is that, as long as the product is sold for more than its variable cost, it is making a **contribution** towards the fixed costs and profits.

Contribution pricing is often used for one-off orders. For example, the Alpha Company's monthly fixed costs (FC) are £3000, variable costs (VC) are £3 per product. It regularly sells 2000 alarm clocks each month.

So:

fixed cost per product, i.e. average fixed cost (AFC) = the fixed costs divided by the sales volume, i.e.   = $\frac{£3000}{2000}$ = £1.50

total cost per unit   = AFC + VC
                         = £1.50 + £3.00 = £4.50

A new customer, Beta Holdings Ltd, wants to buy 500 clocks, but is only prepared to pay £4.00 per clock. This will not cover the total cost of making the clock, but it will cover the variable costs; anything over £3.00 makes a contribution.

Should Alpha accept the order? It depends on:

▶ whether the fixed costs are actually already covered by other orders

▶ whether they have enough capacity to make the new order

▶ how much goodwill the acceptance of this order will generate – will Beta Holdings turn into a regular customer, maybe at a better price?

▶ how much bad feeling may be created if other, regular, customers find out and feel over-charged.

This is similar to the technique that economists call **marginal cost pricing**. Marginal cost is the cost of making additional units. So, in the example above, Alpha would work out what *additional* cost was involved in making the extra 500 clocks; it would need components, use more electricity, and perhaps would have to pay some overtime. Often, these additional costs will be the same as the variable costs of the order.

However, it is possible that Alpha would have to buy more machinery and, in that case, the additional cost (marginal cost) would be more than just the variable cost as additional fixed costs would be incurred too.

In a highly competitive business, a company may have the opportunity to achieve significant extra business by putting in a low bid.

Advantages of contribution pricing are that:

▶ it may mean keeping workers on, when otherwise they would have been laid off causing hardship for them and their families

▶ it keeps workers' skills honed; if they spend time idle, or doing other work, they are likely to get out of practice and will not be so efficient in the future

▶ if you let workers go, your competitors may snap up the best of them

▶ idle machinery sometimes seizes up and may require more maintenance in the future

▶ idle machinery is a wasted investment, and still costs money in service agreements, etc.

A related concept is that of **loss leaders** (see below).

It would be useful for the firm to know how much (i.e. what **sales volume**) it has to sell in order to cover its costs. Then it can see if it is likely that the product will sell that many, and so if it is worthwhile. Clearly, price is one of the main determinants of how many products people will buy. The law of supply and demand (as well as common sense) tells us that higher prices result in lower sales, and vice versa.

The firm can work out the required sales volume, *at a given price*, that will cover costs. This is called the **breakeven point**.

Breakeven analysis

Breakeven analysis can be done graphically (see Exhibit 10.4) or as a calculation.

A breakeven chart is a clear, visual way of analysing a firm's profit at various levels of output, and a set price. By drawing a new chart, managers can see the impact of a change in price on the firm's profits, breakeven point and margin of safety. If costs change, a new chart will also show the impact of that. Increases in costs will push the breakeven point higher; increases in price will result in a lower breakeven point.

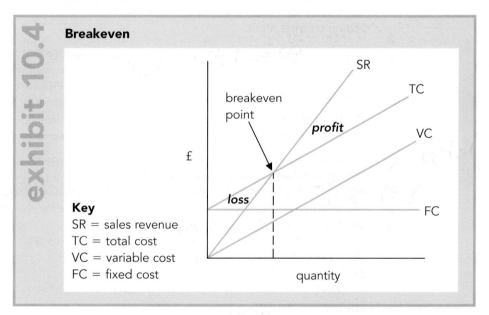

exhibit 10.4

Breakeven

Key
SR = sales revenue
TC = total cost
VC = variable cost
FC = fixed cost

At any given price, the firm will break even at the point where total cost (TC) = total sales revenue (SR). It can then draw further graphs to work out the breakeven points at different prices.

If it sells a larger quantity than the breakeven point, it makes a profit. If sales fall below breakeven, it makes a loss.

If you would like to try drawing a breakeven chart, have a go at the additional activity at the end of this chapter ('Appendix: additional cost-based pricing activity').

Margin of safety

If a firm sells more than is required to break even, then that extra quantity is referred to as its 'margin of safety'. In Exhibit 10.5, a firm sells 100,000 products, but breaks even when it sells 75,000. The margin of safety is 25,000. The significance of this is that the firm knows how many sales it can afford to lose before it hits crisis point.

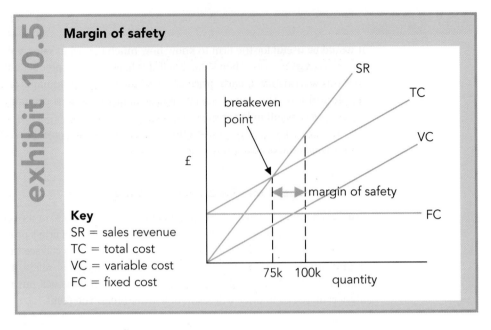

exhibit 10.5

Margin of safety

£

Key
SR = sales revenue
TC = total cost
VC = variable cost
FC = fixed cost

breakeven point

SR

TC

VC

margin of safety

FC

75k   100k

quantity

Setting a target profit

When firms use target profit pricing, they want to set a price that will result in a defined overall profit. This method of price setting is popular with the privatized utilities, which have a duty to provide fair prices and not to make excess profits. Firms set a target profit by, on a normal breakeven chart, finding the point at which the difference between sales revenue and total cost equals the target profit. Then they simply draw a line down to the quantity axis and read off the sales volume required to achieve that target profit (see Exhibit 10.6).

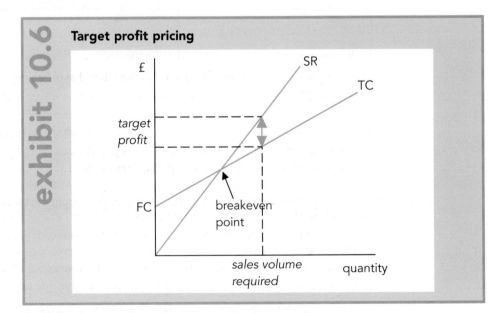

exhibit 10.6

Target profit pricing

£

SR

TC

target profit

FC

breakeven point

sales volume required

quantity

Target profit pricing can also be calculated. The formula for this is:

$$\frac{\text{fixed cost} + \text{profit target}}{\text{contribution per item}} = \text{required level of output}$$

For example, the Roadrunner Co wants to make £600,000 profit on its bicycles. Fixed costs total £1.2 million, variable costs are £800 per bike. The bike is priced at £2000.

$$\text{contribution} = \text{selling price} - \text{variable cost}$$
$$= £2000 - £800 = £1200$$
$$\frac{1{,}200{,}000 + £600{,}000}{£1200} = 1500 \text{ bicycles}$$

So it knows that if it sells 1500 bicycles at a price of £2000 each, then it will make £600,000 profit (see Exhibit 10.7). Alternatively, it could read this figure off a breakeven chart by finding the point at which the SR and the TC lines are £600,000 apart.

Remember that a breakeven chart works for one price only – you need to draw a new chart to try out the profit target at a new price.

exhibit 10.7

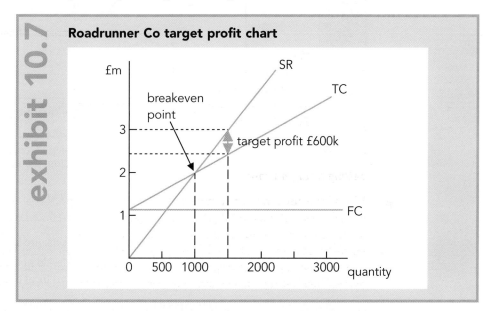

Roadrunner Co target profit chart

Drawbacks to breakeven analysis include:

▶ it assumes that all the products made will be sold

▶ it is a static model; if costs change, then a new chart has to be drawn

▶ as with all analysis tools, its effectiveness depends upon the quality of the figures it uses: rubbish in = rubbish out

▶ it is actually more complicated than the example in Exhibit 10.7 shows; fixed costs are not always linear, they can increase (for example, when the capacity of a machine is reached and a new one has to be bought). (See Exhibit 10.8.)

FOREIGN CURRENCY PRICING

Firms that have customers in other countries have to decide which currency to use when pricing goods and services. It is generally considered to be good marketing practice to price in the customer's currency. However, this has some disadvantages for the seller:

▶ the foreign currency has to be converted into the seller's own currency; this costs money and, if the exchange rate changes (as it often does), the seller may get less than expected

▶ some currencies are non-convertible (i.e. they cannot be exchanged for another currency); this is usually because the country's economy is unstable

▶ some governments impose strict exchange control regulations, limiting the amount a company can take out of the country; this is an attempt to protect the nation's wealth.

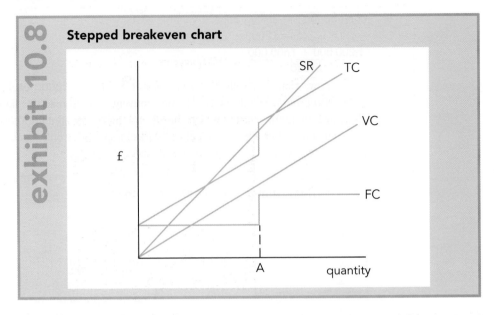

exhibit 10.8

Stepped breakeven chart

For an explanation of protectionism and its impact on pricing, see any good international marketing textbook, such as Cateora and Ghauri (2000).

Additional complexities of pricing in a foreign currency are:

▶ less reliable market information

▶ different prices, in different currencies, for multiple markets, are hard to manage

▶ varying pricing laws (for example, many Muslim countries do not allow credit, some governments will not allow foreign companies to undercut local ones).

There are a number of things an exporter can do to minimize the risk in their foreign currency dealings:

▶ **hedging** is making a deal to buy/sell currency in advance; that way, the exchange rate is fixed and so cannot change adversely

▶ some companies put a clause in their contracts stating that if the exchange rate fluctuates by more than x per cent, the contract price will be adjusted so that the loss is split between buyer and seller

▶ the use of foreign currency bank accounts is a well-established practice worldwide; companies pay in their earnings from sales in that country, then use the accounts to pay local wages, buy supplies, etc.

Despite the difficulties, firms have to work out their policy for handling foreign business. Almost all business today has an international element – the rest of the world is just not going to go away.

globalfocus

The Uzbekistani *som*

Uzbekistan is a landlocked central Asian country, just north of Afghanistan with about 25 million inhabitants. Uzbekistan is now a republic, having won its independence from the Soviet Union in 1991.

Despite natural resources that include petrol, coal, gold and uranium, Uzbekistan is a relatively poor country. In the second half of the 1990s, its government imposed strict import and currency controls in an attempt to combat the country's economic problems.

The Uzbekistani *som* (UKS) is an **unconvertible currency**. It cannot be exchanged for **hard currency** and foreigners are not allowed to take *soms* out of the country.

globalfocus

This makes Uzbekistan a much less attractive market for foreign companies, as *soms* earned there have to stay there.

In such situations, exporters may have to insist on payment in their own currency, or in that of a third country such as American dollars or euros. Some countries prefer to deal in dollars as a matter of course.

Source: 2001 census; US Government, 2002

PRICING STRATEGIES

New product pricing strategies

The price is one of the most difficult things to get right for a new product. Many products fail because they are either too expensive, and therefore do not sell, or too cheap and so the company is unable to meet its costs. It is often difficult to raise a price once a product has been launched on to the market as customers by then have a view of the right price and are reluctant to pay more. This is why so many new products declare that they have an introductory price. This leads customers to expect a price rise in the near future.

The two major new pricing strategies are:

1. market penetration
2. market skimming.

Market penetration

When a company first enters a market, it needs to build **market share**. A low price should tempt people to try the new product. If they like it, they will buy it again. So product trial may lead to product adoption. The main objective of a penetration pricing strategy is to establish the product in the market: to build a customer base.

Advantages of **market penetration pricing** are that:

▶ it encourages people to try a product
▶ it encourages retailers to build up stocks – then they will not have room for competitors' products.

Disadvantages are that:

▶ it may provoke retaliation from existing companies
▶ it is not suitable for products with a short product life cycle as there may not be enough time to recover from the initial, low revenue.

The big disadvantage to the consumer is, of course, that the price does not stay low forever. New credit cards offer low, or no, interest. Then, when they are established, the 'introductory offer' disappears and they hope that their cardholders will not bother to change cards again.

Market skimming

This is really the opposite of penetration pricing. Firms following a skimming strategy set their prices higher than they need to, in order to maximize profits. The key to the success of a market-skimming strategy is that there should be no significant competition – otherwise people will just buy the cheaper alternative. The company may be launching an entirely new product, or entering a new market.

This strategy works well where:

▶ there is insufficient market capacity and competitors cannot make more of the product

▶ there are no competitors

▶ the demand for the goods in question is relatively **price inelastic**

▶ a high price is seen as an indicator of high quality.

Advantages of market skimming are:

▶ early cash recovery – particularly important if this is a new product and the firm has made a significant investment in its development; it needs to get its money back before other firms copy the invention and the market becomes more crowded.

Disadvantages are that:

▶ there is a high danger of encouraging other firms to enter the market – they see high profits being made, and they want to make them too

▶ depending upon the type of product and the market in question, there may be an ethical issue over charging high prices, e.g. for prescription drugs, or in less-developed countries.

General pricing strategies

General pricing strategies are:

▶ prestige pricing

▶ pre-emptive pricing

▶ product line pricing

▶ price discrimination.

Prestige pricing

Prestige pricing sets a high price for a product. Unlike price skimming, this is an ongoing strategy – the product stays expensive throughout its life. The high price is designed to associate an image of quality and high status with the product. This high price is itself an important motivator for consumers. Customers with higher incomes are less price sensitive and more interested in buying high-quality, prestigious products that enhance their image. Promotional strategies revolve around these aspects of the product, helping to justify the high price in the customer's mind. Typical prestige brands include Chanel, IBM, Bang & Olufsen, Cartier and BMW.

Rolls-Royce: a prestige product at a prestige price

Pre-emptive pricing

A company following a pre-emptive pricing strategy sets low prices to deter new entrants to the market. This is especially suitable in markets where there are few other **barriers to entry** – for example, the company does not hold a patent and/or entry costs are low. (For more on barriers to entry, see Chapter 3.)

Pre-emptive pricing should not be confused with **predatory pricing** (see below). Pre-emptive pricing is a perfectly legitimate strategy, whereas predatory pricing, which sets prices below costs in order to drive another firm out of business, is illegal in many countries including Britain.

Product line pricing

Many companies develop product lines, rather than just single products. A company's product range may contain a number of product lines – for example, Ford produces the Ka, Fiesta, Focus, Fusion, Mondeo, Galaxy, Maverick . . . and all of these lines have a number of models with different engine sizes, different finishes and different features.

The product manager has to set price steps within the product lines. How much more will a customer pay for a Focus with 1.6-litre engine rather than 1.4? How much extra should be charged for a Zetec? There will be some overlap between the top of one line and the bottom of the next one up; but how much can they overlap without the top of the line losing business?

Some sellers use well-established price points for the products in their line: so a restaurant's main courses may be premier price (for a particularly special dish, such as lobster), top price (for more expensive ingredients such as steak), mid-price (for most dishes) and low price (perhaps for the vegetarian options).

314

exhibit 10.9

Summary of basic pricing strategies

	new	ongoing
high	market skimming	prestige pricing
low	market penetration	pre-emptive pricing

Price discrimination

This strategy can be dangerous, but can also be very profitable. It relies heavily upon **market segmentation** (see Chapter 4). Price discriminators charge different prices, *for the same goods*, to different market segments. The most common segments used are time, geography and age. Some examples are outlined below.

Time-based discrimination:

▶ many train services are more expensive if you want to travel before 9.30 am

▶ British Airways' return economy air fare from London to Sydney is £1628 over Christmas, but only £686 in June (prices at October 2002)

▶ many entertainment venues give a discount if you book in advance.

Geographic discrimination:

▶ CDs are cheaper in the USA than they are in many European countries

▶ cars are cheaper on mainland Europe than they are in Britain (see e-focus box, opposite)

▶ African countries are (at last) being allowed to buy AIDS drugs for a fraction of their normal price.

Age discrimination:

▶ children travel on public transport at reduced prices

▶ OAPs get discounts on cinema and theatre tickets

▶ if you are under 26, you can get a one-month Inter-rail ticket, valid for trains in 28 European countries, for about 70 per cent of the price that over-26s pay.

activity

Search the World Wide Web. What's the best price you can find for a current top 10 CD?

The key to successful price discrimination is that customers should not be able to move between segments. It is surprising how many teenagers will happily take a couple of years off their age in order to get a cheaper bus fare. If people can move themselves into a cheaper segment, they will.

The great British rip-off

For years, British consumers have been paying far more than their European counterparts for cars. The car companies have given a number of reasons for this, including the additional manufacturing costs incurred by putting the steering wheel on the other side and the additional distribution costs caused by having to cross the Channel.

They got away with it so long largely because not enough people knew about it, but recently there has been a stream of car buyers catching ferries or the Eurostar, across to France and Belgium, and bringing their new car home. They've saved several thousands on the deal. So what changed?

One of the main reasons for the change was the advent of the Internet. It is so easy now to to do price comparisons across the world. The Internet gives customers almost perfect pricing information, making it far harder for sellers to get away with high prices. Internet shopping agents (programs that automatically search a number of websites for the best price for a particular product) make it even easier for customers to get a better deal.

The car price differentials between Britain and mainland Europe are so large that there are now several companies that will organize the purchase and delivery of a new car for you. They take a commission, of course, but, even so, car buyers save substantial sums.

In the European Union, borders are easy to cross, and there is no duty on goods brought in for personal use. Europeans frequently visit neighbouring countries to get a better deal – on a car, on alcohol and cigarettes, on Christmas presents. It gets harder to maintain different prices in different countries when people are able to travel freely.

The Internet has been a major blow to the price discriminators. Now, consumers can surf the World Wide Web looking for bargains. They can check out prices all over the world and either buy online or use their superior pricing knowledge to drive down high-street prices.

PRICING TACTICS

Shorter term, or special situation, pricing options include:

▶ predatory pricing
▶ psychological pricing
▶ loss leaders
▶ promotional pricing and discounts.

Predatory pricing (destroyer pricing, extinction pricing)

This pricing tactic is considered an anti-competitive practice in a number of countries, including the UK (i.e. it is against the law, but it is notoriously hard to prove).

66 Predatory pricing occurs when a dominant undertaking incurs losses with the intention of removing a rival and/or deterring other potential competitors. 99 (Offiice of Fair Trading, 2002)

economies of scale

unit costs fall as larger quantities are produced; a cost advantage associated with large organizations

The larger firm can carry this because it benefits from **economies of scale**. There have been some notorious examples of predatory pricing in the airline business and also in publishing.

The Times newspaper was accused of this back in 1998, when it reduced its cover price from 35p to 20p (€0.49 to €0.28) seriously undercutting its broadsheet rivals. However, the allegation was never proven. In 2002, Aberdeen Journals Ltd was fined £1.328 million (€1.86 million) for abusing a dominant market position. The Office of Fair Trading (OFT) decision followed a Competition Act investigation into allegations of predatory pricing by Aberdeen Journals, a sister paper of the *Daily Mail* (Office of Fair Trading, 2002).

ethicalfocus

Microsoft vs Netscape

In 1996 Microsoft started giving away Internet Explorer, its web browser. In fact, it was argued that in some cases Microsoft effectively paid people to use Internet Explorer in preference to their existing browser, by giving them free software and marketing assistance. The strategy was crucial to the company's success in taking the market leadership away from arch-rival Netscape, which was, up until then, the most popular web browser. 'Even though Netscape constantly revised its pricing structure, it was impossible to stay competitive with "better than free"', testified Netscape CEO James L. Barksdale in the Justice Department's anti-trust suit against Microsoft (France and Hamm, 1998).

Psychological pricing

A surprisingly large number of products are priced at x number of pounds and 99p: £4.99, and £9.99 are particularly popular prices. The idea, of course, is to fool the customer into thinking that the item is cheaper than it really is. £1000 sounds so much more than £995 – or so the theory goes.

This links to **psychological price barriers** (see above). If a customer's top price for a bunch of supermarket flowers is £3.00, then it makes sense to price some at £2.99. The customer feels he or she got a good deal; the supermarket has only lost out on a penny.

Loss leaders

This tactic is often employed by retailers as a means of getting customers into a shop. Getting customers into the shop is a major retail objective as, once inside, they are more susceptible to the in-store promotional displays and impulse buys. A loss leader is a product, prominently displayed and advertised, that is priced well below its normal price, even below its cost to the seller. It is a lure.

Advantages are that:

▶ the lower price provides a competitive advantage

▶ this can build the brand if people associate the company with value for money

▶ there may be opportunities to sell **complementary products**, upgrades or follow-on goods/services, e.g. a maintenance agreement

▶ it stimulates word-of-mouth promotion.

How can businesses afford to do this? Well, as with **contribution pricing** this is not a tactic that can be employed for everything, or all the time. Profits from the other items on sale have to cover the losses of the loss leader. Some retailers even put their other prices up in order to compensate, so watch out.

Seasonal sales and special offers are types of sales promotion

Promotional pricing and discounts

Short-term special offers are really **sales promotions** rather than price reductions, so see Chapter 8, which covers marketing communications, for discussion of those. Discounts are often part of the pricing policy, especially if offered as a matter of course, for a reason. For example, many firms give a discount for bulk purchase.

Sainsbury's gives a 5 per cent reduction to customers who buy six bottles of wine. Clearly this is to encourage people to buy more, and, if they do buy more, then Sainsbury's can afford to charge a little less and still make a good profit.

Many restaurants have a table d'hôte menu: two, three or even four courses for a fixed price. The restaurant can afford to offer diners a good deal because this helps with its ordering and planning. If it knows that a lot of people will order the same dish, then there is less waste, and so less cost.

CHANGING THE PRICE

For many businesses, changing prices is expensive and time consuming, so it is not something they want to do frequently. They have to rework the figures, recalculate VAT, redraw breakeven charts and work out new profit forecasts. Mail-order companies have to reprint their catalogues (the larger, glossier ones can cost as much as £5 (€7) each). Restaurants have to reprint their menus. Shops have to change price labels and tills have to be reprogrammed.

So, given the trouble and expense involved, why would a firm change its prices? There are a number of possible, pressing reasons:

▶ there is a substantial change in business costs; perhaps because raw materials have become cheaper, or because of new, more efficient production techniques (lower price can be charged), or materials or wages have become more expensive (an increase in prices is needed to compensate)

▶ there is an imbalance between supply and demand, i.e. customers want to buy more than the company has to sell; if there's a shortage, then prices may rise – possible causes include production hold-ups, such as strikes, shortages in materials, machine breakdowns, and the product suddenly becomes fashionable (the latest craze)

▶ there is an imbalance between supply and demand, i.e. customers do not want to buy as much as the company has to sell; if there's a surplus, then prices may fall – possible causes include a bumper harvest, a better product hitting the market, a health or safety scare (e.g. news stories about red meat being bad for you caused a massive drop in the sales of beef, pork and lamb)

▶ a change in competitors' marketing, e.g. a price decrease, a major advertising campaign, new stores opening up

▶ a changed economic situation, e.g. inflation

▶ new laws, new taxes or other government pressure, e.g. government-appointed regulators review the prices charge by privatized utilities (BT, water companies, gas and electricity providers)

▶ as a result of a change in the firm's marketing strategy, e.g. as part of a repositioning exercise.

Price wars

A price war is a destructive spiral of reducing prices. It starts with one seller trying to under-cut competitors by reducing prices. Others follow suit, meaning that the first firm has to reduce prices again in order to maintain its competitive advantage. So it goes on, sometimes until the weaker competitors (those with fewer financial resources) go out of business.

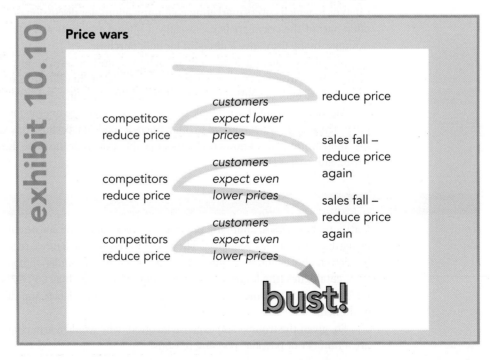

exhibit 10.10

Price wars

In the short term, a price war is popular with consumers; however, it is bad for business and, in the longer term, it is bad for consumers too.

Businesses lose profits; they are cutting prices and, because others are matching their price cuts, they are not gaining **market share**. So they are just selling the same amount but at a reduced price. Eventually, either firms will go out of business, thus reducing consumer choice, or the firms involved will call a truce. Then they may have to put prices back even higher to recoup the profits they lost during the price war.

PRICE ELASTICITY OF DEMAND

Price elasticity of demand is a measure of price sensitivity, i.e. it measures how many more, or fewer, products are sold when the price changes.

We know from basic demand theory (and from common sense) that if the price of a product goes up, then fewer people will want to buy it, and vice versa. If a product's demand is very sensitive to a change in price, i.e. when the price goes up just a little, then far fewer products are sold, then it is said to be **price elastic**. If the product's sales do not vary by much when price changes, then its demand is said to be **price inelastic**.

insight

Price rise or price cut?

Although few marketing managers work out the exact elasticity of their products' demand curves, this is a concept that everyone involved in setting prices needs to be aware of. It is a vital consideration when changing prices as it determines whether lowering, or raising, prices is most likely to result in a revenue increase.

If a product has a price inelastic demand, then putting prices up will result in increased total sales revenue. Very few customers will stop buying the product, and their loss will be amply covered by the higher price that remaining customers pay.

If a product has a price elastic demand, then to increase revenue, the price should be lowered. Many more people will buy the product. So many that they will compensate for the lower price.

Most essential goods (bread, petrol, power, etc.) are not particularly price sensitive (inelastic). Whereas inessentials (cream cakes, bubble bath, meals in restaurants, etc.) are usually more sensitive to price changes (elastic).

This can be seen from the demand curves in Exhibits 10.11 and 10.12. The shallow curve is for a product with a price elastic demand, i.e. very sensitive to a change in price. A small price change results in a large change in the quantity of the product demanded.

exhibit 10.11

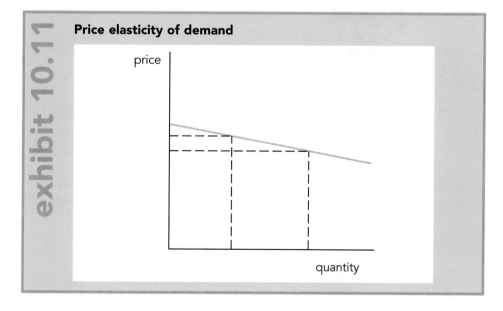

Price elasticity of demand

The steep curve is a price inelastic demand curve for a product such as cigarettes. As they are addictive, few people give up even after a significant price increase.

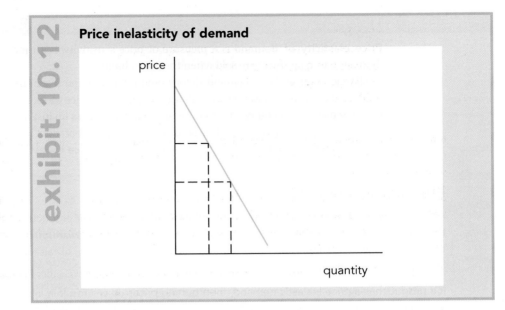

exhibit 10.12

Price inelasticity of demand

Calculating elasticity

insight

In order to calculate elasticity, the price *change* needs to be expressed as a *percentage* of the *original price*.

$$\text{Price elasticity} = \frac{\text{\% change in quantity demanded}}{\text{\% change in price}}$$

The bigger the answer, the greater the elasticity. For example, **Le Café** is considering increasing the price of its café latte. It wants to know whether this price increase will achieve the aim of increasing revenue. This depends on how many customers stop buying the lattes because they are too expensive. Last time it increased the price, it went from £1.50 to £1.65, and Le Café sold 480 cups a week instead of 600. Price elasticity can help.

step one
work out price change:
£1.65 − £1.50
= 15p

step two
to express the price change as a percentage, divide the *change* in price by the *original price*:
15p/150p × 100
= <u>10%</u>

step three
to express the quantity drop as a percentage, divide the *change* in quantity by the *original quantity*:
480 − 600
= −120
−120/600 × 100
= <u>−20%</u> (don't worry about the minus – it will be explained later)

insight

step four
now sub the figures into the elasticity equation:
% change in quantity demanded
% change in price
−20/10
= −2

If the answer is higher than −1, the product's demand is elastic. The product is significantly sensitive to price changes and raising the price will lead to a large fall in sales. This is the case with the café lattes.

So, if you are the marketing manager of **Le Café**, you need to be wary of increasing the price. A better way to increase revenue would be to *decrease* the price; then a lot more people will buy the product, and the increase in the volume of lattes sold will outweigh the price decrease per latte.

If the answer is below −1, then the product in question has an inelastic demand curve. Raising the price will not put many people off and revenue should increase.

The minus sign just means that when price rises, demand falls, i.e. they have a negative relationship. If demand rose with price (as in the case of some antiques, works of art, shares), then there would be no minus sign.

Factors affecting the price elasticity of demand

▶ Necessity or luxury? To an economist, a luxury is anything inessential: chocolate, bubble bath, ready-made meals, videos, etc. Really luxurious products, such as diamonds, sports cars, top designer clothes, etc., are termed **prestige goods**. Generally, necessities and prestige goods have inelastic demand, luxuries have elastic demand.

▶ Close substitutes: if there are many alternative products available, then the demand will tend to be elastic. A substitute is something that a customer could buy instead, e.g. there are lots of different makes of ballpoint pen or pencils.

▶ Habit forming? If it is, then the demand will tend to be inelastic, e.g. cigarettes.

▶ Time period: many products are more responsive to changes in price (i.e. more elastic) in the long term. It takes a while for people to find an alternative, although they eventually will. Also, higher prices will encourage new competitors into the market, and so more choice will be available.

▶ Frequency of purchase: the more often customers buy the product, the more impact a price increase has on their budget, and therefore the more price elastic the demand is, e.g. a student may have a favourite brand of beer, but if the price goes up, he or she may have to switch to a cheaper one.

▶ Customer loyalty: if a brand is well established, then it may have loyal customers who are reluctant to change. The demand will be inelastic.

▶ The price level: elasticity varies along the demand curve. When something is already very cheap (e.g. matches), making it cheaper may have little effect. Similarly if something is too expensive for most people (e.g. a Rolls-Royce) making it even more expensive may have little effect on demand. So very expensive goods may have price inelastic demand above a certain level, but elastic below a certain level; imagine £20 off trips to Australia – it is not enough to make a difference, but £200 off might be.

Necessities are usually price inelastic at lower price levels, but may become elastic at higher levels as more alternative products become economically viable, e.g. cakes instead of bread; or would people take a bus to work if it cost the same as a taxi?

▶ Stage of the **product life cycle**: a new product may have price inelastic demand on introduction (little competition), be more price elastic during the growth phase, less elastic during maturity (assuming brand loyalty has been built up) and have a high level of price elasticity in its decline.

It is important for a company to know how demand for its product will react to a change in circumstances. This chapter has only considered elasticity in terms of price, but the concept can be applied to all marketing variables.

Other elasticities of demand

There are numerous different kinds of elasticity that can be calculated: advertising elasticity of demand measures how responsive sales are to a change in the advertising budget, income elasticity measures the response to a change in people's earnings. Of particular significance is cross-elasticity of demand. This measures the change in one company's sales in response to the change in price of a competitive product. For example, Coca-Cola would expect to sell more if Pepsi raised its price. Calculating the cross-elasticity would help Coca-Cola to know how many more cans to produce.

SUMMARY

Pricing is a much-neglected marketing tool. Too many firms take a mechanical approach to the setting of prices, often purely on the basis of costs. Far too few organizations review their prices regularly enough and so they miss marketing opportunities.

Pricing is a competitive weapon that should be deployed alongside the rest of the marketing mix. A product's price sends a message: of quality, of desirability, of status, of a good buy. It has to vary according to place of purchase: wholesale, retail, Internet. It is a key part of the **brand**.

Common pricing objectives include: maximizing revenue, maintaining brand image, building market share, recovering an investment made (usually in developing the product), enticing customers to the store, and rewarding customers for loyalty.

Pricing methods are largely either cost based or market based. Too great an emphasis on cost can lead to missed profit. Market-based methods take account of what the market can bear, but the price must always be high enough to cover costs in the long run.

Pricing strategies and tactics overlap. There are specific strategies for new product pricing. Firms following a **market penetration** strategy set their prices low. A **market skimming strategy** employs high prices. General pricing strategies include: **prestige pricing**, where a high price is set to confer status; **pre-emptive pricing**, where a lower price is set to discourage competition; **product line pricing**, where related products are sold at a variety of prices; and **price discrimination**, which charges different prices for the same product to different market segments.

Pricing tactics include **psychological pricing**, which sets a price that sounds cheaper (e.g. £999) and **loss leaders**, which are products sold very cheaply but made up for by the profits of others.

Elasticity is a key concept when price changing. Products with **price inelastic** demand will earn more revenue if the price is increased. Prices for products with **price elastic** demand should be lowered if the firm wants to sell more.

Challenges reviewed

Now that you have finished reading the chapter, look back at the challenges you were set at the beginning. Do you have a clearer idea of what's involved?

Hints:

▶ profit margins and price wars

▶ price elasticity of demand

▶ product pricing strategies – new and existing

▶ remember grey importing.

READING AROUND

book chapters

Levela Rickard and Kit Jackson (2000) Chapter 10 in *The Financial Times Marketing Casebook*, FT Prentice Hall.

Hugh Davidson (1997) *Even More Offensive Marketing*, Penguin.

website

visit www.kelkoo.co.uk, a price-comparison site, to find cheaper prices

SELF-REVIEW QUESTIONS

1. How does price affect a product's brand image? (see page 295)

2. How do the forces of supply and demand affect prices? (see page 296)

3. Complete this formula: perceived value = perceived benefits − ? (see page 298)

4. List three possible objectives of a pricing strategy. (see page 299)

5. List the three key influencers on pricing decisions. (see page 299)

6. What is a psychological price barrier? (see page 301)

7. Whose prices are taken into account in 'going-rate pricing'? (see page 301)

8. Which type of cost is mark-up pricing based on? (see page 303)

9. If a new customer wanted to place a large order, but would only accept a low price, what would you take into account when deciding whether or not to take the order? (see page 305)

10. What are the drawbacks to breakeven analysis? (see page 309)

11. Briefly describe two major new product pricing strategies. (see page 311)

12. Define price elasticity of demand. (see page 319)

MINI CASE STUDY

Read the questions, then the case material, then answer the questions.

Questions

1. Why was Levi's so reluctant to sell its jeans to Tesco?

2. How was Tesco able to sell the jeans so cheaply?

3. If large food retailers are able to sell designer brands at cheap prices, what are the long-term implications for branding?

Levi's vs Tesco

The world's biggest brands have spent a fortune building their names and they protect their image jealously. Large retail chains have enormous amounts of marketing power and are used to being able to dictate terms to their suppliers. A clash seemed inevitable.

▶

The court case involving Levi Strauss and British supermarket chain Tesco was part of a power struggle between these two camps.

Britons spend an estimated £20 billion a year on branded fashion goods, and Tesco wants the right to sell those designer brands cheaply, but if it wins, then the brands' exclusivity is lost.

Sourcing the goods was not easy. Tesco had to buy them through the **grey market**. Levi's would not sell to the supermarket directly and bona fide Levi's distributors were worried about selling the jeans on to supermarkets.

Christine Cross, head of Tesco's non-food sales, felt that consumers should not have to pay such high prices: 'Consumers today are very well travelled, they see prices all over the world ... why should Levi's be one price in America, another in France and a third price in the UK?'

However, Levi's was concerned for the future of its business: 'Our brand is our most important asset.

It is more valuable than all the other assets on our balance sheet. It's more valuable than our factories, our buildings, our warehouses and our inventory,' explains Joe Middleton, Levi's European president. 'The true cost of making this jean is not just the factory element. It is much more than that.'

Many were unconvinced by the brand's arguments. If the superstores gained the right to stock anything they wanted to, then Brits could buy cheaper jeans – either with their groceries, or through traditional channels forced to reduce prices or lose sales. Of course, the longer-term casualty would be brand value, which would be unlikely to survive the shame of jeans being sold alongside baked beans.

The court decided that a manufacturer had a right to oversee the distribution of its products. Levi's won and its brand image was saved – until next time.   **Source: adapted from Datar, n/d**

REFERENCES

Anonymous (2001) Vitamin cartel fined for price fixing, *Guardian* 21 November.

Bandyopadhyay, S., Lin, G.B. and Zhong, Y. (2001) Under the gavel, *Marketing Management* 10(4), American Marketing Association (Nov–Dec), 24–8.

Cateora, P.R. and Ghauri, P.N. (2000) *International Marketing* (European edn), McGraw-Hill.

Cox, J. (2001) Pricing practices that endanger profits, *Marketing Management* 10(3), American Marketing Association (September), 42–6.

Datar, R. Battle of the brands, *The Money Programme*, BBC TV, at http://news.bbc.co.uk/1/hi/programmes/the_money_programme/archive/1604636.stm, accessed 20 October 2002.

France, M. and Hamm, S. (1998) Does predatory pricing make Microsoft a predator? at www.businessweek.com (23 November) accessed 15 October 2002.

Lancaster, G., Withey, F. and Ashford, R. (2000) *Marketing Fundamentals*, CIM Workbook, Butterworth-Heinemann.

Office of Fair Trading (2002) Aberdeen Journals Ltd has been fined £1.328 million for abusing a dominant market position, at www.oft.gov.uk/news/press+releases/2002/pn+58-02+oft+fines+scottish+newspaper+publisher+for+predatory+pricing.htm, accessed 20 October 2002.

OPEC (Organization of the Petroleum Exporting Countries) (2002) www.opec.org, accessed 20 October 2002.

Treanor, J. and Elliott, L. (2002) Big four brace for bad news from Brown, *Guardian* (14 March).

US Government (2002) *CIA World Factbook*, at www.cia.gov/cia/publications/factbook/index.html.

APPENDIX: ADDITIONAL COST-BASED PRICING ACTIVITY

activity

Drawing a breakeven chart

You will need proper graph paper, a ruler, pencil, rubber and calculator for this.

The Roadrunner Co produces racing bicycles.

> fixed costs (FC) total £1.2 million
> variable costs (VC) are £800 per bike
> the bike sells for £2000

1. The first challenge is to decide on the scale for the graph. In real life, you would know current output levels and could use that as a guide; otherwise, it is really trial and error. Draw the y (vertical) axis along the short side of your paper. For our Roadrunner example, let's label the (vertical) y axis £m, and take it up to £4m, and the (horizontal) x axis (quantity of bicycles) to 3500.

2. Now, plot the fixed costs. This is the easy one – fixed costs do not change – so we draw a straight, horizontal line across from the y axis at £1.2 million. Label this line 'FC'.

3. Next, draw the variable costs (VC) line. VC are £800 per bike, so pick a number (any number between 1 and 3500) and work out the VC at that level of output.

> For example, 500 × £800 = £400,000

Now make a small mark at the point where 500 on the x axis meets £400,000 on the y axis. Repeat for another random point, say 2000:

> 2000 × £800 = £1,600,000

Next, taking 0 (bottom left corner of the graph) as your starting point, just join the dots to make a variable cost line (it should be a straight, diagonal line; if it is not, then check the two calculations). Label this line 'VC'.

Why 0 as a starting point? It is because if you don't make any products, then there will be no variable costs – they are ingredients and raw materials remember.

4. The next line to draw is the total cost (TC) line and there's a cheat's way to do this.

Take a ruler and lay it along the VC line, then carefully move it up, keeping the angle the same, until it crosses the y axis at the start of the FC line – then draw a straight diagonal line, starting at the y axis. This line should be parallel to the VC line. Label this line 'TC'.

Why does the total cost line start at the FC line? Because total cost = fixed cost *plus* variable cost, so it can never be *less* than fixed cost.

5. The sales revenue (SR) line is drawn in a similar way to the VC line. Pick two numbers (any two numbers within the scale of the graph). Work out the revenue at those sales volumes (quantity × price), then, using 0 as a

starting point, plot a straight diagonal line that joins all three points. Label this line 'SR'.

6. Now you're ready to read off the breakeven point; X marks the spot, i.e. it is where the sales revenue and total cost lines cross. Draw a line down to the quantity axis – the answer should be 1000.

Roadrunner Co breakeven chart

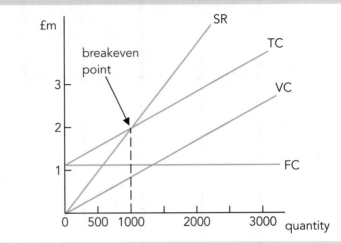

contribution

selling price – variable cost

Of course, if the company wants to know what happens if the price is increased to £2100, it will have to draw a new line for sales revenue.

As an alternative to the graphical method, the firm might calculate breakeven points using this formula:

$$\frac{\text{Fixed costs}}{\text{contribution per item}}$$

Let's revisit the Roadrunner Co figures:

fixed costs total £1.2 million
variable costs are £800 per bike
price is £2000

contribution   = selling price – variable cost
= £2000 – £800 = £1200

$$\frac{1,200,000}{1200} = 1000$$

So, it needs to sell 1000 bicycles at £2000 in order to cover all its costs, i.e. to break even.

answer to full cost pricing activity (page 305)

total cost	= fixed costs + variable costs
fixed cost per unit (box)	= $\frac{£\,40,000}{100,000}$ = 40p
total cost per unit (box)	= 40p + £1 = £1.40
price i.e. total cost + 25%	
	= £1.40 + (£1.40 × 25%)
	= £1.75

THE MARKETING MIX

MARKETING MIX CHALLENGES

The following are illustrations of the types of decision that marketers have to take or issues they face. *You aren't expected to know how to deal with the challenges now*; just bear them in mind as you read the chapter and see what you can find that helps.

▶ Aphrodite is a small, well-known confectionery brand, which wants to change its image to that of a supplier of high-quality, special-occasion sweets. The marketing director has asked you to review current marketing activities to ensure that they support this new market position. What do you need to check?

▶ You are the marketing manager for a well-known designer fashion brand. A chain store has approached your company with a view to placing a large order. The finance manager is delighted and is prepared to discount the price. However, the managing director has some concerns. Do you think this order should be accepted? Do you want to impose any special terms and conditions?

▶ Bargainz r uz, a large discount store, is having trouble getting customers to apply for its store credit card. It has asked you to help find a way to persuade customers to apply for the card. Where would you start?

▶ A friend owns two coffee bars, one in Leicester and one in Edinburgh. She now works in Edinburgh as that coffee bar is new and has no manager yet. Since she left, takings at the Leicester restaurant have dropped right down and she doesn't know why. She has asked you to help her find the problem. Do you know what to do?

KEY CONCEPTS

basic product
augmented product
total product
4Ps
7Ps
integration
mix objectives
marketing programmes
implementation
product (see Chapter 7)
price (see Chapter 10)
promotion (see Chapter 8)
place (see Chapter 9)
marketing strategy and plans
  (see Chapter 12)
branding (see Chapter 7)
product life cycle (see
  Chapter 7)

CHAPTER OVERVIEW

INTRODUCTION

This chapter rounds up Part 3 of the book, on the **marketing mix**, summarizing the techniques and demonstrating how they fit together. If preferred, this chapter could be read first as an introduction to the more detailed chapters on each element of the mix.

The marketing mix is at the heart of modern marketing; it is the means by which most marketing is actually carried out. The **4Ps** is the most commonly used schematic for the marketing mix and has the advantage of being both widely recognized and easy to remember. This 4Ps mnemonic was first proposed by Jerome E. McCarthy in 1960 and, despite some criticism over the years, it is still taught in universities, and used in practice, today.

4Ps

a mnemonic (memory aid) for the marketing mix: product, promotion, place, price

The marketing mix is a set of tools and should be treated as such. No one element can stand alone; they must all support each other. If they conflict, **target markets** will be confused and objectives will not be met. Marketing managers blend their marketing mixes to make an integrated plan that will achieve their marketing objectives. If the organization has products that its customers want to buy, at prices they are prepared to pay, and available from the right places, then all the organization needs to do is tell customers about them – and persuade them that this is a better deal than the one the competition is offering.

MARKETING MIX OBJECTIVES

Before any decisions are taken on what to do with the marketing mix, it is important to know what you are trying to achieve. If you just get into your car and drive, without first deciding where you want to go, then you will drive around aimlessly. To reach a destination, you have to know where you want to be and plan a route to get there. The marketing mix is the organization's route to its marketing objectives (see Exhibit 11.1).

An organization's objectives work in a hierarchy. At the top level are the corporate objectives. All other objectives, including marketing, should be designed to contribute to those overall, corporate objectives.

The illustration in Exhibit 11.2 is insufficiently detailed for the real world, of course. Objectives should always be SMART:

▶ **s**pecific (clearly thought out and worded)

▶ **m**easurable (it is clear whether the objective really has been achieved)

▶ **a**chievable (possible to do)

▶ **r**elevant (of value to the organization and in keeping with other objectives)

▶ **t**imed (with a deadline).

For example, to increase **sales revenue** from the pet food division (specific) by 10 per cent (measurable) by 31 December 2005 (timed). This objective could be relevant if the company

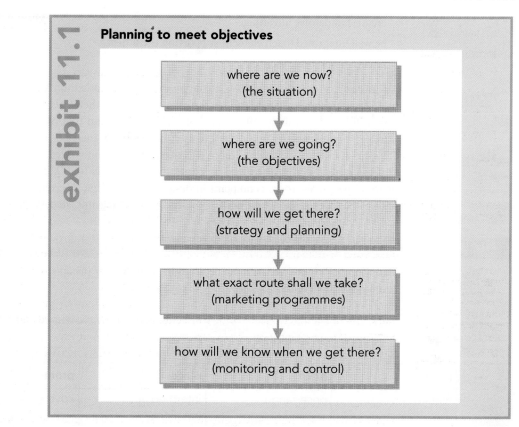

exhibit 11.1

Planning to meet objectives

where are we now?
(the situation)

where are we going?
(the objectives)

how will we get there?
(strategy and planning)

what exact route shall we take?
(marketing programmes)

how will we know when we get there?
(monitoring and control)

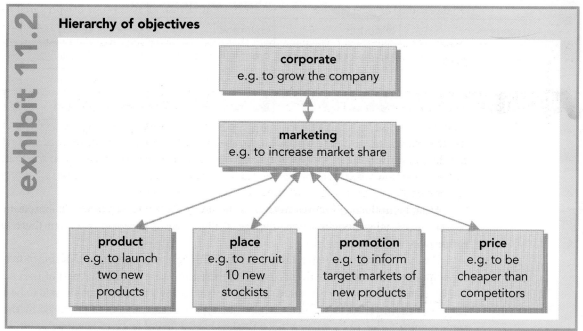

exhibit 11.2

Hierarchy of objectives

corporate
e.g. to grow the company

marketing
e.g. to increase market share

product
e.g. to launch
two new
products

place
e.g. to recruit
10 new
stockists

promotion
e.g. to inform
target markets of
new products

price
e.g. to be
cheaper than
competitors

was seeking to grow, and achievable if it has the resources (money, people, facilities) to put behind the sales drive. (For more on marketing objectives, see Chapter 12.)

A well-designed marketing mix will:

▶ achieve marketing objectives

▶ meet customers' needs

▶ create competitive advantage

▶ be well integrated (each element supporting the others)

▶ fit with marketing resources.

The meeting of customer needs is at the heart of good marketing. Marketers have to get inside their customers' heads and see the offering through their eyes. **Competitive advantage** will be created if the offering is noticeably better than that of the competition. For example, it may be better quality, or cheaper, have a better image or be more readily available. The marketing mix will be more effective if it is well integrated, i.e. each element fits with the others so that there are no contradictory signals (see 'Mixing it' below). With regard to resources, there is no point in designing a mix that the company cannot implement, either because it lacks finance, expertise or a suitable infrastructure.

THE 4PS

Each of the 4Ps is covered in more depth in its own chapter (Chapters 7–10). Exhibit 11.3 summarizes them and shows how they fit together.

exhibit 11.3

The marketing mix: key variables

product	price	place	promotion
features	price range	intermediaries (retailers, wholesalers, etc.)	advertising
range	discounts	coverage	personal selling
support services	allowances	order processing	public relations
brand	negotiation policy	stock control	sales promotion
design	credit policy	delivery	direct marketing
packaging	price changes	transport	sponsorship

Product

The product is at the heart of marketing – without it, nothing else is required. It may seem obvious just what a product is (a pen, a car, a ring, a bar of chocolate, etc.), but there is rather more to it than that.

A car is of course a product, but not all cars are the same. They differ in terms of features, quality, size, speed, shape and colour. All these things are an essential part of the car. They are characteristics (or attributes) of a particular car. So a product could be said to be a bundle of characteristics. Products of the same type, e.g. cars, and even produced by the same manufacturer, e.g. Ford, may none the less have different features (engine size, braking system, colour, interior trim, etc.) and will come in different sizes for different drivers (small car, small family car, family car, executive, limousine, van, minibus, people carrier, etc.).

What makes up a product? A chocolate bar has ingredients: cocoa, sugar and milk. A ring needs raw materials: gold, diamonds, fixings. A car has components: engine parts, a chassis, tyres, etc. It is the quality of these things, coupled with the workmanship that goes into the product, that determines the product's quality. Quality is something that most customers look for in a product, even though they cannot always afford to buy the best. This is an example of how the marketing mix blends. The best components, such as those that go into a Rolls-Royce (e.g. walnut veneer dashboards), cost more than others (e.g. plastic dashboards). This means that a higher price will have to be set for the products that have the higher-quality components. Some customers will be willing and able to pay that price (so long as the quality really is better), some will not. Those that do buy a Rolls-Royce will be buying not just a car but an exclusive image. They will therefore expect impeccable service, both before and after the sale.

activity

Find some products you bought recently (it doesn't matter how small). Why did you buy those products? What are their benefits to you? Why didn't you buy a rival product?

Companies provide a range of products, of differing quality, and with different features, to match the prices that different customers are prepared to pay for that product type.

So, a product is a bundle of characteristics, but it can hardly be a surprise that that is not what customers really want to buy. What the customer really wants is the benefit that the product brings. People do not buy cars, they buy means of transport or status symbols. They do not really buy rings, but tokens of affection, gifts, a badge of engagement. Marketers concentrate on the benefits of their products – the features and quality are really just the means by which those benefits are delivered.

exhibit 11.4

The total product

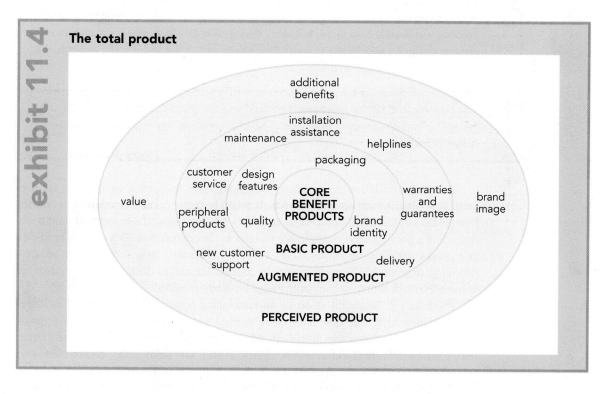

Products have a number of levels, which together make up the total product offering. Customers may decide between two products on the basis of any of the attributes listed in Exhibit 11.4, e.g. new customer support, but they will not buy a product that does not deliver the core benefit required. A pen must write, chocolate must taste good, a car must go.

The basic product is the product itself and includes features, components, quality level, styling and packaging. The perceived product is the product as the customer actually sees it, which may not be in quite the way the supplier intended. For example, a restaurant may wish to be thought of as upmarket, but its **target market** may just think it is overpriced. The augmented product is the surrounding support for the product, including all support services, delivery and installation.

Take a shirt as an example. Its core benefits are that it covers nakedness and provides some warmth. As a basic product, the shirt is blue, fashionably styled, available in most sizes and made of 100 per cent cotton of the highest quality. The supplier offers a no-quibble, money-back guarantee if the shirt fails to live up to expectations. This augments (adds to) the product. The shirt also happens to be made by Armani. So what is your perception of it?

b2bfocus

Augmented products

There is likely to be a greater emphasis on service in b2b markets, both pre- and post-sale. It is important to business customers that products are delivered on time and that they are repaired promptly if necessary. If equipment is down, then this is likely to mean lost sales. Take PCs as an example. It is frustrating enough for a consumer when a computer won't work, but for a firm it might mean that orders don't get through, or customers cannot reach them, or sales cannot be processed because customer details are unavailable. It has much more serious implications.

Businesses usually order larger quantities and so are more valuable customers than individual consumers. They are likely to be more particular about specifications too. Many companies have policies that state which computers must be bought for which purpose and exactly how large, fast, etc., they should be. They may insist on bespoke systems designed specifically to meet their needs and, if the order is big enough, the supplier is likely to provide these.

Customer relationships are more important in b2b markets. It is a lot of effort to win new business and so the emphasis is on retaining the good customers you have and benefiting from their repeat purchases. This often requires high-quality, responsive customer service.

Previously, firms sought to differentiate themselves from their competition through tangible product advantages (their products might be better quality, come in more colours, have additional features). Competitive strategies revolved around development, and maintenance of a product was demonstrably superior to the competition. This came to be known as a **unique selling proposition (USP)**. However, as markets have become more competitive, tangible product differences are harder to maintain and so the augmented product has become the main source of competitive edge for many companies.

The term USP originally stood for 'unique selling point' and was first used by Rosser Reeves, whose idea was that advertising worked best when it made one clear point. Unfortunately, the phrase was picked up and reinterpreted as meaning that a product must have a unique feature (Pickton and Broderick, 2001). The word 'point' caused confusion. Consequently, unique selling proposition is the definition now generally preferred.

The USPs of today are more likely to be derived from additional services or from **brand values**. For more on products and services, see Chapter 7.

The age of the brand

Since it was first devised, the marketing mix has been a major source of competitive advantage for many firms: Aldi and ASDA charge cheaper prices, Mercedes makes superior cars, the founder of Woolworth claimed the three secrets of retail success were 'location, location, location', and most FMCG companies spend millions on promotion. However, towards the end of the twentieth century, branding was seen to be the main contributor to a company's competitive edge. The emphasis was on brand value. Leading brands battled for the loyalty of consumers; few more fiercely than the big sportswear companies, Nike, Reebok and Adidas, who spent millions promoting their brands. They competed as fiercely to sponsor the best, or in some cases the most photogenic, sports stars as those athletes competed themselves.

Known for mobility – Jonny Wilkinson and team mates in training

Some highly successful organizations are just brands – they don't actually make anything and may franchise the selling operation too. For example, Virgin has lent its name to a number of products (vodka, cola, cosmetics) that it has very little to do with.

At the beginning of the twenty-first century, the brand's power looks less sure. Customers seem to want more value than a brand alone can give (Christopher, 2000). Customer service looks set to be the key source of competitive edge over the next few years. What will the sportswear giants come up with next?

Promotion (marketing communications)

Today, consumers have a wide choice of products and services on which to spend their money. Sellers try to influence that choice through the use of promotion. This is the part of the marketing mix that is primarily concerned with communication which is why it is now more commonly known as marketing communications. Unfortunately that does not start with P, though, and so the old term of promotion is still used as well. Marketing communications is preferred because there was always the possibility of confusion between promotion and **sales promotion**. Marketing communications and promotion are interchangeable terms and this text uses both.

The promotional mix traditionally comprises:

▶ advertising

▶ public relations (PR)

▸ sales promotion

▸ personal selling

to which can be added direct marketing and sponsorship.

Advertising uses paid-for media, e.g. television, radio, cinema, Internet. Media relations is a large part of **public relations (PR)** and this uses unpaid-for media through media releases and the placing of stories. Companies use many other PR activities as well, though, including exhibitions, **hospitality**, **sponsorship** and **product placement**. Short-term special offers, (money-off coupons, multibuys, competitions, free trials, etc.) are called **sales promotions** and more money is spent on these than on advertising. Personal selling ranges from sales assistants in shops, through door-to-door salespeople and telesales to the high-level account managers who sell large capital items (such as bridges and ships) to governments and the boards of multinational clients.

All these activities must be integrated so that they support, rather than contradict, each other. The same message and tone should come through from each activity. This is an important part of building **brand image**. Marketing communications activities must also fit with the rest of the marketing mix. The message comes through from all of the mix, not just from explicit communications. Harrods sells quality products at premium prices, and we expect its communications to be similarly upmarket. A gaudy advert in a downmarket magazine offering a **bogof** would detract from its carefully cultivated image.

b2bfocus

Marketing communications

The biggest promotional tool in **b2b** is personal selling. Firms who operate in b2b markets, rather than consumer markets, usually have fewer customers who buy more. This makes the expense of salespeople worthwhile. Salespeople can explain complex products and build relationships with their customers. They are an important source of competitive edge and repeat business.

Trade shows and exhibitions are important in business markets. Most industries have these (e.g. Internet World, the Motor Show, the Boat Show). They are good for networking, product demonstrations, identifying **prospects**, building contact databases, entertaining customers and checking out the competition.

Businesses do use **advertising** to market to other businesses, but they use different **media**. Television would be overkill. Most adverts appear in the specialist trade press, such as *The Grocer, Computing, Accountancy Age, Environmental Engineering* and *The Hat* magazine. Sometimes businesses will do some consumer marketing to help their trade customers sell products on. So diamond miners might promote jewellery to increase the derived demand for diamonds.

For more on marketing communications, see Chapter 8.

Place (distribution and logistics)

Place is perhaps the least descriptive of the marketing mix titles and therefore the most likely to cause confusion. Today, place refers to the whole **distribution** process – from customer enquiry to after-sales service. In consumer marketing, the place where the actual sale happens is part of that, but it is not the whole story. In b2b, the sale often takes place on the customer's premises, where a salesperson has called.

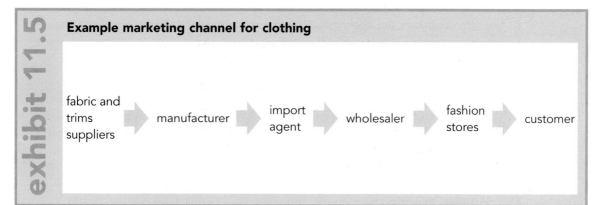

exhibit 11.5

Example marketing channel for clothing

fabric and trims suppliers → manufacturer → import agent → wholesaler → fashion stores → customer

The marketing channel, or distribution channel illustrated in Exhibit 11.5 is a three-level channel (that is, there are three links in the chain between the manufacturer of the product and the eventual customer).

An important task of marketing management is to design the marketing channel. The longer the channel, the more removed the producer of the product is from its customers and the more opportunity there is for things to go wrong. Most manufacturers have little or no customer contact. It is the **retailer** who builds a relationship with the customer. This lack of contact makes it harder for manufacturers to get to know what their customers think of the products, what they would like to see changed, what new products they might like. It also means they have to work harder to build brand loyalty.

The shortest channel is a zero-level (0-level) channel. This is direct selling; there are no intermediaries. The product's producer sells directly to the customer.

Marketing managers not only have to work out the length of a channel, but its breadth. How many retailers, distributors, etc. will handle the product? The answer will partly depend on whether this is an exclusive or a **mass-market** product. Is it cheap or expensive? Again, the mix intermingles. The nature of the product helps to determine the nature of the channel.

Channel design is only the beginning. The **supply chain** for a product may be complex and will require careful ongoing management. Good relationships throughout the chain are essential for long-term success. Distributors need support and encouragement if they are to choose to **push** the right product forward.

Place is about getting the right product to the right customer at the right time. A lot goes on behind the scenes to ensure that this happens.

push strategy
a promotional strategy aimed at distribution channels

e-focus

Channel conflict

The Internet has opened up new markets for all members of the supply chain, from raw materials suppliers through to retailers. This freer market access has brought new competition with it: not just from companies at the same level in the supply chain that could not previously reach the market, but also from members at different levels.

For example, a number of sportswear **retailers** have set up e-commerce sites to offer their customers an alternative way to buy sporting goods. These retailers, in theory at least, will have to deal with competition from retailers in other countries (in practice, many retailers cannot cope with supplying overseas orders and so only deliver to specific locations). Most of these retailers get their stocks from **wholesalers**, who buy large quantities from manufacturers or importers and then split the products into smaller lots to sell on (this is called breaking bulk).

Wholesalers do not operate from smart high-street stores and so, in the past, were not equipped to deal with end customers. Now they can. With an Internet site, the wholesalers can cut out the retailers and sell direct. It doesn't stop there. If the wholesalers can do this, why not the manufacturers themselves?

This merging of customer bases is a cause of channel conflict. **Supply chain** members are able to compete with other members higher up, or lower down, the chain. Some manufacturers choose not to compete. They may offer products direct to customers but make sure that the deal is not as good as can be obtained at online retail sites. There is sound reasoning behind this strategy, often to do with order administration and the problems of dealing with thousands of customers when you are only used to dealing with tens.

For more on place, see Chapter 9.

Price

Price is the one element of the marketing mix that does not need a budget. The other three tools all cost significant amounts. Price really costs nothing. It just brings the money in.

At one level, the price is what a business charges its customer for the goods and services it provides. However, the product that the customer is buying may actually cost more than the price suggests. This may be because of hidden costs, such as a computer upgrade required before the software will run, or it may be more subtle, like the time it will take the customer to install the new software (time is money), or the loss of the benefits they would have got if they had bought a different package. So the organization needs to bear these other things in mind when setting the actual price.

Now with added extra!

Some organizations add new features to their products in an attempt to make them seem better value. However, if customers see no benefit to the additions, this ploy will only add to the firm's costs, necessitating a higher price that customers may be unhappy to pay. An online retailer offered a reduced-price DVD player in its clearance sale. As an added incentive, the player came with 50 free films. They were not well-known films. Is this a good deal or might customers be put off by the prospect of giving house room to a lot of unwanted DVDs?

The price of a product is usually the most significant part of the value that a customer hands over in exchange for a product. Therefore, the perceived value of the product must be at least equal to the price. Other elements of the mix can be used to increase the perceived value and therefore allow the charging of a higher price.

Price sends a message to potential customers: high quality, cheap and cheerful, bargain, or somewhere in between. It is important that this message accords with the actual product. If Rolls-Royce halved its prices people would be likely to think that the quality had dropped significantly. If Toshiba drops the price of its computers because a new model will be out soon, people may see this as a bargain and snap them up. The price and the product must match up if marketing is to work successfully.

Price must also be in accord with place. If a restaurant wants to charge high prices it needs good food and excellent surroundings. Then perhaps the restaurant critics will give it good write-ups (which is good **PR**).

For more on price, see Chapter 10.

Packaging – the fifth P?

Whether or not we grant packaging the status of fifth P, it certainly warrants our attention. Packaging really transcends the traditional 4Ps.

It is part of the product. Many products have to be packed or they cannot be sold. For example, the product may be liquid (e.g. cough syrup), dangerous (e.g. acid), potentially damaging (e.g. hair dye), delicate (e.g. contact lenses) or perishable (e.g. foodstuffs). As well as protecting the product, the packaging may be there to protect consumers. Childproof tops protect the young from accidental ingestion of harmful medicines. Tamper-proof packs prevent the malicious from poisoning, or otherwise spoiling, products.

Sometimes the packaging is more than a means to contain the product; it is an integral part. Products such as toothpaste turn packaging into a feature: pump or tube? Food can be packaged in different ways and this turns it into different products. For example, peas may be sold in tins, jars, packets, vacuum packs or their original pods. Individual drinks cartons have straws attached to make them easier to drink on the go. Some packs are deliberately made attractive so that people will use them rather than put the product into something else (for example, some of Marks & Spencer's desserts come in glass bowls). This can be good promotion too if the pack has the product's name on it. How many people, even in cafés, bother to decant ketchup out of the bottle rather than have it sitting on the table advertising Heinz?

activity

Next time you go grocery shopping, look carefully at the different types of packaging used. Who are they designed to appeal to? Are *you* influenced in your choice of product by the packaging?

Packaging can be a key consumer decision criterion, especially for commodity products. Take milk as an example. Milk can be packaged in a number of ways: glass bottle, plastic bottle, paper carton, tin or packet (for dried milk). Some customers may choose the milk with the carton that is easiest to open (some are really quite difficult), or the one that pours best, or keeps the milk freshest longest, or survives freezing.

Innovative packaging can confer **competitive advantage**. A supplier who invents a new and better way of packaging has an advantage over its competitors – at least until they catch up. Imagine having been the first to put fruit juice in a small carton with a straw, milk in an easy-pour carton, shampoo in a sachet or tissues in a pocket-sized pack.

The packaging is a key part of the **brand image** and so is jealously guarded by brand owners. Coca-Cola watches competitors carefully and is quick to object if any rival product looks too similar to its own (the first can design for Sainsbury's Cola was too close). Distinctive packaging becomes associated with the product and is the means by which the product is recognized: Jif's lemon juice is packed in a yellow plastic lemon. Perrier has a distinctive green bottle.

Marmite and Tesco's own brand yeast spread – packaged inspiration

Packaging is sometimes referred to as the silent salesman because of its **marketing communications** role. Packaging sends a message about the product inside. This may be explicit (i.e. it may be a slogan or **on-pack promotion**) or it may be implied through the packaging's style. Advertisements often contain a **pack shot**, usually at the end of the ad. It is hoped that this image of the pack will stay with the consumer and then, when they see it in the shop, they will remember the message of the advert. This is particularly useful for products that rely on recognition, i.e. when the customers may browse shelves looking for a suitable product to buy (this applies to most **FMCG**).

Packaging is also informative. It states country of origin, lists ingredients, gives instructions for use and carries warnings (e.g. not suitable for children under three).

The packaging can also be used to persuade people to use more of the product. Allegedly, Domestos increased its sales substantially by changing the instruction 'use sparingly' to 'use liberally'. Foodstuffs regularly carry recipes designed to encourage cooks to see how else the product could be used. Imaginative packaging can help to sell the firm's other products: include other products in the recipes, attach a trial-size packet of biscuits to the coffee (or vice versa) – there are many possibilities.

Packaging can be varied to give a company more pricing options. Refill packs are cheaper than original products. Larger sizes are often better value.

Good packaging is essential to protect products during distribution. Secondary packaging (large cartons and palettes) may be needed here to make sure goods are easy to handle, can be stacked safely, and arrive at their destination in good condition. Sometimes this secondary packaging can be turned to good promotional advantage. Packets of crisps, which are notoriously hard to keep on the shelves (they sell fast and so run out, and they also slip about), are normally supplied to retailers in large brown boxes. One innovative crisp company decided to use these boxes to give their crisps an edge. They perforated a hole in one side of the box so that, when the hole was punched in, customers could reach into the box and pull out the crisps. The boxes had become display stands (all bearing the crisp manufacturer's name and logo, of course). Shops no longer had to unpack the crisps and restock shelves. When a box was empty they just brought in the next box.

Carrier bags: carrying the message home

THE 7PS OF SERVICES MARKETING

These are:

▶ product

▶ price

▶ promotion

▶ place

▶ physical evidence

▶ people

▶ process.

Services present the marketer with additional challenges. They are intangible (i.e. they cannot be touched, picked up, put on a shelf). This makes customers more wary of them. Their quality is hard to be sure of until it is too late. You can send a meal back, but your evening has already been spoilt. People provide services and therefore the quality of provision is often inconsistent.

Also most services have to be used at the time they are provided and in the place they are provided. It is not possible to store a manicure and have it later, nor to ask an entertainer to do their act now so that you don't have to visit the theatre to watch it later. For more on the special nature of services, see Chapter 7.

Services companies need to build the customer's trust in the services they offer. They need to reassure the customer that the service will be a quality experience. Many papers and articles have been written on customer perceptions of service quality. Perhaps the most famous model used to measure these perceptions is SERVQUAL (Parasuraman *et al.*, 1988), which employs five dimensions that contribute to service quality: tangibles, reliability, responsiveness, assurance and empathy.

One obvious strategy to overcome fears associated with the service product's intangibility is to turn it into something more tangible. It is generally recognized that the surroundings in which a service is delivered are a key part of customer satisfaction. The ambience of the restaurant, the plates, the music, the state of the toilets – all these things contribute as much to a meal out as does the quality of the food. These more tangible aspects of services are called **physical evidence**. The delivery of a service is usually reliant on people, so people are also part of the services marketing mix.

Then there is the question of the actual provision of the service. When a customer buys a product, such as a video, it is put in a bag, taken home and watched whenever the new owner feels like watching it. They do not actually see the product being made, they just buy the end result. However, a service only exists while it is being delivered. When a customer

exhibit 11.6

The additional 3Ps of services marketing

physical evidence, includes	people, includes	process, includes
ambience	skills	service delivery
peripheral products	manner	booking
documents	appearance	payment

has a haircut, the only thing that gets taken home is a new look – and if it is a bad look, then there is little can be done about it. The actual process of hair cutting is the important thing.

These 7Ps of services marketing are discussed individually below.

Service product

It is harder to maintain consistency with a service product than it is with a physical product because of the reliance upon people to deliver the service (see 'People', below). Fast-food chains get round this by tightly controlling what their staff do. Kitchen staff walk along set paths from fryer to sink to serving hatch. Bells ring when it is time to turn the burger or take the chips out of the fat. Nothing is left to chance. This heavily proscribed way of working has the added advantage of meaning that trained chefs are not required. The work, however, is repetitive and can soon become boring. Staff turnover is often high in such restaurants.

Price

The same pricing tactics and strategies apply to services as to physical products, although there are additional difficulties. The intangibility of services, and the mistrust that evokes, tends to make customers rely even more on price as a determinant of quality. Some fashionable London hairdressers charge women £150 (€210) for a cut and blow dry. Outside Mayfair, it is possible to get a haircut for less than £20 (€28).

The provision and consumption of services must (usually) take place at the same time. This means that an oversupply cannot be sold off cheap later, nor can a service be put on back order and delivered to the customer another day. **Demand** prediction is critical to profitability. Marketing has to be imaginative to overcome this problem. The airline industry handles it through over-booking some planes (knowing that not all customers will turn up) and also advertising cheaper, stand-by seats so that it can fill unsold places.

Place

Services cannot be stored and so physical distribution is not usually a problem. Certain aspects of **physical evidence** (see below) may, however, need to be stored and distributed, e.g. tickets. As this is not their prime area of expertise, many service providers use agents to handle this for them. Travel agents book airline tickets. Ticket agents, such as Ticketmaster, handle bookings for theatres and shows. In London, drivers buy the congestion charge permits required for driving into the central zone from newsagents.

Promotion (marketing communications)

As services are likely to vary in their delivery (because they rely on people and people are not automatons), it is often wiser to stress the benefits rather than the specific features of the service. Again physical evidence has a part to play here. Restaurants talk about the excellence of their food; airlines show off their extra-wide seats with additional leg room; beauticians stress the all-natural ingredients in their products.

People

It is the organization's people who deliver the service, and their attitudes, skills and efficiency often determine how satisfied customers are. It is therefore important that customer-facing staff should be well trained, appropriately turned out and courteous. It is often people that build relationships rather than companies. (In some industries, notably hairdressing, employees have to sign a contract preventing them from working in the same area for a specified time period in an attempt to prevent them from taking customers with them when they leave.)

If the service personnel are on the end of a telephone line, then it is good telephone manner that is essential. If they are communicating by e-mail, it is their written communication and efficiency that is important.

Technology does not replace people in the delivery of most services, it just makes them more remote (and means that the company needs fewer of them). The loss of the personal touch means that it is even harder to build customer relationships. The Internet has the potential to remove all human interaction from transactions, reducing them to mere routines (Pincott and Branthwaite, 2000). Amazon and other online booksellers work really hard to build relationships with their customers. They personalize web pages and greet their returning visitors by name. However, there is growing evidence that too much personalization is unpopular with some customers who do not want so close a relationship with their bookseller (O'Connor and Eamonn, 2001).

Physical evidence

peripheral product
a secondary product often provided as part of a service, e.g. the complimentary mints at the end of a meal, shampoo at the hairdressers

Most services do have a tangible element. Even dentists give you appointment cards and occasionally free toothpaste, and they certainly have instruments and a chair.

These tangible aspects are known as physical evidence and are key in shaping the customers' perception of the quality of the service. Physical evidence takes many forms. It may be a **peripheral product**, e.g. the oil used in a car service or the soap provided in a hotel. It may be the surroundings in which the service is delivered: the ambience. This comprises décor, music, colour scheme, etc. – particularly important in places of entertainment such as bars and restaurants. It may be a ticket or a contract; the physical proof that you have paid for the service. Tickets may sound trivial but they play a vital role in reassuring customers that their flight, theatre seat or concert is booked. There is no real need for an airline to issue a ticket, indeed some Internet-based airlines do not, but the ticket tells the customer where to go to catch the plane and is a chance to check that the flight is correctly booked. Even the Internet airlines usually send a confirming e-mail.

activity
Next time you use a service, whether it is the dentist, hairdresser, a bar, a library or any other, note down all the items of physical evidence you can spot. What is their role in the service's marketing?

Process

Process is the way in which the service is provided. McDonald's is self-service whereas many other restaurants offer waiter or waitress service. The processes involved are different, although each scenario is capable of providing competitive advantage.

How bookings are made and how customer enquiries are handled is part of the service process. This is an aspect of service management that is becoming increasingly outsourced and automated through ticket agents, and Internet and telephone sales. Where, and how, cars are parked at cinemas, theatres, restaurants and airports is all part of the service. This outsourcing is potentially damaging for the customer relationship. Customers may actually build relationships with the firm's subcontractor rather than the firm itself. This makes the customers harder to retain in the future. Even worse, it has been known for companies that started as subcontractors to expand and take on the whole business themselves (e.g. plumbers contracted to a home services company could decide to take on the customers themselves).

The ambience in this upmarket hotel is an important contributor to the high price of the rooms

MIXING IT (BLENDING THE MARKETING MIX)

Each element of the marketing mix should support the others. They should build to a consistent whole that accords with the organization's brand values. For example, an upmarket, exclusive fashion brand would:

▶ require high-quality products, made with top-class fabrics, well styled and well made, perhaps finished by hand

▶ command premium prices

▶ be sold in more exclusive stores

▶ be promoted in a tasteful, creative way, perhaps with adverts placed in fashion and lifestyle magazines, and with suitably upmarket celebrities wearing the clothes.

A mass-market clothing brand, however, might:

▶ use cheaper fabrics and mass-production techniques, keep fancy trims to a minimum

▶ undercut competitors' prices

▶ be sold everywhere

▶ be promoted extensively, in the newspapers and magazines that the customers read, on billboards, even on flyers.

These mixes send clear, but very different, messages about the company's offering. If the messages get mixed, then customers will become confused. You cannot charge a high price but use cheap materials (at least not for long). If your products are on sale everywhere, they lose their exclusive image (this is why Levi's was so keen to stop Tesco selling its jeans, and why perfumiers such as Calvin Klein do not want their products sold in high-street stores such as Superdrug and Littlewoods).

The marketing mix is used to implement marketing strategies and plans. It is the marketer's tool kit, and deciding how to use each tool is a key part of the marketer's job. Those decisions are made in the light of the organization's objectives and its overall strategy to meet those objectives. Look back at the above example: if a brand wants to maintain its upmarket position, then clearly it must be in the best shops and be made of high-quality materials. The desired market position informs the choice of how to use marketing tools. With the marketing purpose firmly in mind, marketing managers are able to design effective marketing programmes, which must be based on a well-coordinated marketing mix.

globalfocus

Cheap imports

Where do they come from, those piles of branded goods in the local supermarket? How can Superdrug afford to sell perfume so cheaply? Sometimes the goods are legitimate supplies – perhaps excess stock or the end of lines that the manufacturers are selling off. Sometimes their route to market is murkier – grey in fact. **Grey importing** is when someone outside the official supply chain buys goods, often in another country, for sale back home. Some of these products come from less developed countries where prices have to be lower (otherwise people could not afford to buy them). This **price discrimination** tempts buyers from the more expensive markets who know they can then substantially undercut the manufacturer's recommended price and still make a profit.

THE PRODUCT LIFE CYCLE

The product life cycle (introduced in Chapter 7) is a useful tool in determining the optimal marketing mix. As a product goes through its life, its support requirements change. Exhibit 11.7 illustrates how this might happen.

exhibit 11.7

Mixing it through the product life cycle

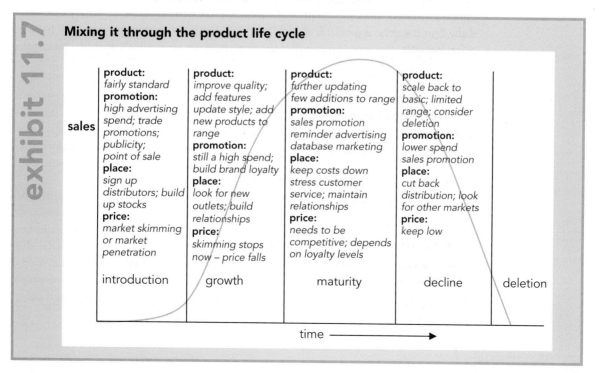

The product life cycle model was originally devised for generic products, i.e. the product type not the individual branded item (shoes, not Clark's shoes). It can, however, be applied to any new product (for new product types, see Chapter 7).

Products are often very expensive to launch. The research and development that goes into a new product can cost hundreds of thousands and will have to be recouped in the early life of the product. Initially, the promotion budget will be at its highest. People do not know about this new product and so they must be told. There may be no **distribution channel** and so that needs to be built up. If the product is a new-to-the-world invention (e.g. 3G phones), then the company may be able to use a price-skimming strategy to help recover some of its costs more quickly. However, this will encourage competitors into the market (unless the new product is protected by patents – though often even these are not enough).

The growth stage is the time to focus on building **brand loyalty**. The product should be settling down, any teething problems out of the way. Now is the time to introduce new members of the product range and add features. A more heavily featured product may attract more customers. The **early majority** (see the section on the **product adoption process** in Chapter 5) should be displaying an interest by now and they are likely to be tempted by a lower price. However, if the initial strategy was **penetration pricing**, perhaps for a **me-too product**, then now is the time to put the price up. Otherwise it will have to stay cheap forever. Distribution coverage is vital to build up sales. A good **push strategy** will encourage **retailers** and other intermediaries to stock the product.

Competition hots up in the maturity stage. The market is likely to have been split into numerous segments. For example, when chocolate was first introduced into the UK market, it was sold as cocoa to be mixed in drinks or added to other confections. In today's mature confectionery market, just think how many different types of products, aimed at different types of people, are chocolate based. There are likely to be standard products by now although they may be more sophisticated than the original basic ones. This makes manufacturing easier and cheaper. However, there may still be a number of variations. For example, kitchen furniture may have a standard, modular design but come in a choice of colours, finishes, handles, etc. There may also be special editions available for limited time periods. Promotion will be geared towards maintaining market share and extending the maturity stage (the next stage is decline and the firm will want to put that off as long as possible). There will be an emphasis on good customer service and on rewarding loyal customers. Generally speaking, the price of a mature product needs to be competitive; however, if the firm has done a good job of building brand loyalty, then demand may now be more **price inelastic**. This would mean that the firm could get away with a slightly higher price than its competitors.

Now is the time to look for an **extension strategy** in order to delay decline. The product might fare better in another market, e.g. another country, there may be new uses for it, or perhaps it can be repositioned. A classic case of repositioning as an extension to the product life cycle is provided by the Guinness story. Many years ago, Guinness was regarded as an old person's drink with its slogan, 'Guinness is good for you'. There was a distinct problem. Its market was dying – literally. Award-winning advertising helped to make the drink trendy and so make it appeal to a younger market segment, and it lives on today.

In the decline stage, everything starts to wind down. Product ranges and features are cut to a minimum with unprofitable products and less popular features being phased out. The customer has a lot less choice. Expensive promotion is unlikely to be worthwhile. Less busy or profitable distributors may be dropped. The demand is likely to be very **price elastic** and so prices need to stay low. The exception to this is when a product has built a highly loyal following (perhaps it has gained the status of a cult product) when people may be prepared to pay very high prices to obtain their beloved product before it disappears forever.

CRITICISMS OF THE MARKETING MIX

The mix has been at the heart of marketing since the 1960s, but it is not universally acclaimed. There are those who find the **4Ps** too limiting and so add further elements to the list. Some authors feel the fifth P should be packaging, others that it should be people. The element of 'people' is formally included in the **7Ps** of services marketing but packaging still moves around.

Jones and Vignali (1994) added an S, for service. It is today recognized that all products have a service element and that this is key to their acceptance and success (see Chapter 7). Customer service must be at the heart of a **marketing-orientated** organization and the responsibility of everyone in the company, not just the marketing team. Gronroos (1997) considered that to view service as another element of the marketing mix would be disastrous for an organization as it would isolate customer service as a distinct function apart from the rest of the organization.

Modern marketing stresses the importance of building good relationships with customers and intermediaries, and one problem with the marketing mix is that it emphasizes techniques rather than customers and their needs. We could see relationship building as part of promotion; however, this brings a danger of inducing customer cynicism. Card-based **loyalty schemes** are viewed by many as mere **sales promotion** – and customers are likely to have cards, and collect points, from all competitors.

The marketing mix has occasionally evolved into other letters. For example, Lauterborn (1990) proposed the 4Cs:

▶ customer needs and wants

▶ cost to the customer

▶ convenience

▶ communication.

The 4Cs have the advantage of being more customer focused. However, the 4Ps are indelibly lodged in the minds of several generations of marketers and are likely to be the preferred model for some time to come.

SUMMARY

Most marketing plans rely heavily on the marketing mix for their implementation. The 4Ps has been the most commonly used framework for many years but this is extended to 7Ps when considering services marketing. As so many products now have service elements to them (warranties, guarantees, after-sales service, etc.), the **7Ps** framework has become more commonly used. Packaging is another important marketing tool and often proposed as the fifth P. Although it remains the most popular framework, the **4Ps** model is not without its critics, mainly on the grounds that it is insufficiently customer focused.

The marketing mix should be integrated, each element working with the others to present a united front and support the organization's marketing objectives. An uncoordinated mix sends conflicting messages to target customers and is much less effective in terms of marketing goals.

Challenges reviewed

Now that you have finished reading the chapter, look back at the challenges you were set at the beginning. Do you have a clearer idea of what's involved?

Hints:

▶ the marketing mix must be integrated so all elements should support the organization's desired position in its market

▶ price is seen as a determinant of quality

▶ consumer trust is harder to establish when the product in question is intangible

▶ the 7Ps of services marketing are key determinants of the attractiveness of services to customers.

READING AROUND

book chapters

Chaston, I. (2001) E-services marketing, Chapter 12 in Chaston, I., *E-marketing Strategy*, McGraw-Hill.

Slater, J.S. (1999) Product packaging: the silent salesman, Chapter 42 in Jones, J.P., *The Advertising Business*, Sage Publications.

journal articles

Gronroos, C. (1997) From marketing mix to relationship marketing – towards a paradigm shift in marketing, *Management Decision* 35.

Joachimsthaler, E. and Aaker, D. (1999) Building brands without mass media, *Harvard Business Review on Brand Management*, Harvard Business School Press (originally published in the *Harvard Business Review*, Jan–Feb 1997), 1–22.

website

www.cim.co.uk

SELF-REVIEW QUESTIONS

1. What are the 4Ps? (see page 330)

2. What are the 7Ps? (see page 339)

3. Where does packaging fit in the marketing mix model? (see page 337)

4. What are the five 'hallmarks of an effective marketing mix'? (see page 329–30)

5. Name, and describe, the levels of the total product offering. (see page 331)

6. What are the main tools of the promotional mix? (see page 333)

7. What is another name for 'promotion'? (see page 333)

8. How can packaging give a product a competitive advantage? (see page 337)

9. What is ambience? What might contribute to it? (see page 339)

10. Why is it especially important to build customer trust when you are selling services? (see page 339)

11. Why is it important that all elements of the marketing mix match and support each other? (see page 342)

12. What faults can you find with the marketing mix as a framework for marketing activity? (see page 345)

MINI CASE STUDY

Read the questions, then the case material, than answer the questions.

Questions

1. Identify, and explain, examples of the 7Ps at work in the case study.
2. What is Rock Planet doing well? Where does it fall down?
3. Using the 7Ps to guide you, recommend three improvements the restaurant could make. You should explain and justify your ideas.

Rock Planet

The Rock Planet restaurant opened with a burst of publicity and a celebrity launch party just over a year ago. For the first few months it was the place to eat, although even then there were mutterings about slow service and rude waiters. Now it's a familiar London landmark, particularly popular with tourists who like the inexpensive set lunch menu. Its reasonable prices and rock star connections also attract the young for celebrations such as birthdays and leaving parties. The bouncers look formidable, but they've never been known to refuse anyone entrance unreasonably.

The restaurant is usually full, so diners wait in the bar, which is loud and crowded. A 1960s-style jukebox adds to the din. Customers get a Rock Planet buzzer, one of five designs (each a model of an artist), which lights up and sings when their table is ready. Flamboyant waiters shake cocktails in dramatic style against a backdrop of rock memorabilia. Electric guitars adorn the walls alongside pictures of their famous former owners. One of Jimi Hendrix's guitars has pride of place above the bar. To its right, under thick glass, is a scrap of paper on which John Lennon jotted some of the words to 'She Loves You'. On the left is Badly Drawn Boy's hat.

The rock décor is carried through to the restaurant, as is the music. All the waiters are young and dressed up. There are the teddy boy suits and the flared skirts and short socks of the 1950s, glam rock, grunge and some of the latest club styles. The restaurant serves fast food American style: hamburgers (and a veggie burger), fries, salads, chicken and ribs. It also does take-aways and delivers within a five-mile radius.

The biggest complaint is that food doesn't come to the table fast enough – something that is rubbed in by the lights that flash on a neon map of the USA to tell the waiters when an order is ready for collection. However, many diners find the friendly service makes up for their building hunger. And they tend to order more drinks. Home-delivery customers have to order at least two hours before they want the food.

Rock Planet is a place where people like to celebrate their birthdays and so the staff have a birthday routine. They dance through the restaurant carrying sparklers and then, when they reach the birthday table, they sing 'Happy Birthday' and encourage the rest of the diners to join in. The birthday boy or girl is presented with a cup cake with an everlasting candle on it and a small bag of inexpensive Rock Planet merchandise.

Further entertainment comes from the Rock Planet Moments. Each day, the manager chooses three dishes to be the special commendations of the day. When the 20th order for that dish is delivered to a table, there is a fanfare and lights flash. The lucky diner gets the featured dish on the house and a complimentary cocktail (alcoholic or non-alcoholic) of their choice. For the 50th order, the diner gets their whole meal free.

Very lucky diners may get to sit at a table next to the stars. The restaurant is owned by a group of well-known musicians who make a point of eating there as often as possible. Sometimes, you might even get 'Happy Birthday' sung by a megastar.

One of the biggest challenges for the management is keeping the place clean. It's a large, busy restaurant and lots of children eat there. Inevitably this means that there are spills and it can be hard to get them cleaned up while people are eating. The toilets are checked every hour but they still sometimes run out of towels or soap. The floor seems always in need of a clean. The problem in the bar is even worse. Staff have trouble fighting their way to tables to collect glasses and wipe down tabletops. A dropped tray of glasses means dangerous glass on the floor, so staff are reluctant to collect too many at once. Frequently the bar staff run out of clean glasses altogether.

Rock Planet has had some bad reviews recently.

Critics say the food is unimaginative and of low quality, the restaurant too loud and too dirty, the service too slow and the waiters often get the orders, or the bill, wrong. But apparently the diners disagree – it's still packed out every night.

REFERENCES

Christopher, M. (2000) Customer service and logistics strategy, in Baker, M.J. (ed.) *The Marketing Book*, Butterworth Heinemann.

Gronroos, C. (1997) From marketing mix to relationship marketing – towards a paradigm shift in marketing', *Management Decision* 35.

Jones, P. and Vignali, C. (1994) Commercial education, *Journal of Retail Education*.

Lauterborn, R. (1990) New marketing litany: four Ps passe; C-words take over, *Advertising Age* 26.

McCarthy, J.C. (1960) *Basic Marketing: A Managerial Approach*, Irwin.

O'Connor, J. and Galvin, E. (2001) *Marketing in the Digital Age*, FT Prentice Hall.

Parasuraman, Z.a.B. *et al.* (1988) SERVQUAL: a multiple-item scale for measuring customer perceptions of service quality, *Journal of Retailing*.

Pickton, D. and Broderick, A. (2001) *Integrated Marketing Communications*, FT Prentice Hall.

Pincott, G. and Branthwaite, A. (2000) Nothing new under the sun? *International Journal of Market Research* 42.

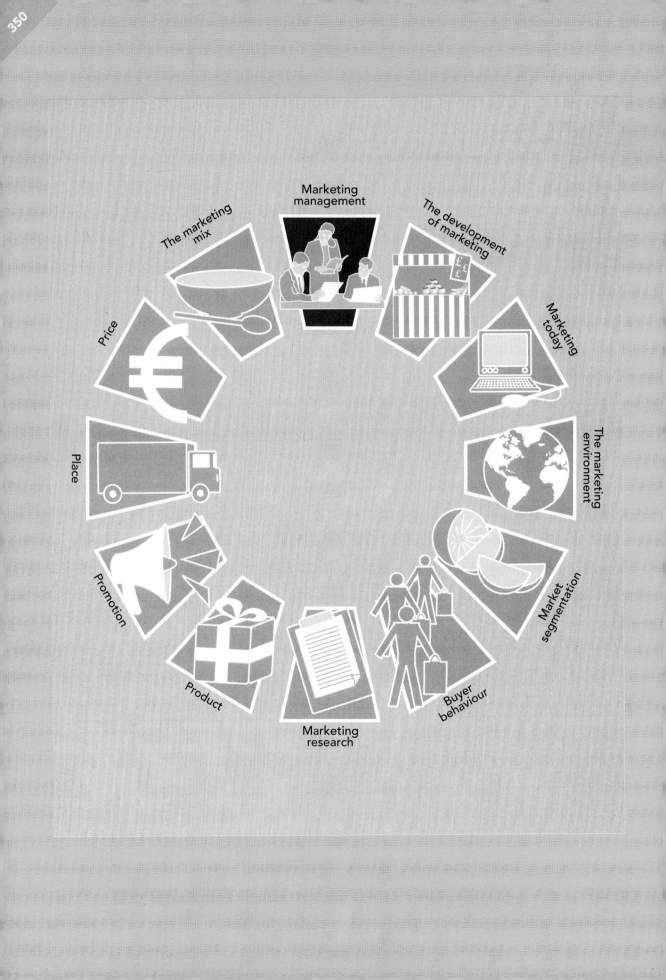

Marketing
management

The development
of marketing

Marketing
today

The marketing
environment

Market
segmentation

Buyer
behaviour

Marketing
research

Product

Promotion

Place

Price

The marketing
mix

THE MARKETERS

WHAT THIS PART IS ABOUT:

The final section of this book draws together all the previous areas and shows what marketers really do with the resources at their disposal. It takes a practical approach to marketing management and planning, and then looks at some of the different roles within the marketing function.

CHAPTER 12

MARKETING MANAGEMENT

BY TRACY HARWOOD

MARKETING MANAGEMENT CHALLENGES

The following are illustrations of the types of decision that marketers have to take or issues they face. *You aren't expected to know how to deal with the challenges now*; just bear them in mind as you read the chapter and see what you can find that helps.

▶ Your uncle runs a shoe factory that is struggling to compete with cheaper, developing-world manufacturers. He knows you've done a business course so he invites you to a management meeting to discuss the way forward. Do you have anything to contribute?

▶ A friend wants to start up her own company and needs a bank loan. The bank won't give her the loan without a marketing plan. She doesn't know how to write one. Can you help her?

▶ You run a medium-sized import/export agency. The international environment is turbulent and you are concerned that some of your markets, and sources of supply, will dry up. What should you be doing?

▶ You are the marketing director of a successful UK chain of restaurants. The company has money to put into expansion and you have been asked to present the options to the board.

▶ You work for a major British bank that is thinking of moving into the insurance market. You have to assess how well your bank is likely to be able to compete with the other insurance companies. How will you do this?

KEY CONCEPTS

marketing analysis
marketing budgets
marketing control
marketing management
marketing metrics
marketing planning
marketing objectives
marketing operations
marketing organization
marketing strategy
portfolio analysis
PRESTCOM analysis
product life cycle
SWOT analysis

CHAPTER OVERVIEW

INTRODUCTION

Marketing decisions are key drivers to success in the modern marketplace. Marketing has the power to influence every part of the business and affect how organizations meet the needs of their customers, how they respond to competitors, deal with suppliers and financiers, as well as how they treat their employees.

This chapter will consider marketing's place in the company's overall plan and how marketing can help the organization achieve its goals. It will cover the basic planning process and introduce some of the analysis tools that marketers use to help make those plans.

How organizations manage their marketing activities is affected by many factors, not least whether they are **marketing orientated** (see Chapter 2), what management style they choose to adopt, what preferences they have for organizational structure and the extent to which they carry out their planning as a **top-down approach** or a **bottom-up approach**.

Top-down or bottom-up?

The top-down process refers to the senior managers specifying objectives, budgets, strategies and plans that are passed down to operating functions to put into action. The bottom-up approach works in reverse. Objectives, budgets and plans are set at operational level and are passed up to senior management for approval and consolidation into the company's overall plans. Both processes have their advantages and disadvantages but they do not need to be mutually exclusive. It is possible to use both approaches together to avoid the problems that can occur when constructing plans in relative isolation.

Another consideration is the extent to which companies adopt an **outside-in approach** (Schultz, 1993) to their management and planning, in contrast to an **inside-out approach**. The former is outer-directed. The organization looks outward to focus on the needs of the marketplace to determine appropriate courses of marketing action. Customer perspectives are adopted and, as such, this approach corresponds with a strong marketing orientation, as discussed in Chapter 2. The latter is inner-directed and focuses on the needs of the organization first, and customers and the marketplace second. Clearly, a balance of the two is required if the basic outcomes of marketing are to be achieved as identified in the Chartered Institute of Marketing's definition:

hierarchical management structure

each manager has a set place within a vertical chain of command

exhibit 12.1

Focus of planning and management

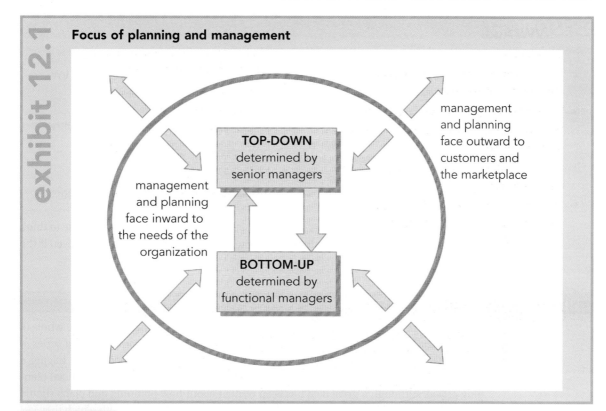

management and planning face outward to customers and the marketplace

TOP-DOWN
determined by senior managers

management and planning face inward to the needs of the organization

BOTTOM-UP
determined by functional managers

“Marketing is a management process responsible for identifying, anticipating and satisfying customer requirements profitably.”

Carrying out marketing well is not an easy task. The structure of organizations may make it difficult to coordinate and manage the different departments and specialisms as one entity. Management's response when faced with large, many-faceted tasks has been to divide them into sub-units (departments) in order to cope with the magnitude of operations. While project teams and cross-functional assignments can help to break down organizational barriers, there remain problems of **hierarchical management structures**, **vertical and horizontal communications**, **turf battles**, power struggles and **functional silos** (Shultz, 1993) in which individuals and groups (**stakeholders**, see Chapter 2) experience conflict as they protect their own specialization and interests. These stakeholders may be within the organization or outside it, and their vested interests can vary significantly.

Shareholders will be looking for profits and returns on investment. Suppliers will be looking for continuity of custom. Employees will want security, a good working environment and good wages. They will be concerned with fulfilling their own departmental objectives, which will differ between departments even though they may share the same organizational objectives, and so on.

Somehow, the organization as a whole, needs to balance these interests to achieve a level of satisfaction for all. An added complexity is that marketing departments frequently also make use of a wide variety of external agencies. These can be external researchers, marketing communications agencies and members of the distribution channels.

VW/Audi

The VW/Audi Group organizes itself in relation to its brands and principal activities. It is a very complex organization. There are separate marketing groups for each of its major brands: Audi, VW, SEAT, Škoda and Bentley (among others). There is a separate marketing department for VW Commercial Vehicles and another that handles VW Finance. Within the departments, there are internal marketing staff based at headquarters and regional marketing staff throughout the country. Each brand has its own dedicated dealership. If that is not complicated enough, each of the marketing departments deals with its own external agencies. For example, one of the smaller departments, VW Commercial Vehicles, has 12 agencies with whom it works, which range from advertising, PR, sales promotions and media buying, to research, a call centre and a fulfilment agency.

If you thought marketing was only about satisfying customers, now is the time to think again; the management of marketing is very much more complicated than that, even if the final result may be described in terms of customer satisfaction.

THE MARKETING PLANNING PROCESS AND MARKETING MANAGEMENT

Marketing management and planning is part of a wider activity that involves the whole of the organization. The output of the total planning process is the production of a series of plans covering the various functional areas of the business. Such plans, while having a longer-term focus, usually cover a 12-month duration to coincide with the financial planning period. Although a great deal has been written about how planning and plans should be developed, organizations and their managers tend to adopt processes with which they feel most comfortable. Sometimes this results in plans not always being fully documented.

At its highest level, the organization has to set its corporate (business) mission and goals that act as an overall direction for the business. To achieve these goals, each of the functional areas within each of the **strategic business units (SBUs)** (if an organization has them) needs to set their own plans involving objectives, strategies and tactics. In the 'insight' box illustrating the VW/Audi Group, each of the brands makes up a different SBU for the Group. As pointed out earlier, the approach can be top-down or bottom-up or a combination of the two. For this reason, the arrows shown in Exhibit 12.2 point in both directions. Collectively, the plans for production, finance, marketing, human resource management, etc. form the composite that becomes the plan for the SBU. The plans for the SBUs come together to create the corporate plan for the organization as a whole. For companies that do not have SBUs, the functional plans simply form the basis of the corporate plan. It is important to recognize that

strategic business unit (SBU)

a distinct part of an organization which has an external market for its products and services

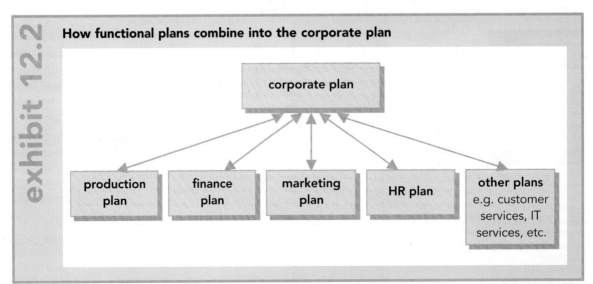

exhibit 12.2

How functional plans combine into the corporate plan

corporate plan

production plan | finance plan | marketing plan | HR plan | other plans e.g. customer services, IT services, etc.

marketing planning does not take place in isolation from the rest of the organization but is an integral part of it.

The process for setting each plan is similar but we will concentrate solely on the marketing management and planning process.

There are five basic questions that need to be answered in marketing management and planning:

▶ Where are we now?

▶ Where do we want to be?

▶ How are we going to get there?

▶ Are we getting there?

▶ Have we arrived?

While there are a variety of marketing planning process models, there is general agreement on the stages involved that relate directly to the five basic questions. They are presented in Exhibit 12.3. These stages enable marketers to produce plans that form the basis of how the company will approach and operate in the marketplace.

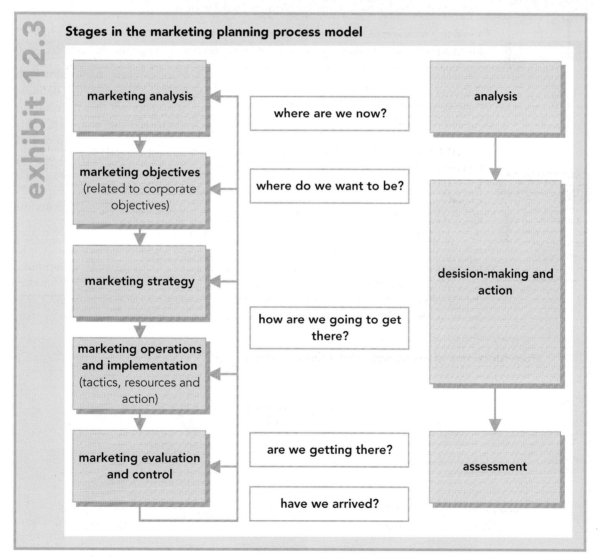

exhibit 12.3

Stages in the marketing planning process model

marketing analysis

where are we now?

analysis

marketing objectives
(related to corporate objectives)

where do we want to be?

marketing strategy

desision-making and action

how are we going to get there?

marketing operations and implementation
(tactics, resources and action)

marketing evaluation and control

are we getting there?

assessment

have we arrived?

Exhibit 12.3 illustrates how the evaluation and control of marketing activities feeds back into the rest of the planning process to check that current plans are being achieved on an ongoing basis, that they have been achieved (or not) at the end of the planning period and to provide a basis for the development of future plans. The feedback process (frequently known as **tracking**) allows plans to be modified as necessary throughout the planning period. It is important to understand what works and why. If there have been changes in the marketing environment, perhaps competitor activity has changed, then the plans need to take account of these changes and the marketing activities modified as appropriate. Changes to plans may be at the strategic level or at the more operational, tactical level. The tactical level of marketing is often thought of as the use of the marketing mix elements and this is a useful simplification that you might find helpful. Aspects of marketing strategy that are broad-level decisions are considered later in this chapter.

Within the overall framework of the planning process model, there are a number of marketing management tools that can be used at the different stages in order to aid analysis and managerial decision-making. They help us achieve what is, basically, a systematic approach to identifying and analysing competitive advantage in the marketplace for our products, i.e. goods and services, thus helping to achieve long-term benefits for companies. Let us now examine each of the stages in the model in turn.

MARKETING ANALYSIS – WHERE ARE WE NOW?

Marketing analysis involves an understanding of the how the company is operating in its business environment. It comprises a complex set of factors that affect marketing decisions and plans, and ultimately affects business performance. It is important that the company monitors itself and its environment in order to prepare for future activities and, particularly, build and maintain **competitive advantage**. This type of analysis is not just a one-off, never to be repeated activity but something that successful businesses do on an ongoing basis. So important is this area of marketing management that a whole chapter has already been devoted to it that readers might want to reacquaint themselves with (see Chapter 3). Some overview points are presented here to show how and why marketing analysis fits into the marketing management and planning process.

In thinking systematically about marketing analysis, it maybe helpful to consider a sporting analogy, for example, a tennis match (see Exhibit 12.4).

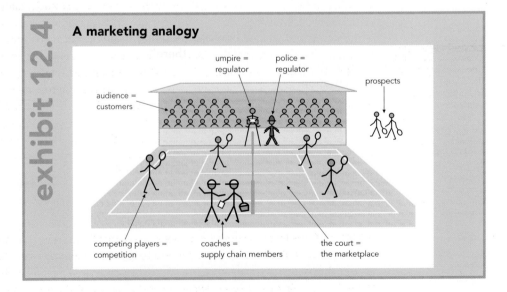

exhibit 12.4

A marketing analogy

umpire = regulator

police = regulator

prospects

audience = customers

competing players = competition

coaches = supply chain members

the court = the marketplace

▶ The sports ground, including car park, changing areas, stadium and play area or pitch, is the environment.

▶ The marked areas on the pitch indicate where you can play the game, i.e. the marketplace.

▶ There are specific rules for playing the game and entering certain areas of the pitch, as well as for how long the game will last. This could represent government and industry regulations. Some rules will apply to the car park, where other forms of competitive behaviour are going on (such as between fans or customers discussing who will play best), or the governing bodies debating new rules for the pitch. Although the car park games do not affect you immediately, they could do if customers support competitors or new rules come into force.

▶ Each weekend you will play opposite a different team in your league. This is your competition and, even though you do not play against the same team every week, the cumulative scores for each team in the league will determine who wins outright, who goes up to the next league and who drops out.

▶ The performance of individual players, from all teams in your own league and others, also has a key role and there is likely to be much activity around securing the best ones for your game – the more you offer them, the more likely you are to acquire the best ones!

▶ You may have different umpires, i.e. economic, social and technological forces, who see different events on the pitch and penalize or support you accordingly.

▶ As your team moves up the league, you will attract a bigger crowd who become more actively involved in your game. These could represent your customers, your potential customers who are there in support of the competition, and also those who just like to watch the game in order to report on aspects of it – these represent industry watchers.

▶ Your team will not only include all the company employees (and some of those may be giving inside information to the opposition) but it will also include your suppliers and distributors, and you will possibly invite some of your best customers on for guest appearances. These make up the membership of your supply chain – individuals and companies that it is particularly important you keep happy in order to continue trading successfully.

With the advent of databases and the growth in marketing research data, there is a wealth of information available to marketers, who are increasingly being required to assess their performance and measure the effectiveness and efficiency of marketing activities, this has been called **marketing metrics**. Marketing is an expense to any organization – a necessary one, but an expense none the less. It is important that measurement systems are in place to analyse the value of marketing and to use those systems to improve marketing performance in the future. This information is fed into the analysis process from the marketing evaluation and control mechanisms that form part of the total marketing planning process.

There are a variety of tools and approaches that can be used in marketing analysis. Readers should familiarize themselves with some of the more important ones, as identified below.

marketing metrics
measurements that help with the quantification of marketing performance, such as market share, advertising spend, and response rates elicited by advertising and direct marketing (source: CIM)

PRESTCOM and SWOT analysis

PRESTCOM was first introduced in Chapter 3 as a tool that can be systematically applied to analyse an organization's internal and external environment. External factors are usually outside the control of an organization or else they are only likely to have limited control over them. Internal factors are completely under the control of the organization. PRESTCOM is a mnemonic to remind us of the main areas that should be analysed by organizations. It stands for Political, Regulatory, Economic, Social, Technological, Competitor, Organizational and Market factors.

Having identified the key factors impinging on an organization, a SWOT analysis can then be undertaken to identify which of the factors represent the organization's Strengths and Weaknesses as part of the internal environment, and which of the factors represent Opportunities and Threats to the organization. Opportunity and Threat analysis can be made more meaningful by using Opportunity and Threat matrices in which the likelihood of the factor occurring and the potential impact it might have can be assessed. For example, if a threat is not likely to occur, or if it does, its impact is assessed as minimal, then this can probably be ignored or relegated as being of low concern. If an opportunity has low cost implications, is within the capabilities of the organization and is likely to be very profitable with limited competitive interference, then it might be a good opportunity to pursue.

Porter's five forces model

In analysing competitive activity, a useful tool is **Porter's five forces model**, which was described in Chapter 3. This model enables businesses to analyse their competitive environment by focusing particularly on the competition and the bargaining power in the supply chain – suppliers through to customers. Assessment can be made of the intensity of competition and the threat of new competitive entrants, the threat of substitute products, and the bargaining power of suppliers and customers.

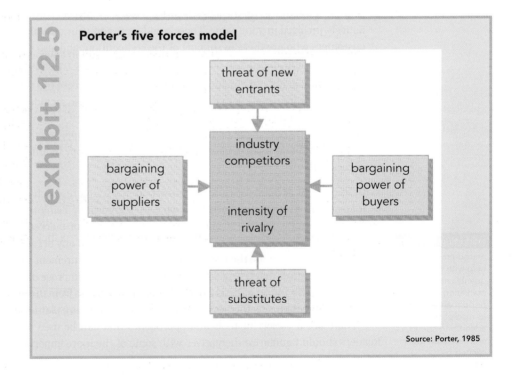

exhibit 12.5   **Porter's five forces model**

Source: Porter, 1985

Suppliers are powerful when:

▶ there are few other sources of supply for the company

▶ the suppliers threaten to integrate up the supply chain, in effect becoming a direct competitor to the company

▶ the costs of switching to other suppliers is great

▶ the company's business is not key to the supplier.

Customers (*buyers*) are powerful when:

▶ there are few main buyers in the marketplace

▶ products are commoditized or standardized, i.e. there is little or no differentiation from the customer's perspective

▶ the company is not a key supplier to the customer.

The threat of *substitution* may be determined by:

▶ the pricing of substitute products and, therefore, the sensitivity of customers to pricing

▶ the costs of the customer switching to a competitive product are low

▶ the customer has a high propensity to substitute.

The threat of *new entrants* to the marketplace may be determined by how high the barriers to entry are. These may include:

▶ the costs of producing for the marketplace

▶ the capital expenditure required to establish a business

▶ access to appropriate distribution

▶ the reaction of existing competitors.

The intensity of *rivalry* between competitors may depend on:

▶ the number of competitors in the market – the more there are, the more intense the competitive activity

▶ the cost structure – high capital investment may result in lower costs because management will want to ensure that its machinery operates at optimum capacity, rather than laying idle, waiting for orders

▶ the differential advantages between products, i.e. those products perceived by customers to be differentiated are less likely to attract competitive behaviour

▶ the costs involved in customers switching to competing products – if these are high, then customers are less likely to switch, negating the need for such intense rivalry

▶ the strategic objectives being pursued by the competitors – if a competitor is holding or harvesting its products, then it is not as concerned with highly competitive behaviour

▶ the exit barriers, i.e. if these are low, then more competition will be encouraged into the market, resulting in highly active competitive behaviour as they try to gain market share.

activity

Imagine you are the manager of your favourite football team ... Apply Porter's five forces model to identify who has the greatest power in your market. Consider:

▶ who potential entrants into your market could be

▶ who the competition is and how competitive the game is

▶ who could be a substitute for your team

▶ who your suppliers are, what they supply you with and how important they are

▶ who your customers are, what they buy from you and how important they are to you and your team.

Competitor analysis and marketing information systems

It is particularly important to understand how the company's products compare with those of the competition. **Competitor analysis** is, therefore, a significant part of the process of understanding whether or not the products marketed by a company have a sustainable advantage in the marketplace. This is not something that should be done just once at the launch of a new product or service, but should be undertaken on a continuous basis throughout the life of the product. It is important because it is something that customers and potential customers will also be doing and, if they find that a competing product is better value for money . . . well, what would you do?

The process of competitor analysis must involve an analysis of the strengths and weaknesses of competitive products and, usefully, some identification of the costs and quality issues they have. It may involve some form of **benchmarking** – this is where companies compare themselves to the best-in-class companies in their industry, typically the market leader. The purpose of this is to identify areas for potential improvement. A useful tool for this has been developed by Hooley *et al.* (1998) (see Exhibit 12.6).

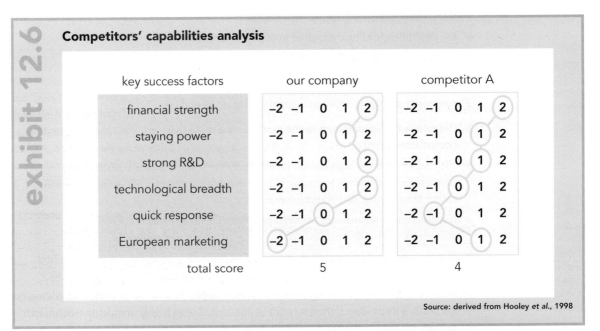

exhibit 12.6

Competitors' capabilities analysis

key success factors	our company	competitor A
financial strength	–2 –1 0 1 (2)	–2 –1 0 1 (2)
staying power	–2 –1 0 (1) 2	–2 –1 0 (1) 2
strong R&D	–2 –1 0 1 (2)	–2 –1 0 (1) 2
technological breadth	–2 –1 0 1 (2)	–2 –1 (0) 1 2
quick response	–2 –1 (0) 1 2	–2 (–1) 0 1 2
European marketing	(–2) –1 0 1 2	–2 –1 0 (1) 2
total score	5	4

Source: derived from Hooley *et al.*, 1998

The issues around analysing the competition are discussed further in Chapter 3.

Competing companies market their products in a similar way to the company using the elements of the **marketing mix** (the 4Ps or 7Ps). It is important to understand not only how competitors succeed in the market but also how they fail. You can learn from their mistakes just as well as your own and it is a lot cheaper! This sort of information can be gathered by talking to customers and other industry or market 'informants'. Sources may include the press, suppliers or other competitors with whom you have contact. Very often, companies will attend high-profile conferences and trade exhibitions with a view to gathering **competitive intelligence** quite openly, although some may engage in underhand corporate espionage (the latter is obviously not ethical or, indeed, recommended). Clearly the closer you are to market intelligence, the better you will be able to make decisions – third- or fourth-hand data can be twisted out of all recognition, not unlike a game of Chinese whispers, and result in ineffective decision-making.

Recently, Souhami (2003) has argued that companies must stop 'staring at the same information and get the most out of competitor intelligence'. Souhami argues that 'competi-

competitive intelligence

information on rivals, their products and environments compared with one's own

tive myopia' sets in when companies do not monitor their competitors systematically, which involves continuously gathering up-to-date information. An approach to systematic gathering and disseminating competitive intelligence together with other relevant marketing information is referred to as a Marketing Information System (MkIS). For a review of a MkIS see the insight box.

insight

MkIS

The Marketing Information System (MkIS) comprises four components:

1. internal continuous data, gathered from continual analysis of the business from, e.g. financial accounts and salesforce productivity records

2. internal ad hoc data, from analyses undertaken of specific events within the business, e.g. to see how well a particular promotion has performed

3. environmental scanning, from monitoring the business environment (PRESTCOM factors), and

4. marketing research, undertaken either continuously or as needed for particular purposes on an ad hoc basis to determine such things as customer attitudes to and opinions on product offerings.

The data derived from these activities is distilled and disseminated to the right people at the right time in order for them to make optimum strategic, tactical or operational decisions. The sheer amount of data now available to managers in modern times, however, highlights particular management issues. Imagine all the sources of information: TV, web, spoken (recorded and conversation) word, videoconferences, written word, reports, publications, industry analyses, trade and press articles, internal documents. Consider how difficult it is to extract the wheat from the chaff, i.e. identify what is important.

Data was originally managed manually and sometimes with the assistance of press cuttings agencies, who helped companies to gather data. Now, the growth in the range of media, facilitated by the development and growth of technologies, has resulted in the development of specialist computer software, e.g. SAS Textminer (www.sas.co.uk). This software helps manage the extraction of key information using techniques that industry frequently refers to as 'data integration management' (Proctor, 2002). The use of such a wide array of data has given rise to the general term 'database marketing'. It is frequently thought of in relation to customer data but need not be so confined.

Schultz (1997) comments:

❛❛To integrate marketing you must integrate sales and selling, and to integrate those functions, you must integrate the entire organization ... The goal is to align the organisation to serve consumers and customers. Databases are rapidly becoming the primary management tool that drives the organisation's business strategy.❞❞

Today's databases are very much more than simple customer listings. Computing power has created the ability to store and cross-analyse vast amounts of data, such as service and sales data, purchasing records, and attitudinal and behavioural data. There are many fields of data, covering millions of transactions and relationships. Without this information, it is unlikely that truly integrated marketing could exist. It is the heart of a marketing intelligence system. Exhibit 12.7 illustrates an overview of the MkIS.

The aim with an efficient and successful MkIS is to turn data into information that, in turn, needs to be turned into management knowledge and action.

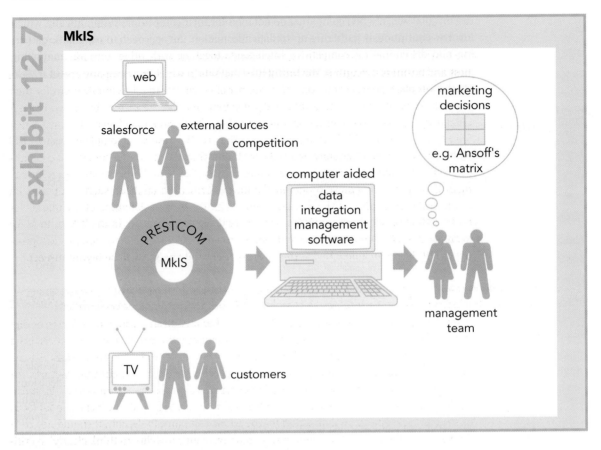

exhibit 12.7

MkIS

web

salesforce external sources

competition

PRESTCOM
MkIS

computer aided

data integration management software

marketing decisions

e.g. Ansoff's matrix

management team

TV   customers

Product life cycle (PLC) analysis

Product Life Cycle

a product analysis tool based on the idea that a product has life stages: introduction, growth, maturity, decline and deletion

The **PLC** was introduced in Chapter 7 and elaborated upon in Chapter 11, which should be read for more details. It is based on the idea that products, like people, go through different stages in their lives. As a product reaches a new stage, particular emphasis is placed on different aspects of the marketing mix. During launch, for example, promotion becomes important to make potential customers aware of the new product. Before the decline stage begins, it is possible to re-invigorate the product with a new, improved version, and so on. It is, therefore, important to have a realistic understanding of where a product is currently situated in its life cycle in order to develop appropriate marketing plans for its future. This is not to suggest that this is an easy task. Identifying exactly where a product is on the PLC requires an understanding of past sales and a prediction of future sales. The PLC, itself, is not a predictive tool.

Portfolio analysis

While the PLC is a useful tool for looking at individual products, it is also necessary to think very carefully and strategically about the company's range of products and how they relate to one another as well as to competing offerings. An approach known as **product portfolio analysis** is helpful here and a number of different tools are available. These can be used to analyse individual products as well as the strategic divisions within companies called SBUs (strategic business units).

   As with the product life cycle, portfolio analysis has already been covered in Chapter 7. Briefly, we can identify two portfolio tools here. One is the **Boston Consultancy Group (BCG) matrix** or the Boston Box, so called because the analysis places products (or SBUs) in a 2 × 2 box whose axes are relative market share and market growth rate. Another tool is the **General Electric (GE) matrix**, initially devised by McKinsey & Co during its work with the General Electric Company in America, and whose axes are industry/market attractiveness and business strength in the industry or markets in which the company operates. Both these tools place products into one of a number of categories that has implications for their competitive positioning, their strategic development and their resource allocation. The significance of this type of analysis is that companies should seek to achieve a balanced portfolio (just as one would do in financial investment). The resultant completed matrix will place all the relevant company products or SBUs within the matrix for an overall comparison of their positions. Some products will be very profitable and others will require investment if they are to achieve profits in the future. Critical to analyses such as these is an accurate determination of the markets operated in. Too broad a definition of the market for each product or SBU being analysed will render the analysis invalid. In the BCG matrix, for example, it is *relative* market share and market growth rate that are important for each product or SBU being included. Define the markets badly and analysis will be highly suspect.

BUSINESS MISSION AND OBJECTIVES – WHERE DO WE WANT TO BE?

Just as you set out on your studies to obtain a higher qualification, such as a degree or diploma, in order to become, perhaps, a marketing management expert, successful advertising executive or an entrepreneur, so a business will set out to achieve some broad aims. A **business mission**, or vision as it is sometimes called, is an explicit statement that captures the broad aims of the company. This is used to communicate those broad aims to all its stakeholders, both internal and external. Its purpose, ideally, is to provide an inspirational focus or strategic and operational direction for the whole company. Preferably, it should not be 'a long awkward sentence that demonstrates management's inability to think clearly', a criticism laid by Dilbert, one of the greatest cartoon characters who ever poked fun at business and management.

There are a number of general components to a good business mission statement. It should:

▶ identify the company's philosophy, i.e. its approach to business

▶ specify its product–market domain, i.e. where the company will operate in the marketplace

▶ communicate key values for those involved, i.e. how it will operate

▶ be closely linked to critical success factors, i.e. the things the company has to be good at to survive.

insight

Mission possible . . . ?

Nike's mission statement is:

❝To bring inspiration and innovation to every athlete* in the world.❞

This appears quite narrow since it implies customers are purely those competitive athletes. Its market, however, extends much wider. Do you own Nike clothing? Why? Perhaps you consider yourself to be a competitive sportsperson? No? Its purpose is, of course, not to limit its market to competitive sportspeople only. So, in order to qualify what it means by 'athlete' (notice the asterisk in the mission statement), it goes on to use a quote from one of its legendary role models and co-founder of the company, Bill Bowerman: *'If you have a body, you are an athlete.'

This very cleverly puts Nike into the domain of every person in the world. It implies some of the components outlined in this section and it clearly incorporates the core values of the senior management.

To explore the many global Nike brands and products, go to www.nike.com.

For more about Nike's business and to read more about its mission statement, go to www.nike.com/nikebiz.

Source: www.nike.com

Compare Nike's mission (in the insight box) with that of the global activist organization Greenpeace (www.greenpeace.org), whose mission statement is as follows.

66 Greenpeace is an independent non-profit global campaigning organization that uses non-violent, creative confrontation to expose global environmental problems and their causes. We research the solutions and alternatives to help provide a path for a green and peaceful future. 99

This is less succinct than Nike's statement, but still incorporates the main components of a mission.

It also qualifies its statement and goes on to say:

66 Greenpeace's goal is to ensure the ability of the earth to nurture life in all its diversity. 99

GREENPEACE

activity

Write a mission statement for yourself, incorporating the components outlined above. Remember, you do not have to have a sentence for each of these components – consider Nike's and Greenpeace's missions.

This, again, clearly implies what the organization is trying to achieve and incorporates the strong beliefs that we know and see in some of its highly creative, attention-seeking behaviour reported in the news.

According to Levitt (1960), who is responsible for having created the concept of the business mission, in order to develop an appropriate mission a company's managers should ask some basic questions such as 'What business are we in?' 'What business should we be in?' and 'What business can we be in?' The answers should be given in terms of customer needs, rather than the products the company makes (and are, therefore, another good indicator of marketing orientation). See the example in Exhibit 12.8.

This type of extrapolation enables a company to identify much broader-based competition and think about how it could be more competitive and avoid 'marketing myopia' (Levitt, 1960). Marketing myopia is where a company forgets that a customer wants a product to solve a problem. The classic example highlighted by Levitt is a drill – he states that the customer actually wants the holes it makes. This can be taken further, however, because in fact customers do not usually want holes in walls, they want hooks for pictures or brackets for shelves.

exhibit 12.8

Defining the business

Traditional definitions of business	Customer need-based definitions
railways	transportation
gas	energy
computers	information processing
photocopiers	office productivity

Source: Piercy, 2002

Thinking about products in this way also gives the company greater scope in its development of new products, as well as highlighting the full range of products that may be competing for its customers.

Consider the computing example and how narrowly defined the view of a traditional computer is: it is a rigid, plastic box containing various electrical and silicon-based components, it has a screen and requires a keyboard and sometimes a mouse to produce some output, based on some input from the user. The customer, however, is really only interested in the output – hence, the need is identified as information processing. Information processing can be achieved by a traditional computer or other form of silicon-enabled technology (e.g. a laptop, a palmtop, a PDA, a calculator, a mobile phone or perhaps in the future a home entertainment system including TV). It can, however, also be achieved by a clever person, i.e. without any need for silicon-based intervention!

activity

Can you identify any other types of customer need than information processing for the computer product? Think of how and why you use your own personal computer.

None the less, information processing is only one need that computers fulfil. What else could customers be interested in?

The process of identifying what business it is in, and could be in, will enable a company to develop an appropriate business mission. Having decided on a business mission, a company will use this to inform and develop its business objectives from which it will decide on specific strategies. The next paragraphs look at how business and marketing objectives are formulated, based on a systematic analysis of the marketplace.

Objectives should conform to three basic conventions (Walker *et al.*, 1992).

1. What performance dimensions should the company and employees focus on?
2. What is the target level of performance for each of these dimensions?
3. What is the time frame in which the targets should be achieved?

In addition, it is clear that objectives need to be achievable and, therefore, a well-known acronym that captures these conventions is **SMART** (Specific, Measurable, Achievable, Relevant and Timed).

The following are examples of typical business and marketing objectives that a company may specify:

▶ to develop and implement marketing plans for launching the Cherryblobs product line into Europe within two years

▶ to become the number one supplier of Cherryblobs in the target market within five years

▶ to develop a new product development programme for Cherryblobs by end of year

▶ to gain a 40 per cent level of awareness of Cherryblob advertising within nine months of launch

▶ to achieve 15 per cent profitability for Cherryblobs by end of quarter three.

Of course, the business and marketing objectives must be informed by a thorough analysis of the current market position.

Having set objectives, the next section will look at setting strategies to achieve them.

MARKETING STRATEGY – HOW ARE WE GOING TO GET THERE (STRATEGICALLY)?

With a clear picture of the business environment and of the objectives it wishes to achieve, the company can now decide how it is going to take its business forward into the next trading period. It can think about this in terms of shorter or longer time periods. It is often much easier for managers to make decisions for the short term because they will have more detailed, and accurate, information about the marketplace.

Long-term decisions require managers to see into the future – longer-term success is about being visionary, reading the market, knowing the business well and, sometimes, getting lucky. Even Marks & Spencer's experienced managers have not been able to do this with complete accuracy or total success in the last ten years but, on the other hand, Stelios Haji-Ioannou of easyGroup fame has been an artful player.

The next paragraphs look at how some marketing management tools can be utilized to develop strategic direction for the business (Johnson and Scholes, 1998). It is the choice of strategic direction that provides focus for the company's longer-term continuation.

Porter's generic strategies

Porter's generic strategies is one model that provides an overview of strategic direction for the company (see Exhibit 12.9).

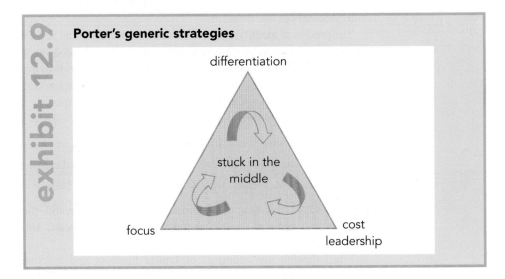

exhibit 12.9

Porter's generic strategies

differentiation

stuck in the middle

focus

cost leadership

It highlights that the company can pursue one of three main competitive strategic directions based on its identification of competitive forces and view of the market:

1. differentiation, where the company chooses to differentiate itself based on some competitive advantage it has identified, e.g. brand or service offering

2. cost leadership, where the company is able to offer low prices thanks to its low production costs

3. focus, where the company concentrates its efforts on a **niche** of the market.

If the company chooses to ignore these choices, or attempts to pursue two simultaneously, Porter argues that it could be in danger of being stuck in the middle, i.e. where it has no clear direction and merely reacts to market conditions, wandering between these three points, and is, therefore, vulnerable to competitive activities.

insight

MADE to win

Recently, a Graduate Enterprise company start-up, MADE, comprising six students from De Montfort University, entered the marketplace with a new 'street' branded clothing range. The GE scheme gives students an opportunity to run their own company for one year, supported by a range of expertise in business and marketing. Their first tentative steps to success were entirely due to their planning and implementation of the business objectives they had specified at the outset of their year. They remained tightly focused on a niche strategy, which required them to identify and align their brand with key influencers in their target market, including test marketing. They used a cult Radio 1 DJ in order to position their product and subsequently won a national award: Graduate Enterprise Company of the Year 2003. They are now looking to run their company for real.

So, the basic approaches outlined in this chapter can work just as well for entrepreneurs with new start-ups as they do for large established businesses.

Source: Opportunities@dmu

Ansoff's matrix

Ansoff's matrix is another management tool managers use to help decide on their strategic direction, or thrust. It looks at the product in relation to its market and helps managers to define the direction in which the business will grow.

exhibit 12.10

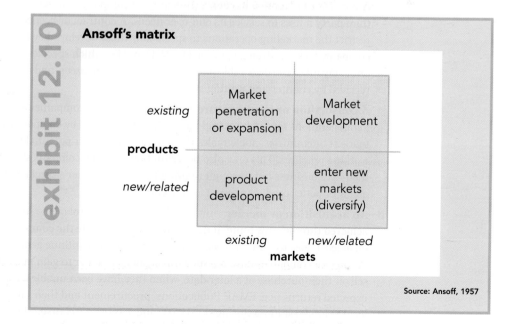

Ansoff's matrix

Source: Ansoff, 1957

▶ **Quadrant 1**: existing products in existing markets – *market penetration or expansion strategy*. This is about focusing effort in existing markets and encouraging existing customers to use the product more (more at each use, or more frequently, or use competing products less).

▶ **Quadrant 2**: new or related products for existing markets – *product development strategy*. Involves some element of product development or improvement for existing customers. Car manufacturers are continually striving to improve their products – consider, for example, the Ford Escort now replaced (mostly!) by the Ford Focus.

▶ **Quadrant 3**: existing products in new or related markets – *market development strategy*. This is about finding new uses for products or may involve launching into different geographic areas of the world. Lucozade was originally a drink for recuperating children but when the company found that mothers were using it as a 'pick-me-up' during the day, it decided to relaunch the product, which is now firmly established as a 'sports' drink.

▶ **Quadrant 4**: new or related products in new markets – *diversification strategy*. Taking new products into new markets is the hardest of the four directions from a company's perspective. This is because it involves moving into an area of business it is unfamiliar with and, hence, the risks of potential failure are high. The strategy works best when there is a close match with existing experiences.

Alternative strategic directions depend on the company's view of how much it wishes to control the activities related to the marketing of its products. Such expansion can be achieved through **vertical** or **horizontal integration**, which form different types of **strategic alliance**. Options include the following.

▶ **A network** – this is a loose association between a company and, for example, a series of distributors, such as pursued by many car manufacturers who sell through a range of different types of outlet. It could also be a network of agents, which is pursued by some companies when they enter an unfamiliar market or a new country. With a network, the company may have relatively little control over how the third party markets the products to end users, or how end users (consumers) are treated.

▶ **A contract or licence agreement** – here the company imposes conditions on the third party it uses to service its end-user needs. A contract or licence agreement may restrict the marketing operations to specifically those developed by the originating company. This is a strategy pursued by McDonald's, which specifies everything from outlet layout to the disposable packaging used by franchisees, and even the training received by counter and waiting staff.

▶ **A consortium or joint-venture** – where two or more companies agree to develop joint operations on a contractual basis. This may be used by companies entering new markets or countries, and enables them to maximize their potential by taking on local working practices. This may also be a situation whereby companies remain focused on their core business but, through utilization of each partner's specialisms, they develop a new or better product offering for the end user.

▶ **An acquisition or merger** – ultimately, complete control of the supply chain is achieved through this route. It does, however, necessitate the company to be cash rich or, at least, able to raise sufficient capital to invest and continue generating a profit. A number of companies have pursued this strategy in order to gain market share only to sell off their purchase at a later date, when they have been unable to realize the expected returns (e.g. EMAP Publications' procurement and then sale of a series of local FM radio stations during the 1980s and 1990s). Of course, the reason for a procurement or merger may be because a firm wants only a part of another company to add to existing operations, such as a brand name, or to achieve economies of scale by focusing on what each are good at, e.g. 3i's Go airline and easyJet merger in August 2002, whereby they have agreed both will use the easyJet flight booking system, among other things.

Competitive positioning

The company must further determine the position it wants in the marketplace, based on its assessment of the attractiveness of different market segments relative to business strengths. Positions the company may adopt include:

- ▶ leader
- ▶ challenger
- ▶ follower
- ▶ nicher.

b2bfocus

Too few cooks

Normally, b2b is about marketing to business customers, often with the aim of some form of alliance between them that benefits both parties. AWOL, a small recruitment company specializing in the placement of chefs and catering staff in the north-west of England, however, has a unique business problem: good-quality chefs are few and far between and notoriously prone to leaving jobs. Indeed, many are self-styled one-man businesses in their own right. So, as well as building relationships with restaurant and pub owners in its catchment area, who are the 'bread and butter' of AWOL's business, AWOL is also active in building strong relationships with its chefs. This means that as the chef rolls from one job he takes his recruitment company with him too, thus building a pyramid with a genuinely strong footing for the company.

This is a strategy of focused differentiation, which enables AWOL to retain its identity distinct from other recruitment agencies with both restauranteurs and chefs.

Source: Kim Brown, AWOL Recruitment (www.awolrecruitment.com)

Clearly, these positions will necessitate particular approaches to the market. For example, it would be anticipated that market leader or challenger positions will require aggressive defence or attacking behaviour of competitors' positions, actively choosing to engage in pricing or promotional wars; consider the quote 'It's far easier to stay on top than to get there' (Ries and Trout, 1986). Indeed, analogies between war and marketing have been extremely popular. On the other hand, a market follower is a company that is quite happy to take a background position, while a market nicher is one that focuses only on a small part of the overall market, thus avoiding direct attention or confrontation with the market leaders or challengers.

The application of marketing management tools enables the company to develop its strategic focus, by providing the detail behind the business objectives and strategies. In turn, these must be operationalized. The next section looks at marketing operations and implementation in more detail.

MARKETING OPERATIONS AND IMPLEMENTATION – HOW ARE WE GOING TO GET THERE (TACTICALLY)?

Operational and implementation decisions necessitate the blending of different elements of the company in order to achieve its goals; in other words, make it happen (still part of the 'How are we going to get there?' question). A framework for understanding the interaction between the different elements of a company in implementing strategy is McKinsey's 7S framework (see Exhibit 12.11).

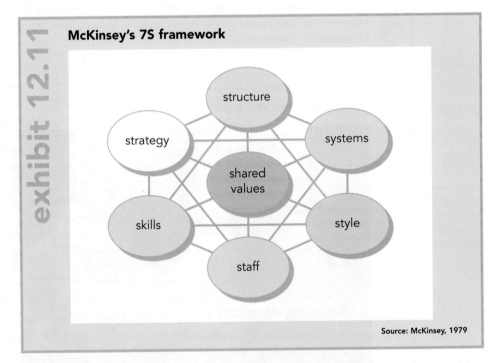

exhibit 12.11

McKinsey's 7S framework

Source: McKinsey, 1979

A company uses the particular Skills of many different Staff who require organizing (Structuring) in a way that maximizes their benefit to the company. The company uses different Systems in order to operate, e.g. computer systems, decision-making systems, work-processing systems. It adopts a distinct Style based on its leaders and historical culture, and all employees must Share values that are similar in order to meet the Strategic goals.

Making strategy happen, however, presents a distinct set of problems to many managers, which requires them to address change of one form or another within the company.

Change is something that few employees welcome with open arms because it generally means a painful moving of goal posts. Consider your own reaction to a plan for change in the structure of the programme of study you are currently following, e.g. 'We are no longer going to study business and marketing at this institution but have decided all our students will follow a course on mathematics. This is because we perceive future employers will only want those students who are mathematically literate.' It would not matter how much the decision is justifiable, there would still be a large number of students who would pursue their studies elsewhere. None the less, a negative attitude to change is something that managers must overcome in order to meet the strategic goals they have specified.

Successful implementation of strategy, therefore, necessitates an understanding of attitudes to change. People may resist change, support it or be uncertain about it.

Addressing issues such as this requires **internal marketing**. The purpose of internal marketing is to address the concerns and, therefore, needs of different groups or segments of employees. For some, concerns may come from a lack of information on the changes, while others may not possess the know-how or skills to act upon the changes proposed. Others may have both the knowledge and the know-how but lack the will power.

For each of these internal **segments**, management must inform, develop through appropriate training and incentivize appropriately. Needless to say, failure to implement successfully the changes proposed may ultimately result in the failure of the company or, at least, a swift change of position for those responsible for the failure. Failure may, however, be due to reasons other than a lack of support from employees. Quite simply, it may be the wrong strategic choice (see Exhibit 12.12 for possible reasons for failure).

---

exhibit 12.12

Reasons for failure in strategic planning

- lack of chief executive officer (CEO or MD) support
- too narrow an outlook
- irreversible decline of the company or market
- emphasis on *where* to complete, rather than *how* to compete
- 'me-too' instinct
- not enough emphasis on *when* to complete

- failure to take account of individuals within the company
- using the wrong measures of success
- managerial conflict
- lack of information, or wrong information, or information withheld from key decision-makers
- results of planning ignored

Source: Chartered Institute of Marketing, 2002

Internal marketing is an important activity that will enable a company to remain focused on the needs of its customers. As stated by Greene *et al.* (1994):

> ❝firms that do not or will not embrace the issues of internal marketing and incorporate those ingredients into their strategic marketing plan will see their market share and profit base erode. Internal promotion can create a positive and/or superior image of the firm and its products in the mind of the customer. ❞

Organizational structure

The organizational structure will give clues as to the degree of its focus on customers and, therefore, its likely attitude towards marketing. Although many companies have a marketing department, roles within this department will vary depending on the type of business conducted or types of customer it serves. For example, the marketing department in a b2b company, i.e. one that does not have direct contact with end users or consumers, may just be a sales team, while a company managing a number of brands is likely to have product, brand and category managers.

The following are examples of different types of typical organizational structure:

▶ product, based on the products, groups of products or brands the company manages

▶ functional, based on the different management functions that run the business, e.g. sales, human resources, finance

▶ geographic, based on the regions where the company operates, e.g. Europe

exhibit 12.13

Illustration of two organizational structures

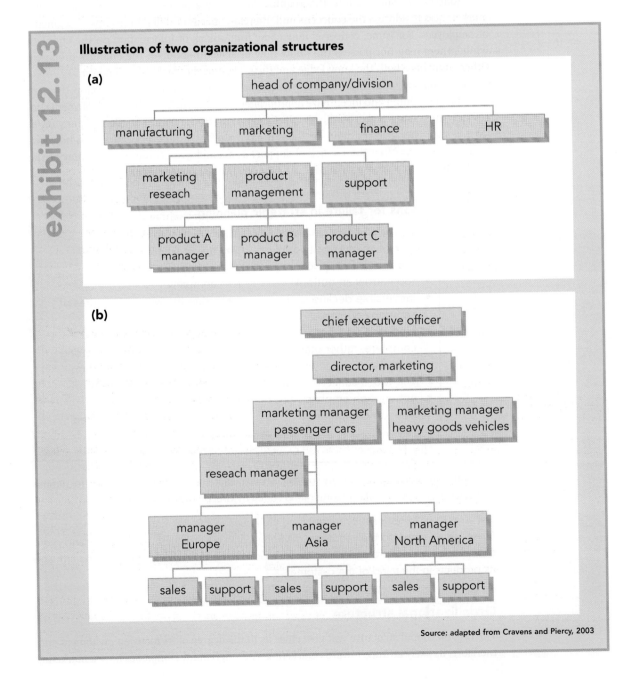

Source: adapted from Cravens and Piercy, 2003

▶ market, based on the markets the company operates in, e.g. Dell operates in both customer and b2b markets, which includes education, and small and medium-sized businesses

▶ customer group, based on the segments of the market the company serves or even individual 'key' customers, i.e. those that are strategically important to the company

▶ matrix, a hybrid-type structure where the company incorporates all functions into teams supporting different products or brands

▶ network, a highly versatile and relatively new approach that is, in essence, a coalition between a number of independent specialist firms, coordinated by a 'control centre' organization; specialist firms may be product designers, component manufacturers or distributors.

Structure (a) is product. It is one of the most common structural designs and depends on the size and scope of the company's operations. It is argued (Cravens and Piercy, 2003) that this approach may be adapted in time to incorporate, rather than products, groups of customers at the lowest level indicated. The structure clearly illustrates that products are supported by individual managers.

The second structure (b) is a typical hybrid of the product, geographic and functional structures. It incorporates the needs of customers by aligning operational teams close to different, albeit geographically orientated, customer segments. It is also a global structure, which aims to serve the company's market across the world.

The structure adopted by a company will depend on the core values and strategies of the management team in line with the organizational aims and objectives. It is important to recognize that structure is evolutionary since companies operate in a dynamic environment and, in order to retain position, will evolve to ensure they remain at the forefront of their customers' minds. Such changes must be managed particularly well in order to ensure that the company's stakeholders are not alienated. It is why, for example, internal marketing is an important part of the process in aligning the business to meet the needs of customers.

Contingency plans

Analysing the market is not just a means to facilitate strategic choice; it also helps to plan for an uncertain future. The theory, of course, is that by analysing the past, one can extrapolate forward. Consider what happens if there is a recession, a war, a new unknown competitor, a new alliance between two small firms that wish to steal your market share, a takeover bid for your main customer, further **market fragmentation**, a new form of telepathic media developed obviating the need for advertising, Internet meltdown, an increase in average life expectancy to 145 years, an invasion of sophisticated aliens who start trading on Earth ... Clearly, some of these are more likely to happen than others, so events can be ranked by probability of their occurrence and their potential impact on the business.

Although continuous market research (see Chapter 6) provides good clues as to the nature of the problems that may arise in a market, there is always room for the unexpected. Piercy and Lane (2002) coin the term **market sensing**, which is the need for an understanding of the market rather than merely knowledge of it. Understanding is about synthesized knowledge – you may know a lot of 'stuff' but do you understand it? (Prove it!) Piercy has produced a framework to help managers categorize the potential series of events that may impact on their business (see Exhibit 12.14).

The purpose, of course, in identifying potential problems is so the company can prepare itself to take some action, referred to as contingency planning (which may be called crisis management in another guise), i.e. plan B through to plan F, etc. This is so that businesses can be proactive in their reactions, which is not really the oxymoron it appears to be!

market fragmentation

a market characterized by a large number of relatively small players, none of whom have significant competitive advantage

market sensing

the need for an understanding of the market, rather than merely a knowledge of it

exhibit 12.14

Piercy's framework for market sensing

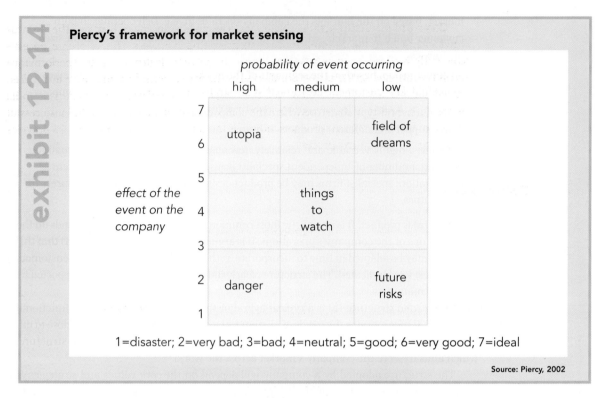

1=disaster; 2=very bad; 3=bad; 4=neutral; 5=good; 6=very good; 7=ideal

Source: Piercy, 2002

It is, however, not possible to develop a great number of options as they will take as much time and effort to develop as 'plan A'. It is prudent, having said that, to have some rudimentary ideas that can be picked up relatively quickly should things go wrong.

What is often difficult, however, is to know when to implement the contingency plans. This calls for continuous careful analysis of the business and market environment, referred to as marketing evaluation and control.

MARKETING EVALUATION AND CONTROL – ARE WE GETTING THERE, HAVE WE ARRIVED?

From the outset, every business needs to plan its finances carefully. At an operational level, this will require some form of cash-flow analysis by which the company can manage its day-to-day spending and income requirements. The company will also have to meet legal requirements. Whether incorporated into a private or public limited liability company, this necessitates the production, maintenance and management of profit and loss accounts and balance sheets.

From the marketing management and planning perspective, it is important to work the figures through to ensure there is enough funding available to achieve the intended goals. This is known as budgeting. Other questions to consider are: what are the options available if targets are not met, by whom and through what process does financial investment reach the operational level, how much is needed to achieve the target sales? To make a profit, the company must achieve its targeted sales. Clear profit is net of all expenditure. Revenue generated from sales, therefore, impacts on every area of the business from research and development through to human resource management, financial planning and marketing activities, whether they are directly or indirectly related to sales activities. Marketing's role is both to plan for sales activity and to ensure that customers and relationships are managed efficiently and effectively in order to achieve those sales.

Control of marketing activities amounts to an understanding of how well the business is performing given the decisions made by its marketing managers. This, of course, necessitates analysis of the variance between planned (target or budgeted) and actual performance across the range of activities that are affected by the decisions made. It may also, and indeed often does, take into account how well the company has performed in comparison to its competitors, especially the industry leaders. Effective control, therefore, results in successful adjustments to activities in order to achieve the intended objectives. Exhibit 12.15 provides a summary of the control process.

Control process

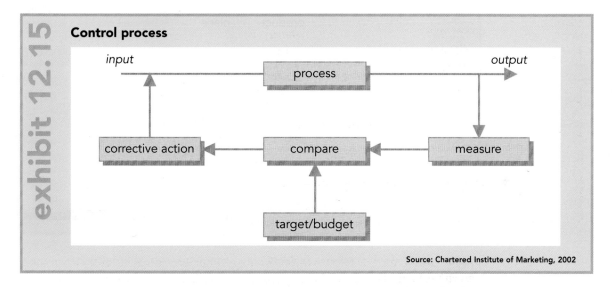

Source: Chartered Institute of Marketing, 2002

The range of control mechanisms is vast. The following are just a few examples:

▶ profitability analysis
▶ production analysis
▶ sales analysis
▶ customer service analysis
▶ benchmarking and competitor analysis.

There are four main considerations when designing control mechanisms: effectiveness, efficiency, strategy and profitability (see Exhibit 12.16). For example, if a business is performing inefficiently, this means it is not utilizing its resources effectively and will not, therefore, be as profitable as it could be. To rectify this, the business may adapt its tactics or implement a new strategy.

All elements of the product offering and the marketing plan can, and should, be examined. **Marketing metrics** highlights the need to measure and assess all possible aspects of marketing that can be measured. The level and quantity of detail can be extensive. Measurements will include the following and a great deal more:

▶ market share
▶ sales by segment and customer group
▶ performance of new products
▶ level of complaints
▶ competitive response to marketing activity.

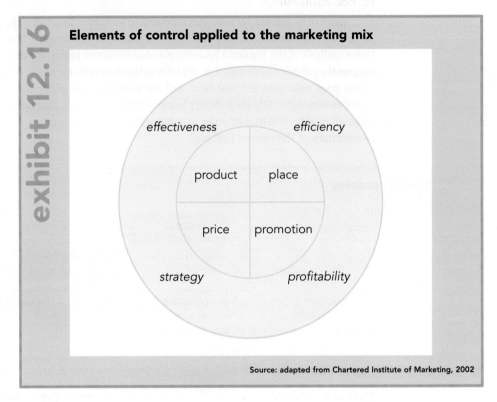

exhibit 12.16

Elements of control applied to the marketing mix

effectiveness   efficiency

product   place

price   promotion

strategy   profitability

Source: adapted from Chartered Institute of Marketing, 2002

Price:

▶ profit margin

▶ discounts offered and level

▶ price analysis by customer segment

▶ comparisons to competing products

▶ level of contribution.

Place:

▶ channel costs

▶ channel volume

▶ delivery time

▶ stock levels

▶ performance of individual channel members.

Promotion:

▶ cost per contact made

▶ media coverage

▶ customer awareness levels

▶ customer enquiries generated.

It is also possible to think about the additional elements of the marketing mix in this way.

Physical environment:

▶ customer awareness of and attitudes towards the physical aspects of service provision

▶ efficiency of store or outlet layout.

Processes:

▶ length of time from beginning to end

▶ number of people involved.

People:

▶ skills and competences

▶ training delivery

▶ qualifications

▶ rewards and incentives.

Having identified any areas of business that are underperforming, managers must decide how to address the shortfalls – either strategically or tactically, which is where contingency planning comes into force. The decisions, of course, will depend on the nature of the problem identified. For example, if there is a shortfall in sales, the company may decide to:

▶ target a new segment of the market (strategic)

▶ put prices down or up (tactical)

▶ redirect the sales effort or send salespeople on a training programme (operational).

The speed and efficiency with which shortfalls are addressed is often crucial to the ongoing success of the business. As stated earlier, it is far easier to defend a leading market position than it is to challenge a major competitor. It is important, therefore, not to let the business slip too low before attempting a retrieval. Consider how difficult it is in the current competitive climate for Marks & Spencer to regain its leading position in retail clothing and fashion. Control is not something that should be left until the end of the trading period, but is something that is ongoing. It is one of the key reasons for undertaking a systematic analysis of the market. Furthermore, it is important to control for those things that are important, not just easy to collect (Souhami, 2003).

---

activity

The idea of control can also be applied to your own studies. Consider how you measure your performance. You will think about:

▶ the results you have from previous assessments, say at A-level

▶ your intended results

▶ the amount of effort you have made to study

▶ the results of your other assessments at university

▶ the results of your friends' and colleagues' assessments.

How do you rectify your performance if you did not get the result you expected? Do you monitor your performance regularly and make continual adjustments, or do you just carry on regardless? Have you made contingency plans?

This chapter has reviewed the marketing management and planning process. Consideration has been given to the types of question that managers need to ask.

The planning process, which can be undertaken through a combination of top-down, bottom-up, outside-in and inside-out approaches, comprises five key stages:

1. marketing analysis
2. mission and objectives
3. marketing objectives and strategy
4. marketing operations and implementation
5. marketing evaluation and control.

The planning process results in the development of a series of business plans that include the marketing plan or multiple marketing plans.

Within these five stages, a variety of marketing frameworks or management models have been highlighted:

▶ PRESTCOM and SWOT analysis
▶ Porter's five forces model
▶ competitor analysis and marketing information systems
▶ competitors' capabilities analysis tool
▶ product life cycle (PLC) analysis
▶ portfolio analysis (the BCG and GE matrices)
▶ Porter's generic strategies model
▶ Ansoff's matrix
▶ competitive positioning
▶ McKinsey's 7S framework model
▶ Piercy's market sensing framework
▶ control process model.

Challenges reviewed

Now that you have finished reading the chapter, look back at the challenges you were set at the beginning. Do you have a clearer idea of what's involved?

Hints:

▶ Porter's generic strategies and competitive positioning
▶ see 'marketing planning process model'
▶ see 'contingency planning' – and environmental scanning in Chapter 3
▶ Ansoff's matrix
▶ marketing analysis, particularly the 'five forces' model.

READING AROUND

articles

Thomas, D. (2003). A good clean fight, *Marketing Week* (3 July), pages 20–23: a topical strategy-in-action article about how Procter & Gamble and Unilever are attempting to refocus their businesses – try to identify the business objectives and respective strategies in the markets identified for each of these consumer-market giants.

Wyner, A.G. (2002) Top down or bottom up? *Marketing Management* 11(5) (Sept/Oct), page 6: a short article which discusses two different management approaches to strategy formulation and implementation written by the vice president of strategy at Millward Brown.

Waggoner, R. (1999) Have you made the wrong turn in your approach to market? *The Journal of Business Strategy* 20(6) (Nov/Dec), pages 16–21: discusses the importance of getting strategy right in the marketplace and identifies the types of objectives that organizations work towards.

SELF-REVIEW QUESTIONS

1. What are the main stages of the marketing planning process? (see page 357)

2. List three marketing planning analysis tools. (see page 359)

3. How can the product life cycle be used by an organization? (see page 364)

4. What is portfolio analysis? (see page 364)

5. What axes are used with the GE matrix? (see page 365)

6. What are Porter's three generic strategies? (see page 368)

7. Define the four generic strategies from Ansoff's matrix. (see page 369)

8. Name four competitive positioning strategies. (see page 371)

9. Identify five possible reasons for strategic failures. (see page 373)

10. What is 'market sensing'? (see page 375)

11. Why is marketing control important? (see page 376)

MINI CASE STUDY

Read the questions, then the case material, then answer the questions.

Questions

1. Why would P&G and Unilever want to take such apparently drastic actions by cutting the number of brands to a core few?

2. Which marketing tools discussed in this chapter could they have used to analyse their market situations? Why would they use them? How would they use them?

All Change!

Procter & Gamble and Unilever have been cutting down their product portfolios recently in order to enable them to refocus their businesses. P&G has been making cuts for nearly 10 years now, including global restructuring of its business operations, which in 1996 appeared to be 'bloated and fragmented' (Thomas, 2003). Its aims were to double sales within a 10-year time frame. Since December 2002, the restructuring complete, its net income had risen from £1.76 billion (2001) to £2.62 billion (2002).

Meanwhile, in August 2003, Unilever announced a lower sales target for the year, down from an anticipated 5–6 per cent to 4 per cent. It has been selling off a considerable number of its long-established brands, such as Brut ('splash it all over') and Mentadent (the toothpaste with baking soda and peroxide) – some 850 in all since its restructuring began – but was still 350 brands over its target of just 400 core brands.

So, what is the slimline P&G going to do now? Apparently, the focus is going to be on household 'soaps' – that's not the *EastEnders* variety, but Ariel, Bold and Daz! It planned a £20 million relaunch of Ariel in September 2003 with a new product formulation that is claimed to be even more effective at getting rid of those stuck-on stains. Its aim was to attract a bigger customer base, which, with its Bold and Daz brands, currently accounts for 49 per cent of the market.

None the less, Unilever's Persil brand remains the strongest contender in the marketplace, growing at a rate of around 6 per cent per year, mainly as a result of constant innovation and advertising. It claims the title of the most trusted soap brand (in spite of its blip in 1995 when its reformulation quite literally shredded clothes) which leaves the market in a bit of a stink. Indeed, it seems poised for a good old-fashioned dust-up as both P&G and Unilever try to out-market each other for the top spot.

Source: Thomas, 2003

REFERENCES

Ansoff, I. (1957) Strategies for diversification, *Harvard Business Review* (Sept–Oct), 113–24.

Cravens, D. and Piercy, N. (2003) *Strategic Marketing* (7th edn), McGraw-Hill.

Greene, W., Walls, G. and Schrest, L. (1994) Internal marketing: the key to external marketing success, *Journal of Services Marketing* 8(4), 5–13.

Hooley, G., Saunders, J. and Piercy, N. (1998) *Marketing Strategy and Competitive Positioning*, Prentice Hall.

Johnson, G. and Scholes, K. (1998) *Exploring Corporate Goals*, Prentice Hall.

Levitt, T. (1960) Marketing myopia, *Harvard Business Review* (July/August), 45–56.

Piercy, N. (2002) *Market-led Strategic Change* (3rd edn), Butterworth-Heinemann.

Porter, M.E. (1985) *Competitive Advantage: Creating and Sustaining Superior Performance*, Free Press.

Proctor, A. (2002) in Harwood T., *Negotiations in Buyer–Seller Relationships*, PhD thesis, De Montfort University.

Ries, A. and Trout, J. (1986) *Marketing Warfare*, McGraw-Hill.

Schultz, D.E. (1993) How to overcome the barriers to integration, *Marketing News* (19 July), 27(15), 16.

Schultz, D.E. (1997) Integrating information resources to develop strategies, *Marketing News* (20 January), 31(2), 10.

Souhami, S. (2003) Competitive myopia, *Marketing Business* (April), 32–4.

Thomas, D. (2003) A good clean fight, *Marketing Week* (3 July), 20–3.

Walker, O. Jr, Boyd, H. Jr and Larreche, J.-C. (1992) Marketing strategy in Cravens, D. and Piercy, N. (2003) *Strategic Marketing* (7th edn), McGraw-Hill.

www.greenpeace.org.

www.nike.com.

www.sas.co.uk.

www.cim.co.uk.

WHAT DO MARKETERS DO?
POSTSCRIPT: CAREERS IN MARKETING

PART FOUR: THE MARKETERS

CHAPTER OVERVIEW

- Introduction
- What do managers do?
- What do managers of marketing do?
- Jobs in marketing

- Marketing qualities, skills and competences
- Background and education
- Summary
- Reading around

INTRODUCTION

The format of this chapter is different to the others. It appears here as a postscript to the first 12 chapters, which provide a basic introduction to marketing. Those chapters helped to provide an insight into what marketing is, what principles and concepts it covers (the discipline of marketing); but not much has been said so far about what marketing managers actually do (the management of marketing). Chapter 12 introduced some aspects of marketing planning and organization, both important aspects of marketing management. This chapter will focus on the jobs and skills of managers of marketing by, first, providing an overview of what managers do in general and then going on to consider managers of marketing in particular.

In contrast to the other chapters in this book, no challenges will be set at the outset nor will self-review questions or a case study be given at the end. There are some activities, though, and by carrying them out you will improve your understanding. Also, take a look at the list of websites given at the end of the chapter; you can find out a great deal by surfing the net.

Chapter 1 gave a definition of marketing, one set by the Chartered Institute of Marketing (CIM), in which marketing was closely related to management. This final chapter returns to that theme by focusing on the different management jobs of marketing.

The first thing to appreciate is that referring to 'marketing managers' all of the time can be misleading. There is a rich diversity of marketing jobs and they do not all carry the title 'marketing manager'; in fact most do not. The duties, tasks and responsibilities undertaken are many and varied, requiring a range of skills and abilities. These create an array of opportunities for those starting out in marketing and for those developing their careers as they rise to higher levels of seniority. This chapter will provide an insight into some of the roles undertaken by managers of marketing and its related specializations, and some of the skills and qualities needed to carry out the jobs effectively.

Over the years, the marketing profession has been subject to some disapproval for how effectively it has performed. Some of its most ardent critics have been marketing managers themselves. They have criticized their colleagues for being ill-equipped to carry out their jobs and insufficiently rounded to understand the total business implications. In one survey, marketers rated their colleagues as having only average capabilities, with a little more than 10 per cent believing them to be fairly poor or even worse. In another survey (conducted by a leading international management consultancy) of managing and marketing directors in large FMCG, retail and service-sector organizations, while marketing was identified as being more vital than ever, marketing departments were viewed as increasingly failing to match up to expectations. The departments were criticized as being too short-sighted and being an ill-defined mixture of activities. To add to the confusion, managing directors and marketing directors did not agree on the nature and extent of marketing's role. Perceptions have been that the discipline has been insufficiently commercially orientated and too narrowly focused. Clearly, what has been happening is that the quality of marketing practices has been highly variable.

Studies on the development of marketing within organizations suggest that the marketing management function has been, or is being, subsumed into those of other professional groupings and management functions. The inescapable conclusion is that marketing managers do not manage marketing. It may be argued that they never fully did. The reasons for this are numerous.

Marketing as a business approach has a widespread effect on the whole organization. It is too diverse for any one manager to manage. Any pretence that this is not the case represents a gross misunderstanding of the nature of marketing. It has been said that 'Marketing is too important to be left solely to the Marketing Department.'

Another way of looking at this quote is to recognize that so many people within companies affect the marketing output that it would be impossible to control all marketing activities from one department and it would be unwise to try. Not only is marketing a business approach (the marketing concept and orientation), it is a range of varied activities, some of which are carried out by non-marketing personnel as well as some others that are carried out by managers responsible for only part of the marketing function. The criticism that organizations adopt the trappings without the substance of marketing can often be levelled with the result that the managers who are given the task of managing marketing do not, and cannot, do so. Nigel Piercy's research over a number of years has made it quite clear that departments other than marketing control many of the critically important marketing activities. Other research, such as that by Peter Doyle, has identified that marketers are infrequently appointed as chief executive officers (CEOs) or to board positions and, therefore, cannot exert the level of control and vision that can only be achieved at the most senior levels of a company. A recent analysis of the FTSE-100 companies has highlighted that, compared with 26 from a financial background, only 13 CEOs have marketing backgrounds. Notably, these include the appointments of Luc Vandevelde of Marks & Spencer, Sir Peter Davies of Sainsbury's, and Gerry Murphy of Carlton Communications, all of whom have been successful in turning their respective businesses around in the face of increased competitive climates.

Exacerbating the problem has been the general poor level of professionalism within the discipline. People have moved into marketing positions without necessarily having the appropriate education, training and experience. Numerous studies have borne this out. Sometimes job titles have been changed to include 'marketing' when the jobs themselves may have only limited marketing involvement and responsibility. From the early 1980s onwards, marketing fell victim to its own popularity when it became fashionable to dress up otherwise mundane job titles by adding 'marketing' to them. There was a degree of prestige associated with such titles at the time and, for example, sales managers became marketing managers or sales and marketing managers while their jobs remained as managing the salesforce. A great deal of misunderstanding ensued. In one notable example, a junior employee proudly sported the title of marketing intelligence officer, but his primary task was to collect press cuttings. The job title described neither the position nor the manager with any degree of accuracy.

While some of the criticism of marketing in the 1990s has been justified, a proportion has been less so. Over recent years, marketing has faced the challenge of measuring its effectiveness and achievements, and has been proving its worth. The recent emphasis on such areas as customer relationship management, database management, direct marketing, e-commerce, key account management and marketing metrics has done much to improve the perceptions of its status, raising its profile and helping to overcome the notion that marketing is an isolated function within the company. What is undoubtedly the case is that marketing positions provide some of the most challenging and exciting roles within organizations.

This is what some people in marketing have said about their jobs.

66Those in marketing have to want to make things happen.99   (David Sowter, Nabisco)

66The good marketer must have vision, unlimited energy, the ability to communicate and put plans into action while remaining realistic, practical and down to earth.99   (Ralph Wright, Peter Dominic)

66Marketing is less about expertise, more about general all-round management strength – marketers must be sound in the selling environment as well as in production/development area. Expertise can be bought in – it is the management of all these various activities of product management that is the key to being the best marketers.99   (Ian Trottman, Walls)

66The greatest challenge to marketers today is the management of change.99   (Paul Sartor, Olivetti)

66The most intellectually challenging (and satisfying) role in business today.99   (Mike Hughes, Guinness)

66Marketing is a responsible, challenging role that requires a logical approach and far sightedness. However, a few years ago, many marketers believed that they were bigger than the role – causing animosity with sales people and, in some cases, expensive mistakes for manufacturers.99   (Steve Saunders, Hillsdown)

66It is up to marketers to perform at a level where the results are delivered.99   (Philip Sheldon, Bass)

66The business environment has never been more demanding. The rewards for success have never been higher, but so have the risks of failure. Marketing has never been so vital to the success of the business enterprise. The challenge of marketing will be answered by better skilled, more professional, more commercially-aware managers who will truly accept the responsibility of their task. In the truly successful company, marketing will cease to be just a separate department of managers, but will become a commercial attitude of mind that permeates every aspect of that company's operation.99   (Frank Auton, Beecham)

If you have read and understood the material in the preceding 12 chapters of this book, and the principles they have covered, you will have made an excellent start towards a successful career in marketing . . . that is, if you are willing to accept the challenge.

WHAT DO MANAGERS DO?

Marketing managers, in whatever aspect of marketing they specialize, are, first and foremost, managers. Admittedly, junior posts will involve few management duties but it is interesting to note that even junior marketers find themselves with important responsibilities and many reach senior positions at a young age.

David Bodman of EMR Search, a specialist recruitment agency, had this to say about marketers:

66It takes roughly 10 years for high flyers to reach the level of marketing director and, for others, up to 20 years. They will all be graduates, usually from good universities with at least an upper-second degree. And marketing, it seems, is a young person's game. Not one of the candidates I've placed in recent months has been over 40.99

Jerry Daniels of the Michael Page executive recruitment agency comments:

66Beyond extensive and in-depth marketing knowledge and experience, we look for key leadership skills such as communications, especially the ability to communicate across different areas of company operations. Vision, innovation skills, strategic planning, problem solving skills and commercial savvy are also must-haves. We also want them to bring evidence of controlling the overall consumer experience. 99

But before saying more about the jobs of marketing managers, it is worthwhile developing an understanding of what is involved in being a manager. The exhibits that follow identify the findings of a number of management researchers.

Henry Fayol was one of the first people to try to identify the key functions of managers. Other researchers (such as Hales, and Carroll and Gillen) have produced similar findings, as shown in Exhibit PS.1.

exhibit ps.1

Functions of management

Fayol	Hales	Carroll and Gillen
Planning	Planning	Planning
Organizing	Allocating	Supervising
Controlling	Controlling	Investigating
Commanding	Motivating	Evaluating
Coordinating	Coordinating	Coordinating
		Staffing

The degree of commonality between the lists of the different researchers is self-evident and is probably due to attempts to generalize about managers and their jobs, but this does not always produce an accurate picture of what individual managers actually spend their time doing. As Mintzberg has observed:

66 If you ask a manager what he does, he will most likely tell you that he plans, organises, coordinates and controls. Then watch what he does. Don't be surprised if you can't relate what you see to these four words. 99

What may be at issue here is a distinction between the broad functions that managers appear to be responsible for, and how they spend their time in carrying out those responsibilities. Such responsibilities, by their nature, will also be directly related to the manager's specific functional task, whether this is marketing, production, finance, personnel or whatever, and will account for many of the differences we see when we look at day-to-day management activity. By way of an example of this point, Exhibit PS.2 presents the results of a survey conducted by an international executive recruitment consultancy of chief marketing executives in 700 major organizations. It asked these senior executives about how they spent their time. Clearly, the results would be different for managers at lower levels of seniority and those within a particular role within a broad functional area.

exhibit ps.2

Responsibilities of chief marketing executives

Activity	Allocation of time by activity
People management	15%
Corporate and strategic responsibilities	14%
Market development, existing products, etc.	13%
Market development, new products, etc.	12%
Advertising/promotion	9%
Selling/negotiating	9%
Sales management and pricing	8%
Sales forecasting	7%
Market research	7%
Press and public relations	6%

For Mintzberg, a widely quoted management researcher and author, the main roles that managers fulfil fit into three main categories: interpersonal roles, informational roles and decisional roles. Under these, a short series of other significant subroles are carried out. Pedler, Burgoyne and Boydell have investigated what makes managers effective in their jobs and have identified a series of manager qualities. Finally, having undertaken an extensive review of management research studies, Whetten and Cameron have formulated a top ten list of the most frequently cited skills of effective managers. All of these are presented in Exhibit PS.3.

activity

Compare and contrast the listings in Exhibits PS.1 and PS.3. What are their similarities and what are their differences? Why do they seem to suggest that managers should be good at different things? Do managers have to carry out all the functions and roles, and possess all the qualities and skills identified?

Having considered the functions, roles, qualities and skills of managers generally (do not worry about the distinctions between these terms), let us now move closer to considering managers who work specifically in marketing jobs.

Manager roles, qualities and skills

Mintzberg's managerial roles	Pedler, Burgoyne and Boydell's qualities of successful managers	Whetten and Cameron's skills of effective managers
Interpersonal roles Figurehead Leader Liaison **Informational roles** Monitor Disseminator Spokesman **Decisional roles** Entrepreneur Disturbance handler Resource allocator Negotiator	**Basic knowledge and information** Command of basic facts Relevant professional understanding **Skills and attributes** Continuing sensitivity to events Analytical, problem-solving, decision/judgement-making skills Social skills and abilities Emotional resilience Proactivity – inclination to respond purposefully to events **'Meta–qualities'** Balanced learning habits and skills Self-knowledge	Verbal communication (including listening) Managing time and stress Managing individual decisions Recognizing, defining and solving problems Motivating and influencing others Delegating Setting goals and articulating a vision Self-awareness Team building Managing conflict

WHAT DO MANAGERS OF MARKETING DO?

The details above provide a useful starting point to understand what marketing management is all about. Marketing managers do *manage.* So the functions, roles, qualities and skills of managers in general must also apply to marketing managers in particular, but they need to be balanced appropriately to fit the marketing tasks they specifically perform. Furthermore, they need to be tailored to the requirements of individual marketing jobs. This balance will vary according to a variety of factors that can be summarized under the headings of *situation, task* and *manager* (see Exhibit PS.4).

The three main factors influencing management activity and performance

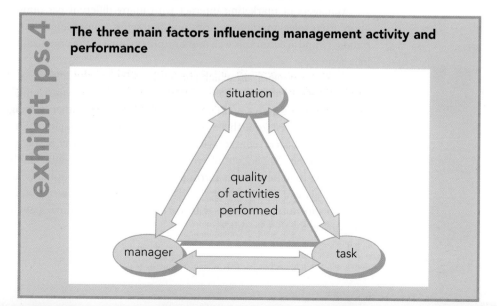

Situation

Situations vary from industry to industry, company to company, and from time to time. Some aspects of the management situation are relatively enduring, such as the organization's culture, its strategic orientation, its departmental structure, interdepartmental relationships and interfaces, levels of collaboration and conflict, and degree of understanding of marketing. All of these factors will have an impact on marketing jobs. If the company practises a marketing orientation, the way marketing is carried out will be different to the approach adopted by a company that has a product orientation (see Chapter 2).

How marketing is organized and its departmental structures (see Chapter 12) will have a major impact on marketing roles. The relationships between employees in different departments may create an environment of collaboration or conflict. Interdepartmental rivalries are typical as the managers in each functional area try to pursue as effectively as possible their own objectives. Marketing is frequently thought of as an expense that may cause difficulties and disruptions to other departments. Although collaboration is obviously sought, it is not always easy to accomplish. Marketing managers often find themselves in particularly difficult positions. Marketing is something that depends on the whole organization working together. A carefully planned marketing campaign for one brand can come to grief because production schedules might clash with those of other brands. Inventory levels may be affected. Planned budgets may have to be revised. The sales department may wish to pursue shorter-term objectives to meet immediate sales targets. Customer services might have different priorities to the finance department, and so on. It is recognized that each department maintains different perspectives, value systems and objectives despite working towards one corporate end. The conflict that ensues and the resistance from other departments is often underestimated.

> **activity**
>
> Think about the sorts of goals and objectives you imagine a sales director or an accounts and finance director might want to pursue, and compare these with what you think would be important to a marketing director. Can you identify points that might lead to conflict?

Lawrence and Lorsch have identified the role of *integrator* as a key management role (this is related to Mintzberg's liaison role in Exhibit PS.3). Given the nature of the marketing function, which spreads throughout an organization, and the fact that the marketing managers need to span organizational boundaries, it may be that they are particularly well placed to help achieve organizational integration if given the opportunity. This can also put a lot of pressure on the managers, who may carry a great deal of responsibility but often have to rely on many others over whom they have no authority to ensure that tasks are completed effectively. This integrator, boundary-spanning role is well illustrated in Exhibit PS.5.

Managers of marketing interact with many different personnel within the organization, from sales, market research and marketing communications to production, distribution, IT and accounts, as well as many others outside the organization in order to get their jobs done.

Stewart's research, in which she has investigated the differences rather than the similarities between managers, has identified the way in which marketing managers find themselves in quite distinctly different situations to most other managers, and that their relationships differ from those of other management groupings. From Stewart's studies, marketing managers' contact with others accounted for over 50 per cent of the marketing manager's time, 20 per cent of which was with external contacts. These levels of contact were higher than for any other grouping, confirming the commonly held view that marketing management requires social skills and is an outward-focused function. Contacts with peers or superiors were high, with correspondingly less time spent with subordinates in comparison to other managers.

exhibit ps.5

Marketing manager and product/brand manager interactions

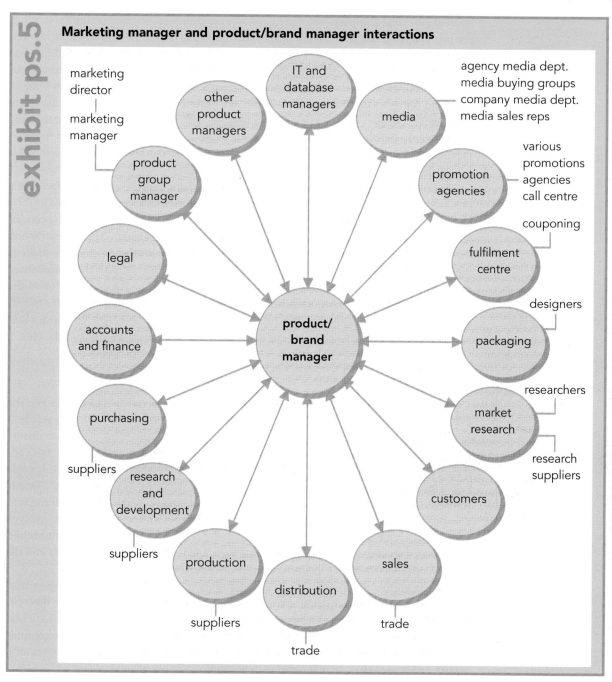

marketing director

marketing manager

product group manager

other product managers

IT and database managers

media

agency media dept.
media buying groups
company media dept.
media sales reps

promotion agencies

various promotions agencies
call centre

fulfilment centre

couponing

legal

packaging

designers

accounts and finance

market research

researchers

research suppliers

product/ brand manager

purchasing

customers

suppliers

research and development

sales

suppliers

production

distribution

suppliers

trade

trade

Task

The tasks set for different marketing managers and those that specialize in particular areas of marketing, such as advertising or market research, vary enormously; so much so that their jobs cannot be considered as similar at all. The section below on marketing jobs gives some details of the many and varied activities of marketers. The actual job specifications, even for jobs carrying the same title, can vary significantly from one company to another and this is particularly true of *marketing manager*, which is a general title that covers a multitude of different possible activities. Exhibit PS.2 gave some indication of the tasks performed by very senior marketing executives and the time spent on each.

Piercy has investigated chief marketing executives in medium-sized manufacturing companies and, after analysing 21 different marketing management responsibilities, isolated five broad groupings: selling (e.g. salesforce operations, pricing); product policy (e.g. product planning, design and launch); marketing services (e.g. marketing research, marketing planning); corporate strategy (e.g. corporate planning, diversification studies); and physical distribution. He concluded that the emphasis placed on these tasks varied according to the situation, which was based on the extent to which the organisation was what he called an 'integrated/full service marketing organization, a strategy/services marketing organisation, a sales-orientated marketing organisation, or a limited/staff role marketing organisation'. Both the findings in Exhibit PS.2 and these details from Piercy's research relate to chief marketing executives. The tasks performed by marketers at lower levels of the organization's hierarchy carry less onerous responsibilities.

One aspect of marketing management that is often under-appreciated is the fact that a great deal of marketing is undertaken by specialist agencies. These are companies in their own right but whose function is to support their clients' marketing activities. Such agencies give the opportunity to specialize in particular aspects of marketing. Whereas marketing managers may be considered generalists, there are many opportunities for people to focus their interests by working in advertising, PR, media, sales promotions, direct marketing, market research or any of the sub-areas of marketing, whether on the client side or on the agency side. Indeed, working in agencies and consultancies offers numerous job options. Advertising agencies employ art directors, copywriters, account planners, handlers, managers and directors, media planners and buyers, production managers, researchers, etc.

Manager

The manager's actual response to the situation and the task will have a major impact on the jobs performed and, importantly, how well they are performed. These responses will be a function of the manager's expertise, background, personal qualities, skills and drivers (ambition, personal goals and perspectives). Management research over the years has confirmed some interesting early findings. For example, Mant has questioned why 'awful people rise with such regularity to high office' and has described two types of 'leader'. One is interested in interpersonal relationships and personal power in which 'the main thing is to control, dominate or seduce the Other in the interests of personal survival'. The second type adopts a more 'balanced' approach in which greater concern is placed on the organization, a purpose or an idea. How far the first type is associated with successful managers and the second with effective managers raises interesting issues.

In contrasting *successful* and *effective* managers, Luthans found that managers who were judged to be successful (in terms of the speed of their promotion) spent quite different amounts of time on activities from managers defined as effective (in terms of quality and quantity of performance, and creating subordinate satisfaction and subordinate commitment to the organization). Langtry and Langtry identified these two types of managers as 'i' and 'o' managers, where 'i' is equated with image, I, me or myself, and 'o' focuses on objectives and others. They comment, 'An i *manager* progresses swiftly through the organization, arriving at a senior position with comparative ease. The *o manager* works hard, is efficient and effective but remains unnoticed. He or she is unlikely to rise above the role of middle manager.' These sorts of findings, while intriguing, are also quite disturbing for the quality of management.

Stewart's research, reported above, highlights some of the particular challenges faced by marketing managers. The amount and type of internal contact highlights the need for strong negotiating and influencing skills. Stewart also found that (as with some other managers) marketing managers experience a high level of exposure – that is, the extent to which they may be directly identified and responsible for particular management decisions. In the case of marketing managers, though, we can appreciate that this exposure may be more strongly felt when the marketing manager lacks authority over others in the organization who directly influence the outcome. These sorts of role demands place particular constraints, choices and pressures on marketing managers in the performance of their duties. Pedler *et al.* in Exhibit PS.3 identified 'emotional resilience' as a key manager quality.

JOBS IN MARKETING

The Chartered Institute of Marketing (CIM) lists as many as 27 different job titles and job descriptions, together with descriptions of a further five agency functions in its latest job descriptions guide produced in association with StopGap recruitment agency. The details below provide a summary of this guide, to which other job positions have been added from other sources, which include PA Sales Selection in association with the CIM, the Association of Graduate Careers Advisory Services, and specialist recruitment agencies.

Even with such an extensive list, the collection is far from complete. There are still more job positions that relate to marketing and its associated activities. Job titles have been grouped together where jobs are similar or where they relate to similar specialisms and their roles have been summarized. Many jobs carry similar titles but at different levels of seniority. The actual nature of the jobs will also vary to some extent based on the industry and size of company. Industrial marketing and sales for a large manufacturing company will be different from a small consumer services company even if the job titles appear similar.

> **activity**
>
> Look through various newspapers and marketing publications at the marketing-related jobs being advertised. Also look on the web for job recruitment sites. These can be found by searching on Google or a similar search engine, or take a look at the sites suggested in the 'Reading around' section at the end of this chapter. Compare the job titles, job descriptions and requirements. How do the descriptions and skills requirements differ? Are there any major differences between jobs with the same title and do some of these differences occur in jobs in different industries and commercial settings?

Company-based positions

Board director

Operating at strategic level involving managing, leading and motivating the department for which the director is responsible (e.g. Marketing Dept, Customer Services Dept, etc.). Involves working with other directors at board level to provide direction and resources for running the whole business.

Marketing director

Operating at the highest level of marketing within the organization, this manager is responsible for formulating and directing the company's marketing strategy and working with a range of subordinate marketing staff.

Marketing manager

Responsible for the strategic direction of all marketing activity for specific goods and services and the production and implementation of detailed marketing plans. In some organizations, this may be the most senior marketing professional. In other organizations, product or brand manager may be used as alternative titles.

(Senior) marketing executive
Marketing executive/assistant

More junior marketing manager positions; support marketing managers in achieving their goals.

Group product/group brand manager
Product/brand manager
Assistant product/brand manager
Category manager

Each of these positions carries direct responsibility for one or more specific brands in their design and delivery of the product and service offering. In effect, these managers are responsible for the development of all marketing plans and activities related to specific brands and have extensive contacts with many other members of the organization (as would be the case with many other marketing management positions) (see Exhibit PS.5). The job title may be used in preference to marketing manager in some companies. The group product or group brand manager will have overall responsibility for a range of managers and brands. Category manager is a term used in some industry and commercial settings to refer to the management of a particular range or category of products. For example, in financial services, a category manager may be responsible for the development and marketing of pension plans and insurance to businesses and individuals. In retailing, the title may be used for someone responsible for a category of merchandise.

Regional/area retail manager
Retail manager
Merchandising manager
Wholesale manager
Agent
Buyer
Channel manager
Distribution manager

Retail, wholesale and distribution management offer many opportunities and environments. Managers can be responsible for the whole store, sections of stores and for groups of stores. Merchandising involves stock allocation and display. Buying is critical to the process – what is bought in are the very products that are then offered for sale to the next group of customers. Channel and distribution management involves the process of managing the distribution chain and the logistics of physical distribution of products.

New media manager

Providing recommendations for the use of emerging new media channels to optimize business performance and objectives, and subsequently developing and executing plans and programmes across the organization.

Online marketing manager

Reporting to the head of marketing, responsible for owning, managing and delivering increase in revenue and margin through the online business channel.

Partnership/alliance manager

Drives and delivers the value proposition for partners/alliance partners by planning, organizing and implementing joint marketing activities, which complement individual company activities.

Market research manager/executive
Marketing information manager
Marketing intelligence officer
Data planners
Market research analyst
Market research interviewer

Junior to middle-management positions involving the collection, analysis and dissemination of market research information. Can involve the management of internal marketing information systems that combine primary research data, internally captured data, and secondary data from a variety of external agencies and secondary sources. Specializations can include data management, quantitative analysis and qualitative research. Research interviewers may be employed on a part-time basis. Data collection can be through a variety of means including face-to-face and telephone interviews, and use of the Internet.

Product development manager
Product research development manager
New product development manager

This area of management focuses on product development of new and modified products to constantly seek improvements in the products being offered to customers. New product development may result in new market opportunities, too.

Sales director/manager
Sales and marketing director/manager
Regional/area sales manager
Sales account manager
Key account manager
Sales Representative
Telesales operators
Sales assistant
Demonstrator

At senior and middle-management levels, involves the management and motivation of a sales department and field salesforce, setting of sales targets, pricing (in conjunction with others), management of key customers and personal selling to key customers. At lower levels, involves personal selling to customers and demonstrating product use. Sales assistant and demonstrator positions are typically associated with retail operations. Telesales will be sales taken over the phone, whereas other sales operatives may travel door to door, visit customer premises or work within retail and wholesale environments.

Marketing controller
Marketing planning manager
Competitive intelligence manager/officer
Marketing services manager
Market/business development manager

These positions generally relate to marketing service functions that act in support of other marketing management activities. They include project management and control of marketing activities, market analysis and identification of market and business opportunities, competitive analysis, the development of marketing plans to take advantage of new markets, control and dissemination of marketing intelligence and information, the control of agency functions such as call centres, promotions agencies, printers, etc.

Export director/manager
International marketing director/manager

Organize and control overseas marketing, sales and distribution activities, working through agents and intermediaries as necessary.

Customer relationship manager
Customer/client services director/manager
Complaints manager
Customer information manager
Database manager

This range of positions has in common a focus on customers. It has only been in recent years that these job roles have developed as companies have emphasized the importance of customer focus and customer satisfaction. Some positions highlight communications between customers and the company, including the management of customer helplines, others emphasize the management of customer databases and customer analysis. They share the intention to understand customer activities, buying practices, loyalty and retention. Customers will be categorized into a variety of groups, forming distinct segments towards which particular offerings will be made.

Director of communications
Director of corporate communications
Campaign manager
Promotions manager
Marketing communications manager
Advertising manager
Public relations manager/officer
Sponsorship manager
Press officer
Public and media relations manager
Public affairs manager
Sales promotions manager
Direct marketing manager
Events/conference manager
Internal communications manager
Media manager
Print account manager

Communications coordinator
Web manager

A wide variety of positions that have in common responsibility for the day-to-day delivery of marketing campaigns. Some management positions will specify particular areas of specialization such as PR, advertising, print production, media relations or relations with key groups such as local and national government, others will be broader in outlook and require the management of campaigns in multiple areas. The level of seniority will vary as will the number of people involved within a department. Some departments will be highly integrated whereas in some organizations departments and managers responsible for different aspects of marketing communications may operate independently of each other. Integration between promotional activities is important to ensure consistent communications not only with external audiences but also internally as well.

Agency-based positions

Board director

Involvement and responsibility for overall strategy, performance and profitability of agency (frequently with other board directors). May have specific responsibility for accounts, finance, creative or production, etc. Also has responsibility for business development.

Account handling

This is the general term given for managing client contact and business within agencies. The role entails day-to-day client contact, ensuring the client's requirements are understood by the agency, and ensuring all work is completed to specification, on time and to budget. Account handlers are the primary liaison point between agencies and their clients. These positions are found in all sorts of agencies from advertising, media, fulfilment and web development to PR, sales promotions and direct marketing, exhibitions, etc.

Group account director
Account director
Senior account manager
Overall responsibility for a number of clients (accounts), development of new business and day-to-day management of a team of account handlers.

Account manager
New business account manager

Middle-management position handling the day-to-day delivery of campaigns for specific clients. A specific role might be in obtaining new business.

Account executive/handler

Entry-level position into account management. Works with account manager. May have primary responsibility for one or a small number of smaller clients.

Traffic manager

A role that ensures the smooth running of agency operations. Traffic managers are project managers who oversee the meeting of schedules and deadlines.

Creative director

The title director may be confusing. In agency positions, this may not be related to a position on the board although senior creative directors may well be board members or even founding partners. Principal responsibility for the creative development and output usually working within teams. May be responsible for a number of art directors. Will be found in agencies whose work involves creative development, e.g. advertising, direct mail, sales promotions, etc. Creative directors, together with art directors and copywriters, form the group known as the creatives.

Art director/visualizer

A title usually conferred on the visualizer, the person responsible for the development of the graphics. Usually works as a team member with a copywriter.

Copywriter

Person who typically works with an art director where visual designs are required and who is responsible for writing the words for promotions.

Account planner

Responsible for fully understanding the client's markets and customers, and delivering consumer insight that drives brand strategy and the communication of it. It is a role that not all agencies employ as a separate function. It involves an understanding of research and analysis, and the development of creative briefs used by the creative team to develop the final creative solutions. It involves teamwork with agency personnel such as the creatives and account handlers as well as the client.

Media planner
Media buyer
Media sales – media owner

This is a range of specialist roles focused on the use of the media, such as mass media (e.g. TV, radio, cinema, press, etc.) and the new media (e.g. the Internet). Planners will be responsible for identifying and scheduling the use of media suitable to achieve the objectives set for a campaign. Buyers will ensure the purchase of airtime and space (e.g. TV/radio and press respectively) at economical rates; media sales are undertaken by staff employed by the media owners, who are salespeople.

Production director/manager/executive

Agencies produce commercials, press advertisements, leaflets, packaging and many more items of promotional materials. Production staff are responsible for liaising with the necessary production companies and fulfilling the briefs set for the production and delivery of the promotional materials.

Market research manager

May be within an advertising agency or marketing research agency. Has similar duties to market research managers employed by client-side companies with the addition of liaison with client managers commissioning the research. Will involve producing and gaining approval for the marketing research brief.

Other

Marketing lecturer

An academic life, maybe, is what is desired. Teaching, administration, research and publication are primary activities.

> **activity**
>
> Visit a local careers advice centre. Pick up information on marketing jobs. Talk to an adviser about all the different job opportunities, and the skills and backgrounds required. Find out about the typical salaries for each job. Do some companies offer training and graduate entry schemes?

MARKETING QUALITIES, SKILLS AND COMPETENCES

A variety of researchers have attempted to list some of the more important skills for marketers. These are compared in Exhibits PS.6 and PS.7. What is important to understand is different skills balances will be needed for particular marketing jobs. For example, some will require analytical skills to be emphasized over creative skills, and vice versa. Although marketing jobs generally require high levels of social skills, some jobs may be more desk based. What is interesting is the limited extent to which many marketers have responsibility to manage subordinates, as they frequently find that more of their activity is based on dealing with peers and superiors in sections outside the control of marketing. The opportunity for delegation to subordinates is reduced while the need for social and negotiating skills is heightened.

Research undertaken in the USA by Abernethy and Gray indicated the most important skills for entry-level positions are oral skills in communication, interpersonal skills, enthusiasm and motivation, written communication skills and related work experience. They simultaneously identified that the greatest weakness of many graduates is their lack of communication skills, unrealistic expectations, lack of practical experience and lack of clear career goals.

Thomas has identified a range of 17 skills held by marketing managers 'who are very good at their jobs' on the basis of contact with practising marketing managers. He describes his list as not being definitive, and an examination shows that some areas overlap. Middleton and Long researched what employers look for when recruiting for marketing jobs. Their list extends to 10 items, while a *Marketing Week* survey asked marketing managers themselves to score those skills they considered most important. Ten skills areas achieved average scores higher than 3 out of 5.

exhibit ps.6

Qualities and skills in marketing management

Thomas's skills of the professional marketing manager	Middleton and Long's marketing skills identified by employers	*Marketing Week's* ten top-scoring skills identified by marketers (scores in order of merit)
Planning skills a continuous process of analysis and decision-making resulting in plans that are used	Planning	Planning and organizing (5)
Environmental awareness a process of monitoring and anticipating change resulting in proactive, not reactive, management	Entrepreneurship	Entrepreneurial flair (4.8)
Organizational ability dynamic organizing of available resources; the skill to change the organization to meet changing environments	Organizational skills	Man management (4.7)
Segmentation and product development skills the ability to make segmentation and product development decisions (and to use the information needed to develop them) to meet the defined needs of the market segments selected	Numeracy	Financial control (4.7)
Behaviour analysis skills skills in identifying consumer perceptions and understanding buyer behaviour	Creativity	Creative flair (4.5)
Market research commissioning skills marketing research and the information it generates is important to marketing decision-making; much of the relevant information is derived from an ability to commission such research from others in cost-efficient ways	Resilience	Time management (4.5)
Information analysis skills the skill to be able to specify what types of information, and what types of analysis, are required, and to be at ease with the use of information technology	Initiative	Risk taking (4.1)
Innovation management skills skills of managing product and service development and launch within the company and in the marketplace	Analytical skills	Staff recruitment (4)

exhibit ps.6

Qualities and skills in marketing management

Thomas's skills of the professional marketing manager	Middleton and Long's marketing skills identified by employers	*Marketing Week's* ten top-scoring skills identified by marketers (scores in order of merit)
Strategic thinking skills skills to think beyond the immediate and the tactical; abilities to use concepts and tools of strategic analysis and decision-making with longer-term implications	Communication	Sales negotiation (4)
Sales and advertising management, and productivity management skills abilities that ensure efficiency and effectiveness, particularly in the context of two large marketing investment areas: sales and advertising	Selling skills	Buying (3.4)
Marketing mix optimization skills the ability to skilfully blend all the elements of the marketing mix		
Interdepartmental cooperation and conflict-resolution skills management skill in working with others to increase cooperation and prevent or reduce conflict		
Financial management skills 'the financial illiterate has no place in the ranks of the marketing department of the marketing company'		
Systems thinking and skills the ability to analyse and understand complex systems in order to make them work more effectively		
Long-term perspective ability to comprehend the long-term interests of the company, to go beyond short-term and personal aggrandisement as 'guardian of the company's future'		
Ability to 'Market' marketing enthusiastically to communicate to others what it is that marketing managers do and the role marketing should have within an organization		
Proactivity the ability to look to the future, to anticipate, to make things happen and get things done		

Exhibit PS.7 shows more research findings. Heidrick and Struggles' research was based on questionnaires completed by chief marketing executives, which they defined as the most senior marketing person within an organization irrespective of title. Mathews and Redman used the Pedler *et al.*'s list of management qualities (shown in Exhibit PS.3) as a basis for their analysis of marketing job advertisements. The final column in Exhibit PS.7 shows one particular large pharmaceutical company's listing of what it looks for in terms of marketing manager skills.

exhibit ps.7

Continuation of qualities and skills in marketing management

Heidrick and Struggles' personal qualities and skills of chief marketing executives	Mathews and Redman's analysis of marketing job advertisements (skills receiving frequent mentions)	Pharmaceutical company's marketing skills listing
Relationships Communications Thinking abilities Taking a wider view Leadership Vision Commercial judgement Planning Professionalism Understanding of modern management Financial appraisal and control Product and market knowledge Numerate and analytical Commercial experience Adaptability and acceptance of change	Social skills Creativity Mental agility Proactivity Problem solving	Calculated influence Creativity Analytical mind Initiative Problem solving Managing others Direct persuasion Efficiency orientation Achievement drive Practical, logical focus Aesthetic sense

Now, finally, we will look at another approach that identifies the important qualities needed by managers in marketing. Some years ago, the British government set up a series of consultative boards to classify the skills and attributes of managers across a range of business and management functions. It referred to these as management competences. One board covered the area of marketing. After extensive consultation, it came up with an initial list of marketing competences and these are shown in Exhibit PS.8.

exhibit ps.8

Outline of marketing competences determined by the Marketing Standards Board

A   Establish strategies and policies
A1   Analyse and determine business and marketing objectives
A2   Formulate policies and strategies
A3   Implement policies and strategies
A4   Determine future action plans for policies and strategies

B   Establish and maintain marketing resources and systems
B1   Identify requirements
B2   Provide resources to meet requirements
B3   Monitor and coordinate the deployment of resources
B4   Maintain effectiveness of resources

C   Anticipate, stimulate and satisfy customer needs
C1   Identify business opportunities
       Commission the provision of information
       Produce proposals for marketing research
       Contract for the provision of marketing research
       Provide information through desk research
       Set up quantitative research
       Provide quantitative information
       Set up qualitative research
       Provide qualitative information
       Analyse and interpret quantitative information
       Analyse and interpret qualitative information
       Present findings
C2   Produce business case
       Develop new and existing products and services
       Develop markets
       Determine fit to organizational requirements
       Evaluate opportunity
       Propose recommendations
C3   Develop marketing plan
       Determine product and service specification
       Determine pricing structure
       Obtain proposals for the provision of marketing communications
       Provide proposals to supply marketing communications
       Construct campaign plan
       Determine sales plan
       Determine distribution channels
       Develop an export strategy
       Produce marketing plan
C4   Implement marketing plan
       Set up distribution channel
       Install and monitor pricing plan
       Commission the provision of marketing communications
       Fulfil marketing communication plan
       Provide customer service

exhibit ps.8

Outline of marketing competences determined by the Marketing Standards Board

C5   Evaluate marketing plan
Obtain, monitor and evaluate data
Identify deviations from planned activities
Evaluate achievement against business objectives
Identify and recommend action

D   Organize, control and monitor marketing resources
D1   Manage operations
Maintain operations to meet quality standards
Create and maintain the necessary conditions for productive work
Lead meetings and group discussions to solve problems and make decisions
Contribute to discussions to solve problems and make decisions
D2   Manage resources
Manage people
Manage finance
Manage information
Coordinate and integrate resources and strategies
D3   Manage change
Contribute to the evaluation of proposed changes to services, products and systems
Implement and evaluate changes to services, products and systems

activity

Think about your own strengths and weaknesses. Compare them to the skills and qualities of managers in different marketing management positions. Use Exhibits PS.6, PS.7 and PS.8 and your findings from earlier activities to help you. The CIM offers a skills analysis service that you may be able to use by visiting its website at www.cim.co.uk. Or you may find visiting the Prospects website interesting, at www.prospects.ac.uk. From its home page, click on the 'What job would suit me?' button; this will take you to the 'Prospects Planner'. As a first-time user you will need to register, which only involves filling in a few boxes to set up your own Prospects Account, which is saved for you for later visits. It is free of charge. The Prospects Planner asks you to answer a few simple questions about what you would look for in a job. The questions cover your interests, motivations, general skills and people skills. It will then list a range of job areas that match your profile that you can then look at in greater detail. This is also a good site for simply finding out about jobs.

BACKGROUND AND EDUCATION

Managers in marketing have a wide range of backgrounds, education and experience. In general, the more senior the role, the broader the base of marketing, business and people management knowledge and skills that is required. Senior roles are often, for example, more about managing people than they are about implementing marketing plans. For this reason, the skills and competences required of senior marketing managers are similar to those of other managerial groups, e.g. production and finance.

Marketing is a profession that can be practised without any professional or academic qualification, unlike law, accounting, architecture or engineering, say. Many practising marketing managers have no marketing qualifications at all and some have only limited training. They rely on their experience. For many marketers, the route to their marketing career may well have started in a totally different function (engineering and sales have been common starting points in the past). Increasingly, graduates are entering businesses with general business or marketing degrees, and increasing numbers now hold the CIM diploma qualification.

However, *Hobson's Graduate Career Directory* (2001) still highlights that many graduates entering marketing jobs do so holding numerous non-marketing or non-business degrees (see Exhibit PS.9). For some marketing positions, specialist degrees can be an advantage. A qualification in psychology can be helpful in applying for marketing research posts; one in biology can be useful in pharmaceutical marketing; English can be favoured in posts involving copywriting, and so on. What is important in each case is that graduates should be abe to demonstrate their general intellectual level by obtaining a degree in whatever the subject may be.

exhibit ps.9

Degree qualifications of new marketing graduates

Degree background of new marketing graduates	%	Degree background of new marketing graduates	%
Business studies	34	Biology	4
Modern languages	13.5	Economics	4
English	10	Law	4
History	9.5	Chemistry	2.5
Psychology	8	Mathematics	2.5
Geography	7	Physics	1

Although somewhat dated, one piece of research sponsored by the CIM summarized the backgrounds of marketing executives as shown in Exhibit PS.10.

exhibit ps.10

Summary of findings on the backgrounds of marketing executives in the UK

1. Marketing practice in the UK appears to be still a largely male preserve.
2. In company terms and in job terms, mobility appears to be a characteristic. Around 66% of respondents had held their present jobs for less than three years and 45% had been with their present company for less than three years. Nearly 50% were appointed externally to their present jobs.
3. 50% of respondents were educated to at least degree level. In less than half of these cases had marketing been included in their studies. Marketing was included in some subgraduate and postgraduate qualifications but the amount was undisclosed.
4. Sales is the most likely area from which UK marketing executives come into the marketing profession.
5. Over one-third of respondents felt they had not had enough training to do their present job.

In another piece of research, the backgrounds of senior marketing managers was investigated. The results appear in Exhibit PS.11

exhibit ps.11

Background of UK senior marketing managers

First degree subjects held	%	Professional qualifications held	%
Science, maths or engineering	24	Engineering	12
Classics, arts or modern languages	14	Accountancy	2
Economics, politics or social sciences	12	Law	less than 1
Marketing, commerce or business studies	5	Other	14
Law	2		
Other	1		
Total	58	Total	29

What Exhibits PS.10 and PS.11 indicate is that marketing as an occupation has some way to go to reach professional maturity. This should not be considered a problem. Marketing is a much newer discipline than most people realize. Today's graduates will have the opportunity to make a significant difference. The CIM and other professional marketing bodies are working hard to raise marketing's professional profile and standing. Details of some of the professional bodies and their qualifications are given below. This list is far from complete as there are many other bodies, too, each focused on its own area of specialization.

The Chartered Institute of Marketing (CIM) www.cim.co.uk

▶ Foundation Certificate in Marketing – basic-level understanding of marketing

▶ Certificate in Marketing – for junior-level marketers

▶ Advanced Certificate in Marketing – for operational marketers

▶ Postgraduate Diploma in Marketing – the highest professional qualification

Chartered marketer, the highest professional status, is an award given by the CIM in recognition of achievement of both theoretical knowledge and practical experience and expertise.

The Market Research Society (MRS) www.mrs.org.uk

▶ Advanced Certificate in Market and Social Research – entry-level qualification on the basics of research techniques

▶ Diploma of the Market Research Society – higher-level practical and relevant emphasis on qualitative and quantitative research studies

The Institute of Direct Marketing (IDM) www.theidm.com

▶ Diploma in Interactive and Direct Marketing

▶ IDM Certificate in E-Marketing, a vocational e-marketing qualification

The Communications, Advertising and Marketing Education Foundation (CAM) www.camfoundation.com

▶ A range of six Advanced Certificates; candidates are required to obtain all six to achieve the Advanced Diploma

▶ Advanced Diploma in Communication Studies

▶ A range of four Higher Certificates, two lead to the Higher Diploma in Integrated Marketing Communications, two lead to the Higher Diploma in PR

▶ Higher Diploma in Integrated Marketing Communications

▶ Higher Diploma in PR

Marketing and general masters programmes: MA, MSc and MBA

These are academic postgraduate qualifications studied over a one- or two-year period.

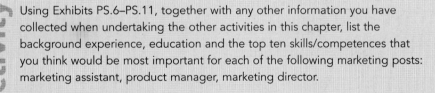

activity

If you can, make an appointment to interview a marketing manager to find out more about the job she or he does. Prepare in advance of your meeting. What questions will you ask?

activity

Using Exhibits PS.6–PS.11, together with any other information you have collected when undertaking the other activities in this chapter, list the background experience, education and the top ten skills/competences that you think would be most important for each of the following marketing posts: marketing assistant, product manager, marketing director.

Choose one of these posts, or another in which you are interested, and write a job description assuming that the employer is a national insurance company. Again, if you prefer, you can choose a different sort of company that may better reflect your personal interests.

SUMMARY

This chapter has attempted to give you a flavour of the roles and skills needed in the management of marketing by, first, looking at what managers do and then taking a closer look at what managers of *marketing* do. There are many different marketing jobs available and they are not all called 'marketing manager'. The actual tasks performed and the skills needed will differ from job to job. Some brief details are presented here, but you are encouraged to do some investigating for yourself into jobs that may be of particular interest. Marketing managers have a wide variety of backgrounds and qualifications. Marketing offers an exciting and challenging career for those who wish to take up the challenge.

books

Hobson's Graduate Career Directory (2001), information on marketing, retailing and sales.
Karen Holmes (2000) *Advertising, Marketing and PR: The Insider Career Guide*, Industrial Society.
Shirley Jenner (2000) *The Graduate Careers Handbook*, FT Prentice Hall.
Adela Stanley (2000) *Careers in Marketing, Advertising and PR*, Kogan Page.

Useful websites

Adecco	www.adecco.com
AF Selection	www.afselection.co.uk
Antal International Ltd	www.antal.com
AppointmentsPlus	www.appointments-plus.co.uk
Armadillo Executive Resourcing	www.armadillo-uk.com
Association of Graduate Careers Advisory Services	www.agcas.org.uk
Association of Graduate Recruiters	www.agr.org.uk
Best International	www.best-people.co.uk
BigBlueDog.com	www.bigbluedog.co.uk
ChangeJobs	www.changejobs.co.uk
Chartered Institute of Marketing	www.cim.co.uk
CityJobs.com	www.cityjobs.com
Careers Research and Advisory Centre	www.crac.org.uk
CVStore	www.cvstore.net
Datascope Recuitment	www.datascope.co.uk
Direct Recruitment	www.direct-recruitment.co.uk
DoctorJob.com (1)	www.doctorjob.com
DoctorJob.com(2)	www.gti.co.uk
dotjobs	www.dotjobs.co.uk
Fish4Jobs	www.fish4jobs.co.uk
FreeAgent.com	www.freeagent.com
Gallery Resources	www.galleryresources.co.uk
Graduate Appointments	www.gradapps.co.uk
gradunet	www.gradunet.co.uk
Guru.com	www.guru.com
HARP Wallen	www.harpwallen.co.uk
Hcareers	www.hcareers.co.uk
Heywood Associates	www.heywoodassociates.com
Hotjobs (US)	www.hotjobs.com
hotrecruit.co.uk	www.hotrecruit.co.uk
IGC Limited	www.igc.co.uk
InterviewMe.co.uk	www.interviewme.co.uk
Irene Anderson Associates	www.iaa.co.uk
Jobpilot.co.uk	www.jobpilot.co.uk
JobShark	www.jobshark.co.uk
Jobsite	www.jobsite.co.uk
Jobs Online (US)	www.jobsonline.com
Jobworld	www.jobworld.co.uk/
Joslin Rowe	www.joslinrowe.com
Justpeople.com	www.justpeople.com
Major Players	www.majorplayers.co.uk
Manpower	www.manpower.co.uk

Marketing Resource InfoCentre	www.marketingresource.com
Marketingmoves	www.marketingmoves.com
Mercury Search & Selection	www.mercurysearch.co.uk
Michael Page International	www.michaelpage.net/index.asp
Monster UK	www.monster.co.uk
Monster Germany	www.monster.de
Monster France	www.monster.fr
Moves Recruitment	www.moves-recruit.co.uk
PeopleBank	www.peoplebank.com
Pertemps	www.pertemps.co.uk
Phee Farrer Jones	www.pheefarrerjones.co.uk
prjobs.net	www.prjobs.net
Prospects	www.prospects.ac.uk
PSD Group International Recruitment	www.psdgroup.com
Ragtime	www.ragtime.co.uk
Recruit Media	www.recruitmedia.co.uk
Reed New Media	www.reednewmedia.co.uk
Reed Online	www.reed.co.uk
Reedon.net	www.reedon.net
Revolution Recruitment	www.revolutionrecruitment.co.uk
Ruth Halliday Associates	www.ruth-halliday.co.uk
Senate	www.senate.uk.com
Spectrum	www.spectrumrecruit.co.uk
Stepstone	www.stepstone.com
Stepstone Germany	www.stepstone.de
Stopgap	www.stopgap.co.uk
SwiftWork.com	www.swiftwork.com
Telegraph recruitment	www.jobs.telegraph.co.uk
Tempz.com	www.tempz.com
The Canto Consultancy	www.canto.co.uk
The Davis Company	www.daviscompany.co.uk
The Resource Connection	www.resourceconnection.co.uk
Top Jobs on the Net	www.topjobs.net
Top Jobs World	www.topjobs.co.uk
Total Jobs	www.totaljobs.com
Where its @ 2	www.wia.co.uk
Workthing	www.workthing.com

GLOSSARY

4Ps a mnemonic (memory aid) for the marketing mix: product, promotion, place, price

7Ps a mnemonic (memory aid) for the services marketing mix: product, promotion, place, price, process, people, physical evidence

above the line advertising in commission paying media, e.g. TV, posters, press, radio, cinema

adoption see *product adoption*

advertising paid-for promotional messages

agent represents other businesses and sells products on their behalf, does not usually hold stock or take ownership of the goods, just takes orders and is paid a commission

AIDA a sequential model showing the steps that marketing communications should lead potential buyers through: Attention, Interest, Desire, Action

ambient media outdoor (usually) media, classically posters but now including more imaginative forms, e.g. laser-light shows, tickets, students (wearing promotional clothing or tattoos)

Ansoff's matrix comprises four possible growth strategies: market development, product development, market penetration/expansion, and diversification

aspirant (aspirational) groups groups to which an individual would like to belong, e.g. a professional football team or a particular club

asset-led see *asset-led marketing*

asset-led marketing basing marketing strategy on the organization's strengths rather than on customer needs and wants (e.g. by developing products that can be made with existing equipment or through *brand extension*)

attitude describes a person's consistently favourable or unfavourable evaluation, feelings and tendencies towards an object or idea

audience profile a detailed description of audience characteristics used by marketing communicators to tailor their promotional efforts

awareness set range of products or brands that may satisfy a customer/consumer need or solve a problem

b2b (business to business) business dealings with another business as opposed to a consumer

barrier to communication anything that gets in the way of a message and prevents it from being received correctly

barriers to entry things that make it difficult, or impossible, for new competitors to enter a market, e.g. patents, high set-up costs

behavioural segmentation dividing a market into subgroups (segments) of customers/users according to how they buy, use and feel about products

belief how or what a person thinks about something, usually based on knowledge, opinion or faith

below the line non-commission-paying promotion, typically all forms except advertising

benchmarking a process of systematic analysis and comparison of one company's performance, measured against another's (the industry leader's), in order to improve business performance

biographical research an individual's story or experiences told to a researcher or found in other materials

bogof buy one get one free

boom when an economy experiences a rapid rise in spending, often accompanied by higher prices and raised investment levels

Boston Consultancy Group (BCG) matrix a product portfolio analysis tool involving classifying products, or *SBUs*, according to their relative market share and market growth rate, as stars, cash cows, problem children or dogs

bottom-up approach functions and departments recommend objectives, budgets, strategies and plans to senior management

brand the essence of a product, what it is (physical characteristics), and what people believe it to be and expect from it

brand equity the monetary value of a brand

brand extension offering further products under an existing brand name but in a new category within the same, broadly defined market (e.g. Mars ice cream built on the Mars bar brand)

brand identity all the outward trappings of the brand, e.g. logo, name, colours, strap line and packaging

brand image people's perception of the brand

brand leader the brand with the highest sales within its particular market

brand loyalty the attachment that a customer or consumer feels to a favourite product

brand manager similar to a product manager, responsible for marketing a particular brand

brand map diagram of competing brand positions resulting from the perceptual mapping process, also called perceptual maps, position maps and space maps

brand name the product, or product line's, given name

brand personality the heart of the brand, the sum of its values, its character traits, e.g. bubbly, elegant, friendly

brand promise the way the brand sets out to fulfil a customer need, e.g. Pepsi Cola might promise to be thirst quenching

brand stretching using an existing brand name on products in a different market

brand-switching buying an alternative brand

brand values how a brand is perceived by the market

branding the process of building a brand

break even see *breakeven point*

breakeven point the amount of goods a firm needs to sell in order to cover its costs

breaking down the process of reducing the quantity of product to be moved

business mission the broad aims a business hopes to achieve

buying centre comprises all the individuals that participate in the business buying decision process

buying economies i.e. economies of scale; companies may buy goods in large quantities and so obtain favourable terms

capital goods (fixed assets) substantial purchases that are not used up in one go but are expected to be used multiple times

cartel group of companies that get together and fix prices between them

case study contains in-depth information, built from multiple sources, that forms a detailed picture of a particular situation

cash cows a category within the *Boston Consulting Group matrix*, products or *SBUs* with relatively high market share in low-growth markets

cause-related marketing a form of *sponsorship* whereby funds are raised for a worthy cause, often a charity (e.g. Tesco's Computers for Schools, Pizza Express's support of the National Trust through sales of its Neptune pizza)

census a survey that includes all members of a population

channel members the businesses that make up a distribution channel; intermediaries

classical conditioning the process of using an established relationship between a stimulus and a response, which can then be used to evoke the same response

classified advertising the small ads, usually placed into specific classifications, e.g. cars for sale, help wanted

closed questions questions that expect a one-word (usually yes or no) answer

co-branding when two companies' brand names appear together, e.g. Intel on IBM computers

cognitive dissonance when a consumer is psychologically uncomfortable about a purchase

cognitive learning active learning using complex mental processing of information

cold call when a salesperson calls on a *prospect* without an appointment

competitive advantage or *competitive edge*, something about an organization or its products/services that is perceived as being better than rival offerings

competitive advertising highlights and illustrates the uses, features and benefits that the advertised brand has and its rivals do not

competitive edge see *competitive advantage*

competitive intelligence information on rivals, their products and environments compared with one's own

competitor analysis the process of obtaining an in-depth understanding of rival firms and their offerings

complementary product one that is required by another product, e.g. a printer needs paper, a DVD player needs DVDs

concentrated marketing where only one market segment is chosen for targeting

consideration set range of preferred products or brands that may satisfy the need or provide a solution to the problem

conspicuous purchases a product or service that is likely to stand out, perhaps because it is unusual, or high status or will be consumed in public

consumer the individual end user of a product or service

consumer durables products for use by individuals that could be expected to last for some time, e.g. a washing machine

consumer goods goods that are bought/used by individuals rather than by companies

consumer models representations of consumer buying behaviour, usually as diagrams

consumer panels a primary research technique that seeks the views, attitudes, behaviour or buying habits of a group of consumers

consumerism the belief that increasing consumption is economically desirable

consumerist someone who believes in *consumerism*

contribution the amount of money remaining from the sale, when the variable costs have been paid

contribution pricing pricing method based on variable costs

controllables events, issues, trends, etc., within the *internal environment*

convenience goods products that customers buy frequently and think little about

convenience sample picked on the basis of convenience to the researcher, e.g. work colleagues

copy text

copywriter writes the words for promotional materials, e.g. adverts

core product the minimum benefits a product should confer, e.g. a pen must write, a car must go

corporate brand a company brand name

corporate image audiences' perception of an organization

costs a firm's payments to suppliers, etc.

creative execution the way an advert is designed in order to put a message across

creative team an *art director* and a *copywriter*; they work together to create ads

cross-selling persuading a customer to buy extra products

culture the set of basic values, perceptions, wants and behaviour learnt by a member of society from family and other institutions

customer buyer of a product or service

customer lifetime value a calculation of the longterm worth of a customer using estimates of expected purchases

customer loyalty a mutually supportive, long-term relationship between customer and supplier, which results in customers making multiple repeat purchases

customer orientation the whole organization is focused on the satisfaction of its customers' needs

customer profile a description of the firm's customer base, used to target customers more accurately

customer value pricing pricing a product or service according to the value placed on it by the customer

customized marketing producing one-off products/services to match a specific customer's requirements, e.g. a made-to-measure suit or the organization of a product launch party

DAGMAR acronym for Defining Advertising Goals for Measured Advertising Results, a hierarchy of effects model describing the stages individuals go through when making a purchase, or consumption, decision

data mining using specialist software to analyse large amounts of data (held in a database or a *data warehouse*) to predict trends and likely customer behaviour

data warehouse large database holding copies of customer and environmental data taken from the organization's other systems, and designed specifically to make it easier to raise queries and produce reports

database marketing the use of computerized customer data to communicate with customers and promote further sales

decision-making unit (DMU) all the individuals who participate in and influence the customer's purchase decision

demand quantity of goods that customers buy at a certain price

demand driven when a surplus, or potential surplus, of goods to be sold gives the buyers more power than the sellers

demographic segmentation markets segmented by population characteristics such as age, gender, occupation and income

depression when an economy experiences a severe fall-off in sales, usually accompanied by unemployment, lower prices and low levels of investment, sometimes called a *slump*

desk research (secondary research) the search for good-quality data that has been validated and is now published for use by others

destroyer pricing see *predatory pricing*

differentiated marketing differences between market segments are recognized and two or more target markets are selected, each receiving a different marketing programme

direct costs costs that are clearly due to the making of a particular product, e.g. cocoa and sugar are direct costs of chocolate bars

direct mail promotional material delivered by post

direct marketing 'all activities that make it possible to offer goods or services or to transmit other messages to a segment of the population by post, telephone, email or other direct means' (CIM)

direct-response advertising 'advertising, or selling, through any medium inviting the consumer to respond to the advertiser' (IDM *Direct Marketing Guide*)

direct sales when a manufacturer deals direct with customers rather than through intermediaries in the *supply chain*

disassociative groups groups to which the individual does not want to belong or be seen to belong, e.g. an upmarket shopper may not wish to be seen in a discount store

discount a deduction from the price

disintermediation the removal of levels of intermediaries in distribution channels, often associated with the trend towards direct sales facilitated by the Internet

display advertising mainstream press advertising, usually with illustrations or other attention-drawing features

distortion a barrier to communication; poor coding skills, e.g. a badly devised ad or a badly worded sales promotion, that prevent the message from being received correctly

distribution the processes involved in moving goods from the supplier to the customer or user

distribution channel a chain of organizations through which products pass on their way to a target market

dogs a category within the *Boston Consulting Group matrix*, products or *SBUs* with relatively low market share in low-growth markets

dumping an anti-competitive practice whereby a company exports its products at a very low price and so undercuts competitors in the target country

dyadic comparisons technique used in perceptual mapping in which two products are compared to each other at a time

early majority a substantial group of customers who follow early adopters in buying a new product or service

economies of scale unit costs fall as larger quantities are produced; a cost advantage associated with large organizations

elasticity a significant response to changes in a marketing variable, most commonly price; quantity demanded changes by a greater percentage than the percentage change in price, i.e. if the price rises the revenue falls

embargo(es) a ban on the trade of a particular category of goods (e.g. arms) or between certain areas (e.g. USA and Iraq)

emergency goods infrequently purchased but needed at short notice, e.g. rain capes, sun hats, plasters

end user the person who actually uses the product or service; this is not always the customer, e.g. a computer may be bought by a company's purchasing officer for use by the marketing manager (the end user)

environmental scanning monitoring the forces that influence the organization in order to identify changes that may affect performance

environmental variables factors within an organization's environment that may change, i.e. *PRESTCOM* elements

EPOS (Electronic Point Of Sale) a computerized system that collects sales data at a retail checkout

e-tailers online *retailers*

ethnography the description, or interpretation, of the patterns of behaviour in a social group or setting; the researcher will immerse himself or herself in a variety of ways into the culture of the group to be studied

evoked set the shortlist of products from which a purchaser will make a final choice

exchange when two parties swap items perceived to be of approximately equal value

exclusive distribution the distribution channel has only one or two specially selected outlets within a specified area

experimentation a primary research technique that seeks to understand the behaviour of specified variables under controlled conditions (i.e. not real-world)

exploratory (research) initial research to see whether a more comprehensive study is called for

extension strategies means of prolonging the *product life cycle*

external environment organizations and influences that are not under the organization's control, e.g. government, competitors, legislation

extinction pricing see *predatory pricing*

extrapolate use already established data (or experience) to predict the unknown, e.g. using last year's sales figures, adjusted for current conditions, to forecast this year's

family brand a brand name that covers a group of related products

family life cycle a form of *market segmentation* based on the recognition that we pass through a series of quite distinct phases in our lives

feedback a part of the two-way communications process whereby the receiver sends a message back to the original sender

field research (primary research) carried out specifically for the research task in question

first mover advantage the first significant company to move into a market is often the most successful

fixed costs costs that do not vary with production levels, e.g. insurance premiums

flyer a short brochure

FMCG (fast moving consumer goods) low-value items that are bought regularly (the shelves empty quickly), e.g. toothpaste

focus groups a qualitative research technique using a group discussion overseen by a moderator, used to explore views, attitudes and behaviour with regard to a marketing issue; common in advertising research

fragmented industry one in which there are a lot of players, few of whom have any significant power

free trade trade across international boundaries without government restrictions such as *import duties* and *quotas*

frequency the number of times that an average member of the target audience is exposed to an advert during a campaign

full-cost pricing prices are set by adding an amount (usually a percentage) to the full (i.e. total) costs of making and selling the product

functional silo when departments or workgroups act as independent entities rather than as components of a much larger system despite having many overlapping activities and information needs

General Electric (GE) business screen matrix a portfolio analysis tool developed by McKinsey & Co and GE involving classifying product lines or *SBUs* according to their competitive position and market attractiveness

geo-demographic segmentation markets segmented by a combination of geographic and demographic approaches using house location and house type

geographic segmentation markets segmented by countries, regions and areas

globalization the process of growing to a worldwide scale; often involves standardization of offerings and cultural convergence

grey importing when someone outside of the official supply chain buys goods (usually very cheaply) in another country for sale in their home country

grey market see *grey importing*

grounded theory starts from the intention to generate, or to discover, a theory by studying how people interact in response to a particular phenomenon; theoretical propositions are developed from interview data and field research

hard currency freely exchangeable currency, usually from one of the more developed countries, e.g. the euro, pound, US dollar

hedging making a deal to buy or sell foreign currency in advance so that the exchange rate is fixed

hierarchical management structure each manager has a set place within a vertical chain of command

hierarchy of effects models describe the stages individuals go through when making a purchase, or consumption, decision

high-involvement purchases purchases that customers expend time and effort on, usually high cost or high risk, e.g. cars, holidays, wedding dresses

horizontal communications happen sideways within an organization, e.g. between workgroups or departments

horizontal integration where a company owns a number of different business at the same level in the supply chain, e.g. Currys and Dixons electrical retailers are part of the same company

hospitality hosting clients (e.g. providing refreshments in a private room) at events

hypothesis a proposition put forward for testing

import duties taxes paid when goods are brought into a country from outside

in-depth interviews one-to-one research interviews; commonly used in qualitative research

indirect costs costs that cannot be attributed to a particular product as they are not directly associated with its production or sale, e.g. the running costs of the chief executive's car

inelasticity little response to changes in the marketing variable being measured (commonly price, advertising, competitive products, income); the percentage change in demand is less than the percentage change in price (or other variable); so if price rises, revenue rises

infinite elasticity the product can only be sold at one price, there is no demand at any other; this is really just a theoretical term

inflation when the prices of goods rise without a matching (or greater) increase in their actual value

information framing the ways in which information is presented to people to ensure selective distortion does, or does not, happen

information search identifying the various ways a need or problem can be satisfied

innovative products a really new product, possibly a technological or medical breakthrough

inside-out approach focuses on the needs of the organization first, and customers and the marketplace second

integrated marketing communications the process of ensuring that all elements of the promotional mix are complementary in order to avoid mixed messages and strengthen the brand

intensive distribution products are available at numerous outlets

inter-media decision the choice of *media class*

intermediaries businesses that form part of the distribution channel, passing goods on towards the end customer

internal environment the organization itself, its functions, departments and resources

internal marketing also called internal PR, addresses the needs (particularly information needs) of employees

Internet worldwide computer network linking smaller networks via satellite and telephone links, and providing access to e-mail services and the *World Wide Web*

intra-media decision the choice of *media vehicle*

iTV interactive television

judgemental sample see *quota sample*

junk mail unwanted promotional material sent by post

just in time (JIT) a lean manufacturing technique where little, or no, stock is held

knowledge-based economy one in which knowledge is the primary wealth creator

lead time the time it takes for an order to reach the customer

learning changes in an individual's behaviour arising from their experiences

legitimate power influence over others conferred by law or regulations

level of confidence the degree to which the researchers are sure that data are accurate

level of involvement the extent to which the purchase is important to the purchaser

Likert scale subjects are asked to indicate their agreement, or disagreement, with a statement by use of a five-point scale

line extension using the brand name on products within the same category

lobbying a means of influencing those with power, particularly politicians and legislators

logistics the flow of goods and services through the supply chain

logo a graphical device associated with an organization

loss leader a product that is sold at a loss, usually to tempt shoppers to make other purchases

loyalty schemes ways in which companies try to retain customers and encourage repeat purchases, often accomplished by awarding points (e.g. Tesco Clubcard, Air Miles)

macroenvironment the broad, external influences that affect all organizations in a market, e.g. the political situation in a country

mailing lists any list of names and addresses to which mail is sent, often potential customers'

marginal cost pricing similar to contribution pricing, a margin is added to the marginal cost (the cost of making an additional product) to arrive at a price

market a composite of individuals or organizations that have a willingness and ability to purchase products; a market can consist of a single or multiple segments

market attractiveness an assessment of how desirable a particular market or market segment is to an organization

market followers take their lead from competitors and copy their successful ideas and strategies (see *market led*)

market fragmentation a market characterized by a large number of relatively small players, none of whom have significant competitive advantage

market growth rate the percentage increase in total sales within a category or market

market leader the company with the highest sales within a *market* (also sometimes used to refer to a groundbreaking firm that others follow)

market led companies take their lead from competitors and copy their successful ideas and strategies (they are also called *market followers*), i.e. they are more cautious and wait for more radical ideas to be tested by others first

market penetration pricing pricing a product lower than competitors, in order to gain market share

market segmentation the process of dividing a total market into subgroups (segments) such that each segment consists of buyers and users that share similar characteristics but are different from those in other segments

market sensing the need for an understanding of the market, rather than merely a knowledge of it

market share a firm's sales expressed as a percentage of the total sales of that type of product in the defined market

market skimming setting a relatively high price to take advantage of limited competition

marketing channel another term for *distribution channel*

marketing communications another name for *promotion*; communication designed and implemented to persuade others to accept ideas, concepts or things; to motivate audience members to action

marketing environment the forces and organizations that impact on an organization's marketing activities

marketing metrics measurements that help with the quantification of marketing performance, such as market share, advertising spend, and response rates elicited by advertising and direct marketing (source: CIM)

marketing mix (see *4Ps*, *7Ps*) the basics of marketing plan implementation, usually product, promotion, place, price, sometimes with the addition of packaging; the services marketing mix also includes people, physical evidence and process

marketing opportunity a chance to reach a particular group of customers with a product or service offer

marketing orientation provision of customer value determines an organization's direction

mark-up pricing the price is set by adding a percentage (a mark-up) to the direct cost

mass customization tailoring product offerings almost to meet individual needs

mass market a homogeneous market, i.e. no distinction between segments

mass marketing delivering the same marketing programme to everybody without making any significant distinction between them

mass media communications channels that reach a large, relatively undifferentiated audience, e.g. posters, the Internet, press; plural of mass medium

McKinsey/General Electric matrix a portfolio analysis tool developed by McKinsey & Co and GE, involving classifying product lines or *SBUs* according to their competitive position and market attractiveness

media class or media category, type of media, e.g. television, press, posters, cinema

media vehicle the actual TV programme, newspaper, magazine, film, etc., in which adverts appear

mediagraphic segmentation markets segmented by reading and viewing habits

membership groups groups an individual already belongs to and which therefore have a direct influence on his or her behaviour, e.g. students belong to a class

merchandise see *merchandising*

merchandising (1) selection and display of products within a retail environment; (2) a form of licensing spin-off products often inspired by entertainments (e.g. T-shirts at a concert)

message the impression a promotion leaves on its audience

me-too product a new product that is an imitation of an existing, competitive one

microenvironment comprises an organization's competitors, distributors, suppliers and its own internal resources

Minitab a software program for statistical analysis

modified rebuy the buyer wants to modify an element of the rebuy, e.g. change colour, size, price or delivery time

monopoly a market in which there is only one supplier

Multi-attribute Attitude Mapping (MAM) a form of perceptual mapping comparing a product's key features (according to their importance to target customers) with features offered by competitive brands

multichannel distribution the use of different types of channel to reach the same target market

multibranding a strategy employed by companies that have multiple products within the same category

Multidimensional Scaling (MDS) a form of perceptual mapping that establishes similarities and differences between competing brands

multinationals corporations with subsidiaries in multiple countries

multivariate analysis two or more variables are analysed at the same time

new media makes use of modern technologies, e.g. the Internet, *iTV*, mobile phones, CD/DVD

new task when someone buys a product for the first time

niche market a market segment that can be treated as a *target market*; a small, well-defined market, often part of a larger market

niche marketing a form of concentrated marketing in which the target market is relatively small, well defined and very focused

noise a barrier to communication, usually from an external source, e.g. technological breakdown

not for profit organizations whose primary goal is something other than profit, e.g. government, charities, clubs, pressure groups

observation a primary research technique that involves watching how subjects behave in their normal environment

oligopoly a situation where the market is dominated by a small number of very large companies

omnibus surveys a large questionnaire that provides data for multiple clients

on-pack promotion a promotional offer printed on the product's packaging

one-to-one marketing personalized marketing, typically on the Internet

open-ended questions questions that invite the respondent to comment rather than just give a one-word answer

operant conditioning (instrumental conditioning) the learner's response produces a reinforcing stimulus

opportunities to see (OTS) a measure of media effectiveness

opportunity cost alternatives that could have been had/done instead, e.g. the opportunity cost of a lunchtime sandwich may be a pre-packed salad, and an evening at the cinema costs a night's study

outside-in approach the organization looks outwards to focus on the needs of the marketplace to determine appropriate courses of marketing action

own-label products that bear a retailer's brand name, e.g. Tesco; sometimes called 'private brands'

pack shot a picture of the product, in its packaging, used in an advert to aid recognition

patent a legal protection for inventions that prohibits unauthorized copying

penetration pricing see *market penetration pricing*

perception the process by which people select, organize and interpret sensory stimulation (sounds, visions, smell, touch) into a meaningful picture of the world

perceptual map results from the perceptual mapping process and shows brands' relative positions (also called a brand map, position map or space map)

perceptual mapping the process of visually representing target-market perceptions of competing brands in relation to each other

perfect competition a theoretical market situation in which all product offerings are identical, and there are many small buyers and sellers, none of which are able to influence the market and all of which have perfect market knowledge

peripheral product a secondary product often provided as part of a service, e.g. the complimentary mints at the end of a meal, shampoo at the hairdressers

personal selling an oral presentation, in a conversation with one or more prospective purchasers for the purpose of making sales

personality a person's distinguishing psychological characteristics that lead them to respond in particular ways

PEST an acronym for the macroenvironment (part of an organization's external environment): Political, Economic, Social, Technological

phenomenological research describes the experiences of individuals concerning some specific phenomena or occurrence

physical distribution the process of moving goods and services between businesses and consumers

physical evidence the tangible aspects of a service, e.g. a bus ticket, shampoo (at the hairdressers); one of the 7Ps of services marketing

pioneer advertising informative advertising, usually for a new product or service

place one of the elements of the marketing mix, concerned with distribution, delivery, supply chain management

PLC most commonly, public limited company but often used in marketing to stand for the *product life cycle*

point of sale (POS) the place where a product or service is bought

population a complete group of people, cases or objects which share similarities that could be studied in a survey

portal a website that acts as a gateway to a number of other sites

Porter's five forces model a competitive environment analysis tool

Porter's generic strategies three main competitive strategies: cost leadership, differentiation or focus

portfolio analysis the process of comparing *SBUs* or products/services to see which are deserving of further investment and which should be discontinued

position map graphical representation of brand positions resulting from the perceptual mapping process; also called a brand map, perceptual map or space map

positioning the place a product (brand) is perceived to occupy in the minds of customers/consumers of the relevant target market relative to other competing brands

post-testing evaluating the effectiveness of a proposed marketing communication with its target audience after release

predatory pricing also know as destroyer pricing or extinction pricing, it is when a dominant company sells products at a loss with the intention of driving a rival firm out of the market

pre-emptive pricing setting prices relatively low in order to deter others from entering a market

premium price a relatively high price

press the types of media written by journalists, most commonly newspapers, and magazines and directories

press advertisements adverts placed in printed media such as newspapers and magazines

press conference a meeting at which journalists are briefed

press release publicity material sent to editors and journalists

PRESTCOM an acronym for the marketing environment: Political, Regulatory, Economic, Social, Technological, Competitive, Organizational, Market

prestige goods high-status goods, e.g. Rolls-Royce, Rolex

prestige pricing pricing a product high in order to enhance its status

pre-testing evaluating the effectiveness of a proposed marketing communication with its target audience before release

price how much each product is sold for

price discrimination charging different prices for the same products/services to different market segments, e.g. off-peak fares

price elastic when the demand for a good changes significantly after a price change, e.g. price goes up by 10 per cent, demand falls by 20 per cent

price elasticity of demand a measure of the degree to which demand for a good changes when its price is changed

price followers firms that set their prices in accordance with others in the market, notably a price leader

price inelastic demand product sales are not very sensitive to price changes; see *inelasticity*

price leaders set prices for a market, other firms follow their lead

price makers another term for *price leaders*

price premium a high price charged to give the impression of superior quality

price takers another name for price followers

price war two, or more, firms keep undercutting each other in an attempt to build market share until one or the other backs off or goes out of business

primary data first-hand data gathered to solve a particular problem or to exploit a current opportunity

primary research (field research) carried out specifically for the research task in question

problem children a category within the *Boston Consulting Group matrix*, products or *SBUs* with relatively low market share in high-growth markets

procurement buying of goods and services for use within organizations

product adopters model (product diffusion model) categorizes product buyers/users according to their take-up rate of new products

product adoption process the stages a buyer goes through before purchasing a product

product breadth the number of *product lines* a company supports

product depth the number of items within a *product line*

product life cycle a product analysis tool based on the idea that a product has life stages: introduction, growth, maturity, decline, deletion

product line a product and all its variants (models, colours, styles, sizes, etc.)

product line pricing coordinated pricing for a group of related products

product manager responsible for the marketing of a specific product or product line

product orientation the philosophy of an organization that focuses on making the best possible product rather than on its customers' needs

product placement arranging for products to be seen, or referred to, in entertainment media, e.g. during TV or radio programmes, films, plays, video games

product portfolio all a company's, or *SBU's*, products

product portfolio analysis the process of comparing products/services to see which are deserving of further investment, and which should be discontinued

production orientation the philosophy of an organization that focuses on production rather than marketing

profit the difference between what something costs to make and the price for which it is sold

profit margin the difference between cost and price, expressed as a percentage

promotion another name for marketing communications, communication designed and implemented to persuade others to accept ideas, concepts or things; to motivate consumers to action

promotion mix traditionally, advertising, PR, sales promotion and personal selling

prospecting looking for prospective customers

prospects prospective (i.e. possible future) customers

psychographic segmentation using lifestyles, values and personalities to split up markets

psychological price barrier the top price a customer is prepared to pay

public relations (PR) planned activities designed to promote goodwill between an organization and its publics

public sector government-owned organizations

publicity stunt an event designed to capture the attention of the media or other *publics*

publicity the stimulation of demand for goods, or services, by generating news about them in the mass media

publics PR term for target audiences, the groups of people that the organization communicates with

pull strategy a promotional strategy aimed at end customers or consumers

purchase decision the selection of the preferred product to buy

push strategy a promotional strategy aimed at distribution channels

qualitative research investigates people's feelings, opinions and attitudes, often using unstructured, in-depth methods

quantitative research seeks numerical answers, e.g. how many people have similar characteristics and views

question marks an alternative name for *problem children*, also sometimes called *wild cats*

questionnaire a set of questions for use during a survey

quota a limit on the amount of foreign goods that can be imported into a country

quota sample picks respondents in proportion to the population's profile, e.g. if 25 per cent of the population are under 25 and female, then researchers set a quota of 25 per cent females under 25 for the sample

random sample a probability sample, see also *simple random sample*

reach the number (or percentage) of the target audience exposed to an advert or other promotion during a campaign, also referred to as coverage or penetration

recall remembering things (e.g. products, brands, adverts); may be prompted (i.e. aided by stimulus material such as part of an advert) or unprompted (i.e. unaided)

recession when an economy experiences reducing sales and investment; if this continues, it may go into a *depression*

recognition being aware of something (e.g. a product or an advert, when shown)

reference groups the groups that an individual belongs to or aspires to

referent power influence over others gained through superior knowledge or expertise

relationship marketing a long-term approach that nurtures customers, employees and business partners

repositioning involves moving existing perceptions to new perceptions relative to competing brands

reseller a business that buys products in order to sell them on to another business further down the marketing channel

response a reaction to a stimulus

retail selling goods to customers for their own use, i.e. not for resale

retail audit a research implement that provides information on retail product sales, e.g. value, volume, market/brand share

retailer a sales outlet that deals with end customers, a shop

return on investment (ROI) profit expressed as a percentage of the capital invested

revenue (sales revenue) the income a firm receives from the sale of goods and services

reward cards similar in appearance to credit cards, used to register points given away with purchases (e.g. Nectar card, Tesco Clubcard)

sales orientation a strategic view that focuses on short-term sales

sales promotion a short-term special offer, e.g. two for the price of one

sales quota target number (or value) of sales set for a salesperson

sales revenue the income a firm receives from the sale of goods and services

sales volume the quantity of goods sold, expressed in units, e.g. 2 million apples

sample a smaller number of people, or cases, drawn from a population that should be representative of it in every significant characteristic

sampling frame a list of the actual members of a population from which a sample is then chosen

SBUs see *strategic business unit (SBU)*

secondary data data previously collected for other purposes that could be used in the current research task

secondary research (desk research) the search for good-quality data that has been validated and is now published for use by others

segments distinct parts of a larger market; customers and consumers in each segment share similar characteristics

selective attention the process by which stimuli are assessed and non-meaningful stimuli, or those that are inconsistent with our beliefs or experiences, are screened out

selective distortion occurs when consumers distort or change the information they receive to suit their beliefs and attitude

selective distribution the distribution channel is restricted to a few outlets

selective retention the way consumers retain only a small number of messages in their memory

self-liquidating special offer a sales promotion that pays for itself (usually because the company making the offer has bought the promotional items in vast quantities and so obtained a substantial discount)

semantic differential scale research subjects are asked to indicate the strength of their views by choosing a point between two extremes, e.g. was the Rosannica Restaurant's service: good – – poor

service encounter the time during which a customer is the recipient of a service, e.g. the duration of a meal in a restaurant

service recovery trying to retrieve a situation caused by a bad product or poor *service encounter*

services intangible products

shopping goods carry a relatively high risk, perhaps because they are a high price or it may be that the cost of product failure is high

SIC (Standard Industrial Classification) system of classifying products by a allocating numbers (codes) to every product category, industry or business sector

simple random sample the Rolls-Royce of sampling methods, every member of the population has an equal chance of being selected; this can be expensive and often difficult

slump when an economy experiences a severe fall-off in sales, usually accompanied by unemployment, lower prices and low levels of investment, sometimes called a *depression*

SMART a mnemonic for the setting of objectives, which should be: Specific, Measurable, Achievable, Relevant and Timed

social costs the costs incurred by society generally as a result of business processes or decisions, e.g. the clearing up of pollution, the provision of transport infrastructure

social grading segmentation by occupation of head of household; the typical classifications used are A, B, C1, C2, D and E groups

social responsibility a sense of duty towards all organizational stakeholders

societal marketing meeting customers needs and wants in a way that enhances the long-term well-being of consumers and the society they live in

space map see *position map*

spam electronic junk mail

speciality goods unusual, probably quite pricey, products

sponsorship giving financial aid, or other resources, to an individual, organization (usually non-profitmaking) or event in return for a positive association with them, e.g. the Coca-Cola Cup

SPSS (Statistical Package for the Social Sciences) a software program for statistical analysis

stakeholders individuals or groups who are involved in, or affected by, the organization's actions and/or performance

standard error average amount of error introduced through the sampling process

staple goods essential goods, regularly purchased, perhaps always kept in the cupboard, e.g. coffee, milk, shampoo

stars a category within the *Boston Consulting Group matrix*, products or *SBUs* with high market share in a high-growth market

statement stuffers promotional inserts sent with a statement (e.g. bank statement, credit card statement)

stimulus something that provokes a reaction, activity, interest or enthusiasm

straight rebuy where the buyer routinely reorders a product or service without any change to the order whatsoever, it may even be an automatic process

strap line a subheading in a press article or advertisement

strategic alliance a form of joint venture in which two organizations work together to achieve their goals

strategic business unit (SBU) a distinct part of an organization that has an external market for its products and services

substitutes other products that might be bought as alternatives; they satisfy the same, or similar, needs

supply quantity of goods that sellers are prepared to put on the market at a certain price

supply chain network of businesses and organizations through which goods pass to get to their final destination

supply led shortages of goods mean that suppliers can dictate terms of business

survey direct questioning of market research subjects

SWOT analysis a situational analysis tool that assesses the organization's strengths and weaknesses (internal) and opportunities and threats (external)

syndicated data services combine data from responses to questions on various topics, e.g. the British Market Research Bureau's (BMRB) Target Group Index's (TGI) questionnaire

syndicated research data consolidated information from various studies

systematic random sampling uses the whole population as a sampling frame but draws subjects from it at regular intervals, e.g. every 10th name on the list

target see *target market*

target audience the people, or organizations, that are selected to receive communications

target market a group of buyers and consumers who share common needs/wants or characteristics, and whom the organization focuses on

target marketing (targeting) the selection of one or more market segments towards which marketing efforts can be directed, sometimes called market targeting

target marketing strategies used to select a single, or group of, target markets

telesales making sales calls by telephone

tender tendering is where firms bid for a contract and, usually, the lowest-priced bid wins

top-down approach senior managers specify objectives, budgets, strategies and plans that are passed down to functions and departments to put into action

total costs the sum of all costs

total product the complete product offering including all marketing mix elements

tracking ongoing campaign information fed back into the marketing planning process

tracking study research exercise that monitors the performances of brands and the effects of marketing communications over a period of time

trade trial promotions sales promotions aimed at members of the supply chain, e.g. a prize for selling 100 cases of wine

trading bloc a group of countries that work together to promote trade with each other and present a common front to outside nations, e.g. the European Union (EU), NAFTA (North American Free Trade Association)

transaction exchange a one-off sale, or a sale that is conducted as if it were a one-off

transactional marketing focuses on the immediate sale

triadic comparisons technique used in perceptual mapping in which three products are compared to each other at a time

turf battles when individual managers, or departments, fight for their own interests at the expense of those of other managers/departments

turnover the monetary value of sales, also called revenue or sales revenue

uncontrollables events, issues, trends, etc., within the *external environment*

unconvertible currency cannot be exchanged for another currency

undifferentiated marketing where the market is believed to be composed of customers/consumers whose needs and wants from the product are fundamentally the same; in undifferentiated or mass marketing, the same marketing programme is used for all

unique selling proposition (USP) a clear point of differentiation for a product/service

unit costs how much it costs to make a single item (usually worked out on average)

unit elasticity i.e. price and quantity demanded change at exactly the same rate; as a result, whatever you do to the price, there is no increase in the company's revenue

up-selling persuading a customer to trade up to a more expensive product

variable costs costs that go up as production increases and down when it decreases, e.g. electricity bills

vendor rating a vetting process to help buyers identify where there may be potential benefits or difficulties associated with a particular supplier

vertical communications happen up and down the hierarchical organization structure, e.g. sales manager to salesperson, and vice versa

vertical integration where a company owns a number of different businesses above or below it in the *supply chain*

viral marketing modern form of *word of mouth* promotion, often uses new media (e.g. e-mail and texting)

white goods large electrical appliances for domestic use, e.g. fridges, washing machines (traditionally coloured white)

wholesaler a reseller, buying products in bulk to sell on to other businesses in smaller quantities

wild cats an alternative name for *problem children*, also sometimes called *question marks*

word of mouth where members of the *target audience* pass on information or promotional messages to each other; see also *viral marketing*

World Wide Web the graphical user interface to the *Internet*

write-downs goods reduced for sale

zero elasticity completely inelastic; you can do whatever you like to the price (or other marketing variable), there will be no change in the quantity demanded

INDEX

INDEX